A

Journalism

Reader

Edited, with introductions
by

Michael Bromley

and

Tom O'Malley

London and New York

First published 1997
by Routledge
11 New Fetter Lane, London EC4P 4EE

Simultaneously published in the USA and Canada
by Routledge
29 West 35th Street, New York, NY 10001

Typeset in Perpetua by Florencetype, Stoodleigh, Devon

Printed and bound in Great Britain by T.J. International Ltd, Padstow, Cornwall

British Library Cataloguing in Publication Data
A catalogue record for this book is available from the British Library

Library of Congress Cataloging in Publication Data

A journalism reader/[edited by] Michael Bromley and Tom O'Malley.
    p.   cm.——(Communication and society)
    Consists of previously published works and new contributions.
    Includes bibliographical references and index.
    1. Journalism. I. Bromley, Michael. II. O'Malley, Tom. III. Series:
Communication and society
    PN4733.J595   1997
    070.4——dc21   97–9914

ISBN   0–415–14135–4 (hbk)
           0–415–14136–2 (pbk)

Contents

CONTENTS

vi

PART FOUR
1970 and after

PART FIVE
Practice and Image 1700–2000

Illustrations

Figures

Tables

Preface

This collection of original, scholarly articles and selected readings from the work of journalists and those with direct experience of journalism has its origins in a conference organised jointly by the Campaign for Press and Broadcasting Freedom and the Department of Journalism at City University in February 1994. The title of the conference, 'The End of Fleet Street? The National Newspaper Industry in Historical Perspective', clearly indicated its theme. As organisers of the conference, we felt that while a great deal had been written and said about the events which the title of the conference evoked – the dispersal of the national newspaper sector from Fleet Street in the period after 1986 – little of it had been adequately analytical. Betraying our own primary concerns, we believed that the process of analysis was being hindered by the generally ahistorical perspective of the debates. We hoped that the conference would stimulate interest from scholars, students, researchers, practitioners and others outside, as well as from within, the still small population of historians working in the area of the media in general, and the press in particular. The objective was to foster cross- and inter-disciplinary contacts and approaches.

Some of the chapters in this book derive directly from papers delivered to the conference. Once we embarked on the prolonged process of publication, however, additional papers were offered. We also identified a need to gather together a selection of the work of journalists and others in the media industries with experience of journalism, parts of which we knew were regularly referred to but usually out of context. Scott's observation that 'Comment is free, but facts are sacred' is a case in point. We were also aware that a large number of students interested in journalism had few opportunities to explore its history. It is quite salutary for a former journalist to realise that a prospective generation of practitioners does not know that George Orwell was a journalist as well as a novelist, and has not heard of James Cameron. These factors, and the realisation that, as interest in journalism (rather than the media) rose in the 1990s, there was an obvious shortage of appropriate texts, led us to broaden our focus away from Fleet Street in the 1980s and 1990s.

This book does not attempt to present a history of journalism since 1800. It contains a series of inter-connected readings on specific topics within, and of specific views on, journalism. Our intention is to aid the process of understanding journalism and its role in the development over time of cultures commonly given the epithets 'democratic', 'popular', 'mass' and 'consumer'.

Michael Bromley
London

Tom O'Malley
Glamorgan

January 1997

Acknowledgements

We would like to thank all those who helped to organise and who partici-pated in the Campaign For Press and Broadcasting Freedom and City University conference on 'The End of Fleet Street?' in February 1994. We would also like to thank James Curran and Professor R.N. Franklin for supporting this project, and Rebecca Barden of Routledge for her guidance and help.

The editors and publishers acknowledge the sources of the following, and are grateful to those who granted permission to reproduce the extracts iden-tified:

Chapter 1: James Mill, 'Liberty of the Press', *Edinburgh Review* 18 (May 1811), 98–123; Chapter 2: J.S. Mill, 'Of the Liberty of Thought and Discussion', *Essay On Liberty* (1859); Chapter 4: W.T. Stead, 'The Future of Journalism', *Contemporary Review* (November 1886), 663–79; Chapter 7: Edward Dicey, 'Journalism Old and New', *Fortnightly Review* 83 (1905), 904–18; Chapter 8: C.P. Scott, 'The *Manchester Guardian*'s First Hundred Years', *The Guardian* (1921) © *The Guardian*; Chapter 9: Lord Riddell, 'The Psychology of the Journalist', *Journalism by Some Masters of the Craft*, Pitman Publishing (1932), 49–63; Chapter 10: Tom Clarke, *My Northcliffe Diary*, Gollancz (1931), 262–98; Chapter 11: Henry Wickham Steed, 'The Ideal Newspaper', *The Press*, Penguin Books (1938), 243–8; Chapter 13: George Orwell, 'The Prevention of Literature', *Selected Essays*, Penguin Books (1957), 159–74 © Mark Hamilton as literary executor of the estate of the late Sonia Bronwell Orwell and Martin Secker and Warburg; Chapter 14: Francis Williams, 'What Kind of Freedom?', *Dangerous Estate: The*

Anatomy of Newspapers, Longmans, Green (1957) and Patrick Stephens (1984), 251–6; Chapter 15: James Cameron, *Point of Departure: Experiment in Biography* (1969), 71–7 © HarperCollins Publishers; Chapter 16: Nicholas Tomalin, 'Stop the Press I Want to Get On', *Nicholas Tomalin Reporting*, Andre Deutsch (1975), 77–85 © estate of Nicholas Tomalin; Chapter 17: 'Conclusions?', *Journey into Journalism*, Writers and Readers Publishing Cooperative (1997), 103–7 © Arnold Wesker; Chapter 20: 'Call That a Newspaper?', *The 'Sun'-sation: Behind the Scenes of Britain's Best-Selling Daily Newspaper*, Angus and Robertson (1989), 50–62; Chapter 22: 'Why We are Here', *British Journalism Review* 1, 1 (1989), 2–6 © *British Journalism Review*.

General introduction

■   Michael Bromley and Tom O'Malley

THIS READER IN THE HISTORY OF journalism provides a
study aid for undergraduates, teachers and researchers. It contains
material which not only will help to deepen understanding of the practice
and context of journalism history but also raises new questions about the
history of the press and broadcasting industries. It brings together the work
of journalists, philosophers, historians, cultural theorists and specialists in
public policy and industrial relations, amongst others, who provide a variety
of perspectives on the history of journalism. This diversity expresses our view
that print and broadcasting are complex social institutions that need to be
studied using a range of analytical tools.

The material is arranged chronologically (Parts One–Four) and themat-
ically (Part Five). It can be used to underpin the teaching of the historical
development of the ideas and practice of journalism and to supplement available texts on media history (Curran and Seaton 1991; Jones 1996; Brown
1985). The readings can be used comparatively, to note the differences and
similarities across two hundred years of journalism. Equally, the articles can
be used to explore the salience of key themes in the history of journalism,
be they crime, gender, class, regulation, ownership, industrial relations, or
status. We hope that the volume will encourage a more historically informed
approach to the teaching of media, cultural and communication studies,
because, arguably, insufficient attention is currently given to the disciplines
and insights of historical analysis in both teaching and research in the
broad field of media, communication and cultural studies (Garnham 1990:
62).

The readings reprinted here are from philosophers (the Mills), editors (Stead, Steed, Dicey, Williams), correspondents (Cameron, Tomalin), owners (Riddell, Scott), and literary figures (Orwell, Wesker) – all with first-hand experience of journalism – and represent a range of perspectives on the purpose, status and craft of that occupation. They illustrate how journalism has been understood at different times and how the audiences for journalism have been conceived. The high minded, high Liberal theory of the Mills (Chapters 1 and 2) represents the peak of nineteenth century philosophising about the relationship between press, government, liberty and truth. The assumed audience for their pieces is middle and upper class, learned and used to tightly reasoned, allusive argument. By the end of the century and the beginning of the next there is a different tone to the pieces. Stead, the pioneer of 'New Journalism', and Dicey (Chapters 4 and 7) speak the language of the Victorian journalists at their most confident. They are sure about their importance and the importance of journalism in political life, yet they are also aware that not all is well with the press or journalism.

Thereafter, as the twentieth century develops, it is the troubled elements in Dicey and Stead which take over in our selections. The growth of a commercial, mass press after the 1890s sets the scene for discussions about the nature of journalism in the twentieth century. Riddell and Clarke (Chapters 9 and 10) reflect the values and assumptions of a proprietor and an editor, respectively, of the popular press during the first thirty to forty years of the century. Their tone recalls the socially superior and culturally insensitive figures ridiculed in Evelyn Waugh's novel *Scoop* (1938). They illustrate how assumptions about social class and gender structured aspects of journalism. Riddell's piece illustrates the continuing class divisions within the occupation and touches on a recurring theme in our collection; the uncertainty of what is the nature and purpose of journalism.

In the context of this collection, Wickham Steed, Orwell and Williams (Chapters 11, 13 and 14) are, in a sense, transitional voices. They articulate the tensions within journalism between the need to make a profit and views which attribute to journalism a social role over and above this goal – one of sustaining an informative, critical and intelligent level of public discussion. This tension underpinned the deliberations of the three post-war Royal Commissions on the press. But the tone of address used by these writers is markedly different to that used by the Mills or Stead and Dicey. It is an increasingly plainer tone, one which assumes a wider, more democratically constituted readership. It is not trivial but neither is it aloof and ponderous.

James Cameron's piece in Chapter 15 reflects the experience of a writer who has lived through these contradictions and has found his own niche within the field of journalism. Indeed Cameron's position is, as Bailey and Williams suggest in Chapter 28, unique. His principled vision of what journalism should be stands out, in sharp contrast to the more cynical perspective outlined in Chapter 16 by Tomalin and the unreflective brevity of Grose (Chapter 20).

Wesker's piece (Chapter 17) revisits the tensions inherent in journalistic practice, with the eye of an outsider and a dramatist. He asks, in a sense, who
are these people who claim so many rights as journalists? His answers replay
the growing awareness in the last decades of the century of a crisis in the
public perception of the role of journalism. As if in response, the extract
from the founding edition of the *British Journalism Review* (Chapter 22) is
full of a sense of crisis in the press and broadcasting and in the role of journalism, while contrarily, the extract from Grose represents the more confident
view of the nature and style of 'popular' journalism since the 1970s, and
takes the form of a defence of *The Sun*.

The articles commissioned for this reader reflect the range of factors
which have shaped journalism, to some extent in the nineteenth century but
mainly during the twentieth. Issues covered include crime, gender, class, and
empire from the nineteenth century. In the twentieth they cover questions of
the Labour movement and the press, ownership, industrial relations, content,
local journalism, and investigative journalism. We supplement these studies
with analyses of key, longer term themes. These touch on the relationship
between place and function in the metaphor of Fleet Street; the evolution of
the concepts of objectivity and impartiality in the press and broadcasting;
the way in which journalists have written about their experiences, and the
vexed question of whether journalism is a craft or profession.

The contributions use a range of published and unpublished sources and
tools of analysis from different traditions of study. There are common themes.
These include the importance of analysing the media in their historical
context; the importance of ownership and regulation; and the way in which
journalism weaves connections across different areas of social experience,
gender, class, politics and geography. The sense of journalism as a shifting,
unreflective activity, trying to capture meanings and to mobilise them for a
variety of different ends, emerges from the readings. Above all, there is the
sense of uncertainty – about the proper role of government in relation to the
media; about the role of commerce; about standards; about regulation and
training; about the effects of technological change. Most often, however, it
is the uncertainty in the voices of the practitioners which strikes home.
Reading these extracts and articles leaves the impression of groups of people
who are unsure of the craft and purpose.

Part of the dilemma of journalism may be located in the fragile nature
of its output. The accumulated works of tens of thousands of journalists over
the past two hundred years tend to 'lie buried in newspaper files; and . . .
like political speeches, rarely survive their hour' (Hayley 1946: 160). There
is little evidence that the pronounced shift in media, particularly in the later
twentieth century, has rendered journalism, recorded now on film and audio
and video tape, any less ephemeral. The Chronology at the end of this collection helps to make explicit the scope and accelerating rapidity of change in
the media – from the first tentative utilisation of steam to power printing

presses in the early nineteenth century to the apparent limitlessness of satellite transmitted digitalised multimedia in the 1990s – which have confronted journalism. Unlike many occupations, especially the 'old trades' of the pre-industrial and industrial eras, including most notably those in printing, journalism appears to have survived more or less intact the shifting contexts of its practice.

The value of the authentic voice of the practitioner in mapping this set of experiences seems clear, yet it is still largely inaccessible. Those whose writing has attained a greater permanence – and thus those represented in this collection – are exceptional. The correlation between this select group and the canon of British journalism (which is normally considered to include at least Stead, Scott, Steed, Orwell, Williams, Cameron and Tomalin – all of whom are represented in the pages which follow) seems clear but is as yet not fully explored. The exclusivity of the group moderates but does not render wholly invalid its experiences: it is among precisely these varied inheritors of the broadly Millsian tradition that we might expect the effects of the industrialisation and commercialisation of the press to have been most acutely felt.

A crucial element in the vulnerability of journalists is their apparently near total dependence on the media in which their work appears. The majority of those represented in this volume edited or wrote for a small number of liberal and left titles – the *Daily News* and its successor the *News Chronicle* (Dicey, Clarke, Williams, Cameron); the *Observer* (Dicey, Orwell, Williams); the (*Manchester*) *Guardian* (Scott, Cameron); the *New Statesman* (Orwell, Williams, Tomalin); and the *Daily Herald* (Cameron and Williams). So vibrant throughout the 1930s and 1940s, this press went into decline from the late 1950s. It has been argued that this had less to do with its political commitment than to the triumph of an alternative 'popular' journalism (Engel 1996: 179). The exemplar of left 'popular' journalism was the *Daily Mirror*, whose editor for most of the 1940s professed the rest of the London press to be 'too niminy-piminy, too nice altogether, too refined'. His successor wrote in 1948:

> The *Mirror* is a sensational paper. We make no apology for that. We believe in the sensational presentation of news and views, especially important news and views, as a necessary and valuable public service in these days of mass readership and democratic responsibility . . .
>
> Sensationalism does not mean distorting the truth. It means the vivid and dramatic presentation of events so as to give them a forceful impact on the mind of the reader. It means big headlines, vigorous writing, simplification into everyday language, and the wide use of illustration by cartoon and photograph . . .
>
> Sensational treatment is the answer, whatever the sober and 'superior' readers of some other journals may prefer.
>
> (Cudlipp 1953: 101–2; 250–51)

There was little new in the 'popular' articulation of social radicalism: it had been one of the hallmarks of much of the nineteenth century Sunday and evening press (Engel 1996: 45–7). The radical London evening newspaper the *Star* promised 'no ... verbose and prolix articles':

> We believe that the reader ... longs for other reading than mere politics, and we shall present him with plenty of entirely unpolitical literature – sometimes humorous, sometimes pathetic; anecdotal, statistical, the craze of fashions, and the arts of housekeeping – now and then, a short, dramatic and picturesque tale. ... Our ideal ... is to be animated, readable, and stirring.
>
> (*Star*, 17 January 1888)

Yet over time, the real struggle was that of making 'serious' journalism profitable (Spender 1930: 245–7).

In the commercialised and industrially organised press, exemplified by Northcliffe's *Daily Mail* from 1896, journalism was made to serve the enterprise through appealing at its lowest to 'the meanest intelligence' (Taylor 1996: 35–7). The 'serious' press recognised the challenges posed by this new paradigm which asserted the primacy of what Scott in Chapter 8 identifies as the 'material' interests of the press over its 'moral' responsibilities, and in which 'serious politics ... [were to] be sacrificed to commercial exigencies' (Spender 1930: 246). The pressure built as advertising became a more important component of newspapers in the 1930s (Hart-Davies 1990: 62). 'Serious' journalism survived by being underwritten by, but protected from, commercialism. The solution reached at the *Daily Herald* was that the original owners, the TUC, continued to dictate editorial policy while the new majority shareholders, Odhams, ran the business (Engel 1996: 121). At the *News Chronicle* the chairman, Walter Layton, secured annual profits for a quarter of a century after 1931, while also defending journalistic standards as editor-in-chief (Hubback 1985: 128ff). In both instances, the arrangement collapsed in the 1960s and the papers ceased publication.

An alternative accommodation then presented itself, based on the premise of the neutrality of commercialism which permitted 'serious' journalism to re-assert its autonomy. Roy Thomson (1975: 219–20) argued that establishing the importance of the press as 'a marketplace for goods and services' permitted newspapers to function efficiently and to avoid conflict between their commercial and editorial activities. At the Thomson-owned *Sunday Times* under the editorship of Harold Evans, as Doig points out in Chapter 18, investigatory journalism apparently unhampered by commercial considerations flourished in the late 1960s and 1970s. The work of the 'Insight' team seemed to transcend many of the limitations of later twentieth century journalism, not least in the publication of a number of books both by the team and by others about its work (Linton and Boston 1987: 156, 207,

236, 269). This partial rediscovery of journalistic confidence was short-lived. After Thomson sold Times Newspapers to Rupert Murdoch, commercial interests became predominant (Leapman 1992: 75–9; Evans 1983). As Grose's paean for *The Sun* suggests, there is a close coincidence between a newspaper's (editorial) 'rapport with its readers' and purely commercial objectives such as 'getting closer to the customer': Simon Jenkins (1986: 218) has seen this phase as the final unification of capitalism and free speech. The extent to which, if it is so, it has diverged from even the utilitarian vision of the elder Mill may be judged from the ways in which newspaper proprietors of the 1980s expressed their ambitions: 'if the readers of pop papers want lower standards, who can deny them?' Eddie Shah observed (Goodhart and Wintour 1986: 292–3); 'I want a tearaway paper with a lot of tit,' Murdoch is supposed to have told the staff of *The Sun* (Engel 1996: 253).

One foreseeable outcome of such an approach is explored by Gall in Chapter 21. While most immediately the consequence of exceptional circumstances, the situation at the post-Maxwell *Mirror* was surely a product of the far more general attempt to impose so-called 'macho management' not only on newspapers in the era of Wapping but also increasingly on broadcasting. Most attention in this respect has fallen on the national newspaper sector: it is noticeable that since the 1980s the media themselves tended to break the unspoken rule of Fleet Street that 'dog does not eat dog', and turned attention upon themselves. Fleet Street suddenly became newsworthy, not simply because, as much of British industry declined in relative terms, the media assumed a new more visible role as 'big business', or because of the close interrelationships with the personalities and policies of the Thatcher governments, but also because, as Harris points out in Chapter 25, it had assumed the character of a national metaphor for the democratic health of the culture (a factor which, it may be argued, was successfully exploited by Thatcher) (Bromley 1995). Franklin and Murphy remind us in Chapter 19 that a parallel trend can be traced in the local press, where, they suggest, the concentration of ownership among a small group of conglomerates was at least as damaging to the perceived role of the journalist in the process that Habermas (1989) calls 'the public sphere'. In this respect, the journalist leans heavily on the slippery concept of 'objectivity'. Allan proposes in Chapter 26 (after E.P. Thompson) that objectivity is a set of historically located relationships, and that attempts to fix it either in 'professional' practice or in statutory obligations of impartiality are likely to create only anachronisms.

Kaul provides evidence in Chapter 5 of the ways in which journalists are compromised by governments, by their media employers, and sometimes by the two acting in consort. News – and views – are valuable assets in politics and business. Indeed, Petley suggests in Chapter 23 that in the contemporary national press the marketability and ideological correctness of a particular style of punditry has all but supplanted, and may be subverting, the role of the press as informer and educator. It is highly ironic that statutory requirements for impartiality in news and current affairs which are imposed on broadcasting have presented newspapers with a unique selling proposition as providers of cheap and nasty entertainment pandering to prejudice. The ecology of this kind of journalism is often assumed to be the tendency toward intense concentration of media ownership since 1945, which has been further encouraged by the deregulatory policies of Conservative governments since 1979, and which is popularly embodied in the rather menacing spectre of 'the Murdoch press'. Yet when Stead surveyed the London press in 1904 he discovered a landscape many of whose main contours must be familiar to the newspaper reader of ninety years later, and for the creation of which, Baylen asserts in Chapter 6, Stead himself must bear some responsibility. This press helped to widen the public sphere, not least through the process of feminisation. The analysis of Carter and Thompson in Chapter 3 delineates some of the late nineteenth century origins of Murdoch's commercial obsession with sensationalism, and proposes ways of problematising it at a time when the media are again inclined to play the 'gender card'.

The experience of some of the journalists represented in this volume (Clarke, Williams, Cameron) and the findings of Doig indicate that for an extended period (from the 1930s to the 1980s) the public service environment both at the BBC and within the current affairs programming areas of Independent Television offered an attractive alternative place to practise the kind of journalism that was being squeezed from the pages of national newspapers. Yet the increasing commercial pressures on both ITV companies and the BBC, resulting largely from the policies of the Thatcher governments, may limit those opportunities in the 1990s and beyond.

Particularly since 1979 Labour, as well as the Conservatives, have drawn back from utilising the mechanism of State regulation of the media. The nineteenth century Liberal origins of the press enshrined a resistance to government oversight. As O'Malley demonstrates in Chapter 12, neither mounting concern over the performance of the press since the turn of the century nor the opportunity for regulation presented by the establishment of the BBC has been sufficient to overcome this. The first Royal Commission on the press is generally criticised for being ineffective. Yet, given the historical development of the press and its enmeshment with the emergence of the liberal, democratic nation-State as 'watchdog' and 'Fourth Estate', what room was there for manoeuvre?

Since the 1980s many proponents of a more 'democratic' media have suggested that the global network of electronic delivery systems may prove more productive in this respect, because it has the capacity to remain free of *all* regulation (see Gilder 1994). The prospect is held out of messages unmediated by journalists travelling directly between citizens. No media, the argument goes, means no requirement for regulation. The debate continues, and Doull presents an alternative picture in Chapter 24 in which the Internet is heavily colonised by journalists. The deep interest shown by many traditional media owners in 'the information superhighway' suggests that they expect there to be 'business as usual' in cyberspace. Bromley in Chapter 27 goes so far as to suggest that the introduction of computerisation has provided capital with an opportunity to routinise the editorial function to an extent which actually threatens the continued existence of journalism as an occupation in any currently recognisable form.

It is perhaps not surprising, therefore, that journalists emerge as a group of people uncertain about how useful their work is or how acceptable they are as a group. The journalist does not have the defined role of the lawyer, cook, cleaner, doctor, building worker or bus driver. Journalism in the last two hundred years has produced many strident advocates rushing to defend its activities and to speculate on its role and function. Yet the journalist's very tendency to write in a swift, unreflective form produces impressionist accounts of the practice and purpose. The prevalence of this form of writing suggests that journalism has existed, in some senses, on the margins of social acceptability. Unlike other activities, there is something about journalism which is permanently troubled and contradictory. These readings should help students to explore this and other themes in the long, complex, important and fascinating history of journalism.

References

Bromley, M. (1995) 'From conciliation to confrontation: industrial relations, Government and the Fourth Estate, 1896–1986', in A. O'Day (ed.) *Government and Institutions in the Post-1832 United Kingdom*, Lampeter: Mellen Press, 361–89.

Brown, L. (1985) *Victorian News and Newspapers*, Oxford: Clarendon Press.

Cudlipp, H. (1953) *Publish and Be Damned: The Astonishing Story of the 'Daily Mirror'*, London: Andrew Dakers.

Curran, J. and Seaton, J. (1991) *Power Without Responsibility*, London: Routledge.

Engel, M. (1996) *Tickle the Public: One Hundred Years of the Popular Press*, London: Gollancz.

Evans, H. (1983) *Good Times, Bad Times*, London: Weidenfeld & Nicolson.

Garnham, N. (1990) *Capitalism and Communication*, London: Sage.

Gilder, G. (1994 edn) *Life After Television: The Coming Transformation of Media and American Life*, New York: Norton.

Goodhart, D. and Wintour, P. (1986) *Eddie Shah and the Newspaper Revolution*, London: Coronet.

Habermas, J. (1989) *The Transformation of the Public Sphere* (trans. Thomas Burger), Cambridge: Polity Press.

Hart-Davis, D. (1990) *The House the Berrys Built: Inside 'The Telegraph', 1928–1986*, London: Hodder & Stoughton.

Hayley, Sir W. (ed.) (1946) *C.P. Scott, 1846–1932. The Making of the 'Manchester Guardian'*, London: Frederick Muller.

Hubback, D. (1985) *No Ordinary Press Baron: A Life of Walter Layton*, London: Weidenfeld & Nicolson.

Jenkins, S. (1986) *The Market for Glory: Fleet Street Ownership in the Twentieth Century*, London: Faber & Faber.

Jones, A. (1996) *Powers of the Press. Newspapers, Power and Public in Nineteenth-Century England*, Aldershot: Scolar Press.

Leapman, M. (1992) *Treacherous Estate: The Press after Fleet Street*, London: Hodder & Stoughton.

Linton, D. and Boston, R. (eds) (1987) *The Newspaper Press in Britain: An Annotated Bibliography*, London: Mansell.

Spender, J.A. (1930) *Weetman Pearson, First Viscount Cowdray*, London: Cassell.

Taylor, S.J. (1996) *The Great Outsiders: Northcliffe, Rothermere and the 'Daily Mail'*, London: Weidenfeld & Nicolson.

Thomson of Fleet, Lord (1975) *After I Was Sixty: A Chapter of Autobiography*, London: Hamish Hamilton.

Waugh, E. (1938) *Scoop*, London: Little, Brown.

PART ONE

1800–1900

Introduction to part one

■   Michael Bromley

FROM HIS TWENTIETH CENTURY vantage point, R.K. Ensor reflected nostalgically on 'the dignified phase of English journalism' of the second half of the nineteenth century. The (almost last) bastions of this journalism 'conducted with a high sense of personal responsibility' were the penny morning newspapers, modelled on *The Times*, and the monthly and quarterly reviews, whose stock-in-trade was political news and views presented in 'long articles, long paragraphs' and 'small treatises'. Although 'incredibly dull and matter-of-fact' when compared to the 'brighter' newspapers of the closing years of the nineteenth century, this press did not confuse journalism with business, nor did it 'cook' the news by 'doctoring the facts' (Ensor 1936: 144–5; 310–14). Newspapers, as Charles Dickens observed in his first leading article for the new *Daily News* in 1846, were not to be run as if they were the trade in patent medicines.

Until the 1850s the press was partially regulated through the imposition of the 'taxes on knowledge', the main effect of which was to provide an imprimatur to 'respectable' publications. The 'freeing' of the press exposed the dilemma of the classical liberal approach to press freedom. Ostensibly 'free' to address directly the demands of an expanding national polity for public information, the press was simultaneously at liberty to pursue the burgeoning consumer market.

A press that was priced by the market, it was commonly argued in the 1850s, 'must be a low sort of thing' (*The People's Review of Literature and Progress*, February 1850), and the 'free' press settlement seemed to many of its supporters to run into trouble in the 1880s and 1890s. Newspapers,

Henry Massingham wrote in horror in the *National Review* in April 1900, were actually run for the readers by their proprietors; editors, he suggested, were no longer necessary. Their 'independence of judgement' was not required; and an editor could not 'give his work that personal note out of which the power of influencing others really comes'. Pessimism about the 'democratic despotism' fostered by a cheap press infected many liberals.

> the whole attitude towards the reader was transformed. The old idea assumed that he was a critical politician, who watched events and would resent the paper's missing any serious news-item. All such items were therefore carefully given, and if none of them happened to be very 'bright' that was the affair of Providence, and must be accepted like rain or sun. The new idea assumed a mass of readers, whose interest in politics was slight, whose memories were short, who would never know or care if half the serious news were left out, but who day by day demanded bright stories to tickle their imaginations ... and if Providence did not supply exciting news, the office must not fail to make some.
>
> (Ensor 1936: 314)

Were the principles of free expression, such as those articulated by James and John Stuart Mill, to be sacrificed on the altar of commercialism? Although coinciding with this commercialisation of the press from the 1880s, the 'New Journalism', as practised by W.T. Stead, represented an attempt to exploit the opportunities presented by the development of more populist journalism to extend participation in public affairs to a wider public. The flavour of Stead's 'utopian objectives' (Baylen 1992: 38) is revealed in the extract reproduced here.

That the 'revolution' in the press could not be contained; that clear distinctions could not be made between 'hard' and 'soft' news, or between politics and consumption (Hartley 1996: 6, 34) is apparent from Kaul's analysis of Imperial communications as they developed rapidly over the latter part of the nineteenth century and into the twentieth. The demand for news from India extended beyond the élite readership of *The Times*, and the news agencies, utilising the facilities offered by the telegraph, were able to supply the raw material of 'factual' reports to 'popular' newspapers whose sub-editors rewrote the dispatches into short paragraphs. Yet, while it may be justifiably claimed that, in conflating what must have still been for many of the new readers the abstractions of global politics with the prospect of meeting tangible if modestly rising material expectations, newspapers such as the *Daily Mail* 'expanded .. horizons' (Engel 1996: 60–3), their exploitative tendencies were all too apparent. Nowhere was this more so perhaps than in the mobilisation of gender which served, as Carter and Thompson indicate, to deny, confine and marginalise issues and events which threatened the violent patriarchal foundations of late Victorian society, while facilitating the identification of women as 'target' consumers.

The newspaper in part created by the period of Gladstone's Free Trade budgets of 1853 and 1860, which removed the duties on more than 500 items, was a consumer good itself, and it made its journalists compete for space with display advertisements for soap, chocolate, department stores and patent medicines.

References

Baylen, J.O. (1992) 'The British press, 1861–1918', in D. Griffiths (ed.) *The Encyclopedia of the British Press, 1422–1992*, London: Macmillan, 33–46.

Engel, M. (1996) *Tickle the Public: One Hundred Years of the Popular Press*, London: Gollancz.

Ensor, R.K. (1936) *England: 1870–1914*, London: Oxford University Press.

Hartley, J. (1996) *Popular Reality: Journalism, Modernity, Popular Culture*, London: Edward Arnold.

Chapter 1

James Mill

LIBERTY OF THE PRESS

OUR LAW IN FAVOUR of the liberty of the press consists in mere general expressions[1], and these not engrossed in statutes, but inserted in the works of individual lawyers, and there accompanied with qualifying clauses altogether as vague and comprehensive as the 'pourvu qu'on ne conspire pas contre le gouvernement', which was found so efficacious in France. Thus, Blackstone tells us – 'Every person has an undoubted right to lay what sentiments he pleases before the public: to forbid this, is to destroy the liberty of the press.' This is nearly equivalent to the general permission of Directorial law. The learned author proceeds – 'But if he publishes what is improper, mischievous, or illegal, he must take the consequence of his own temerity.' Now, where are we to look for authentic definition of these important words *improper*, *mischievous*, *illegal*? Alas, we know not . . . The Lord Chief Baron Comyns, in his justly admired Digest of the English Law, defines a libel to be, 'a contumely or reproach, published to the defamation of the government, of a magistrate, or of a private person'. Now, *contumely*, *reproach*, and *defamation*, include every thing that can be construed into censure. No censure, therefore, of the government, or even of a public functionary, is safe in England. We shall produce only one other authority, as being both a very recent, and a very high one. On the trial in the cause, entitled, The King against Cobbet [*sic*], 24th May 1804, Lord Ellenborough said, 'It is no new doctrine, that if a publication be calculated to alienate the affections of the people, *by bringing the government into disesteem*, whether the expression be ridicule or obloquy, the person so conducting himself is exposed to the inflictions of the law: – It is a crime.' Now, to point out any fault in the government undoubtedly tends to bring, so far, the government into disesteem. Therefore, to point out any fault in the government, is a liberty not allowed to the press by the law of England.

Several years ago, we expressed our sense of this important matter in the following terms:

> The liberty of the press is, indeed, the most inestimable security of that of a people, because it gives the tone to the public feelings on which all liberty must ultimately rest. But how is it that we have learned to deem it one of our constitutional rights? A great deal is said about it in pamphlets; a great deal is said about it in essays on government; it is an acknowledged privilege everywhere, but in Westminster-Hall. *There, unluckily, it has neither a habitation nor a name.* M. de Lolme tells us, that he was struck at not being able to hear of any law which enacted the liberty of the press, till it occurred to him that it existed, because it was not forbidden. But, with a little more inquiry, this ingenious foreigner might have found law enough *against* this *soi-disant* right; though none *for* it. The truth is, the liberty of the press *does not exist*, nor ever did exist in England, but by connivance. And, unless at our distance from the metropolis, we are deceived as to that actual practice of the English courts, the indulgence itself (viz. the connivance) has been reduced within very narrow limits. It is as difficult for the most adroit pamphleteer to arraign public measures, without blaming public men, as for Shakespeare's Jew to take his pound of flesh without a drop of blood; and if this is the fullest extent of the privilege, we may safely pronounce, that *fari quae sentias* will be as much a phantom of right *in practice*, as it has always been in law.

[O]f all the dangers at the present day besetting our liberties, the danger of leaving a door open for the destruction of the liberty of the press, by a vague and indeterminate law of libel, is by far the greatest.

The law of libel in this country presents, indeed, a phenomenon, to which we know not that a parallel is to be found in the history of mankind. Although founded entirely upon recent and practical authority, and claiming no reverence for antiquity or legislative sanction, it is a law at utter variance with the sentiments of every class and denomination of men, both public and private, in the kingdom. Even Attorneys-General themselves, in the very act of arraigning some unfortunate man for a libel, never fail to declare themselves friends to the liberty of the press. Not a man, probably, could be found in the nation capable of understanding the meaning of the terms, who would not declare the freedom of the press to be one of the first of political blessings — to be that sort of security for our liberties, without which all other liberties would prove vain and ineffectual . . . That liberty of the press, so uniformly extolled, the law entirely disallows. There is not a conceivable expression, passing censure upon any institution, any measure, or any member of Government, which the all-comprehending law of libel places not within the verge of punishment, — of punishment short of life, and liable to any degree of severity the Judges please . . . if every thing that *reflects* on those entrusted with the administration of public affairs, — if every thing tending to the *discredit* of any one of them be an *aggravated* libel, — it is absurd and ridiculous to speak of the liberty of the press . . . There can be no doubt, that to pronounce a man in a high situation unfit for his office, would be disagreeable to his feelings; but if the press must not so much as insinuate that any public functionary is only fit for the private walks of life, it is but an idle mockery to tell us we have a free press . . .

Is there any man, however inclined to screw up the springs of authority, who reckons it criminal to lay before the public, expressions reflecting upon the qualifications or practices of public men? . . .

It is sufficiently obvious, that, with regard to political subjects and public men, the liberty of the press may be abused in two ways. The one is, when good public measures, and good public men, are blamed; — the other is, when bad public measure, and bad public men, are praised. Of these two, we should consider the last as being infinitely the worst. It is not only, beyond all comparison, the most prevalent, as being the best paid, and not at all punished: But it is infinitely the most dangerous and the most fatal in its operation. It is the skreen by which, more effectually than by any thing else, power is concealed in that *gradual* progress to despotism . . . And, even when nothing worse than imbecility wields the reins, it is that by which it is chiefly upheld in its blunders, till it ripens national misfortunes into national ruin. Every thing the government performs is asserted, and with pretended demonstration proved, to be excellent. Every plausible circumstance which can be discovered belonging to it, is displayed in the most advantageous light, and fixed habitually in the public eye, while every dangerous or mischievous circumstance is carefully disguised or hidden from the view. To the great mass of mankind whose minds are chiefly passive in the reception of their opinions, nothing more is needed to make them believe that their government is admirable, than perpetually to hear that it is so. And, even upon the strongest minds, it is well known that the tide of popular opinion, if running with any considerable strength, is all but irresistible . . .

It is evident, therefore, that if any exercise whatsoever of the press be an abuse, its becoming that vehicle of undeserved praise of public men and public measures is an abuse; and if mischief be the ground of complaint, no other abuse presents so many and cogent reasons for being restrained by punishment . . .

We have, at the same time, a just sense of the evils which arise from the abuse of censure pronounced by the press. In regard to the public transactions of public men, or their qualifications for public trusts, as we deem no praise to be an abuse but that which is undeserved, so we deem no censure. Wherever real incapacity in a public man is pointed out — wherever the real impolicy or mischief of a wrong measure is stript of its disguise, and made to appear in its own shape, we conceive that the nation is served in the highest instance; and any thing rather than an abuse, has been effected by the press. But we readily grant, that when, by the influence of false censure, a good nation is made to disapprove of a good measure, or a good minister, and to defeat the one, or deprive itself of the other, the press has been the source of mischief. There is, in the first place, refutation of the censure by the same channel; a grand and appropriate cure, and which, considering the force of truth, will generally prevail. And there is punishment, which, as often as a man brings an accusation which he cannot support, may be inflicted in measure and proportion.

There is, however, another danger, real or imaginary, of which certain classes of men hold up to their own eyes a colossal and hideous picture; and labour earnestly with it to appal the hearts of other men; — that is, the danger of anarchy, arising from excessive censure of measures of government and public men. Now, without pretending for the present to measure very accurately the degree in which the press ever has contributed to produce the evils of anarchy, or is every likely to contribute, this we take upon us without any hesitation to say, that the abuse, in the way of censure, has far less tendency to produce the evils of anarchy, than the abuse in the way of praise has to produce the evils of despotism; and that despotism is by far the most imminent danger. It is from the praise, and not from the censure, that society has infinitely the most to dread.

To point out the exact limits of the power of the press to disorder society by the abuse of censure, would require a minute analysis of the nature and constitution of different governments. A few obvious considerations, however, may be presented, which afford no inaccurate standard to judge by. Of those countries which have enjoyed the most of the power of censure by the press; and those which have enjoyed the least: — in which has there appeared the greatest disposition to anarchy, and in which the least? The answer which the experience of history presents to us, will surprise those who have credulously lent their faith to the men who have lately been so active in traducing the application of censure by the press. The only countries in which any tolerable degree of the liberty of the press has ever been enjoyed, have been a few of the Protestant countries of modern times — England, Holland, Switzerland, and the United States of North America. Now, so far from showing the greatest tendency to anarchy, – of all countries that ever existed, these have been the farthest removed from that tendency . . .

But the revolution in France is something which agitates the imaginations of men, and which, without allowing them time to render themselves in any tolerable degree acquainted with the facts of that extraordinary event, makes them fear and detest in the mass all things which, justly or unjustly, have been ever supposed to have had a share in producing it. The abuse of the press was carried to a great height during the excesses of the French revolution; — the abuse, therefore, of the press was, they tell us, the cause of these excesses. This we consider to be . . . [a] fallacy . . . The abuses of the press which attended the excesses of the French revolution, we regard as the effect, not the cause of the public disorders . . .Were there never any cruel and sanginuary revolutions but where there was a press? . . .

It was not the abuse of a *free* press which was witnessed during the French revolution; it was the abuse of an *enslaved* press. The press was at all times the exclusive instrument of the domineering faction, who made use of it to calumniate their enemies and agitate the people; but prevented, by the terrors of extermination, all other men from making use of the press to expose their machinations and character. It was exactly that species of abuse which is committed, in different degrees, by every set of rulers in France, in England, or any where else, who allow more latitude to freedom of expressions on their own side, than on that of their opponents. Had real freedom of the press been enjoyed – had the honest men whom France contained been left a channel by which to lay their sentiments before the public – had a means been secured of instructing the people in the real nature of the delusions which were practised upon them, the enormities of the revolution would have been confined within a narrow compass, and its termination would have been very different . . .

If men would only employ a little patient consideration in forming their notions, we should not despair of getting all but a few, to join with us in opinion, that, so far from the freedom of the press being the cause of the French revolution, had a free press existed in France, the French revolution never would have taken place. It is the natural, nay, we may confidently say, the necessary effect of a free press, so to harmonise together the tone of the government and the sentiments of the people, that no jarring opposition between them can ever arise. By the free circulation of opinions, the government is always fully apprised, which, by no other means it ever can be, of the sentiments of the people, and feels a decided interest in conforming to them. As it must thus, in some degree, mould itself upon the sentiments of the people, so it feels an interest in fashioning the sentiments of the people to a conformity with its views. It is at pains to instruct, to persuade, and to conciliate. It acts not with a proud and negligent disdain of the feelings of the people. In a word, the government and the people are under a moral necessity of acting together; a free press compels them to bend to one another; and any contrariety of views and purposes liable to arise, can never come to such a head as to threaten convulsions. We may safely affirm, that more freedom of the press granted to our own country, would have the salutary effect of harmonising, to a much greater degree, the tone of government and the sentiments of the people, and of rendering all violent opposition between them still more improbable than even at present it is. We may even go further: we may speak of that state of convulsion itself, against which so many of our contemporaries think it necessary to take so many precautions. Were that revolution, which we think so very little probable, really to happen, nothing would prove so strong a bulwark against the abuses, to which a state of revolution is apt to give birth, as the freedom of the press, so clearly established and modified by law, and the utility of its exercise so fully proved by experience, that it would be impossible for the public to be deceived in regard to the shackles which a predominant faction might desire to impose upon that freedom, or in regard to the false glosses which it would endeavour to put upon its own and other men's transactions.

That the press, too, though calculated to produce important effects in the slow progress of ages, is an instrument with which no violent and sudden changes can ever be effects, we should think abundantly evident, upon a little consideration of its very nature . . .

The liberty of the press is a point on which so much depends, and with regard to which there is still in this country so much room for reform, that we shall not be easily induced to remit our efforts, till that sort of legislative provision, which we have here endeavoured to describe, be at last bestowed upon the nation.

Note

1   This extract is taken from a review of an edition of Emmanuel Ralph's *Memoires de Candide, sur La Liberté de la Presse* which appeared in the *Edinburgh Review* (May 1811). Mill (1773–1836) moved to London from Scotland at the beginning of the nineteenth century to pursue a career in journalism. From 1802 he was editor of the *Literary Journal*, and from 1805 to 1808 editor of the *St James's Chronicle*. He helped Jeremy Bentham to found the *Westminster Review* in 1824.

Chapter 2

J.S. Mill

OF THE LIBERTY OF THOUGHT AND DISCUSSION

THE TIME, IT IS HOPED, is gone by when any defence would be neces-sary of the 'liberty of the press' as one of the securities against corrupt or tyrannical government[1]. No argument, we may suppose, can now be needed against permitting a legislature or an executive, not identified in interest with the people, to prescribe opinions to them and determine what doctrines or what arguments they shall be allowed to hear . . . Let us suppose, therefore, that the government is entirely at one with the people, and never thinks of exerting any power of coercion unless in agreement with what it conceives to be their voice. But I deny the right of the people to exercise such coercion, either by themselves or by their government. The power itself is illegitimate. The best government has no more title to it than the worst. It is as noxious, or more noxious, when exerted in accordance with public opinion than when in opposition to it. If all mankind minus one were of one opinion, mankind would be no more justified in silencing that one person than he, if he had the power, would be justified in silencing mankind. Were an opinion a personal possession of no value except to the owner, if to be obstructed in the enjoyment of it were simply a private injury, it would make some difference whether the injury was inflicted only on a few persons or on many. But the peculiar evil of silencing the expression of an opinion is that it is robbing the human race, posterity as well as the existing gener-ation – those who dissent from the opinion, still more than those who hold it. If the opinion is right, they are deprived of the opportunity of exchanging error for truth; if wrong, they lose, what is almost as great a benefit, the clearer perception and livelier impression of truth produced by its collision with error . . .

We can never be sure that the opinion we are endeavouring to stifle is a false opinion; and if we were sure, stifling it would be an evil still.

First, the opinion which it is attempted to suppress by authority may possibly be true. Those who desire to suppress it, of course, deny its truth; but they are not infallible. They have no authority to decide the question for all mankind and exclude every other person from the means of judging. To refuse a hearing to an opinion because they are sure that it is false is to assume that their certainty is the same thing as absolute certainty. All silencing of discussion is an assumption of infallibility. Its condemnation may be allowed to rest on this common argument, not the worse for being common.

Unfortunately for the good sense of mankind, the fact of their fallibility is far from carrying the weight in their practical judgment which is always allowed to it in theory; for while everyone well knows himself to be fallible, few think it necessary to take any precautions against their own fallibility, or admit the supposition that any opinion of which they feel very certain may be one of the examples of the error to which they acknowledge themselves to be liable . . . Nor is his faith in this collective authority at all shaken by his being aware that other ages, countries, sects, churches, classes, and parties have thought, and even now think, the exact reverse. He devolves upon his own world the responsibility of being in the right against the dissentient worlds of other people; and it never troubles him that mere accident has decided which of these numerous worlds is the object of his reliance, and the same causes which make him a churchman in London would have made him a Buddhist or Confucian in Peking. Yet it is as evident in itself, as any amount of argument can make it, that ages are no more infallible than individuals – every age having held many opinions which subsequent ages have deemed not only false but absurd; and it is as certain that many opinions, now general, will be rejected by future ages, as it is that many, once general, are rejected by the present . . .

If even the Newtonian philosophy were not permitted to be questioned, mankind could not feel as complete assurance of its truth as they do now. The beliefs which we have most warrant for have no safeguard to rest on but a standing invitation to the whole world to prove them unfounded. If the challenge is not accepted, or is accepted and the attempt fails, we are far enough from certainty still, but we have done the best that the existing state of human reason admits of . . .

Strange it is that men should admit the validity of the arguments for free discussion, but object to their being 'pushed to an extreme', not seeing that unless the reasons are good for an extreme case, they are not good for any case. Strange they should imagine that they are not assuming infallibility when they acknowledge that there should be free discussion on all subjects which can possibly be doubtful, but think that some particular principle or doctrine should be forbidden to be questioned because it is so certain, that is, because they are certain that it is certain. To call any proposition certain, while there is anyone who would deny its certainty if permitted, but who is not permitted, is to assume that we ourselves, and those who agree with us, are the judges of certainty, and judges without hearing the other side . . .

Let us now pass to the second division of the argument, and dismissing the supposition that any of the received opinions may be false, let us assume them to be true and examine into the worth of the manner in which they are likely to be held when their truth is not freely and openly canvassed. However unwillingly a person who has a strong opinion may admit the possibility that his opinion may be false, he ought to be moved by the consideration that, however true it may be, if it is not fully, frequently, and fearlessly discussed, it will be held as a dead dogma, not a living truth.

There is a class of persons (happily not quite so numerous as formerly) who think it enough if a person assents undoubtingly to what they think true, though he has no knowledge whatever of the grounds of the opinion and could not make a tenable defence of it against the most superficial objections . . . This is not knowing the truth. Truth, thus held, is but one superstition the more, accidentally clinging to the words which enunciate a truth . . .

Whatever people believe, on subjects on which it is of the first importance to believe rightly, they ought to be able to defend against at least the common objections . . . On every subject on which difference of opinion is possible, the truth depends on a balance to be struck between two sets of conflicting reasons. Even in natural philosophy, there is always some other explanation possible of the same facts; some geocentric theory instead of heliocentric, some phlogiston instead of oxygen; and it has to be shown why that other theory cannot be the true one; and until this is shown, and until we know how it is shown, we do not understand the grounds of our opinion. But when we turn to subjects infinitely more complicated, to morals, religion, politics, social relations, and the business of life, three-fourths of the arguments for every disputed opinion consist in dispelling the appearances which favour some opinion different from it . . . He who knows only his own side of the case knows little of that. His reasons may be good, and no one may have been able to refute them. But if he is equally unable to refute the reasons on the opposite side, if he does not so much as know what they are, he has no ground for preferring either opinion . . . Nor is it enough that he should hear the arguments of adversaries from his own teachers, presented as they state them, and accompanied by what they offer as refutations. This is not the way to do justice to the arguments or bring them into real contact with his own mind. He must be able to hear them from persons who actually believe them, who defend them in earnest and do their very utmost for them. He must know them in their most plausible and persuasive form; he must feel the whole force of the difficulty which the true view of the subject has to encounter and dispose of, else he will never really possess himself of the portion of truth which meets and removes that difficulty. Ninety-nine in a hundred of what are called educated men are in this condition even of those who can argue fluently for their opinions. Their conclusion may be true, but it might be false for anything they know; they have never thrown themselves into the mental position of those who think differently from them, and considered what such persons may have to say; and, consequently, they do not, in any proper sense of the word, know the doctrine which they themselves profess . . . So essential is this discipline to a real understanding of moral and human subjects that, if opponents of all-important truths do not exist, it is indispensable to imagine them and supply them with the strongest arguments which the most skilful devil's advocate can conjure up . . . If the teachers of mankind are to be cognisant of all that they ought to know, everything must be free to be written and published without restraint.

If, however, this mischievous operation of the absence of free discussion, when the received opinions are true, were confined to leaving men ignorant of the grounds of those opinions, it might be thought that this, if an intellectual, is no moral evil and does not affect the worth of the opinions, regarded in their influence on the character. The fact, however, is that not only the grounds of the opinion are forgotten in the absence of discussion, but too often the meaning of the opinion itself. The words which convey it cease to suggest ideas, or suggest only a small portion of those they were originally employed to communicate. Instead of a vivid conception and a living belief, there remain only a few phrases retained by rote; or, if any part, the shell and husk only of the meaning is retained, the finer essence being lost . . .

It still remains to speak of one of the principal causes which make diversity of opinion advantageous, and will continue to do so until mankind shall have entered a stage of intellectual advancement which at present seems at an incalculable distance. We have hitherto considered only two possibilities: that the received opinion may be false, and some other opinion, consequently, true; or that, the received opinion being true, a conflict with the opposite error is essential to a clear apprehension and deep feeling of its truth. But there is a commoner case than either of these: when the conflicting doctrines, instead of one being true and the other false, share the truth between them, and the nonconforming opinion is needed to supply the remainder of the truth of which the received doctrine embodies only a part. Popular opinions, on subjects not palpable to sense, are often true, but seldom or never the whole truth. They are a part of the truth, sometimes a greater, sometimes a smaller part, but exaggerated, distorted, and disjointed from the truths by which they ought to be accompanied and limited. Heretical opinions, on the other hand, are generally some of these suppressed and neglected truths, bursting the bonds which kept them down, and either seeking reconciliation with the truth contained in the common opinion, or fronting it as enemies, and setting themselves up, with similar exclusiveness, as the whole truth . . . Even progress, which ought to superadd, for the most part only substitutes one partial and incomplete truth for another; improvement consisting chiefly in this, that the new fragment of truth is more wanted, more adapted to the needs of the time than that which it displaces. Such being the partial character of prevailing opinions, even when resting on a true foundation, every opinion which embodies somewhat of the portion of truth which the common opinion omits ought to be considered precious, with whatever amount of error and confusion that truth may be blended . . .

Unless opinions favourable to democracy and to aristocracy, to property and to equality, to co-operation and to competition, to luxury and to abstinence, to sociality and to individuality, to liberty and discipline, and all the other standing antagonisms of practical life, are expressed with equal freedom and enforced and defended with equal talent and energy, there is no chance of both elements obtaining their due; one scale is sure to go up, and the other down. Truth, in the great practical concerns of life, is so much a question of the reconciling and combining of opposites that very few have minds sufficiently capacious and impartial to make the adjustment with an approach to correctness, and it has to be made by the rough process of a struggle between combatants fighting under hostile banners . . . Only through diversity of opinion is there, in the existing state of human intellect, a chance of fair play to all sides of truth. When there are persons to be found who form an exception to the apparent unanimity of the world on any subject, even if the world is in the right, it is always probable that dissentients have something worth hearing to say for themselves, and that truth would lose something by their silence . . .

The exclusive pretention made by a part of the truth to be the whole must and ought to be protested against; and if a reactionary impulse should make the protestors unjust in their turn, this one-sidedness, like the other, may be lamented but must be tolerated . . .

I do not pretend that the most unlimited use of the freedom of enunciating all possible opinions would put an end to the evils of religious or philosophical sectarianism . . . I acknowledge that the tendency of all opinions to become sectarian is not cured by the freest discussion, but is often heightened and exacerbated thereby; the truth which ought to have been, but was not, seen, being rejected all the more violently because proclaimed by persons regarded as opponents. But it is not on the impassioned partisan, it is on the calmer and more disinterested bystander, that this collision of opinions works its salutary effect. Not the violent conflict between parts of the truth, but the quiet suppression of half of it, is the formidable evil; there is always hope when people are forced to listen to both sides; it is when they attend only to one that errors harden into prejudices, and truth itself ceases to have the effect of truth by being exaggerated into falsehood . . .

We have now recognised the necessity to the mental well-being of mankind (on which all their other well-being depends) of freedom of opinion, and freedom of the expression of opinion, on four distinct grounds, which we will now briefly recapitulate:

First, if any opinion is compelled to silence, that opinion may, for aught we can certainly know, be true. To deny this is to assume our own infallibility.

Secondly, though the silenced opinion be an error, it may, and very commonly does, contain a portion of the truth; and since the general or prevailing opinion on any subject is rarely or never the whole truth, it is only by the collision of adverse opinions that the remainder of the truth has any chance of being supplied.

Thirdly, even if the received opinion be not only true, but the whole truth; unless it is suffered to be, and actually is, vigorously and earnestly contested, it will, by most of those who receive it, be held in the manner of a prejudice, with little comprehension or feeling of its rational grounds. And not only this, but fourthly, the meaning of the doctrine itself will be in danger of being lost or enfeebled, and deprived of its vital effect on the character and conduct: the dogma becoming a mere formal profession, inefficacious for good, but cumbering the ground and preventing the growth of any real and heartfelt conviction from reason or personal experience.

Note

1   This extract is from the *Essay On Liberty*, which was published in 1859 and which has subsequently been widely regarded, particularly in the United States of America, as a founding statement of the liberal journalism ethos with its foregrounding of the rights to individual freedom, especially the freedom of speech. Mill was generally disdainful of journalism, yet he wrote hundreds of newspaper articles.

Chapter 3

Cynthia Carter and Andrew Thompson

NEGOTIATING THE 'CRISIS' AROUND MASCULINITY

An historical analysis of discourses of male violence in the *Western Mail* 1896

Introduction

During the closing decades of the nineteenth century a growing sense of public 'crisis' surrounded white, middle-class, heterosexual masculinity in Wales, as in the rest of Britain.[1] According to Bristow (1991), masculine identity was being incisively reshaped during this period in Victorian history through such things as the public schools, the popular dissemination of imperialist adventure stories for boys, as well as the establishment of sports such as cricket and football as mass cultural events. At the same time, questions around the control of male (as well as female) sexuality, exemplified by the Campaign Against Contagious Diseases Acts, became part of larger public discussions around the double sexual standard (Bland 1992; Smart 1992; Walkowitz 1984). Press coverage of the 'Ripper murders' also contributed to debates around masculinity as a form of gender identity which had become unstable and potentially violent. Additionally, social purity campaigners and feminist writers of the period also suggested that the growing instability around gender identity was related to a radical renegotiation of male sexuality which was taking place at the time (Beetham 1996; Bland 1992; Jeffreys 1985; Walkowitz 1984). It may also be argued that anxieties around masculine identity were tied to the public emergence of discourses around male homosexuality (for example, in the law, medicine, psychoanalysis and literature) (Foucault 1980; Tolson 1978; Weeks 1991).[2] Beetham argues that

> Ideological struggles around gender, sexuality and the body were obviously not 'new' in this period but they took on an unusual intensity

and importance. For a short time, a space opened up in which radically new formations seemed possible. Within that space, however, men and women continued to be differently positioned. There was no positive public discourse, however coded, of female same-sex desire. Since both medicine and Parliament were open only to middle-class men, they enacted the legislative and medical control of sexuality over women, the working class and children as well as 'deviant' men. Gender inequalities complicated the struggles over sexuality and were in turn caught upon in the inequalities of class.

(Beetham 1996: 117)

During this period of radical instability (or crisis) in gender identity, across Britain the successful 'achievement' of 'normal' (heterosexual) middle-class masculinity became increasingly contingent upon the acceptance (particularly by men) of the liberal notions of 'rationality' and 'self-control', as well as hard work in the public sphere (Davidoff and Hall 1987: 21).[3] The 'self-control' attributed to this form of masculinity was used by middle-class men to defend their almost exclusive appropriation of both public and private political power, and to justify attempts to control what they believed to be a working-class propensity to crime and violence which they viewed as a 'threat' to the stability of British society.[4]

The crisis surrounding masculine identity must also be understood in relation to a rising awareness of the instability and even the 'threat' of feminine identity embodied by both the 'New Woman'[5] and 'New Journalism'.[6] The term 'New Woman', coined sometime in the early 1890s, was used to describe a woman who rejected patriarchal restrictions in the areas of paid labour, public and private relationships, physical activity, sex-roles, and so forth. 'New Journalism' refers to a way of presenting the news which relies more heavily on the use of illustration, and one which places a clear emphasis on 'feeling rather than reason, the personal rather than the authoritative tone, the private or "human" interest of its stories as against their public aspect' (Beetham 1996: 126).[7] At the same time, however, such formats discursively define[8] and discipline the lives of women and the working classes so as to disperse the potential 'threat' these groups might pose to hegemonic masculinity.[9]

The scandal of sensation as a quality of the New Journalism was part of a larger debate in which 'sensationalism' was linked either with the working class or with women. Both these groups lacked the objectivity and cool rationality of the middle-class male reader . . . Much of the anxiety about the New Journalism centred on the fear that those characteristics associated with working-class reading would become general. Implicit was a related fear of another kind of deviant reading, that of the feminine. The description of the New Journalism as 'sensational' mobilised these anxieties as well as those around sexuality.

(Beetham 1996: 125)[10]

This chapter looks at some of the ways in which the crisis around white, middle-class, heterosexual masculinity was articulated and negotiated in Wales, across the pages of the *Western Mail*, by examining news accounts of violence against women and girls selected from the paper over a one month period in 1896. One of the most powerful illustrations of the ways in which that crisis was played out in urban Wales, in our view, may be found in the reporting of gendered crime news: it is in such accounts that the *Western Mail* most clearly attempted discursively to manage perceived 'threats' on behalf of middle-class men from both the working-classes and women.

Before analysing these news stories, we begin by sketching out some of the key issues and debates in circulation around male violence in late Victorian society. From there we offer an overview of the historical construction and importance of crime news in the British press generally, highlighting the relationship between crime news and New Journalism, to give the reader an appreciation of the historical significance of crime news in our daily newspapers. We then move on to analyse accounts of male violence in the *Western Mail*, illustrating some of the ways in which the crisis around middle-class masculinity was being continuously renegotiated across its pages. In our view, however, examined on their own, these accounts yield only a partial picture of the management of middle-class masculine anxieties around identity at the turn of the last century. Our examination of the news sample is therefore related, where relevant, to specific editorials, columns and stories taken from the *Ladies' Own Supplement to the Western Mail*.[11] It is in this latter text that negotiations around gender identity underpinning the crisis around middle-class masculinity were most explicit and prescriptive. As such, the *Ladies' Own Supplement* often laid bare many of the cultural assumptions only hinted at by the news accounts we examined in the newspaper.

Male violence in Victorian society

Writing in the *Contemporary Review* in 1878, Frances Power Cobbe, the celebrated Victorian women's rights campaigner, estimated that during the opening years of that decade there were approximately 1,500 'brutal assaults' on women each year in England and Wales. More recent studies (Doggett 1992; Jones 1992; Tomes 1978), however, have suggested that these figures represented a peak, arguing instead that during the latter half of the nineteenth century the official figures point to a gradual decline in the number of violent crimes committed against women by men. Yet in spite of this downward trend, during this period the issue of violent crimes against women, then defined as 'wifebeating',[12] became the focus of growing public concern. Clark, mapping the social history of legislative responses to wifebeating in the eighteenth and nineteenth centuries, seeks to explain this shift in attitude, commenting that 'public concern about wifebeating does not ebb and flow with the actual incidence of the crime, but surges when domestic violence becomes symbolically linked with other concerns' (Clark

1992: 187). The latter half of the nineteenth century witnessed legislative reforms, dealing principally with the contentious issue of divorce, but evolving, under political pressure, to address the broader question of violence against women (and children).[13] There were calls, in both parliament and the press, to bring offenders more firmly into the orbit of the law; politicians of varying political hues railed against the 'brutes' who perpetrated such acts, while in newspapers and periodicals journalists and other social commentators outlined their respective positions on the legal and moral dimensions of the debate. Why, then, did this change of attitude towards the issue of the use of violence against women take place?

During the course of the century a number of factors, such as the burgeoning debate on women's rights, the temperance movement, and increasing unease on the part of the Victorian upper and middle classes about the apparently spiralling levels of violence among the working classes, each contributed to the heightening of public awareness of violent crimes against women and girls. Women's rights campaigners, for example, routinely identified drunkenness as one of the principal factors which led to acts of violence; as Cobbe asked: 'If the English people will go on swallowing million's worth of brain poison each year what can we expect but brutality the most hideous and grotesque?' (1878: 65). In addition, a number of studies (Clark 1992; Doggett 1992; Pleck 1987) have suggested that upper- and middle-class attitudes towards violent crimes were motivated, in part, by their concerns about outbreaks of public violence, as evidenced by the riots and demonstrations of the 1830s and 1840s, as well by the widely held perception of the commonplace nature of the violence which occurred in working-class districts; as Doggett argues:

> There was a connection in the upper- and middle-class Victorian mind between crime and popular rebellion and this was a time when widespread popular rebellion still seemed like a possibility. Just as concern about wife-beating was part of a more general disquiet about violence, this, in turn, was part of an upper- and middle-class urge to regulate working-class behaviour.
>
> (Doggett 1992: 117)

In our view, a further mediating factor in the debate on violence against women, as well as on violent crime in general, was the wider commercialisation of crime by the newspaper press. In the next section of the paper, we explore the role of the daily press in Britain in defining issues of violence against women as a matter for public concern and state intervention.

The Victorian daily press and news of violence against women

Participants in the debate on violence against women regularly cited the daily catalogue of violence documented in the newspaper press as evidence of the widespread nature of the problem. Doggett notes that accounts in newspapers of violent crimes against women were frequently used by interested parties to underscore the seriousness of the problem and to generate public support for legal reform. As she explains: 'politicians who supported increased penalties for assaults on women made heavy use of such accounts, as did concerned lay commentators' (1992: 111). One contemporary remarked that 'it is no exaggeration to say that scarcely a day passes that does not add one or more to the published cases of this description of offence' (Kaye 1856: 233–234).[14] Cobbe, moreover, in waging her campaign for legislative reform, carefully documented press accounts, employing them in her essays as a graphic illustration of the nature of the problem. In her much-debated essay on 'Wife-Torture in England' (1878), for example, Cobbe makes extensive use of accounts from newspapers across the country to buttress her case. In other periodicals, such as the *Women's Suffrage Journal*, contributors followed Cobbe's example, presenting a regular update of cases of violent assaults on women (Shanley 1989).

While this issue provoked impassioned and critical responses, the press accounts were, in themselves, sometimes deliberately misleading or were reported in a sensationalist manner. Cobbe, commenting on journalistic elaborations on court proceedings, explained that 'a few of these cases may have been exaggerated or trumped up'. Moreover, she added that in reading press reports it was important to understand that 'such cases which appear in newspapers are by no means always reliable, or calculated to convey the same impressions as the sight of the actual trial' (Cobbe 1878: 73). Nevertheless, the cumulative effect of the daily reporting of incidents of violence against women, as a number of studies have noted (Clark 1992; Doggett 1992), was that readers were familiarised with the principal features of this problem. Doggett, examining the processes implicated in the social production of wifebeating as a matter of public concern, comments that by the mid-nineteenth century, 'newspapers of the day gave extensive coverage to the details of wife assault cases, and the regularity with which such reports appeared was the subject of frequent comment' (Doggett 1992: 111). The regularity with which incidents of violence against women appeared in the newspaper press engendered contrasting, and often polemical, responses as the commentaries in the periodical press readily testify. One essayist, departing sharply from the views held by liberals such as Cobbe and Mill, exclaimed that women should not blame 'men, as men, for the disabilities and the injustice with which they are in some respects treated' (Browne 1870: 284). A constant feature of the debate, however, in both the newspaper and periodical press, was the extent to which this problem was identified, for varying reasons, as a phenomenon which was largely confined to the working class.

Commenting on crimes of violence against working-class women in Wales during the latter half of the nineteenth century, Jones explains that the 'greatest danger to women lay within the home. A large number of wives, both legal and common-law, were attacked by men.' In spite of changes to the law designed to protect women and children from repeated violent assaults, Jones notes that women who reported violent husbands to the police were often met with a 'mixed reception'. Some sections of the Welsh press, moreover, routinely saw in this issue a source of continuing amusement. 'Wives', he suggests, 'knew when to expect trouble, and the press, in its sardonic coverage of Monday morning's court proceedings, often used the heading "Marriage Bliss"' (Jones 1992: 82–3).

Much of the research on violence against women in Victorian society, and on wifebeating in particular, has also highlighted the significance of gender identities for press debates on this issue (Clark 1992; Doggett 1992; Tomes 1978). Tomes' (1978) analysis of crimes of violence between working-class men and women in mid-nineteenth century London asserts that the comments of magistrates, quoted in an article in *The Times* (1853), and in an accompanying editorial, betray 'a special definition of manliness'; that is to say, one which defined violence against women as 'unmanly' and 'cowardly' (1978: 339). G. Kaye, writing in the *North British Review* in 1856, argued that men in the 'upper classes', as a result of their moral code, exercised a greater level of control over their emotions than their counterparts from the 'lower orders'. As he explained: 'to offer personal violence to a woman is an offence against society for which nothing can atone. Men of education and refinement do not strike women' (1856: 235). In the *Contemporary Review*, Cobbe (1878) acknowledged that wifebeating did occur among the upper and middle classes, but nevertheless explained that there were significant differences in attitude towards the use of violence against women on the part of the upper and middle classes, on the one hand, and the working-class, on the other.

> How does it come to pass that while the better sort of Englishmen are . . . exceptionally humane and considerate to women, the men of the lower class of the same nation are proverbial for their unparalleled brutality, till wife-beating, wife-torture, and wife-murder have become the opprobrium of the land? . . . In his apparently most ungovernable rage, the gentleman or tradesman somehow manages to bear in mind the disgrace he will incur if his outbreak be betrayed by his wife's black eye or broken arm, and he regulates his kicks accordingly. The dangerous wifebeater belongs almost exclusively to the artisan and labouring classes.
>
> (Cobbe 1878: 56–8)

While some authors, such as Cobbe, did not deny that violent assaults on women were committed by upper- and middle-class males, it was their working-class counterparts who were held to be the major cause for concern. A more recent study (Clark 1992) has argued that the demonisation of 'working-class brutes' in the middle-class press shifted public attention away from male violence towards class, and, as a consequence, reinforced a system which continued to leave 'gentlemen' as the protectors of women's rights. We now turn to consider the extent to which crime news contributed to the expansion of the daily press and the implications this had for the reporting of male violence.

New journalism and news of male violence

The reporting of crime news was a significant factor in the expansion of the press during the nineteenth century. Altick, in a consideration of the relationship between the early Victorian newspaper press and the growth of a popular interest in crime, has argued that journalists in this period were 'ready to exploit crime, even ordinary crime, as it had never been exploited before' (Altick 1970: 17). Newspaper proprietors, aware of the financial rewards to be gained from extending coverage of crime as well as concerned by the high level of competition between the various titles, diverted increasing resources to furthering crime journalism. Initially, it was the nascent popular press which, from the 1840s, was the main sponsor of the growth in crime reporting. In particular, the popular Sunday papers, such as the *News of the World* and *Lloyd's Weekly*, were among the first of the new papers to give a prominent position to crime journalism, featuring extensive accounts of the proceedings of the police courts (Brown 1990, 1992). Chibnall (1980) points out that it was this exhaustive coverage of crime news which underpinned the successful growth of the *News of the World*, which appeared for the first time in 1843, and which, before the Stamp Duty was finally repealed in 1855, had secured the largest circulation of any newspaper. Competition, however, was not confined to the popular press; by the middle of the century, the middle-class London dailies, such as *The Times* and, after 1855 the *Daily Telegraph*, were similarly engaged in their own circulation war over crime news (Altick 1970; Chibnall 1980).

The initial success of crime reporting, particularly during the 1840s and 1850s, was that it served to amplify existing fears about the effectiveness of the law in preventing high levels of crime. Reports of particularly horrific instances of violence against women certainly contributed to the introduction of legislative reforms, but also significantly assisted in boosting the sales of the daily newspapers. In our view, media research has tended to neglect the 'ordinariness' or 'everyday' character of most news accounts of violence against women and girls. Many of the crimes reported in newspapers, while rich in detail concerning the specific nature of a given case, were nevertheless routinely accorded little more than a few sentences. However, it was the routine inclusion of reports of such crimes in the press which served to act as a reminder of the continued existence of this problem. Later, in the 1880s and 1890s, the sensationalisation of violent crime, as evidenced in the serial-style coverage of murder trials characteristic of the New Journalism, undoubtedly contributed to the marketability of crime news for the Victorian readership. It was, however, the persistent, almost monotonous, presence of crime in newspapers which gave the press a pivotal position in the public debate on this issue.

The 'New Journalism' was strongly endorsed by the then editor of the *Western Mail*, Henry Lascelles Carr, not least because he viewed women, one of the key groups to whom the New Journalism was designed to appeal, as an important target audience of consumers in the expanding newspaper and domestic goods markets (Cayford 1992). Carr and other press entrepreneurs and advertisers were increasingly keen to reach this growing group of domestic consumers. This being the case, it was clear that more traditional forms of journalism, which were primarily constructed to appeal to middle-class men, were inadequate for reaching women in their increasingly important role as *the* domestic consumer.[15]

> The forms of journalism which were put into place in these decades not only defined femininity but were defined by it. The new press came to be associated with a range of characteristics which were traditionally 'feminine', especially its tendency towards sensation and the personalising of information.
>
> (Beetham 1996: 118)

What is most interesting, and a key site of contradiction within Victorian patriarchal structures in the late nineteenth century, is that while New Journalism sought to secure large numbers of middle-class female readers by appealing directly to what news editors and proprietors believed to be their primary areas of interest (marriage, children, fashion, consumption, etc.), at the same time New Journalism embraced ever more explicit descriptions of and proscriptions around patriarchal violence. It is our opinion that a close reading of this point of contradiction might yield important insights into the ways in which the British press contributed to the discursive management of the crisis around middle-class masculine identity during the period.

In the next section, we move on to examine some of the ways in which accounts of male violence in the *Western Mail* displaced the locus of the crisis around white, middle-class masculinity on to the working classes and women. This consists of a close reading of a news sample of such accounts drawn from the newspaper between Monday, 15 July and Saturday, 15 August 1896, and from the *Ladies' Own Supplement to the Western Mail* from 15 July to 12 September 1896.[16] In our analysis we classified the offender(s) and victim(s) by their gender and social class, the stated or implicit relationship between these parties, the type of crime, the sentence imposed (or the particular stage in the inquiry), if 'drunkenness' was cited as a 'cause' of the violence, and whether there appeared to be sympathy for the victim or the offender in each story. These categories proved to be the most salient in illustrating how news narratives contributed to a renegotiation of the crisis. We found that blame for male violence was often transferred to women, who were represented in ways which implied that they deserved to be assaulted or killed because of their 'unfeminine' (or 'unladylike') behaviour (e.g. drunkenness). At the same time, working-class men were also blamed for male violence because they were deemed to be inherently irrational and to possess an uncontrollable propensity to violence. Where pertinent, we relate these findings to examples drawn from the *Ladies' Own Supplement* to offer a fuller picture of the newspaper's discursive management of anxieties around middle-class masculinity.

News of 'brutes' and gentlemen

Our reading of a sample of 71 news accounts of male violence against women and girls drawn from the *Western Mail* between 15 July and 15 August 1896 confirms the view that middle-class male anxieties around masculinity in Wales were constantly rearticulated with the working classes.[17] Working-class offenders (male and female) and victims (female) were featured in 60 out of 71 news accounts. Middle-class victims featured in 9 of 71 the stories (4 out of this 9 were a continuation of the same story).

Of middle-class male offenders, featuring in only 4 of the 71 stories, without exception their victims were women or girls of either 'working class' or 'class unknown'. Two of these accounts were about the same incident, where a middle-class man, Frederick Saunderson, a schoolmaster of Portland Street, Soho shot and killed Ellis Caley, a domestic servant, then killed himself (*Western Mail*, 31 July 1896: 5). In this instance, it is clear that the two were involved in an affair which, due to their class differences, was inevitably destined to fail, ending in what the paper's headline defines first as 'Double Tragedy in London' (31 July 1896) and later as 'Murder and Suicide Verdict in the Euston Road Tragedy' (3 August 1896: 5). Another news account of a middle-class male offender centres around the Reverend David Evans, vicar of St Mark's, Southshields ('Serious Charge Against a Vicar'), who asked leave to appeal against the decision of the Durham Consistory Court to charge him with misconduct with one woman, living with another outside of marriage and drunkenness at a funeral (27 July 1896: 7). And the final story, 'Charge Against an Army Schoolmaster' (14 August 1896: 5) reports on a case in which army schoolmaster W.H. Gardner, who was married with several children of his own, was remanded on bail for indecently assaulting a 'girl scholar', aged eleven. This case caused 'considerable sensation in the camp'. In all of these news reports, the middle-class offender was known to the working-class female victim.

Without exception in stories where the male offender was middle class, each is treated very sympathetically. In the case of Frederick Saunderson, the murder and suicide is constructed as a 'tragedy'. Saunderson is portrayed as someone to be pitied because a person was blackmailing him over his adulterous affair with a domestic servant. The article declares that 'A letter in the man's handwriting was read, in which it was alleged that the affair was due to the action of a blackmailer, who persistently demanded money by threats of exposing his wife' (3 August 1986: 5). What is less explicit is that our sympathy is also elicited for Saunderson because he found himself attracted to a working-class woman, a love doomed from the outset. The account on 30 July begins by relating that a 'respectably dressed man and woman' rented a room in a hotel on Euston Road in London. 'On Thursday morning, they had breakfast in their apartment, and were, apparently, on the best possible terms. About half past twelve, two shots were heard by the servants, and upon the room being entered both visitors were found to be dead.' Nowhere does the account blame Saunderson for this forbidden passion with a working-class woman, and, as a result, blame is shifted (a) to the blackmailer (who would expose this love forbidden on grounds of class difference and of the offender's marital status); (b) to the offender's wife (one could imply from his affair that she may not have been fulfilling her duties as a wife if her husband sought an affair outside the marriage); and (c) to the victim herself, for being a willing partner in adultery, leading to his and her demise.

In the case of the Reverend David Evans, he is not blamed for 'misconducting' himself with one woman, or for living with another woman outside marriage for four years, nor his drunkenness at a funeral. We are told that his parishioners set up a fund for him so that he could appeal against the Consistory Court decision, which again suggests that the Reverend is not to blame for his behaviour (or at least that his parishioners have forgiven him for his conduct), transferring blame to the woman who was the victim of 'misconduct' (Did she ask for it? Even holy men may become weak in the face of feminine temptation) and to the one who was morally licentious enough to agree to cohabit for several years. The account begins by referring to the defendant by his respected title ('the Reverend David Evans, vicar of St Mark's, Southshields'), whereas the women menioned are not named nor associated with any profession. Discursively, then, the account ex-nominates these women, making it possible for the reader to shift at least some of the culpability in the various charges levied against Reverend Evans to them. Also, by stringing together into one sentence the charges against the Reverend ('he had misconducted himself with one woman, had lived for over four years with another who did not bear his name, and had been drunk at a funeral'), an impression is created that he kept the company of morally suspect women (even if each instance for which he was charged was completely separate and not in any way related to the others).

For the Army schoolmaster, W.H. Gardner, the severity of his alleged crime of indecently assaulting a 'girl scholar' is undercut by the inclusion of the information that he is the 'deputy choirmaster at All Saints Church, and he trained the successful squad at the recent Army schools' physical drill competition before the Duke of Connaught'. The incident is left open to question by inclusion of the information that Gardner is a 'married man with several children'. What is being implied here is that he is a respectable man, one who has taken the vows of marriage and has a number of offspring from this legitimate union. How could this girl be indecently assaulted, one might thus wonder, by such an upstanding citizen? If this charge were indeed true, then the reader is perhaps being urged to decode the account in a way which suggests that the girl must have enticed Gardner in some way.

Here, then we see that the loss of middle-class masculine rationality and self-control is squarely laid on the shoulders of women who by their very presence tempt men into morally reprehensible (typically male working-class) behaviour. This textual sleight of hand exemplifies one of the key ways in which the *Western Mail* mediated the crisis around middle-class masculinity at the time. That is to say, it tended to construct accounts of middle-class male violence such that blame for any failures to live up to the ideals of normative masculinity were apportioned to the 'other' (working-class and middle-class women, as well as working-class men).[18] This point is clearly illustrated by a column entitled 'Don'ts for Wives' appearing in the *Ladies' Own Supplement*. In this column, middle-class women are warned of various things that they must not do if they are to be good wives. Chief amongst these 'don'ts for wives' is the following:

> Don't 'nag' at him. That is the most hateful little word I know of, and the 'nagging' practice is one of the most vicious. Much should be forgiven a husband who has a 'nagging' wife – one whose tongue is never still, and whose every word is a fault finding or complaint.
>
> *Ladies' Own Supplement* (18 July 1896: 2)

Here it is suggested that if middle-class women engage in 'nagging', it might be understandable and even forgivable if their husbands were to lose self-control (either verbally or physically). Blame, therefore, for any violence that might occur would be placed on the shoulders of the woman (who in such circumstances could not really be considered to be a victim of patriarchal aggression).

Such apportioning of blame to the victim in accounts of working-class male violence is nowhere more apparent than in cases where excessive drinking was evident. For example, a news account in the *Western Mail* (10 August 1896: 5), entitled 'He Only Got Drunk: A Man Who Didn't Kill His Wife is Discharged', reported that a German Pole was charged with drunkenness and disorderly conduct by fighting. Answering the complaint, the defendant claimed that he got drunk because he had caught his wife with another man. To this the judge declared, 'It has been held that if you catch your wife with another man you may kill her: but it has not been held that you may get drunk. You are now discharged.' Even more reprehensible was a drunken woman. Thus, at Pontypridd police court on 6 August 1896, a man was discharged from the accusation of attempted murder of his wife (he tried to slit her throat) because she had come home drunk and proceeded to 'bounce' (verbally abuse) him. The Stipendiary in the case declared that there was not enough evidence to send the defendant for trial and in discharging him remarked, 'I'm sorry for you.' Similarly, the item entitled 'Terrible Affair at Swansea Police Court Proceedings' (14 July 1896: 7) recounted the story of a man charged with inflicting grievous bodily harm on his wife, who was drunk at the time of the assault, by kicking her in the mouth and side. The defendant's solicitor claimed that the woman's injuries were incurred as a result of a fight between the husband and wife, sustained by falling rather than assault, and that the prisoner should therefore be granted bail. The Stipendiary decided to maintain the prisoner on remand until the woman's condition improved. In sympathetic tones, however, the journalist asseverated, 'The prisoner, who is a tall, light-haired man, who appeared scarcely to have realised his position, then left the dock in custody.' For either sex of the working classes, but especially for women, drinking was seen to provide an alibi for violent behaviour in men – either as the assailant or as the victim of an assault.

In addition to the disparities between the number of news accounts featuring working-class male and female offenders and victims in relation to those in which middle-class men and women are featured (and here no middle-class women are represented as offenders), there are also significant differences in the ways in which male violence is described when a victim comes from the working classes. One of the most explicit ways in which working-class victims are differentiated from middle-class ones is that the former are primarily referred to as 'women', whereas the latter are described as 'ladies'. At the time, the term 'woman' was still associated with 'common-ness', but also with suffrage (i.e. the 'New Woman').[19] Beetham (1996) notes that during the latter half of the nineteenth century there was still a very clear distinction between females defined as 'women' and those who were considered to be 'ladies'. To be referred to as a 'woman' indicated either working-class status or a belonging to that category of the 'New Woman' who was regularly ridiculed in the British press (as unfeminine, strange and threatening).

Working-class women were almost without exception referred to by their first and last names, their position of employment (delineating their working-classness) and their marital status (being married conferring consid-erably more respectability than being single and certainly more than 'cohabiting' or 'living together'). For example, on 14 July 1896, the *Western Mail* headline 'Derbyshire Murder Trial' indicates that William Pugh, a collier, was indicted for the wilful murder of Elizabeth Boot, a housekeeper. On the other hand, the names of middle-class female victims always included the title of either 'Miss' or 'Mrs', along with their last name (sometimes including a first name), conferring respectability and gentility. To illustrate this point, on 18 July 1896, under the headline 'Threatening a School Mistress

— A Young Lady in Bodily Fear at Bury', the *Western Mail* reported that a working-class woman, Sarah Master ('a maid woman'), had been charged with using threats towards Miss Annie Wood, headmistress at Romilly Road Girls' School, Bury. In the *Ladies' Own Supplement* column entitled 'Single Life', any woman who is not married is directed to keep her

> heart and head in sympathy with the usual work of women. This will not only sweeten and discipline her character in the immediate present, but it will save her from a real and immanent danger. Women who board and who are wholly free from home ties run the risk of becoming exacting and in times querulous. But if there is a family to cling to, cling to it. Do not shirk the responsibility and care involved, but let the family be your chief interest. Though it may be possible to do your work and remain at home, it is usually possible to share, in the best and truest sense, the home and family life.
>
> (*Ladies' Own Supplement*, 5 September 1896: 1)

But perhaps the most direct way in which the *Western Mail* made clear the class of both the victim and the offender was in the explicitness of its descriptions of male violence. In stories reporting on working-class women as victims and offenders, clear and often horrifically detailed descriptions of the violence were supplied. For example, in an article headlined 'A Desperate Man Murders His Wife and Tries to Kill Her Mother – Sentence of Death', Joseph Robert Ellis, aged 22, a seaman, was reported as being indicted for murdering his wife. The couple had been married for only fifteen months, but at the time of the murder were living apart. The article recounts that

> On the date named, the prisoner went to the house of his mother in law, and, after asking his wife to sign a receipt for an instalment of the allowance he contributed towards her maintenance, he seized the girl and stabbed her with a table knife. The mother seized him, whereupon he turned upon her and inflicted several wounds about the head and body. Both women ran out and he pursued them. He caught his wife under a shed, threw her down, and showered more blows on her with the knife, inflicting terrible injuries. The prisoner then deliberately sharpened the knife on the doorstep and was cutting his own throat when a man ran up and seized his arm. The prisoner declared that if any member of the family came up he would stab them, as he wanted to do for the lot, and would hang like a dog.
>
> (*Western Mail*, 4 August 1896: 5)

All of these stories share similar assumptions about what constitutes 'respectable' femininity. None of the assaulted women, all of whom were of working-class origin, is looked upon sympathetically because each transgressed the socially constructed boundaries of normative (middle-class) feminine behaviour. For example, one woman committed adultery and was caught by her husband (driving him to drink), another had too much to drink and then (for reasons not stated) verbally abused her husband. In a separate incident a woman got drunk and had a fight with her husband, and in a final example, a woman was punished for leaving her husband and for using offensive language to him. In a column entitled 'When Marriage is a Failure' in the *Ladies' Own Supplement* (5 September 1896), the acceptable boundaries of (bourgeois) gender roles are clearly delineated. Marriage, and therefore the achievement of heterosexual 'normalcy', is deemed to have failed 'if the husband tries to be mistress as well as master, or the wife master as well as mistress of the house'. One could conclude, then, that the working-class victims exhibited what the *Western Mail* regarded as masculine behaviour (adultery, drinking and swearing), making them responsible for the patriarchal violence to which they were subjected.

Stories in which middle-class women are victims, on the other hand, tend to offer little detail about the alleged crime; most suggest that no physical harm came to the lady in question. For example, on 7 August 1896, the *Western Mail* reported that a man named Charles Smith was remanded in Lymington in connection with an alleged outrage on the London and Bournemouth Express. In this case, two ladies travelling in First Class complained that a man attempted to 'force himself' into the carriage, demanding money and threatening to use a pistol. However, both ladies were unharmed as the offender jumped out of the train when one of the ladies tried to alert the guard. A lady cyclist was at the scene and gave information to some crate layers who 'secured' the would-be thief. The ladies threatened in this case were listed as Mrs Florence Woods and Miss Forbe of Bournemouth. Here we see a very clear example of the different tone, style, and detail of violence used for accounts of male violence against middle-class women than for those referring to working-class women. In addition, one of the strong themes running through the account is that of a disembodied middle-class male protection of these ladies. That is, they were travellers in a first class carriage, a space which ordinarily would be quite safe even if men were fellow travellers, as they would most assuredly belong to the middle classes. But less obvious, perhaps, is the journalist's use of language and description that would serve discursively to protect these ladies and *Western Mail* readers from the full horrors of patriarchal violence. Nevertheless, a related story warns middle-class women that

> It is one of the follies of femininity to ever seek an empty compartment [on a train], under the ostrich-like premise that it is the safest, whereas it is positively the most dangerous. Ladies travelling alone should remember that there is safety in numbers, and should select a compartment in which several passengers are travelling.
>
> (*Western Mail*, 18 July 1896: 6)

Conclusions

By the end of the nineteenth century, the rapid expansion of the newspaper press, and the subsequent widening of the Victorian public sphere, made a significant contribution to growing debates around patriarchal violence. Hitherto viewed as a largely private matter, male violence became the focus of public concern and consideration, especially among the upper and middle classes (Clark 1992). In this chapter, we have argued that in late nineteenth century Wales, as in the rest of Britain, white, middle-class masculinity was in a state of crisis. The anxieties that this group of men experienced were, we suggested, closely related to a number of radical economic, political and social changes occurring at the time. Furthermore, we maintained that during this period the liberal notions of 'reason' and 'self-control' became closely imbricated with a new kind of middle-class masculinity. This emergent form of gender identity was to be realised primarily through an articulation with work (i.e. a middle-class profession). Furthermore, we proposed that the notions of 'reason' and 'self-control' were used to justify the seizure of both public and private political power by this group of men, and fortified what they saw as their legitimate control over working-class 'brutes', whose very existence threatened to undermine the developing bourgeois patriarchal structures of Victorian society.

We then proceeded to outline some of the key issues and debates in circulation during that period around patriarchal violence, concluding that there was a close connection between social concern over violence against women and a (male) middle-class desire to control (male) working-class political rebellion. Attention then turned to a consideration of the contribution of the British press to debates around male violence against women at a time when the press was becoming increasingly competitive and commercialised. Here we outlined the extent to which the attendant changes associated with the 'New Journalism' shaped an increasingly competitive newspaper market in Wales by widening their appeal to female readers, while also becoming more reliant on the daily inclusion of 'ordinary' and sensationalised forms of crime news (including violence against women) to attract ever larger audiences for advertisers.

Finally, we examined some of the ways in which accounts of male violence in the *Western Mail* discursively displaced the locus of the crisis around white, middle-class masculinity onto the working classes and women. Our analysis suggested that *Western Mail* news accounts shifted the blame for patriarchal violence to female victims of such crimes. These women were seen to have deserved their fate because they dared to behave in ways thought to be transgressive of the boundaries of normative (middle-class) femininity. Concomitantly, working-class men were constructed as being naturally prone to uncontrollable and irrational acts of violence (both in general and more specifically against women). These findings were augmented with examples taken from the *Ladies' Own Supplement*, supporting the view that the *Western*

Mail played a key role in the mediation of anxieties around hegemonic masculinity at the time.

Our study has sought to offer a critical intervention into Welsh women's history in general, and in the gendered character of Welsh press history more specifically. Through our examination of the *Western Mail* and the *Ladies' Own Supplement*, we have attempted to foreground historical questions of gender in Wales in relation to the daily inclusion of news accounts of male violence, hereby delineating the role of the press in (re)producing gender identities and inequalities. Finally, it is our hope that this research might offer a direct response to Beddoe's (1996) challenge to researchers to 'trace changing Welsh notions of masculinities and femininities and the relationship between them, to evaluate the impact of the Victorian concept of separate spheres on Welsh urban and rural communities, and to assess the role of gender in constructing social class in Wales' (Beddoe 1996: 61).[20]

Notes

1   Although our analysis specifically examines the ways in which masculine identity was discursively negotiated in Wales via a reading of the *Western Mail* and its *Ladies' Own Supplement*, it is our assumption that many of the arguments we offer here might be usefully taken up to talk about masculinity in the rest of the United Kingdom and related to its different inflections in different parts of the nation.

2   In 1885, the Labouchère Amendment to the Criminal Law Amendment Act 'brought all male homosexuality activity into the scope of the law' (Weeks 1991: 102). In 1895, the trial of Oscar Wilde was a 'dramatic demonstration both of the existence of this deviant male identity and the social necessity for its absolute destruction' (Beetham 1996: 116).

3   Up to that time, middle-class and aristocratic forms of masculine identity were often closely tied to the notions of 'honour', which was to be defended, if necessary, through violence – the 'duel' is an example of one of the ways in which male honour was to be secured.

4   Clark (1992: 196) suggests that at the beginning of the nineteenth century, 'the weakness of the laws against assaults in general began to threaten the legitimacy of the state as violent offenders escaped with light sentences . . . the old system of terror could not suppress political turbulence and violence in general. Instead, the state moved toward more extensive regulation of violence as the middle-class, motivated by evangelicalism and humanitarianism, demanded rational, efficient protection.'

5   'New Woman' was a term also used to dismiss those thought to be somehow 'deviant' in terms of their challenge to middle-class definitions of acceptable femininity.

6   The term 'New Journalism' is attributed to Matthew Arnold in the now famous quotation from his article entitled 'Up to Easter' in the periodical *Nineteenth Century*. He declared, 'It [New Journalism] has much to

recommend it; it is full of ability, novelty, variety, sensation, sympathy, generous instincts; its one great fault is that it is featherbrained' (Arnold 1887: 638). As Beetham notes (1996: 119), 'The class element in this analysis was explicit. It is also significant that the opposition of "reasonable" against "featherbrained" implicitly mobilised the vocabulary of gendered identity. Arnold assumed as his norm the English male middle-class reader to whom the New Press represented those "others" against whom he must define himself.'

7   Commentators have recently described this emphasis as a 'feminisation' of the news (Beetham 1996; Hartley 1996; van Zoonen 1994), offering an expanded range of feminine representations with which female readers might identify (especially in their role as *the* domestic consumer). It also contained news formats which were more appealing to audiences hitherto inadequately catered for by the press, particularly women, and to the working classes. Beetham suggests that the notion of 'feminisation' is helpful in understanding the character of New Journalism. She maintains that, 'Those changes concerned with lay-out and use of illustration worked not just to change the look of the periodical press but also to make the way it looked more important. Since femininity was always located in and defined by appearance, as masculinity was not, the stress on the visual character of the periodical was a further "feminisation". Moreover, the increasing visual importance of advertisement also located the reader as a consumer of commodities rather than as a worker or producer and one therefore with implicitly feminine characteristics' (Beetham, 1996: 126).

8   The term 'discourse' refers to 'any regulated system of statements or language use which has rules, conventions and therefore assumptions and exclusions' (Branston and Stafford 1996: 126). Foucault (1980) extends this notion of discourse to theorise how knowledge is regulated in the interests of specific power relationships, establishing the parameters for preferred ways of understanding these relations.

9   The notion of 'hegemonic masculinity' utilised here draws directly on Rutherford's (1988) definition, as follows.

> Heterosexual men have taken refuge in this idea that our sexual identities are absolute. The dominance of heterosexual masculinity, the ideologies which have supported it by silencing the experience of others, the power structures and privileges that it disguises, the active, daily subordination of women and gay men, the persecution of effeminate men, and the racism of men's colonial legacy – all these have been sustained by its capacity to remain beyond question, its contradictions out of sight. It is an identity that is in continual struggle to assert its centrality in cultural life, yet it attempts to ensure its absence, and to evade becoming the object of discourse. Heterosexual masculinity shifts its problems and anxieties, defining them as belonging to others. Our identity represents its own problems in the image of the compliant female, the black man

as sexual savage, and the perverted homosexual. It organises its legitimacy by constructing the Other, that which is outside and questionable, what is different.

(Rutherford 1988: 22–23)

10 According to Chibnall (1980: 206), 'much of the so-called "new" journalism was not so much innovation as an extension of established styles and techniques. This was particularly the case with the reporting of crime which drew on the colourful layout, profuse illustrations and the sensational "human interest" type of story of publications like the *Illustrated Police News*. Northcliffe was certainly not the first to discover that, in the words of Kingsley Martin, "in times of peace a first class sex murder is the best tonic for a tired sub-editor on a dull evening; but the editor of the *Evening News* was still excited to discover that he was able to calculate with reasonable accuracy the increase in circulation that a really messy murder would secure".'

11 In 1893, the *Mail* began publishing a free eight-page addition to the Saturday newspaper called the *Ladies' Own Supplement to the Western Mail*. Styled very much along the lines of the newspaper itself in length and page layout, the supplement included a high proportion of local advertising for department stores, greengrocers, chemists and so forth. Inside its pages was a mix of extracts from various British newspapers and women's magazines, as well as local notes and editorials (society comment, shopping tips, etc.). It is also interesting to note that during the period analysed here, the *LOS* introduced 'Our Men's Column' which provided female readers with insights into the private cares and concerns of men, including dress, manners, marriage, sex roles and socialising. It would appear that, as with contemporary women's magazines, editors and proprietors were probably aware that men were reading these publications and also wanted to reach that audience, at the very least to make them aware of consumer goods available in Cardiff if not to encourage them to direct their wives to purchase certain goods.

12 Pleck (1987) points out that the term 'wifebeating' was first coined in 1856 during the course of a campaign to secure changes to the divorce laws. The Divorce and Matrimonial Causes Act of 1857 had increased access for women wishing to initiate divorce proceedings, but stopped short of fully addressing the issue of violent marriages.

13 For example, between 1853 and 1860 there were three major attempts to introduce legislative changes designed to deal with the problem of violent assaults on women and children of which only one received Royal Assent: the Act for the Better Prevention and Punishment of Aggravated Assaults upon Women and Children of 1853; and, unsuccessfully, the Aggravated Assaults Bill of 1856 and the Aggravated Assaults Amendment Bill of 1860. The Matrimonial Causes Act of 1878, promoted by Frances Power Cobbe, gave women whose husbands had been convicted of assaulting them the legal right to obtain a Protection Order from the courts, which would effectively constitute a judicial separation (Shanley, 1989).

14   Cobbe, in her autobiography, explained that it was newspaper accounts of violent assaults on women by their husbands which had first stirred her to direct attention towards this question:

> One day in 1878 I was by chance reading a newspaper in which a whole series of frightful cases of this kind [brutal beatings] were recorded, here and there, among the ordinary news of the time. I got up from my chair, half dazed, and said to myself: 'I will never rest till I have tried what I can do to stop this.'
>
> (1895, cited in Shanley 1989: 164)

15   Jones (1993) argues that 'New Journalism' in Wales may be understood somewhat differently than its counterpart in England, on three different levels. Firstly, it affected the 'new elements of style that were introduced into layout, language, coverage, recruitment policies, economic organisation and marketing strategies'. Secondly, it was primarily English in language and, finally, it contributed to the construction of a 'new and crucially undifferentiated audience' of Welsh readers. Rather than seeing New Journalism as a threat — that is, in Arnold's view, 'featherbrained' — Cayford (1992: 191) argues that 'In Wales it was not so much a case of the old versus the new, or of the good or the bad, of the choice between the literate or the entertaining. In its diversity, quality, and, if we are to trust the *Western Mail*'s circulation statistics, also in its appeal, the New Journalism improved Welsh daily journalism and brought it into line with British developments.'

16   We do not claim that this one-month sample is necessarily 'representative' of all *Western Mail* reportage on cases of male violence against women and girls. However, this sample of 71 news accounts does at least provide a starting point for future research of this kind, and is suggestive of what may be 'typical' in terms of such news accounts. We chose this sample period for a variety of reasons. Firstly, we were interested in relating what we found in the news discourses of male violence to the discourses constructing 'femininity' found in the *Ladies Own Supplement to the Western Mail*, published each Saturday beginning in 1893 and ending around the turn of the century. In researching this aspect of our project, we discovered that for the most part the *LOS* had not been retained with the rest of the newspaper. Upon enquiry, the Cardiff Public Library local history staff informed us that if a supplement was not physically part of the main newspaper, it was rarely retained. So, although the *Western Mail* viewed its female readers as an important constituency of its readership (Cayford 1992: 195), historically Cardiff librarians seem not to have considered the *LOS* worthy of retention. Secondly, we discovered, upon further research, that during the period July–September 1896, each Saturday's copy of the *LOS* was included in the bound volumes examined. We felt that including the supplement was important to our main arguments and that therefore this should, to some extent, guide our decision in terms of the sample period. Finally, 1896 represents the year in which the 'popular' tabloid

press came into existence in Great Britain, with the launch of the London based *Daily Mail*. We believe that this further enhanced our decision to choose that year, as it marks the beginning of a shift in terms of thinking about audiences, news presentation, news language, and so forth. We added another month to our sample of the *Ladies' Own Supplement* because, as it was published only once a week, a further month of issues provided us with a wider range of clear examples of the ways in which there was an attempt made to negotiate discursively the position of single women so as to address the potential 'threat' that their marital status posed for normative (middle-class, married) femininity. This was accomplished by re-inscribing such women within an ideology of domesticity and the 'normal' nuclear family.

17   Out of 71 stories, 43 were reports on incidents of male violence against women and girls which took place in either England or Scotland, 26 were from around Wales, one was in the USA, and one in Algeria. Of the Welsh stories, 12 consisted of news reports (roughly more than 100 words in length), while 14 were news briefs (less than 100 words). The Welsh news reports tended to focus on more gruesome and spectacular forms of male violence such as murder and attempted murder, while the news briefs centred on 'mundane' or initial reports of such offences as 'grievous bodily harm', 'unlawful wounding' and 'malicious assault'.

18   Our sample supports this position in that almost all of the accounts included working-class offenders and victims. What we are arguing here is that the absence of middle-class men from most of the accounts of male violence against women and girls contributes to a sense of this violence as largely emanating from (and endemic to) the working classes.

19   Shevelow (1989: 204) argues that as early as the eighteenth century in Britain, 'the general nomenclature of "lady", first shaken loose from its aristocratic attachments to describe the predominantly upper- and middle-class female readers . . . gets reassigned in later periodicals to designate no longer an upper class, but the quality of "gentility" now upheld as a middle-class ideal of behaviour towards which the periodicals guided their readers'.

20   The authors would like to thank Stuart Allen and Tom O'Malley for their insightful comments on an earlier draft of this chapter.

References and further reading

Adburgham, A. (1972) *Women in Print: Writing Women and Women's Magazines from the Accession of Queen Victoria*, London: George Allen & Unwin.

Altick, R. (1970) *Victorian Studies in Scarlet*, London: Dent.

Anderson, P. (1991) *The Printed Image and the Transformation of Popular Culture, 1790–1860*, Oxford: Clarendon Press.

Arnold, M. (1887) 'Up to Easter', *Nineteenth Century* 21: 638–9.

Ballaster, R., Beetham, M., Frazer, E. and Hebron, S. (1991) *Women's Worlds: Ideology, Femininity and the Woman's Magazine*, London: Macmillan.

Bauer, C. and Ritt, L. (1983) ' "A husband is a beating animal": Frances Power Cobbe confronts the wife-abuse problem in Victorian England', *International Journal of Women's Studies* 6: 99–118.

Baylen, J.O. (1992) 'The British press, 1861–1918', in D. Griffiths (ed.) *The Encyclopedia of the British Press, 1422–1992*, London: Macmillan.

Beddoe, D. (1986) 'Images of Welsh women', in T. Curtis (ed.) *Wales: The Imagined Nation*, Bridgend: Poetry Wales Press

Beddoe, D. (1996) 'What about women?: The future of women's history', *Planet* 117 (June/July): 55–61.

Beetham, M. (1996) *A Magazine of Her Own?: Domesticity and Desire in the Woman's Magazine, 1800–1914*, London: Routledge.

Bland, L.(1992) 'Feminist vigilantes of late-Victorian England', in C. Smart (ed.) *Regulating Womanhood: Historical Essays on Marriage, Motherhood and Sexuality*, London: Routledge.

Brake, L. (1994) *Subjugated Knowledges: Journalism, Gender and Literature in the Nineteenth Century*, London: Macmillan.

Brake, L., Jones, A. and Madden, L. (eds) (1990) *Investigating Victorian Journalism*, London: Macmillan.

Branston, G. and Stafford, R. (1996) *The Media Student's Book*, London: Routledge.

Bristow, J.(1991) *Empire Boys: Adventures in a Man's World*, London: Unwin Hyman.

Brown, L. (1990) 'The growth of a national Press', in L. Brake, A. Jones and L. Madden (eds) *Investigating Victorian Journalism*, London: Macmillan.

Brown, L. (1992) 'The British press, 1800–1860', in D. Griffiths (ed.) *The Encyclopedia of the British Press 1422–1992*, London: Macmillan.

Browne, M. (1870) 'The subjection of women', *Contemporary Review* 14: 277–86.

Cayford, J.M. (1991) 'In search of "John Chinaman": Press representations of the Chinese in Cardiff, 1906–1911', *Llafur* 5, 4: 37–50.

Cayford, J.M. (1992) 'The *Western Mail* 1869–1914: A study in the politics and management of a provincial newspaper', unpublished Ph.D. dissertation, Department of History, University College of Wales, Aberystwyth.

Cheesman, T. (1994) *The Shocking Ballad Picture Show: German Popular Literature and Cultural History*, Oxford: Berg.

Chibnall, S. (1977) *Law-and-Order News: An Analysis of Crime Reporting in the British Press*, London: Tavistock.

Chibnall, S. (1980) 'Chronicles of the gallows: The social history of crime reporting', in H. Christian (ed.) *The Sociology of Journalism and the Press*, Sociological Review Monograph 29, University of Keele, Staffordshire.

Clark, A. (1992) 'Humanity or justice?: Wifebeating and the law in the eighteenth and nineteenth centuries', in C. Smart (ed.) *Regulating Womanhood: Historical Essays on Marriage, Motherhood and Sexuality*, London: Routledge.

Cobbe, F.P. (1878) 'Wife-torture in England', *Contemporary Review* 32: 55–87.

Davidoff, L. and Hall, C. (1987) *Family Fortunes: Men and Women of the Middle Class*, London: Hutchinson.

Doggett, M.E. (1992) *Marriage, Wife-beating and the Law in Victorian England*, London: Weidenfeld & Nicolson.

Forbes, J.S. (1996) 'Disciplining women in contemporary discourses of sexuality', *Journal of Gender Studies* 5, 2: 177–89.

Foucault, M. (1980) *The History of Sexuality. Vol. 1: An Introduction*, New York: Vintage.

Hartley, J. (1996) *Popular Reality: Journalism, Modernity, Popular Culture*, London: Arnold.

Hunter, F. (1992) 'Women in British journalism', in D. Griffiths (ed.) *The Encyclopedia of the British Press, 1422–1992*, London: Macmillan.

Jeffreys, S. (1985) *The Spinster and Her Enemies*, London: Pandora.

Jones, A. (1993) *Press, Politics and Society: A History of Journalism in Wales*, Cardiff: University of Wales Press.

Jones, D.J.V. (1992) *Crime in Nineteenth-Century Wales*, Cardiff: University of Wales Press.

Kaye, G. (1856) 'Outrages on Women', *North British Review* 25: 233–56.

Lee, A. J. (1976) *The Origins of the Popular Press in England, 1855–1914*, London: Croom Helm.

McCormick, C. (1995) 'Domestic terrorism: The news as an incomplete record of violence against women', in C. McCormick (ed.) *Constructing Danger: The Mis/representation of Crime in the News*, Halifax, Nova Scotia: Fernwood Publishing.

Pleck, E. (1987) *Domestic Tyranny: The Making of Social Policy Against Family Violence From Colonial Times to the Present*, Oxford: Oxford University Press.

Rutherford, J. (1988) 'Who's that man?', in R. Chapman and J. Rutherford, (eds) *Male Order: Unwrapping Masculinity*, London: Lawrence & Wishart.

Schlesinger, P. and Tumber, H. (1994) *Reporting Crime: The Media Politics of Criminal Justice*, Oxford: Clarendon Press.

Shanley, M.L. (1989) *Feminism, Marriage and the Law: Victorian England, 1850–1895*, London: I.B.Taurus.

Shevelow, K. (1989) *Women and Print Culture: The Construction of Femininity in the Early Periodical*, London: Routledge.

Smart, C.(1992) 'Disruptive bodies and unruly sex: The regulation of reproduction and sexuality in the nineteenth century', in C. Smart (ed.) *Regulating Womanhood: Historical Essays on Marriage, Motherhood and Sexuality*, London: Routledge.

Tolson, A. (1978) *The Limits of Masculinity*, London: Tavistock.

Tomes, N. (1978) "A torrent of abuse": Crimes of violence between working class men and women in London, 1840–1873', *Journal of Social History* 11: 328–46.

van Zoonen, L. (1994) *Feminist Media Studies*, London: Sage.

Walkowitz, J. (1984) 'Male vice and female virtue: Feminism and the politics of prostitution in nineteenth-century Britain', in A. Snitow, C. Stansell and S. Thompson (eds) *Desire: The Politics of Sexuality*, London: Virago.

Weeks, J. (1991) 'Pretended family relationships', in D. Clark (ed.) *Marriage, Domestic Life and Social Change: Writings for Jacqueline Burgoyne (1944–88)*, London: Routledge.

White, C. (1970) *Women's Magazines 1693–1968*, London: Michael Joseph.

Winship, J. (1987) *Inside Women's Magazines*, London: Pandora.

Chapter 4

W.T. Stead

THE FUTURE OF JOURNALISM

THE FUTURE OF JOURNALISM is a large subject.[1] It is but a thing of yesterday, but already it overhadows the world . . . It has part of the necessary garniture of the civilized man . . . A man without a newspaper is half-clad, and imperfectly furnished for the battle of life. From being perse-cuted and then contemptuously tolerated, it has become the rival of organized governments. Will it become their superior?

The future of journalism depends entirely upon the journalist. All that can be said is, that it offers opportunities and possibilities, of which a capable man can take advantage, superior to that of any other institution or profes-sion known among men.

But everything depends upon the individual – the person. Impersonal journalism is effete. To influence men you must be a man, not a mock-uttering oracle. The democracy is under no awe of the mystic 'We'. Who is 'We'? they ask; and they are right. For all power should be associated with responsibility, and a leader of the people, if a journalist, needs a neck capable of being stretched quite as much as if he is Prime Minister. For the proper development of a newspaper the personal element is indispensable. There must be loyalty to the chief far beyond the precincts of the editorial sanctum. Besides, as I shall presently explain, the personality of the editor is the essential centre-point of my whole idea of the true journalism of the governing and guiding order, as distinguished from journalism of the mere critical or paragraph-quilting species. Where there is the combination of the two elements, the distinct personality of a competent editor and the varied interests and influences of an ably conducted paper, it is not difficult to see that such an editor might, if he wished it, become far the most permanently influential Englishman in the Empire . . .

He would be more powerful than any, simply because, better than any other, he would know his facts. Even now, with his imperfect knowledge of facts, the journalist wields enormous influence. What would he be if he had so perfected the mechanism of his craft as to be master of the facts — especially of the dominant fact of all, the state of public opinion?

At present the journalistic assumption of uttering the opinion of the public is in most cases a hollow fraud. In the case of most London editors absolutely no attempt is made to ascertain what Demos really thinks. Opinions are exchanged in the office, in the club, or in the drawing-room; but any systematic attempt to gauge the opinion even of those whom he meets there is none. As for the opinion of Londoners, outside the limited range of their personal acquaintance, that remains to them, as to every one else, an inscrutable mystery. Outside London, everything of course is shrouded in even denser darkness . . .

I am not for a moment advocating the more accurate and scientific gauging of public opinion in order that blind obedience should be paid to its decision, when ascertained. Far from it. The first duty of every true man, if he believes that public opinion is mistaken, is to change it. But whether we regard public opinion as the supreme authority in faith, morals and politics, or whether we merely regard it as so much force to be directed or absolutely checked, it is obviously of the first importance to know what it is that we have either to obey or to transform . . .

The first step, therefore, that must be taken is to require touch with the public, and this, fortunately, is by no means difficult, although it requires some painstaking, and the institution of a very simple but effective organization . . .

What, then, should be the organization of a newspaper office from this point of view? . . .

First, then, the editor of a newspaper should either be personally acquainted with, or should be surrounded by trustworthy assistants who are personally acquainted with, every one whose opinion has any weight on any subject with which he has to deal. Nor should it be mere acquaintance. There should exist such relations of confidence as to render it possible for the editor to be put in possession of the views of any personage whose opinion he desires to know. This of course is a work of time, and even after many years the most successful editor must be content to know many of the most important personages at second-hand. But it is better to be initmate with the confidant of a Minister than to be merely on friendly terms with the Minister himself. There are some Ministers who never tell anything when their journalistic acquaintances seek for information. Others profess to tell everything, and mislead the inquirer in every direction. Those Ministers are very rare who make a confidant of an editor, and still rarer are those who do not make a thorough-going support the condition of such confidences.

These terms are of course absolutely impossible. No consideration whatever, in the shape of exclusive and official information, can compensate for

51

the loss of the right of individuality, of independence, and of criticism. One Minister who will tell you all he knows is worth a dozen Ministers who dole out information as if it were diamonds, and even then leave out some vital item. All that I could contend for is, for instance, that on any given occasion it ought to be possible for an editor to ascertain authentically in twenty-four hours the views of all the Cabinet Ministers and ex-Cabinet Ministers in town – not of course for publication, but for his own guidance and the avoidance of mistakes.

At present that is impossible: first, because Ministers trained in the old school have not yet learned the necessities of the new system; and secondly, because journalists do not as a rule take the trouble to cultivate the acquaintance with Ministers necessary to keep themselves informed. And what is true of Ministers is true to a greater or less degree of ambassadors, judges, generals, and great financiers. Nevertheless, the duty of an editor is absolute. He ought to be able to get at, or know some one who can get at, every one, from the Queen downwards, in order to be able to ascertain what they are thinking about the topic of the day. This is not an interview. Interviewing is the public, this is the private phase of what, after all, must always be the primary department of journalism – that of interrogation. The least confusing of the two, the case of matter spoken in private as if it were material for an interview, would be fatal. If the editor cannot be trusted to keep a secret, if he betrays confidence, the whole edifice collapses. Personal confidence is the foundation of the system . . .

The ideal of the journalist should be to be universally accessible – to know every one and to hear everything. The old idea of a jealously shrouded impersonality has given way to its exact antithesis. Of course, if the personality of the editor is such as to detract from the usefulness of his writings, he had better stick to the old plan. But if the editor is a real man, who has convictions, and capacity to given them utterance in conversation as well as in print, the more people he sees at first hand the better – always provided that he leaves his mind room enough in the crowd to turn round on its own ground. All that I have said concerning the London editor applies *mutatis mutandis* to his provincial brother. The provincial editor has one enormous advantage over the Londoner – one among many. He can cover the whole of his field. He can make the personal acquaintance of every leading public man and of all the local leaders in every department of human activity . . .

This, however, is the mere *A B C* of the subject: it is so obvious that whoever aspires to lead and guide must take counsel with those who have the daily drudgery of administration to do, that there is no need to labour the point. What is much less generally recognized is that the newspaper ought to be in close and direct touch with either extremity of the social system, and with intermediate grades. There is something inexpressibly pathetic in the dumbness of the masses of the people. Touch but a hair on the head of the well-to-do, and forthwith you hear his indignant protest in the columns of the *Times*. But the millions, who have to suffer the rudest buffets of ill-fortune, the victims of official insolence and the brutality of the better-off, they are as dumb as the horse, which you may scourge to death without its uttering a sound. Newspapers will never really justify their claims to be the tribunes of the people until every victim of injustice — whether it be a harlot run in by a policeman greedy for blackmail, or a ticket-of-leave man hunted down by shadowy detectives, or paupers baulked of their legal allowance of skilly — sends in to the editorial sanctum their complaint of the injustice which they suffer. When men cease to complain of injustice, it is as if they sullenly confessed that God was dead. When they neglect to lay their wrongs before their fellows, it is as if they had lost all faith in the reality of that collective conscience of society which Milton finely calls 'God's secretary'. For every appeal to the public is a practical confession of a faith that shuts out despair. When there is prayer there is hope.[1] To give utter-ance to the inarticulate moan of the voiceless is to let light into a dark place;[2] it is almost equivalent to the enfranchisement of a class. A newspaper in this sense is a daily apostle of fraternity, a messenger who bringeth glad tidings of joy, of a great light that has risen upon those who sit in darkness and the shadow of death. I do not say that the editors of the *Times* and the *Daily News* should be on visiting terms with the thieves of the Seven Dials and the harlots of the New Cut, but they should know those who can tell them what the Dialonians feel and what the outcasts in the New Cut suffer . . .

All that, it will be said, is idealistic, visionary, utopian; but it is some-thing to have an inspiring ideal, and it is well to be reminded of the responsibilities that attend upon the power which has come to the journalist as an unexpected heritage from the decay and disappearance of the elder authorities of the bishop and the noble. To be both eye and ear for the community is a great privilege, but power no less than *noblesse oblige*, and much may be done to realize it, if it recognized that the discharge of such responsibilities lie in the day's work of the journalist. It is of course mani-festly impossible for over-worked editors and hard-pressed reporters to undertake new duties without being relieved of some of their functions. But in the large papers much might be done by rearranging duties and the substi-tution of this kind of work for others of a less indispensable description. But I have not yet lost faith in the possibility of some of our great newspaper proprietors who will content himself with a reasonable fortune, and devote the surplus of his gigantic profits to the development of his newspaper as an engine of social reform and as a means of government. And if it be impos-sible for those already in the purple to display such public spirit, then it may be that the same spirit which led pious founders in mediaeval times to build cathedrals and establish colleges, may lead some man or woman of fortune to devote half a million to found a newspaper for the service, for the educa-tion, and for the guidance of the people.

Supposing such a newspaper to be founded, what would be the first step necessary to enable its conductor to gauge and at the same time to influence the opinion of the nation? The necessity for establishing personal relations between the chief of the political, social, and religious leaders of the people in the immediate vicinity of the newspaper office, has already been referred to. But that helps but little towards placing the newspaper in confidential relations with the whole people. What, then, is the best and most effective means of enabling the editor at the centre to keep touch with the people at the circumference? Mere circulation will not avail. There is no London newspaper more circulated among North-country Radicals than the *Daily News*, but the only expression of opinion ever heard up North about the *Daily News* is a groan over its feebleness and lack of grit. Circulation is all very well, and the larger circulation any newspaper has the better for its proprietor; but influence depends not half so much upon quantity as upon the quality of its subscribers. Newspapers with only ten or fifteen thousand circulation have often ten times as much influence as papers with 200,000, the difference being in the character of the readers of the paper. Hence, if the object is to influence the politics of a town, it is better to be read regularly by ten men of the right sort than to circulate a thousand a day among the ordinary newspaper buyers. Democracy has not diminished in the least the power of individuals. It has, indeed, increased their influence by giving them a freer field for the existence of their power. The secret of influence is to get at the right individuals in every town and village . . .

How to attain this end is the problem . . . There are, however, two methods by which a newspaper can work towards that end: the first is by a system of major-generals, and the second by a system of journalistic travellers.

First, the system of major-generals . . . A competent, intelligent, sympathetic man or woman, as nearly as possible the *alter ego* of the editor, should be planted in each district, and held responsible for keeping the editor informed of all that is going on within that area that needs attending to, either for encouragement, or for repression, or merely for observation and report.

That, it will be said, is but a development under a new name of the existing system of resident reporters and local correspondents. That is a great recommendation. But the development is immense — so immense, in fact, that there would be the greatest difficulty in securing persons competent for the discharge of the duties of the post. But by themselves they would be helpless. They need to be supplemented by two agencies — one local, the other central.

There is probably in every constituency in the land some one man or woman keenly in sympathy with the governing ideas of the newspaper in question. That may be said concerning any newspaper which has a soul and a creed . . . In the newspaper whose organization I am sketching there would be so many points of contact with the average Briton that there would be no doubt at all that there would be many persons sufficiently in sympathy with the direction to feel honoured by being asked to co-operate as voluntary unpaid associates with the editor. It would be the duty of the major-general to select with the utmost care, in each important centre of his district, one such associate, who would undertake to co-operate with the central office in ascertaining facts, in focusing opinion, and generally in assisting the editor to ascertain the direct views of his countrymen. There would be endless varieties among those who would act as associates. It might be a squire, or it might be a cobbler; it might be the clergyman's daughter, or a secularist newsagent, or a Methodist reporter . . .

This, however, is but the first tentative approach to an exhaustive interrogation of public opinion. In time, when the associates become more familiar with their work, and the competent and willing workers are ascertained, to these might be entrusted the further and more delicate duty of collecting the opinions of those who form the public opinion of their locality. Each of these select associates would be expected to communicate directly or indirectly with representatives of all classes in the locality, and to collect their opinion as exhaustively as the editor collects the opinions of the leading politicians in London . . . The enormous importance of a system which enabled the editor of a London paper — and of course, on a smaller scale, the editor of a provincial paper — to know at a glance the opinions of, say, even the presidents and secretaries of the political associations throughout the land, are too obvious to be dwelt upon. By degrees, as the returns became more complete, the journalist would speak with an authority far superior to that possessed by any other person; for he would have been the latest to interrogate the democracy — he would have the last word of the leaders of the electors upon the question of the hour; he would, in fact, for the first time be able to say with authority the opinion of the public on this subject is adverse or favourable to the proposed scheme . . .

By this co-operation between a newspaper and selected readers, it will be possible to focus the information and experience latent among our people as it has never been done before, and to take an immense stride towards the realization of the conscious government of all by all, in the light of the wisdom of the best informed. The mere fact that in every town a score of persons, from the mayor to the bellman, were certain to be called upon, as a matter of course, to express a deliberate opinion upon social or political problems, before a leading journalist ventured to declare what was the public opinion of the nation, would have an incalculable influence in vivifying our democracy, in compelling thought, and in quickening popular interest and public questions.

That, however, is by no means the only duty that would be required from the hands of the volunteer deputy major-generals. Once or twice a year . . . a crisis may arise in which it is urgently necessary that the Cabinet and the House of Commons should be presented with an unmistakable demonstration of what the opinion of the people really is . . . Whenever such a time arrived it would be the duty of a deputy major-general to take steps to secure public expression of the popular feeling. He, or it might be she, might not be able to attend a public meeting, much less speak at one. But they could nevertheless set one going by setting the right people in motion . . . Under the proposed scheme the local deputy would be the live coal which sets the place ablaze, and he would be able to have at his command exactly the kind of information needed for the locality.

Just imagine the consequences, under our present system of government, of an arrangement by which a leading newspaper, convinced that the Government was pursuing a policy contrary to the general wishes of the community, was able to issue a three-line whip to its representatives which would secure the holding of a public meeting in every town-hall in the country, in order to express the popular view . . . No more simple and effective method of educating the democracy in the functions of citizenship could be imagined, and yet how could it possibly be worked so cheaply and so efficiently as from the office of a great daily newspaper?

Each of the major-generals would have a general oversight of all the associates in his division, but the whole organization would be kept together, and the personal sense of a common interest kept up, by the periodical visits of the journalistic traveller . . . Not until we introduce something of commercial common-sense and the practical method of business into the profession of journalism will we even have begun to fulfil our *rôle* as exponents of public opinion. The journal, then, which essays to enter into the dominion open to the first comer must engraft the traveller upon its system of organization. It must have at least two constantly on the road, each the perambulating *alter ego*, as far as is possible, of the editor at the centre, filled with his central fire, saturated with his ideas, and with a clear grasp of the system here sketched out.

These peripatetic apostles of the new journalism would make it their duty to visit the associates in every town, to infuse into each a sense of the importance of the common work, and to make every one feel that he or she is an important and indispensable part of the system.

By this means full and accurate knowledge would be secured of each associate: the indifferent could be dropped, suggestions could be interchanged, and, in short, the whole organization made alive and instinct with a common interest and a common enthusiasm.

If this was done – and of course this is merely the crudest and most imperfect outline of what would be necessary – the newspaper that was so worked would be much the most powerful and one of the most useful institutions in the country . . .

It is a new field that is opened up – a new field, and a most tempting one, for it offers to the capable man or woman opportunities of public usefulness at present beyond his utmost dreams, and while apparently making them the humble interrogators of democracy, in reality enrols them as indispensable members of the greatest spiritual and educational and governing agency which England has yet seen. Such a newspaper would indeed be a great secular or civic church and democratic university, and if wisely directed and energetically worked, would come to be the very soul of our national unity;

and its great central idea would be that of the self-sacrifice of the individual for the salvation of the community . . . It may be that the editor is not yet born who is destined thus to organize the new journalism, and take this vast new stride in the direction of intelligent and conscious self-government. But unless our race is destined to decay, both the editor and the occasion are certain to arrive. Parliament has attained its utmost development. There is need of a new representative method, not to supersede but to supplement that which exists – a system which will be more elastic, more simple, more direct, and more closely in contact with the mind of the people. Other than that, the groundwork of which is already supplied by the Press, I see no system, not even a suggestion of a system. And when the time does arrive, and the man and the money are both forthcoming, government by journalism will no longer be a somewhat hyperbolic phrase, but a solid fact . . . nowhere on this planet will there be such a seat of far-extended influence and world-shaping power as the chair from which that editor, in directing the policy of his paper, will influence the destinies of the English race.

Note

1   This article was one of two written by Stead while serving a three-month sentence in Holloway prison. It appeared in the *Contemporary Review* (November 1886). The other article, 'Government by Journalism', appeared earlier in the May issue of the same journal. Stead had been imprisoned for the technical abduction of a child while exposing the practice of child prostitution in the *Pall Mall Gazette*, which he edited from 1883 until 1890. A kind of prototype campaigning journalist, Stead is also closely associated with the introduction of the so-called 'new journalism' into the English press.

Chapter 5

Chandrika Kaul

IMPERIAL COMMUNICATIONS, FLEET STREET AND THE INDIAN EMPIRE c. 1850s–1920s

Introduction

Raymond Williams (1966: 17) has defined communications as the institutions and forms in which ideas, information, and attitudes are transmitted and received. In general governments, considered as networks of decision and control, are dependent on processes of communication, that is to say, their ability to receive, process, and disseminate information (Deutsch 1963). Technological determinists such as Harold Innis and Marshall McLuhan argue that media are never neutral, and that patterns of human social relations are intimately linked to the systems of communication predominant in given eras. The British Empire was, Innis remarks, sustained as much by cheap pulp paper as by the gunboat (Innis 1972). However, the effects of new technology on imperial news reporting were not direct. Imperial news, both in its gathering and its discussion, had always to operate within an imperial political context.

The telegraphic revolution

The second half of the nineteenth century saw an expanding system of imperial communications made possible by the electric telegraph, which, says Headrick (1981), inaugurated a genuinely new form of imperialism.

> For the first time in history, colonial metropoles acquired the means to communicate almost instantly with their remotest colonies . . . The

world was more deeply transformed in the nineteenth century than in
any previous millennium, and among the transformations few had results
as dazzling as the network of communication and transportation that
arose to link Europe with the rest of the world.

(Headrick 1981: 129–30)

As Jorma Ahvenainen (1981: 7) has similarly observed, 'international telegraphic communication made *Weltpolitik* possible'. In this sphere Great Britain
led the world: Britain owned or had an interest in 80 per cent of all submarine cables before the First World War.

The British government was conscious of the strategic importance of the
developing telegraph system. From the 1880s, the expansion of the cable
was dictated by the needs of government offices, and ever more distant lines
with less and less economic value were laid for political reasons (Headrick
1981: 162). The epitome of strategic cables was the 'All Red Route', a cable
passing only through British territories, which by 1911 connected the far
flung colonies and dominions with the metropolis. Under the severe test of
the Great War this work received its vindication, as these channels of communication were utilised not only to gather and transmit information, but to
disseminate official news and propaganda throughout the Empire and neutral
countries.

Telegraphs and the Indian empire

News of the Indian Empire had traditionally been regulated by the distance
and difficulty of access. In 1825 the mails from Calcutta to Falmouth took
nearly four months. Though the sea voyage was much reduced by the opening
of an overland route from Suez to Alexandria ten years later, the time taken
was still nearly seven weeks. The average time taken for mail to reach England
in 1852 from Bombay via Suez was thirty-three days and from Calcutta forty-
four days (Finn 1973: 10; Headrick 1981: 129–39). Imperial communications
with India were irrevocably transformed by the introduction of the telegraph
in 1865, when the distance was electrically traversed in days. By 1906 submarine telegraphy had reduced the average time in transit to thirty-five minutes
(MacDonagh 1906: 35).

The British government was involved with the telegraph to India from
the outset. John Merrett (1958: 92, 97) claims that 'Of all the cable projects
between 1858 and 1865 none was more spectacular than the line to India.'
For the next five years – until the Eastern Telegraph Company came on the
scene – this line earned 'over £100,000 each year for its promoters' (Merrett
1958: 101). Shortly afterwards the Indian government also financed the
building of a land line across Persia from Bushire to Teheran. Another service
was then inaugurated between Teheran and Moscow under an 1866 conven-
tion between Russia and Persia, and this was connected to the earlier line.
Thus there were by the end of the 1860s two telegraph routes between

Western Europe and India: one via Constantinople and the other via Moscow (Ahvenainen 1981: 16).

Recognising the opportunity for providing a line entirely in the hands of one private company, the German firm of Werner von Siemens founded The Indo-European Telegraph Company. Commencing operations in 1870, this was an amalgam of land and sea lines which joined up with the Indian government lines in Teheran, providing an efficient connection that regularly conveyed messages 'in about five hours' (Headrick 1981: 160). Yet it almost immediately faced rivalry from The British Indian Telegraph Company, whose submarine cables connected Alexandria and Bombay via the Red Sea and Aden. The ensuing competition meant prolonged losses for the Indo-European until in 1878 the two companies entered into an agreement to pool revenues and share profits (Ahvenainen 1981: 17).

At the turn of the century there accordingly existed three main telegraphic routes between India and Great Britain:

1   That of the Eastern Telegraph Company (formed by the amalgamation in 1872 of five British companies including the British Indian Telegraph Company), via Aden, Egypt, and Gibraltar.
2   The Indo-European via the Persian Gulf, Persia, Russia and Germany.
3   The Turkish route via the Persian Gulf, Constantinople, and across Europe.

The first two were the more dependable, but the Turkish route, though slow and prone to disturbances, was the most direct and therefore cheapest. Table 5.1 provides a comparison of the various distances involved.[1]

The expense of the telegraphic connection effectively confined its unofficial use to the largest of the metropolitan dailies. Merchants devised various ways of reducing charges, such as clubbing together or 'packing' and the use of code words, yet there was a limit to the extent to which newspapers could reduce costs by similar means. A prominent critic of the system was Charles Bright (1903, 1905, 1909), engineer of several submarine cable networks including that to India, who was convinced of the crucial role of imperial telegraphic communication. Concern at the high level of charges was also

Table 5.1   Length of telegraphic routes between Britain and India

Routes		Miles
Eastern Telegraph Co.		7,664
Indo-European Telegraph Co.	3,735	
Indo-European Department	1,883	
Indo-European (total)		5,618
Turkish		5,155

expressed in official circles in Britain. Sir Edward Sassoon (1900), spokesman of the Imperial Telegraph Committee of the House of Commons, complained of the 'unbridled control' of the telegraph companies. The Eastern Telegraph and its associate companies had become in practice 'an oppressive monopoly with tariffs so abnormal, so arbitrary, and so capricious in relation to comparative distances traversed, that the telegraphing public has at last risen in revolt'. He blamed the government of India for failing to address the problem. Having entered into agreements with the cable companies, it seemed 'powerless' and deaf to the protests of commercial communities at home and in India. 'It is apparent that there is something radically wrong in a state of affairs where we find the Indian Government apparently inert and enmeshed in agreements in consequence of which it can make no move to advance the interests of the Indian public by the reduction of rates' (Sassoon 1900: 596–7). Sassoon alleged that the Indian Telegraph Department encouraged the private companies to make excessive profits through artificially high prices on Indian business in order to subsidise their transmission to areas beyond India such as Australia. No reduction, he concluded, 'of less than 75 per cent, on the Indian tariff at all events, can be regarded as satisfactory' (Sassoon 1900: 597–8; Kieve 1973: 289–300).

The Eastern Telegraph Company's route consisted entirely of submarine cables, and the whole tariff was retained by the company – with the exception of the small royalty payable on land lines in Britain. The Indo-European route was made up of land lines, and the tariff for that part between London and Teheran was subject to royalty payments to Great Britain, Germany, Russia, and Persia. The Indo-European Telegraph Department of the government of India (with lines from Teheran to Karachi) also had to pay a royalty to Persia, but retained the whole cable rate from Bushire to Karachi. Thus, while the Eastern Telegraph Company retained approximately the whole charge on messages sent by their route, the Indo-European Telegraph Company and the Indo-European Telegraph Department each retained only about 90 per cent. A Joint Purse Agreement existed at the turn of the century between these three parties, according to which each partner paid into a common fund the whole of its net receipts from traffic and then drew out at a fixed proportion calculated on the basis of the average revenue generated by each route.[2]

The first Imperial Press Conference 1909

The issue of high rates for telegraphic communication was given prominence at the first Imperial Press Conference in London (Hardman 1909). The conference, which was the brainchild of the journalist Harry Brittain, later Conservative MP for Acton (1918–29), was fully supported by the British government and Fleet Street. It acknowledged the importance of communications for the British Empire, and support for rate reduction, particularly for press telegrams, was forthcoming from notable politicians, including prime minister Asquith, ex-premiers Balfour and Rosebery, and Lords

Cromer and Morley. A resolution, passed with the Colonial Secretary Lord Crewe in the chair, stated that it was of 'paramount importance that telegraphic facilities between the various parts of the Empire should be cheapened and improved so as to ensure fuller intercommunication than at present' (Mills 1924: 109). A direct outcome of the conference was the formation of the Empire Press Union (EPU), which established a system of autonomous branches across the Empire, including India, with access to centres of power in London. The proprietor of the *Daily Telegraph*, Lord Burnham, concluded that the two press conferences (a second was held in Ottawa in 1921), and the activities of the EPU in general, 'carried Imperial solidarity to a further point in newspaper affairs than it has as yet been found possible to do in our Parliamentary relations' (Mills 1924: xvi).

The conference also highlighted the particular problems surrounding the flow of information to and from India. The seven delegates from India, Burma, and Ceylon, out of a total of fifty-four overseas representatives, included E. Digby of the *Indian News* and Surendranath Banerjee of *The Bengalee* (both Calcutta papers), Stanley Reed of *Times of India* (Bombay), G.M. Chesney of *The Pioneer* (Allahabad), A.E. Lawson from the *Madras Mail*, F. Crosbie Roles representing the *Times of Ceylon*, and J. Stuart of the *Rangoon Gazette* (Burma).[3] Stanley Reed delivered spirited arguments in favour of cheap and easy telegraphic facilities for the press, arguing that the 'conditions under which India is now kept in telegraphic touch with the outer world can only be described as grotesque' (Hardman 1909: 140–41). The press rate on telegrams to India, at a shilling a word, was the same as that charged to Australia, even though the latter country was double the distance. The transit and terminal charges for India were higher than for Canada, even though the distance from east to west in Canada was greater. The ratio between press and private cablegram charges to India was a full one-half higher than in any other part of the British Empire. By systematic coding the charge for private cablegrams had been reduced to 'little more than 2d. per word', but even with the 'most conservative computation the cost of every word of news is between 9d and 10d'. Consequently press telegrams were, in general, 'so short that we see overseas affairs as through a glass darkly'.

> In every other part of the world news is considered of so much public importance that it is entitled to a specially cheap rate . . . [but] the picture of India, represented in large sections of the English Press, sometimes cannot be recognised as the land we live in . . . that is not only an enormous inconvenience, but a serious Imperial menace . . . May I ask how you are going to guide the [British] democracy on the affairs of India at one shilling a word?
>
> (Hardman 1909: 140–41)

Banerjee, the only 'native' newspaper representative present, supported his colleague's resolution, but interpreted its importance in a different light.

He argued that times were critical for the Indian Empire, with the spread of political violence and the reforms of Lord Morley. It was therefore of great importance that the 'truth' should be accurately conveyed to the people of Great Britain.

> If we had cheap cablegrams, the false, misleading telegrams regarding Indian affairs would not be sent to this country. They would be wired back for confirmation and correction . . . The mischief would be palliated if not prevented altogether.
>
> (Hardman 1909: 151)

Changes in the system

Largely as a result of the Imperial Press Conference, concerted efforts were made by the government and private companies to reduce the cost of press telegrams and increase the press service to India.[4] A revision in press rates took place on 27 July 1909 when the council at the India Office authorised the director-in-chief of the Indo-European Telegraph Department to agree to a reduction of the rate from 12d. to 9d. per word. Shortly after a system came into operation whereby deferred telegrams in plain language could be sent at half-price.

A year later more thorough-going organisational reform was undertaken to meet the demand for cheaper and more extensive news in overseas dependencies. At that time over 500,000 words were transmitted to India, South Africa, and Australia per annum, and it was estimated that about half of the news sent to each place was general to all. It was consequently suggested that arrangements be made for 'a single message to be sent over the lines of the Eastern Company to a given point, and thence distributed to various parts of the Empire'.[5] As the secretary of the Indian Joint Purse Committee explained, the object was to establish an imperial news service throughout the British Empire. It was contended that the only agency in a position to provide a news service of this character was the Reuters Telegram Company. The Eastern Telegraph Company had therefore made arrangements with Reuters for the 'placing of 150,000 words (per annum) of general and Imperial news at Aden', from where it could be distributed to India, Australia, South Africa, and other places. The rate from Aden to India of the re-transmitted messages would be reduced to 2d. per word provided that the government of India accepted a pro rata reduction of tariff. 'Reuters at present supply Indian newspapers with about 128,000 words of news per annum of which 117,000 is sent to Bombay, and 11,000 direct to Calcutta.' It was suggested that of this total, 58,500 should continue to be sent direct from London to Bombay and 11,000 to Calcutta at the ordinary press rate of 9d. per word, and that 'in lieu of the other moiety of Bombay news, the 150,000 words . . . available at Aden shall be re-transmitted to Bombay at the low rate of 2d. per word.' (See Table 5.2.) Further, Reuters would request the

Indian government to assist them in inland distribution. Reuters was willing to increase the annual sum that it paid to the government from an average of £1,400 to £1,600, if the latter undertook to distribute the additional words that were proposed.[6] The projected effect of these changes on actual news flows was given by the Eastern Telegraph Company to the chairman of the cable rates sub-committee of the Imperial Press Conference.[7]

After detailed negotiations, the government of India accepted this system and it became operational from July 1910.[8] The press rate continued at 9d. per word till the beginning of 1912, when concrete proposals were put forward to lower the press rate to 4¹/₂d. These moves partly reflected the concern of the Secretary of State for India, Lord Crewe.[9] He was anxious to see further reductions in the terminal and transit rates of the Indian government, reductions in the costs of press telegrams, and an increased news service to the subcontinent. The cable rate was eventually reduced to 4d. per word in 1913 (Table 5.3).[10]

During the Great War special arrangements were also made to provide an outward imperial news service. This was practically confined to the official communiques of the allies and was transmitted by the Eastern Telegraph Company 'immediately on receipt in precedence of all other traffic and consequently would reach India with only an hour or two delay'. Some effort was made to introduce a similar service for 'important news from overseas', but the London papers were 'unwilling to accept a news message in common and each desired to receive messages from its own correspondent'.[11]

Table 5.2   Particulars of news service in words

Destination	*Present* (1909)	*Proposed* Direct	*Proposed* Aden to	*Total*
India	128,000	64,000	150,000	214,000
South Africa	146,666	73,333	150,000	223,333
Australia	266,666	133,333	150,000	283,333
TOTALS	541,332	270,666	450,000	720,666

Table 5.3   Cable rates for India, 1908 and 1923

1908 Ordinary		*1908* Press		*1923* Ordinary		*1923* Deferred		*1923* Press	
s.	*d.*	*s.*	*d.*	*s.*	*d.*	*s.*	*d.*	*s.*	*d.*
2	0	1	0	1	8	0	10	0	4

Source: Mills 1924: 81

Conclusion

The effective control by London of two-thirds of the world's cables had a threefold political importance: it made possible the speedy implementation of an imperial grand strategy, military and naval; it placed public administrators more directly under Colonial Office, India Office or Foreign Office surveillance; and it enabled British newspapers to convey detailed reports faster to the British public.

Fleet Street and imperial news

For the press, also, the late nineteenth and the early twentieth centuries were a period of profound change, with access to the new communication networks, advances in printing technology, and a greater number and circulation of newspapers. The Edwardians were better informed than any previous generation. The number of daily newspaper readers doubled between 1896 and 1906, and doubled again by 1914 (Read 1972: 60). In 1920 the combined circulations of national dailies stood at five million. The London press enjoyed an unparalleled influence, for besides being the most significant medium of political debate, it was also the chief source of information on foreign events, providing much of the material from which political opinion was formed. Editors of the quality press such as Garvin, Strachey, Spender, and Dawson were 'journalists for Empire'. 'By their ongoing commentary on imperial issues,' says Startt (1991: 214), 'they helped to make the Empire one of the . . . commanding subjects of the time and extended the parameters of discussion about it.' The mass circulation popular papers sought out the human interest in imperial stories, and in so doing made such news accessible to a much wider audience: the Empire, their readers were reminded, was kith and kin.

Indian news coverage

The early lead of *The Times* in establishing a news network in India was challenged from the late nineteenth century by other major metropolitan dailies. A small core staff of salaried correspondents were supplemented, when necessary, with additional reporters, largely drawn from the ranks of journalists working for the burgeoning English language press in India. Amongst these journalists we find an eclectic mix of the professional and the amateur, the full time and the *ad hoc*. On the one hand, it was said to be possible for the resourceful English-speaker 'to combine planting, racing and journalism' (James 1929: 3). More soberly, H.E.A. Cotton, son of Sir Henry Cotton the Liberal Anglo-Indian, worked for the *Daily News* as its Calcutta correspondent as well as practising in the Calcutta High Court.

Journalism in India also derived from that in England and was conducted along similar lines (Lovett 1926; Barnes 1940). Thus G. Pilcher, the foreign editor of the *Morning Post* between 1909 and 1914, went as the paper's correspondent to Calcutta, where he was joint editor of the *Statesman*,[12] which indeed recruited most of its editorial staff from England. In 1903 S.K. Ratcliffe, a former editor of the London *Echo*, was made editor of the *Stratesman* after serving on the staff as a leader writer. Alfred Watson, who edited the paper from 1925 to 1932, had worked for more than twenty years on the *Westminster Gazette*. Malcolm Muggeridge, previously on the *Manchester Guardian*, became assistant editor in 1934. In 1906 B.G. Horniman, who had also worked for the *Guardian* and some London dailies, took charge of *The Statesman*'s news lay-out. His editorial services were acquired by the *Bombay Chronicle* in 1913.[13]

Apart from correspondents based in India, there were 'roving special correspondents' who moved between metropolis and periphery. A good example was the traveller and journalist Henry Newman, who replaced Kipling on the staff of the *Civil and Military Gazette* and often worked on 'specials' for other Calcutta and London papers as well as for Reuters (*c.* 1900–14) (Newman 1937a, b). For ceremonial occasions, such as the royal visits of 1905 and 1921–22 and the Delhi Durbars of 1903 and 1911, major Fleet Street figures such as J.L. Garvin, Sidney Low, Herbert Russell, and J.A. Spender journeyed to India. Metropolitan papers often collaborated to send reporters to cover a particular crisis. Henry Nevinson, for example, was sent in 1907 on an extended visit financed by the *Daily Chronicle*, *Nation*, and *Manchester Guardian*. Lord Northcliffe, who himself visited India in the 1890s and again in 1922, often shared men and resources between his papers.[14]

Underlying developments in the quantity and form of Indian news reporting were changes in the technology of news collection. With the extension of the telegraph system from the 1860s a radical shift in the quality of overseas news coverage had become possible. However, the effect of the new telegraph technology upon newspaper coverage of India was ambiguous. The charges for press traffic at the turn of the century stood at the exorbitant rate of £1 per word (equivalent to £60 in today's prices), so although information was potentially more available, its effective utilisation was precluded by disproportionate expense. Though by 1908 the press rate had been reduced to a shilling per word, this remained high and its implications for Indian news coverage were expressed by Moberly Bell, manager of *The Times*. The telegraph rate to India was, he complained,

> very high as compared with America at 5d. Taking a column at 1,200 words it is £60 from India as against £25 from the USA. It would seem to me that even in ordinary circumstances a column a week would not be too much to give to our greatest dependency but that which would only cost £1,300 a year from Canada would cost £6,120 from India.[15]

However, by the First World War, as we have noted, the rates for press traffic had been substantially reduced, thus making it possible for the press to better exploit the new networks of information available.

One product of the new telegraphic technology were the international news agencies, of which Reuters was by far pre-eminent in India. By using its services newspapers could obtain access to an extensive system of foreign reporting without having to incur the costs of a large foreign staff. Such agencies had significant implications for the character of foreign news coverage. Since Reuters selected and processed a large part of the foreign news relayed by the metropolitan papers a greater uniformity in the reporting of overseas events was created.

Two case studies

Reuters news agency

In a recent company history, Donald Read (1992: 83) has stated that India was 'the most profitable part' of the British Empire for Reuters, constituting 'a great market for political and commercial news, both incoming and outgoing'. The first Reuters telegram datelined Calcutta was sent in 1858, and four years later Edwyn Dawes became the company's first named agent at Bombay.[16] In 1864 the government of India arranged with the Bombay agent to be 'furnished on the arrival of each mail with a copy of Reuters' telegram.'[17] This relationship was to develop rapidly, especially under Edward Buck, the company's chief representative in India (also appointed correspondent with the government of India in 1897), who formed close links with successive viceroys and the political élite in Simla (Buck 1925; Storey 1951: 83). Reuters' presence in India grew steadily. A Bombay office was established in 1866, and by 1868 this had been joined by offices at Calcutta, Karachi, Madras, Colombo, and Point de Galle.[18] In 1871 the private telegram service between India and London was started by Henry Collins, a venture which proved extremely lucrative. The year 1891 saw the establishment of Reuters telegraph remittance service between England and India, and later between India and South Africa.

Though news and press business formed a significant element of Reuters' activity, the company drew the greater part of its revenue from the supply of commercial intelligence and private telegrams. From this source came the profits which financed its pathbreaking ventures in news reporting, ventures which in turn provided the basis of Reuters' prestige and reputation. Reuters' efforts to expand its business with the sub-continent entailed significant costs which were a cause of concern. As the chairman informed the annual general meeting in 1908: 'we have to proceed very cautiously in opening new agencies in so expensive a country as India.'[19] However, the substantial earnings generated from commercial and private services and the ever increasing demand for news meant that in 1898 the total revenue raised from Indian business was £11,500, a figure which increased to £18,400 in 1908 and £35,200 in 1918. As a share of Reuters' total revenue from all sources, these sums represented 8.1 per cent, 9.4 per cent, and 13.2 per cent respectively (Read 1992: 83). The annual report of 1910 noted that there was

> a growing demand for news, more especially on the part of India and Australia, which found expression in the Imperial Press Conference held last year . . . We, for our part, have done our share, and the service, for instance, which we made to India, regarding the General Election, has been admitted on all hands to have eclipsed anything previously attempted in that direction.[20]

Further, the company's service from India had 'also been greatly in evidence'.[21] Besides the day-to-day work of the branch offices, Reuters responded directly to major political events in India by increasing the number of correspondents at the crisis centres, many of whom would be senior reporters who could send telegraphs without pre-payment and thus respond quickly to events. Table 5.4 shows how the political crisis in India in the years 1919–21 saw an increase in the number of such correspondents employed.

These years saw burgeoning demand for telegraphic facilities from the public, the press, and the government in India, and the internal telegraph network expanded rapidly. Construction of telegraph lines within India first began in 1850–51 and by 1906 the number of paid messages exceeded ten million per year. The internal network served to extend the potential reach of Reuters' services. The Associated Press of India (API) was formed in Madras in 1908 as a domestic news agency for the Indian press. A leading spirit behind the API was the Indian journalist K.C. Roy, who was paid Rs80 per month by Reuters in 1908 'for assisting Mr Buck to organise internal

Table 5.4 Employment of correspondents by Reuters[22]

| Year | Total number of correspondents | | India as a percentage of world total |
	India	Worldwide	
1915	12	66	18.2
1916	13	70	18.6
1917	13	71	18.3
1919	16	74	21.6
1921	17	70	24.3
1923	14	72	19.4
1925	12	74	16.2

Indian service'.[23] In 1910 API merged with Reuters. From 1907 a rival Indian News Agency was run by Everard Coates, formerly the Indian correspondent of the *Daily Mail*, but this was taken over in 1910 by Reuters with the formation of the Eastern News Agency (ENA), of which Coates was a joint-owner and manager until he was bought out by Reuters in 1918. Thus Reuters also became the predominant domestic news agency in India.

News network in India

There was much variety in the types of correspondents utilised and their terms of engagement.[24] Some were permanent Reuters men in India, others were journalists (often editors) working for Anglo-Indian newspapers, contracted on a half-yearly or yearly basis and paid a fixed stipend. Many were also entitled to commission on the profits made by the company. There were, in addition, local 'stringers' employed whenever need arose to supplement existing services or to arrange cover in remote parts, and they received a separate payment for every telegraph published.

There was a core area of Reuters' coverage, which was made up of the major cities, such as Allahabad, Bombay, Calcutta, Colombo, Peshawar, and Simla, and was staffed by senior correspondents with a brief to cover the whole range of news events, and a periphery into which Reuters extended its operations during the first two decades of the century, and which had fewer senior correspondents, who were often part-time and contracted to provide a more limited service. A significant degree of flexibility is discernible in the functioning of these peripheral centres, with some – Quetta and Kanpur being examples – having correspondents posted only temporarily to cover local events.

What were the major areas of Reuters' coverage during these years? Political developments of all kinds received significant coverage. Wars were a Reuters speciality,[25] and the Indian frontier wars and the Tibet Campaign provided ample opportunities for its correspondents. In the N.W. Frontier campaign of 1898, its special correspondent gave such extensive coverage that 'nearly all the papers relied solely upon our service'.[26] The Delhi Durbars of 1903 and 1912 were lavishly covered, as were tours by the Prince of Wales in 1905–6 and 1921–2. But Reuters always had an eye for an exclusive. The 1913 annual report boasted that

> our greatest success in the department of news was with the account of the attempt on the life of the Viceroy [Lord Hardinge], with which we were absolutely alone for many hours, the Government receiving the intelligence first through our medium.
>
> (Annual Report 1913, RA)

Newspapers run by the British in India began subscribing to Reuters from the 1860s, and they were joined from the 1890s by Indian-run papers as well.[27] Paying a monthly fee of Rs.600, these papers undertook not to use the information thus received for any purpose other than publication in their own columns with full acknowledgement.[28] The Indian National Congress, too, made arrangements with Reuters through its London branch to report, for example, proceedings of annual Congress meetings.[29]

By the late nineteenth century, Reuters news service consisted of two main categories. First there was the general service covering world news of importance which was chronicled in brief telegrams for a fixed annual payment.[30] In 1906 there were thirty-four London newspapers thus subscribing to Reuters, and most had been doing so for several decades. The established dailies paid £1,600 p.a., while the smaller evening and weekly papers paid on average between £100 and £400.[31] Owing, however, to the continued growth of the press and demand for news, Reuters decided to introduce a 'supplementary service of lengthy telegrams on occasions of great importance or of exceptional interest, to be supplied to the Press as a Special Service for a special payment of so much a word published.'[32] It was not necessary for Reuters' correspondents to discriminate between the general service and the special service, as this could be done by 'responsible Editors at Head Quarters' (Read 1992: 73). In 1914 the editorial work was shared between European, American, Asiatic, and Dominion rooms (Read 1992: 73). The Reuters archives do not throw any light on the amount spent by individual papers specifically on Indian news coverage. Even when information was available there was no guarantee that it would actually be taken up by the press. Thus the annual report for 1906 acknowledged that despite, the very full coverage accorded by Reuters to the visit of the Prince and Princess of Wales to India,

> We did not reap the pecuniary benefit from our reports of the Royal progress which we expected, in view of the fact that the General Election at home directed public attention from the brilliant pageants which took place in our great Indian dependency.[33]

Reuters and Empire

Reuters had always seen itself as an Empire company, conscious of the necessity of maintaining the good favour of the imperial government. The preamble to its contract of August 1897 read:

> Reuters Agency being desirous of establishing more intimate relations with the India Office, particularly with a view to ensure as great accuracy as possible in its intelligence and furthermore wishing to allow the India Office to avail itself of its various channels of information . . . and to communicate . . . all news received by it concerning or having any bearing on India . . .[34]

In return for £500 per year, the agency undertook to have its representative

> attend periodically or when required at the India Office in London and at the Government Offices in India to receive communications, denials, rectifications of mis-statements etc. appearing in the British or Indian Press, and other matter which it might be desired to make public both here and in India.

Any special telegraphic services required by the India Office were to be paid for separately.[35] The Indian government had a separate contract with the company, which in 1906, in accordance with an agreement made in 1878, meant paying Rs1,200 per month for the ordinary outward service and Rs600 per month for the extended service.[36] From August 1922 the Reuters government service was entirely separated from the press service and consisted of an extended summary of 500 words per day from Bombay with a provision to incorporate any additional news when necessary. The Reuters full service (i.e. government, press and special services) was available to all subscribing newspapers and also to the viceroy, vicereine, and commander-in-chief.[37]

Criticism of the service

Reuters' news service did not escape its share of contemporary criticism, from both the press and the government. The *Manchester Guardian* and *India*, for example, claimed that Reuters correspondents were often inaccurate in their portrayal of events, embroidering fact with fiction. From ministers and officials in London and New Delhi came the same charge, attention being drawn to excessive coverage of 'trivia' and a supposed pro-nationalist bias (Read 1992: 83). Reuters was always vigorous in its defence. Certainly, as its contract with the Indian National Congress suggests, the agency treated that body as a source of demand and did not appear to take a partisan position on the political crisis unfolding in India. A special correspondent was sent to the INC meeting at Allahabad in 1910, because 'Late events in India tend to impart special interest to this gathering . . . and to emphasize the need of an independent and impartial record of the discussions' (Read 1992: 63–5, 88–9).

Though Reuters stressed that it was a private company, independent of government, and placed great emphasis upon the objectivity and professionalism of its news coverage, it is questionable whether it always managed to maintain this impartiality (Boyd-Barrett 1980: 223). Reuters was frequently used by the India Office to telegraph additional words of a meeting or a speech which it thought desirable to publicise in the Indian Empire, or to counteract articles in the London press (Read 1992: 140). This relationship between government and Reuters strengthened further under the pressure of war and the integrity of the agency began to be questioned. Edward Buck was engaged by the Indian government to "'cook up suitable telegrams for transmission, through Reuters, to all parts of the British Empire'" with the object of conveying an impression of loyal Indian support for the war effort (Read 1992: 40). In London Roderick Jones, the company's general manager, became head of the department of propaganda at the Ministry of Information, and Reuters also started a special 'Agence Reuters' to transmit propaganda to assist the allied cause, which took precedence over other messages. The service was financed by the government, which paid trans-mission costs at the rate of £120,000 per annum (Boyd-Barrett 1980: 223). Criticism was voiced in public and parliament at these developments and Jones ultimately bowed to pressure and resigned his governmental post.[38] Nevertheless when, after the war, the government of India appointed a perma-nent committee to advise on publicity and propaganda, its non-official members were journalists representing Reuters (Mr Kingston) and the Eastern News Agency (Mr Roy).[39] 'The close Reuters relationship', says Read (1992: 148), 'with the Indian Government and with the India Office continued throughout the interwar years.' Indeed intimate links with government suited Reuters since official business helped to balance the company's books in a more competitive commercial environment (Read 1992: 148). It is difficult to avoid the conclusion that Reuters, imbued as it was with a self-professed patriotism (most conspicuous during its coverage of the world wars), and conscious of the importance of Empire to its success, tended to reflect the British point of view more sympathetically than the Indian. Graham Storey is of the opinion that, throughout most of the nineteenth century, Reuters was 'essentially part of the British scheme of things in India'. Only gradu-ally did it adapt itself to the growth of Indian nationalism (Storey 1951: 123–4).

'The Times'

The Times had the largest financial outlay on Indian news coverage, and was considered the most influential British newspaper in the treatment of Indian affairs (*History of 'The Times'* 1952: 17). In 1909 its foreign depart-ment consisted of four men, Valentine Chirol and D.D. Braham being chiefly responsible for foreign affairs, Lovat Fraser for Indian affairs, and Edward Grigg for Imperial coverage: 'One or other of these four is continually in direct relations with the Foreign Office, India Office and Colonial Office.'

The India Office was anxious to shape the policy of the paper, or at least to keep it informed of its point of view and secure sympathetic treatment. To this end secretaries of state often met and dined with its chief leader writers.[40] In 1921, when an information officer was first appointed at the India Office to deal primarily with the press, a *Times* man, Owen Lloyd Evans, was selected for the post. The two subsequent appointments, Edwin Haward in 1928 and Hugh MacGregor in 1930, had also served with the paper.

Chirol (foreign editor, 1899–1911) was widely respected as one of the best informed authorities on the affairs of the sub-continent, and was consulted by politicians in India, including viceroys such as Curzon and Hardinge (both of whom were close personal friends), and by the India Office.[41] He served on the Indian Public Service Commission in 1912 and wrote several books on India. Though he left *The Times* in 1912, he continued writing for the paper and served as its special correspondent till after the First World War. Influential as he undoubtedly was in determining the line of the paper in imperial policy, he was not supreme. Power resided ultimately with the proprietor and the editor. A striking illustration of this was provided by the controversy involving Curzon and the commander-in-chief Kitchener in 1905, which ultimately led to the viceroy's resignation. Though Chirol was pro-Curzon and endeavoured to make the paper's line as supportive of the viceroy as possible, his position was ultimately eclipsed by the strong pro-Kitchener line of the military correspondent, Colonel Repington, who enjoyed the backing of the management as well as the Secretary of State, St John Brodrick. As Chirol wrote in explanation to the disappointed viceroy:

> I am sorry my view has not prevailed in Printing House Square against the 'expert opinion' of our military advisor and the general reluctance to criticise unfavourably the policy of His Majesty's Government . . . I cannot press beyond a certain point in matters which do not really lie within my province.[42]

The system of Indian reporting

During the 1890s there were two main *Times* correspondents in India: Howard Hensman and J. MacGregor. Hensman was also employed by the Anglo-Indian *Pioneer*, for which he served as correspondent permanently attached to the government of India – a position similar to that held by Edward Buck of Reuters (Kaul 1993). MacGregor, a lawyer in the Calcutta high court, had earlier played a prominent role for the paper in the Ilbert Bill controversy 1883–4. Both men were well established in India and well connected, but in difficult moments *The Times* did seek assistance from the India Office, though striving to keep such contact to a minimum.[43]

The management kept tight control over the system of reporting in India, as is apparent from instructions issued to each of the correspondents in the 1890s. Telegrams from Hensman had been passing through MacGregor's hands in Calcutta before being wired back to London, sometimes undergoing alteration in the process. This arrangement was considered 'not altogether satisfactory' by the foreign manager D.M. Wallace, who felt that Simla opinion could best be gauged by Hensman. Whilst MacGregor was free to offer any remarks from the Calcutta viewpoint, 'we should prefer to have your telegrams in their original form . . . In this way the present dual correspondent will be bisected into two mutually independent units and I shall be able to make allowance, if necessary, for the personal equation.'[44] Explaining the system to MacGregor, Wallace wrote: 'India is big enough to hold two correspondents and there is no necessity for their always agreeing on doubtful points . . . I can always suppress anything here' (*The Times*, 21 April 1926).

The paper was keen to establish good contacts among the official and non-official British community in India to strengthen its news team. Frequently correspondents were recruited from among conservative sections of the Anglo-Indian press establishment. Lovat Fraser and Stanley Reed, successive editors of the *Times of India*, were prominent in this category. Fraser relinquished his Indian editorship in 1905 due to ill health, but worked as a special correspondent for *The Times* till 1922, serving in India, China, Australia, and elsewhere. Reed, although never working directly for *The Times* in London, was its chief liaison officer in India. Like Fraser, Frank Herbert Brown served an apprenticeship in India before joining the staff of *The Times* in 1902.[45] He specialised in political and constitutional issues, and contributed, from 1916 to 1942, a weekly article on Indian education to the Educational Supplement. Brown covered the three sessions of the Round Table Conference 1930/31. Woolacott of the *Pioneer* and his successor Edwin Haward were English journalists working in India who were recruited to act as *Times* correspondents. Haward was 'our correspondent' in Lahore from 1914 to 1920. On moving from the *Civil and Military Gazette* to Simla to be political correspondent of the *Pioneer*, he became 'our own correspondent' from Delhi/Simla until 1926, when Haward was appointed editor of the *Pioneer*.[46]

The Times sent more special correspondents to India than any other metropolitan newspaper and enjoyed repute for its coverage of special events and issues. Lionel James, a trusted war reporter, visited India in 1907 for a period of three months. For the Delhi Durbar of 1912 *The Times* dispatched Fraser and Grigg. Walter S. Scott, foreign chief sub-editor, wrote to Reed in August 1918 emphasising that the proprietors desired to increase the cable service from India. Reed was therefore instructed to cable weekly 500–700 words of general Indian news for publication on Mondays, in addition to cabling important news at urgent rates. The object was 'to make Indian news a regular and special feature of the paper'.[47] Chirol made a number of special visits. In 1920, when the situation in India was 'disturbed', the management decided that the time was ripe for

> a special investigation, and so far as we can help to improve an ugly situation. Recognising this, we are now negotiating with Sir Valentine Chirol to go out to India in the autumn and send us a series of articles which will be helpful to the British public in explaining the real position, and, so far as possible, also to troubled India.[48]

The policy of the paper was not determined by correspondents, but formulated at head office. Yet it was not expected of correspondents that they should simply expound the 'official line'. As an editorial note to Grigg stated,

> *The Times* is not a department of the Foreign Office and correspondents are not supposed to 'hold' a certain 'language' like diplomatists in conformity with a preconceived policy in London. The policy of the paper . . . is expounded in its leading articles and not in the reports of its correspondents, which deal with matters of fact. A correspondent's whole value to the paper lies in telling the truth as he knows it; special qualifications, long experience and intimate knowledge of a subject become worthless if he has to 'write up' a certain view — almost anyone can do that.[49]

Wallace explained to MacGregor in 1892 that overseas reporters were encouraged to send in their 'impressions', which would 'always receive attentive consideration'.[50] In a letter to Chirol on the question of possible misrepresentation of a correspondent's message by the leader, Wallace contended that a 'correspondent can only do his best to enlighten those at head quarters and leave the rest to the Editor, who has to use his own judgement with regard to the policy of the Paper'.[51] Further, even an influential correspondent, as Chirol undoubtedly was when touring India, suffered rebuke from the manager if he transgressed too far from the paper's official line. Buckle, the editor, telegraphed Chirol in Bombay with reference to the Curzon–Kitchener controversy: 'Through confidence your judgement published greater portion telegram but grave misgivings strongly feel unwise reopen heated controversy beginning Royal tour likely hamper Minto.'[52] In the determination of the paper's line, advice from senior Indian correspondents was of course appreciated. MacGregor thanked Reed for his occasional notes which were 'extremely valuable, and especially helpful in correcting the more or less academic views of those of us whose knowledge of India was gained by reading rather than by personal experience'.[53] The paper had on occasion to temper its line in accordance with the situation in England, especially if it represented a response to a particularly delicate issue likely to inflame sentiment. B.K. Long, writing to Reed in February 1921 at the height of the Non-Cooperation Movement and in the wake of disturbances in Rae Bareli, explained:

> You will understand that we have to balance the pros and cons of a situation like that in India at the moment as carefully as we can. Often our decisions are liable to seem unintelligent to you on the spot; whereas they are due to causes which seem insuperable to us here . . . I think that unless things become really desperate it is better for *The Times* to err on the side of moderation.
>
> (*History of 'The Times'* 1947: 787)

75

Rivalry in foreign news reporting

In the middle of the nineteenth century *The Times* was the only British daily paper with an extensive system of foreign correspondents. The lead it consequently enjoyed in news reporting was the basis of its pre-eminent reputation. Yet developments from 1850 onward progressively undermined its unique position. The repeal of the newspaper stamp duties in 1855 saw the rapid growth in competition from a penny press. Still charging 3d. per copy, *The Times* felt a need to 'offer the public more than the penny papers' (Palmer 1978: 208). This took the shape of increased and better foreign news coverage, but this was seriously affected by the most important technological development of the later nineteenth century – the growth of the telegraph network.

By the 1870s the telegraph had displaced the 'news letter' as the preferred medium for hard news reporting (Palmer 1978: 206). With its commitment to foreign news, *The Times* was forced to follow the trend, but the much greater cost of sending messages by cable meant that the financial burden of the overseas network of correspondents was much increased. And this development coincided with a general decline in the paper's resources – especially following its heavy losses in the Parnell forgery case in 1887. In addition it had to deal with a powerful rival. By creating a system of foreign correspondents on the basis of the new telegraph system, Reuters was soon able to offer a comprehensive service of international news to the world's press. Reuters had secured, by 1858, the subscriptions of seven London morning dailies. Through this medium a large part of the advantage which *The Times* possessed over other metropolitan papers disappeared. As its official historian remarks: 'the effect of the telegraphic agencies in generally levelling-up the standard in foreign correspondence hit *The Times* as it hit no other paper' (*History of 'The Times'* 1947: 787). Indeed, in 1858 *The Times* itself subscribed to Reuters, and by 1870 it was finding the agency's foreign news service 'indispensable' (Palmer 1978: 208). The difficulty of matching Reuters' international coverage was especially great for *The Times* since, unlike an agency, it did not sell its foreign news service to others. By 1890, says Palmer (1978: 214), '*The Times* had lost its superiority in coverage of foreign news; the *Daily Telegraph*, *Standard* and *Morning Post*, using their own correspondents and Reuters, held their own'.

This rivalry for information among foreign correspondents made itself felt in India. In 1892 the manager of *The Times* wrote to Hensman expressing concern that the paper had been slow to report a communique from the Amir of Afghanistan.

> The other day the *Standard*'s correspondent anticipated not only you but also the event which he described! I refer to the Ameer's reply . . . Is it possible that the correspondent got a telegram from Peshawar informing him that the letter had been received there? If so – you too have some one there who could give you the wink when anything important happens.[54]

The threat posed by Reuters was taken especially seriously. Hensman was warned 'to keep a sharp eye' on Reuters' agent in Simla, 'for he runs you very close'.[55] With Reuters matching the paper in hard news reporting, *The Times* sought to differentiate itself by the quality of its commentary and analysis. As Moberly Bell wrote:

> Reuters' agent has one business, to pick up facts, not to bother his head about anything but bare facts, and to wire them at the earliest moment he can acquire them. A *Times* correspondent has a great deal more to do [his] duty being to comment on news rather than to give it: it is only natural that in the mere getting of facts Reuters should forestall him.
>
> (Moberly Bell 1927: 166–7)

This was the policy adopted in reporting Indian affairs. Correspondents in 1892 were instructed to 'Stick chiefly to facts and explanations. The latter will make a distinctive feature compared with Reuters' (*History of 'The Times'* 1947: 768).

Changes in response to deteriorating finances

The reputation of *The Times* for foreign news coverage increasingly failed to be reflected in sales, and the need for economy was pressing from the 1890s till after the First World War. When the Walter family sold the paper to Lord Northcliffe in 1908 its average daily sale was only 38,000. There followed re-organisation in every department, including the system of Indian correspondence, with the responsibility resting primarily with Fraser. Under the new arrangement, all messages to and from India were to pass through the hands of Reed.[56] Reed was to be assisted by Hensman in Simla, Long for the United Provinces, and Fernandez in Peshawar.[57]

Significant advantages were realised from this centralisation of command, as Reed explained in 1914 to the new foreign editor, Wickham Steed, on the occasion of an even more thorough re-organisation of the imperial and foreign service. It was

> thought desirable to prevent any waste in telegraphing, any overlapping of correspondence, and so that the whole news service of the "Times of India" which so far as foreign telegrams are concerned is reserved for the service of "The Times", may be available for any messages which were sent on.[58]

Reed noted that the last condition was 'very often of material value, because . . . no daily paper is published at Delhi or Simla and it is very often practicable to incorporate in a telegram which comes from a correspondent further authentic information which is at our disposal'. The possibilities of cooperation between an Anglo-Indian paper and Fleet Street were well exemplified by this case. According to Reed, the system 'on the whole works to the advantage of *The Times* better than any which can be set up in its place. It secures a very wide service of Indian news on which to draw and it secures also I think a very great economy and accuracy in the cable service.'[59] This arrangement persisted substantially unchanged throughout the war years and into the early 1920s.[60]

Despite re-organisation the scale of foreign news gathering came under pressure to contract. Wallace and Moberly Bell were very cautious managers. Telegraphic costs were a major part of the paper's expense account and the management was always urging its correspondents to be 'more concise'. In 1891 MacGregor had transmitted 49,505 words at a cost of £2,480. Writing to MacGregor in August 1892, Wallace stated that 'we find it desirable to diminish the telegraph expenses from India and Burmah' by 'about one-fourth', as other extra expenditure was foreseen for the following year.[61] Wallace stressed however that, 'If any *important* events should unexpectedly occur, we must be kept fully informed, whatever the *necessary* expense may be.'[62]

The situation regarding telegraphs was a persistent source of concern for *The Times*. It had a contract with the Eastern Telegraph Company by which it was bound to pay for a minimum number of words per annum; during the 1890s this figure was usually 40,000.[63] As the actual amount telegraphed was left to the discretion of correspondents, it was possible both to exceed and to fall short of the minimum.[64] The latter occurred in 1895 and the paper therefore had 'some dissertations transmitted to make up the amount'.[65] With the monopoly of news transmission, the telegraph companies were in a strong position and so newspapers had either to pay the whole fee or else receive no foreign intelligence at all. This was a major hindrance to the metropolitan press, and when nothing much happened in India that had sale value in Britain (as was often perceived to be the case), papers were reluctant to pay for the telegraph facilities. Smaller papers were particularly affected.

As Table 5.5 indicates, there were sharp declines in annual outlay after 1897 and 1901. With the exception of 1904, the totals for the early twentieth century were always under £1,000. Whereas an average of 300 words had been sent each day in 1897, by 1906 the average was only 26.[66]

Table 5.5   Telegraph expenditure from India by *The Times*, 1897–1906[67]

Year	Amount (£)	Year	Amount (£)
1897	4,785	1902	446
1898	2,584	1903	850
1899	1,817	1904	1,186
1900	2,194	1905	755
1901	1,570	1906	407

Another major expense was, of course, the correspondents stationed in India. Upon the re-organisation of the Indian network in 1908–9, Reed was put in charge of all telegraph expenses from Bombay and paid £25 per month for his services.[68] Hensman, who had earlier sent telegrams directly to London, was paid a retainer of £200 per annum and had to work under Reed.[69] He was subsequently dismissed, then reappointed in 1914 on a lower annual retaining fee of £100. The accounts too were centralised in Bombay and Reed appointed to 'furnish us every month an account the amount of which we can pay into some branch here'.[70]

Apart from salaried correspondents there were others who received a retaining fee and a fixed amount per telegram published. In most cases this was 10s., but for cables of 'exceptional interest or length' a payment of £1 was made. For any mail matter published, payment was made at the rate of £3 a column.[71] Correspondents were shared with other papers and transferred around the world depending on the local situation. When, for instance, Arthur Moore was shifted from Teheran to India on a six-month contract from 1 February 1922 with a monthly salary of £125, the *Daily Mail* shared half of the expenses with *The Times*. In addition *The Times* paid an allowance of £2 per day towards hotel fees, defrayed all travelling charges, and made a grant of £30 towards kit expenses.[72] Lastly there was the system of special correspondents. The visit of Lionel James in 1907 cost the paper £200.[73] When Fraser and Grigg went to India to cover the Delhi Durbar of 1912 both were paid £200 and presented with court suits. Their additional expenses in India were covered by a 'very high' sum, only grudgingly accepted by the management. For the special investigation undertaken by Chirol in 1920 it was agreed that he should receive travelling expenses, a living allowance of £2 a day, £4. 4s. a column for matter published and a honorarium of £250.[74] Haward, who received a retainer of £100 p.a. besides the ordinary message and mail rate, was paid £50 and 'any out of pocket expenses' for special work connected with the Mount Everest expedition in 1922.[75] Prolific leader writers on India, such as Lovat Fraser, who were engaged on the London staff, were paid between £700 and £1000 per annum in the years leading up to the First World War.[76] In 1920 the imperial and foreign news editor (formerly foreign news editor) commanded a salary of £900 per annum.[77]

Summary

India occupied a special position in the coverage by *The Times* of imperial issues. The paper's prestige in the sub-continent was unparalleled. According to Reed, it was 'the only English newspaper which is read in India with respect; it is the only English newspaper which influences opinion here, and which has honestly sought to guide the British public on Indian questions.'[78] Yet apart from being an influential organ of opinion among the decision making élite in London and Simla/Delhi, *The Times* was also a business enterprise, and one under increasing financial difficulties. When Northcliffe became proprietor his most immediate concern was the restoration of commercial viability. Cuts in finance and space affected the foreign department and produced understandable consternation amongst the staff. As Chirol complained to Steed in 1910,

> the difficulty of reconciling the exigencies of space under the new dispensation with the full and serious treatment of foreign politics which was one of the best features of the old, is, I fear, increasing every day with a growing tendency to consider what the general public wants in news rather than what the relatively small class of readers who never-theless constitute the backbone of *The Times* and give it its prestige expect to find in the paper.[79]

This change in perspective was reflected in the motives, outlined by the editor, for the decision to send Chirol to India in 1920. His dispatches were intended to appeal more to the generally interested reader than to those with a special interest in Indian affairs

> The idea is that he should write not exactly a numbered series but a number of articles on "India Today" from the point of view of an expert who goes to India with the definite intention of trying to make Indian conditions and Indian problems interesting and comprehensible to the general reader. There would be as much "impression" as erudition in the articles. I think, and Lord Northcliffe agrees, that on these condi-tions the articles ought to be a very valuable feature next winter, which we could advertise before beginning publication.[80]

This need to attract the general, as well as the specialist, reader was the essential dilemma faced by *The Times*. However much it prided itself upon the quality of its reporting and the weight of its contribution to contempo-rary debates, *The Times* remained, like all other newspapers, dependent upon sales if it were to flourish or even survive. And these financial claims made themselves felt in the coverage of Indian affairs. Hugh MacGregor was forced to write to Reed in 1920 that, after a decade of concentration chiefly on political news,

> You will be doing a great service if you can induce our men in India to replace politics as far as possible by a variety of subjects. Newspaper conditions here are becoming rather critical, in that the public are strongly reacting against political matter . . . This is regrettable to serious students of the world's affairs, but has to be recognised by jour-nalists as businessmen whose newspaper prosperity depends at least on a minimum circulation, and so the public must be humoured for a little.[81]

Conclusion

From the turn of the century the London press as a whole devoted increasing attention to the affairs of the Indian Empire. A series of important political developments, such as Curzon's partition of Bengal in 1905 and his enforced resignation from the viceroyalty, and growing nationalist unrest, provided a focus for heightened coverage, while India's contribution to the First World War raised still further the sub-continent's profile. The war and post-war years also witnessed, for the first time, the active involvement of the British government in propaganda. Issues pertaining to the control and accessibility of information came to a head during these years, altering fundamentally the nature of India Office involvement with the British press (Kaul 1994).

A factor underlying the developments of these years was the expanding system of imperial communications. The late nineteenth and early twentieth centuries were an age of information revolution, issuing forth a larger volume and greater variety of information upon the Empire than had ever before been available. Telegraphs, railways, telephones, linotype machines, type-writers, and rotary presses all combined to transform, not only the extent and speed at which information moved around the globe, but the character and presentation of the news conveyed. A radical shift in the quality of over-seas news coverage was made possible. The heightened expectations of their readers ensured that all serious newspapers sought to exploit these oppor-tunities. Much of the impact of these technologies made itself felt by means of international news agencies, such as Reuters, since by their means the sort of costs which had been necessary for a paper like *The Times* in establishing and maintaining a large foreign staff were circumvented.

Telegraphic news agencies were thus great levellers in the sphere of foreign reporting, promoting, especially, the growth of the cheap daily press. Yet the greater average volume of overseas coverage was purchased, in part, at the cost of a uniformity of treatment which had important ramifications for the understanding of political developments. The advent of 'telegraphic journalism' forced newspapers to reconsider the nature of their foreign coverage. With agencies seeking to supply purely 'factual' reports, papers such as *The Times* emphasised the distinctive commentary and perspective upon these events which their own correspondents provided.

Notes

1   Memo by the director-in-chief, Indo-European Telegraph Department for the information of the inter-departmental cables committee, 18.3.01, no. 4, appendix A, L/PWD/7/1390, India Office Records (IOR), India Office Library, London.
2   Inter-departmental committee on cable rates, London, 1900, L/PWD/7/1390, IOR.

3   Others included Canada (15), W. Indies (1), Australia (14), New Zealand (6) and S. Africa (11).

4   Telegrams, the 'text of which contain only information and news relative to politics, commerce, &c., intended for publication in Newspapers', were admitted as press telegrams.

5   The Eastern Extension Australasia and China Telegraph Company Ltd. Special Press Service. 28/2/10. Reuters Special Press Agency and Imperial News Messages, L/PWD/7/1551, IOR.

6   Ibid., letter dated 23 March 1910.

7   Ibid., No. 4.

8   Hibberdine, Eastern Telegraph Company, to H.A. Kirk, Indo-European Telegraph Dept. India Office, 9/7/10, L/PWD/7/1551, IOR.

9   Crewe to the Governor-General-in-Council, 15 March 1912, Tele No. 7; 2 August 1912, Tele No. 18; 27 September 1912, Tele No. 26. L/PWD/7/1573, IOR.

10 Press rates quoted by Sir Basil Blackett, chairman of Imperial and International Communications Ltd, at the fourth Imperial Press Conference, London, June 1930, cited in Desmond (1937).

11 Note on Press Telegrams 12/9/18, P/W 2460/18, L/PWD/7/1573, IOR.

12 He served variously as special correspondent in the North West Frontier and during the Indian tours of the Duke of Connaught and the Prince of Wales.

13 Horniman was deported in April 1919 for supporting the nationalist cause against the excesses of the martial law regime in Punjab.

14 Manager, *The Times*, to Arthur Moore, 1 February 1922. TA. For Northcliffe's views on India see *Daily Mail*, 25 January, 9 March 1922.

15 Moberly Bell to Lovat Fraser, 2 December 1908. Managers' Letter Books, No. 50, TA.

16 Account Book, IOLR directory.

17 National Archives of India, HP/B/111. J. Taylor notes, RA.

18 Reuters Annual Report, RA.

19 Annual Report 1908, RA.

20 Chairman's speech, Annual Report 1910, RA; cf. Annual Report 1908.

21 Annual Report 1908, RA.

22 Compiled from LN325 Databook, RA.

23 Agreements with Agents and Correspondents, Contract Book 1909, LN 293 883309, p. 32, RA.

24 The Contract Books 1906–26 show this clearly, LN 293 883309, LN 279 883301, LN290 883307, RA.

25 During the Boer War, Reuters employed 108 special correspondents in addition to its ordinary staff, Annual Report 1902, RA.

26 Chairman's Address, Annual Report 1898, RA. Similarly for the Tibet Campaign, Annual Report 1904, p. 221, RA.

27 In 1867 Colombo provided Reuters with its first newspaper subscriber in Asia, the *Ceylon Observer*. Among the earliest Indian newspapers were the Calcutta *Englishman*, Bombay *Gazette*, *Madras Times*, Allahabad *Pioneer*, *Civil*

and Military Gazette, Lahore – all in 1879. For details of these contracts refer to Copies of Contracts No. 1, Box 317 1/8818001, RA.

28 India and Ceylon, Agreements Colonial and Foreign, Contract Book 1906, LN 293 883309, pp. 18–19, RA. For changes in this refer to the successive Contract Books arranged chronologically 1906–26.

29 Letter from William Digby, Secretary of the British Committee, Indian National Congress to the Secretary of Reuters, W.F. Bradshaw, 24 November 1891, Copies of Contracts Box 318 1/8818002, RA.

30 Memo on 'General Instructions for the Guidance of Correspondents', August 1897, LN17 863813; cf. similar memo in March 1906, RA.

31 Agreements – Great Britain, Contract Book 1906, pp. 2–7, RA.

32 Ibid.

33 Annual Report 1906, p. 237, RA.

34 Copy of Contract III, India, Burmah and Ceylon. 12 August 1897, LN 391 1/8818003, RA.

35 Ibid.

36 Contract Book 1906, pp. 18–19 and p. 16 respectively, RA.

37 Special Traffic Routine Circular No. 17, Calcutta, 19 July 1922, P&T (Telegraph Traffic), L/PWD/7/1551, IOR.

38 Refer to Reuters Service Bulletin, October 1917, p. 5; September 1918, pp. 2, 10, RA.

39 Reuters Service Bulletin, no. 12, June 1921, p. 19.

40 Arthur Hirtzel Diaries, IOR. Cf. Bell to Fraser, 27 May 1908, Managers' Letter Books, No. 47, TA.

41 Dunlop-Smith, writing to Minto, characterised Chirol as 'very able' and possessing 'the gift of expression', though he added that these qualities were compromised by excessive obstinacy, 23 June 1910, Dunlop-Smith Papers, MSS Eur F 166/9, IOR.

42 Chirol to Curzon, 23 June 1905. Similarly 7 July 1905; 3 August 1905. Curzon Papers, MSS Eur F111/183, IOR.

43 Wallace to Macgregor, 6 July 1892. Foreign Managers' Letter Books, No. 1, TA.

44 D. M. Wallace to H. Hensman, 6 July 1892. Foreign Managers' Letter Books, No.1, 18 November 1891 to 28 August. 1893, TA.

45 Asst. Ed. *Bombay Gazette*, Ed. *Indian Daily Telegraph*, Lucknow, London Correspondent of *Times of India*. He also wrote for other papers such as the *Westminster Gazette*.

46 Edwin Haward, Managerial File, TA.

47 Scott to Reed, 5 August 1918, W.S. Scott Correspondence, TA.

48 MacGregor to Reed, 5 August 1920. MacGregor Correspondence, TA.

49 Unsigned editorial memo to Grigg, 1 May 1912. Grigg Correspondence, TA.

50 Wallace to MacGregor, 6 July 1892; 10 July 1893. Foreign Managers' Letter Books, No.1, 18 November 1891 to 28 August 1893, TA.

51 Wallace to Chirol, 27 June 1892. Foreign Managers' Letter Books, No. 1, TA. For example, Reed and Hensman's telegrams were not used in the

summer of 1911 as they did not follow the line of *The Times* on the Indian Army, Grigg to Chirol, 27 July 1911. Grigg Correspondence, TA.

52 Buckle to Chirol, 8/9 November 1905. Managers' Letter Books, No. 41, TA. Similarly, MacGregor to Reed, Bombay, informing him that it was the 'general principle that Correspondent cannot dictate the policy of the paper', 16 March 1920. MacGregor Correspondence, TA.

53 MacGregor to Reed, 22 June 1920. MacGregor Correspondence, TA.

54 Wallace, Foreign Manager, to Howard Hensman, 23 September 1892. Foreign Managers' Letter Books, No. 1, TA.

55 Ibid.

56 Bell to Hensman, 3 November 1908. Managers' Letter Books, No. 50, TA.

57 Bell to Fraser, 6 April 1909. Managers' Letter Books, No. 52, TA.

58 Reed to Steed, 23 Febuary 1914, Steed Papers, TA.

59 *The Times* also operated an exchange system with Anglo-Indian newspapers. In 1906 these included *Englishman*, *Indian Spectator*, *Madras Weekly Mail*, and *Times of India*, Letters to their Editors from Bell, 14 December 1906. Managers' Letter Books, No. 44, TA.

60 Reed to Dawson, 28 March 1923, Dawson Papers, MSS D69, Fol. 196, Bodleian Library, Oxford.

61 Wallace to MacGregor, 23 August 1892. Foreign Managers' Letter Books, No. 1, TA.

62 Ibid.

63 Wallace to Hensman, 22 July 1896. Foreign Managers' Letter Books, No. 3, TA.

64 Wallace to Hensman, 29 December 1896, ibid.

65 Wallace to Hensman, 16 April 1896, ibid.

66 Bell to Fraser, 2 December 1908. Managers' Letter Books, No. 50, TA.

67 Ibid.

68 Bell to Reed, 24 December 1908, 3 Febuary 1909. Managers' Letter Books, Nos 50 and 51 respectively, TA.

69 Bell to Fraser, 12 March 1909. Managers' Letter Books, No. 51, TA.

70 Bell to Fraser, 12 March 1909. Managers' Letter Books, No. 51, TA.

71 Asst. Manager to Hensman, c/o *Pioneer*, 24 June 1914, TA.

72 Manager to Moore, 1 February 1922. Managers' Letter Books, TA.

73 Bell to James, 23 May 1907. Managers' Letter Books, No. 45, TA.

74 Chirol, Managerial File, TA.

75 Memo from Manager, 16 February 1922, Managerial File, TA.

76 Manager to Fraser, 4 October 1912 (£700) and 1 April 1914 (£1,000), Managers' Letter Books, Nos 56 and 57 respectively, TA.

77 Editorial memo to Macgregor, 1 January 1920, Managerial File, TA.

78 Reed to Dawson, 2 March 1919, Dawson Papers, MSS D68 f170, Bodleian Library, Oxford.

79 Chirol to Steed, 14 December 1910. Chirol Correspondence, TA.

80 Steed to W. Lints Smith, Assoc. Manager, 9 August 1920, Chirol Managerial File, TA.

81 MacGregor to Reed, 19 May 1920, MacGregor Correspondence, TA.

References

Ahvenainen, J. (1981) *The Far Eastern Telegraphs*, Helsinki: Soumalainen Tiedeakatemia.

Barnes, M. (1940) *The Indian Press*, London: George Allen & Unwin.

Boyd-Barrett, O. (1980) *The International News Agencies*, London: Constable.

Bright, C. (1903) 'Imperial Telegraphs', *Quarterly Review* (April).

Bright, C. (1905) 'Imperial Consolidation by Telegraphy', *Monthly Review* (October).

Bright, C. (1909) 'Imperial Telegraphy at a Popular Tariff', *Fortnightly Review* (March).

Buck, Sir E.J. (1925 edn) *Simla, Past and Present*, London: The Times Press.

Desmond, R.W. (1937) *The Press and World Affairs*, New York: D. Appleton–Century.

Deutsch, K.W. (1963) *The Nerves of Government*, London: Collier-Macmillan.

Finn, B.S. (1973) *Submarine Telegraphy: The Grand Victorian Technology*, London: Science Museum.

Hardman, T.H. (1909) *A Parliament of the Press*, London: Horace Marshall.

Headrick, D.R. (1981) *The Tools of Empire*, Oxford: Oxford University Press.

The History of 'The Times' 1884–1912 (1947) vol. 3, London: The Times Publishing Co.

The History of 'The Times' 1912–1948 (1952) vol. 4, part 1, London: The Times Publishing Co.

Innis, H.A. (1972) *Empire and Communications*, Toronto: University of Toronto Press.

James, L. (1929) *High Pressure*, London: John Murray.

Kaul, C. (1993) 'England and India: The Ilbert Bill Controversy, 1883. A Case Study of the Metropolitan Press', *Indian Economic and Social History Review* 30, 4: 413–36.

Kaul, C. (1994) 'A New Angle of Vision: The London Press, Governmental Information Management and the Indian Empire, 1900–22', *Contemporary Record* 8, 2 (Autumn).

Kieve, J. (1973) *The Electric Telegraph*, Newton Abott: David & Charles.

Lovett, P. (1926) *Journalism in India*, Calcutta: The Banna Publishing Co.

MacDonagh, M. (1906) 'The Wires and the Newspapers', *Sells Newspaper Directory*, London: Sells.

Merrett, J. (1958) *Three Miles Deep*, London: Hamish Hamilton.

Mills, J.S. (1924) *The Press and Communications in Empire*, London: Collins.

Moberly Bell, E.H.C. (1927) *Life and Letters of C.F. Moberly Bell*, London: The Richards Press.

Newman, H. (1937a) *Indian Peepshow*, London: G. Bell and Sons.

Newman, H. (1937b) *A Roving Commission*, London: G. Bell and Sons.

Palmer, M. (1978) 'The British Press and International News', in G. Boyce, J. Curran and P. Wingate (eds) *Newspaper History*, London: Constable.

Read, D. (1972) *Edwardian England, 1901–15*, London: Historical Association.

Read, D. (1992) *The Power of News*, Oxford: Oxford University Press.

Sassoon, Sir E.A. (1900) 'Imperial Telegraphic Communication', *Journal of the Society of Arts* (June).

Startt, J.D. (1991) *Journalists for Empire*, Westport, CT: Greenwood Press.

Storey, G. (1951) *Reuter's Century, 1851–1951*, London: Max Parrish.

Williams, R. (1966) *Communications*, London: Chatto & Windus.

1900–1945

Introduction to part two

■ Michael Bromley

WHILE THE DEVELOPMENT OF a more 'popular' press in the 1880s and 1890s alarmed many among even the liberal élite (Carey 1992: 6), the most significant growth in newspaper readerships did not occur until after about 1910, and the press – both daily and Sunday – began to reach 'something like the full reading public' in the 1920s (Williams 1961: 176–7). The conversion of large numbers of working-class people into readers demanded a change in style, which drew from the techniques and appeal of the cinema, advertising, photography and even the radio, whose own audience grew significantly in the 1920s and 1930s (Stevenson 1984: 404–11). The BBC under John Reith exemplified one aspect of a polarisation which manifested itself across the media. Although initially only one newspaper published in tabloid format (the *Daily Mirror*), the most successful paper of the period, the *Daily Express*, was close to being tabloid in approach (Williams 1961: 208). One attempt to categorise the London dailies suggested that alongside the 'serious, comprehensive, careful, discreet' papers there existed the 'kaleidoscopic, flippant and careless'. British journalism, as Dicey reflected in 1905, had changed a great deal since the abolition of Stamp Duty.

Despite the appearance of the *Express* (1900) and *Mirror* (1903), Dicey clearly remained sanguine about the expanding readership. The leading 'popular' half-penny paper was still the *Daily Mail* which, in spite of its reputation, was extremely conservative in practice. Moreover, its owner, Northcliffe, aspired to own *The Times*, which he managed in 1908. With the further growth of daily newspaper readerships – by 58 per cent in the 1920s

(Williams 1961: 207) – and an increasing concentration of press ownership (at one time, Northcliffe owned the *Mail*, the *Mirror* and *The Times*), the threat of commercialisation appeared even greater. Yet it was difficult for a Liberal, provincial newspaper owner/editor such as C.P. Scott to decry the press being run as 'a business, like any other'. As an attempt to reconcile the materialism of the daily press in the 1920s with nineteenth century liberal free press ideology, Scott offers an ethic founded in ideals of the 'free' market.

In reality, the market called not for principled autonomy but for hired hands. Another newspaper proprietor, Lord Riddell, acknowledges but does not debate the 'difficulties' that face the journalist who is 'selling' a story. The issue is evaded: journalists perform as required, and need to be all things to all people. It is the nature of such demands which are put upon them which somehow set them apart, and which Riddell can claim distinguish journalism as a profession (incidentally, in a talk about the 'craft' of journalism). If such an assertion appears rather baseless, then Tom Clarke, in his reminiscence of his period as Northcliffe's news editor at the *Daily Mail*, offers concrete evidence of the vulnerability of journalists arising from what was in fact their uncertain and often precarious status. Gender, class, title, relationships, physical appearance, name could be appropriated in the name of circulation.

In the 1930s the press was subjected to mounting criticism from both the left and the right (Carey 1992: 7–8). The so-called circulation 'wars' in which newspapers canvassed for readers by means of promotional stunts, and the increased concentration of ownership and development of the press as 'big business' which lay behind them, caused particular concern (PEP 1938: 34–5). From the left especially there emerged a number of suggestions for reform, and pressure for a government review. As someone who had worked, at times rather unhappily, for Northcliffe, Wickham Steed may perhaps be expected to have yearned for a newspaper which could profess indifference to circulation figures, sales performance, and advertising revenues. Nevertheless, the functional separation of the self- and public interest dimensions of the press has been, as Wickham Steed recognised, a recurrent ideal among journalists, and the belief that corporate ownership was seriously curtailing the press's ability to pursue its public interest responsibilities provided the impetus for three Royal Commissions on the Press in the post-war period.

References

Carey, J. (1992) *The Intellectuals and the Masses: Pride and Prejudice among the Literary Intelligensia, 1880–1939*, London: Faber & Faber.
Political and Economic Planning (1938) *The British Press*, London: PEP.
Stevenson, J. (1984) *British Society, 1914–45*, Harmondsworth: Penguin.
Williams, R. (1961) *The Long Revolution*, London: Chatto & Windus.

Chapter 6

J.O. Baylen

A CONTEMPORARY ESTIMATE OF THE LONDON DAILY PRESS IN THE EARLY TWENTIETH CENTURY

IN THE 'INTRODUCTION' TO HIS MAGISTERIAL STUDY, *The Rise and Fall of the Political Press: The Twentieth Century* (1984), the late Stephen Koss used W.T. Stead's perceptive 'inventory' of London's twenty-one daily newspapers at the end of 1904 (Stead 1904) as a convenient 'framework' for his book. Koss deemed Stead's assessment significant because, following 'a heady burst of late-Victorian expansionism' of the daily press, during the first decade and a half of the twentieth century, Fleet Street had begun to retrench in a series of acquisitions, amalgamations, and closures with 'the base of proprietorial control continually narrowing'. Generally, the evening papers were the most vulnerable; thus the *Echo* was terminated and the *St James's Gazette* amalgamated with the *Evening Standard* in 1905, the old *Sun* expired in 1906, and the *Morning Leader* was absorbed by the *Daily News* in 1912. All of these events were largely the consequence of greatly increased competition, inflated production costs, and saturation of the newspaper market. Stead, himself, became a victim of this trend by failing to understand the situation when he launched his *Daily Paper* in early 1904; it lasted hardly over a month, broke his health, and almost ruined him financially. What befell Stead was worse for the founders of the *Tribune*, who suffered an even greater disastrous failure when the paper expired in 1906. Yet, as Koss noted, London had 'a staggering array' of daily papers, which included a large number of specialised journals catering to the important business community and other special interests in the metropolitan area. And, as Stead's survey indicated, 'proportionally fewer newspapers qualified as political organs with identifiable affiliations', and even fewer seemed to desire any political affiliation (Koss 1984: 2).

But what inspired Stead, as editor of the monthly *Review of Reviews*, to undertake his survey and critique of the London daily press? He was certainly well qualified to attempt the task, since he knew personally (but not always on friendly terms) virtually all of the editors of the major and significant papers – some of whom began their careers in journalism as his protégés or with his encouragement and help. By 1904, he was one of the 'elders' of British journalism, although with a declining reputation as a result of his deep involvement with spiritualism, his uncompromising anti-war stand during the late Second Boer War, and his association with some movements viewed, at that time, as 'cranky'.

Stead's long career in British journalism began and quickly flourished as the enterprising young editor of the Darlington *Northern Echo* (1871–80), as Assistant Editor of the *Pall Mall Gazette (PMG)* under John Morley (1880–83), and as the innovative and controversial Editorial Director of the paper (1883–90). Stead reached the apogee of his career in London daily journalism by his bold use of the techniques of the 'New Journalism' in the *PMG* to launch such campaigns, agitations, and crusades as the 'Bitter Cry of Outcast London' on behalf of slum clearance (1883), the fatal dispatch of 'Chinese' Gordon to the Sudan (1883–4), the renovation and modernisation of the Royal Navy (1884), and the sensational 'Maiden Tribute of Modern Babylon' revelations (1885) which raised the age of consent for young girls to sixteen (and, unexpectedly, outlawed sexual relations between consenting males).

However the 'Maiden Tribute' agitation was really the high point of Stead's career in daily journalism and his last four years on the *PMG* were an anti-climax. Although he acquired the affection of many Radicals and Socialists by his courageous defence of freedom of assembly and free speech during the Trafalgar Square disturbances in 1886–7 and achieved a great scoop by being the first known foreign journalist to interview a Russian Emperor in 1888, Stead incurred intense dislike and obloquy for himself and the *PMG* as a result of his moralistic 'Social Purity' campaign, and its use to destroy the political career of Sir Charles Dilke, and his ill-advised and credulous advocacy of dubious causes.

After his breach with the long-suffering proprietor of the *PMG*, Henry Yates Thompson, Stead left the paper in January 1890 to establish (with a high interest loan from the Salvation Army and in a brief partnership with George Newnes) the monthly *Review of Reviews*. Despite his use of the periodical to advance the enterprises of Cecil Rhodes and to make Rhodes a national hero, to help to destroy the career of Charles Stewart Parnell, to continue to hound Dilke, and (as in the *Northern Echo* and the *PMG*) to expound his gospel of Anglo-American unity and Russophilism, Stead made a great success of the *Review of Reviews*, but he never recovered the influence he had possessed on the *PMG* during the years 1883–6.

Stead cherished the hope to return to daily paper journalism and persistently (but unsuccessfully) importuned such wealthy friends as Rhodes and

Andrew Carnegie for the capital to establish, own, and edit a daily paper. As the revenues and circulation of the *Review of Reviews* declined in consequence of his unrelenting opposition to the Boer War at the turn of the century and his subsequent preoccupation with pacifist movements and spiritualism, Stead again sought to realise his dream of establishing a new type *Daily Paper*, which would promote the cause of international amity and arms limitation in an era of increasingly dangerous Great Power rivalries and conflicts, and to advance at home social and economic reform. Mustering all the assets he possessed and the funds he could borrow, Stead launched his *Daily Paper* in early January 1904, but, because it was the wrong time for such a venture, and because of poor management, lack of capital to sustain the enterprise, and an unfortunate nervous breakdown, the paper collapsed during the second week of February. Stead was saved from utter financial ruin and even the loss of the *Review of Reviews* by friends and the secret intervention of the Rhodes Trust.[1]

Even before this disaster, Stead had become increasingly concerned and alarmed by the efforts of the metropolitan daily papers – in their practice of the new 'Daily Journalism' – to maintain and increase their circulation in a highly competitive market by sensationalising the news, even to the point of distortion. Above all, Stead, like other contemporary observers of the deteriorating international situation and the unsettling alignments of the Great Powers, viewed with alarm the tendency of the press to exacerbate diplomatic crises and (as in the case of William Randolph Hearst's American 'Yellow Journalism') to prevent or hinder the peaceful resolution of international disputes by misrepresentations, half-truths, and falsehoods which excited public hysteria to the point of war.

At no time was this more apparent to Stead than in the Dogger Bank incident during the Russo-Japanese War which strained Anglo-Russian relations to the breaking point in late October and early November 1904. As the Russian Baltic Fleet was passing through the North Sea on its voyage to the Far East, during the night of 21 October and the early morning of 22 October, the Russian warships encountered British fishing trawlers off the Dogger Bank and, as a result of faulty intelligence reports, believed that the trawlers were Japanese torpedo boats. One or two Russian warships opened fire on the trawlers; they sank one, killing two and wounding four of its crew, and damaged four other trawlers.

The press reports on what had occurred provoked intense indignation in Britain to the point where it seemed that war with Russia was imminent. Meanwhile, following the unfortunate event, British warships shadowed the Russian fleet across the Bay of Biscay until the Russian government ordered the responsible officers to account for what they had done and agreed to international arbitration of the affair. As the Russian fleet sailed on to destruction at the hands of the Japanese in the Far East (27–28 May 1905), the Tsarist government accepted the report of the international tribunal in February 1905 and all claims for compensation. This eased the tension, and the reasonableness of the Russian Foreign Ministry and the British Foreign Office actually facilitated the important and wide-ranging Anglo-Russian understanding in 1907 (Neilson 1989: 80–81).

Stead decided to analyse and review the reaction of the London daily press to the 'sharp and sudden' crisis, from October 23, the day on which the news of the Russian blunder had reached London, until October 29, when the Prime Minister, Arthur Balfour, announced that the crisis was resolved by the Russian government's compliance with British demands. He studied each of the six days' issues of the twenty-one London morning and evening dailies to examine and test 'the gravity, the sanity, the veracity, the temper, the wisdom, and the sagacity' of these journals and their editors.

In a long article, published in the December issue of the *Review of Reviews* under the rubric, 'Character Sketch: His Majesty's Public Councillors: To Wit, The Editors of the London Daily Papers', Stead presented the results of his study prefaced by a commentary on his view of the role of the press and what it aspired to do in and for the nation. The editors of the London dailies, said Stead, regard themselves as 'The unsworn . . . members of the King's Public Council, or . . . as the Public Councillors of King Demos' and 'In either capacity . . . represent the most influential body of men in the three kingdoms.' Indeed, said Stead, what makes the London press and their editors so important is the fact that the government – the Cabinet – is greatly influenced by the press because 'It fears its hostility, and rejoices in its support'. Hence, Stead proposed 'to examine, in the light of the recent [Dogger Bank] incident, the nature of the counsel tendered by these Public Counsellors . . . in order that we may, from this single sample, form some estimate of the value of these Journalistic Advisers.' Although all of these metropolitan dailies professed to be both journals of opinion and journals of news (with the exception of the *Evening News* which claimed to confine itself merely to 'the gathering of the news'), Stead (1904: 593–5; Koss 1984: 1) divided them into four categories:

1   *Councillors of the First Class* This were 'journals which influence opinion and which make the influencing of opinion their chief business', as distinct from those whose major objective is 'to make money by the purveying of news'. The most important of these newspapers were the two 'which every one who is in public affairs must read. No Minister, no diplomatist, no public man can afford to miss reading the [pro-Tory] *Times* [edited by G.E. Buckle] in the morning and the [pro-Liberal] *Westminster Gazette* [edited by J.A. Spender] in the evening.' Both had modest circulations of approximately 35,000 and 20,000, respectively, and were read by the leadership and activists of both parties.

2   *Councillors of the Second Class* These included the *Standard* (C. Byron Curtis), *Daily News* (A.G. Gardiner), the *Morning Post* (J. Nicol Dunn), the *Daily Chronicle* (Robert Donald), the *Star* and the *Morning Leader* (Ernest Parke), the *St James's Gazette* (S.J. Prior), the *Daily Graphic*, the

Globe, the *Echo* (F.W. Pethick Lawrence), and the *Pall Mall Gazette* (Sir Donald Straight).

3   *Councillors of the Third Rank* These comprised papers, 'quite distinct from the first two categories', the circulation of which Stead judged as 'out of proportion to their importance as organs of opinion' and which combined 'the maximum of advertisements and circulation with a minimum of influence'. The most important of these were the *Daily Telegraph* (J.M. Le Sage) and the *Daily Mail* (Thomas Marlowe), followed by the *Daily Express* (which, Stead remarked, was edited by 'the champion hustler, C.A. Pearson, and his bright shining example, Sir Alfred Harmsworth').

4   *Councillors of the Fourth Rank* These included papers which published political opinions which, noted Stead, had neither 'weight nor influence' with any public man or in the settlement of any public issue. These were the *Morning Advertiser* (Thomas Hamber), the *Daily Mirror* (Hamilton Fyfe), the *Sun* (G.H. Jackson), the *Evening News* (Walter J. Evans) and the *Evening Standard* (H.A. Gwynne).

Stead noted that the twenty-one 'responsible conductors of the London dailies', eleven in the morning and ten in the evening, had ample opportunities throughout the six days of the crisis to purvey accurate news on the Dogger Bank affair to the nation, but most of them — especially those editors producing the afternoon or evening editions of their papers — 'flaunted their opinions abroad on newsbills which met the eyes of a hundred times as many citizens as those who purchased their journals'. In fact the 'newsbills' of these papers had a greater influence on 'inflaming or depressing the public' than what was actually printed in the journals and therefore greatly enhanced the enormous power wielded by the press in London. However, 'fortunately for the liberties of the common citizen, the twenty-one [papers] differ among themselves . . . But sometimes . . . the whole one and twenty pipe to one tune and, when they do, nothing can stand against them.' Hence 'Unanimity among London newspapers may usually be regarded as the hall-mark of the devil.' Why? Because 'the different idiosyncrasies, prejudices, and party ties of . . . [the] . . . journals are so tangled and so complex that nothing but some fierce blaze of passion can smelt them momentarily into one homogenous unit. And . . . [these] . . . fierce blazes of passion are appealed to the lower nature of man.' This, averred Stead, had occurred as a result of the Dogger Bank incident and counteracts the two duties or responsibilities which the London dailies owe to their readers: first, to tell the truth and 'keep cool' and, second, to 'avoid wounding words' and inflammatory rhetoric which mislead and excite the public (Stead 1904: 596).

In compliance with the first duty, the papers must 'ascertain the facts, to report them accurately, and to do what they can to place them in their true light, and in the right perspective'. In fact, 'the greater the peril' threatening the nation, the more necessary it is for the press 'to keep a cool head, an open eye, and to carefully . . . guard against allowing passion or resentment to overpower . . . prudence'. The press, Stead insisted, must base its commentaries on facts and restrain 'even the most normal feelings of indignation, lest by giving free rein to their expression they might arouse a temper in the nation which would endanger the preservation of the calm, keen vigilance . . . so necessary when the clouds of war threaten on the horizon'. It is absolutely essential, said Stead, for every editor 'to keep cool' and to do his utmost 'to prevent blind rage or furious anger' from possessing the public. To fulfil the second duty, the editor 'must not provoke war or inflame the controversies that may lead to war by wounding words and savage invective . . . He may deem it his duty to counsel war should there be no other ways of settling the dispute', but only when he can safely assume that no other 'honourable' methods for settling difficulties are possible. However the responsibility of advising or urging war should be undertaken 'as reluctantly as in private life we should undertake the responsibility of killing our brother' (Stead 1904: 606).

How, asked Stead, did the editors of the twenty-one dailies conform to the criteria for dealing with a domestic or international crisis when reacting to the 'regrettable' Dogger Bank incident which, 'with all its gruesome details . . . flashed across to the newspaper offices on . . . October 23?' The first thing they did *not* do was to wait for the exact details or facts before rendering judgements on what they were reporting. They immediately poured scorn on the report that the Russian naval officers might have mistaken the fishing trawlers for Japanese torpedo boats. Worse yet, charged Stead, the editors 'absolutely ruled out as inconceivable' that the action of the Russians was not motivated by any hostile design or intent against Britain. They also failed to take into account, first, that Britain is an ally of the nation at war with Russia and, second, that the latent Russophobia of the British public can all too easily be aroused by incendiary rhetoric in the press.

Even more serious, said Stead, is that his study of the twenty-one papers revealed that their editors used 'printed words' which were intemperate and 'inflamed' public concern and anger. Almost every one of the journals repeatedly used the word 'outrage' to describe the incident and the deliberate use of this harsh word, 'when a milder term would have sufficed', indicated how far the editors had failed in their responsibility to tell the truth. And, worse yet, not content with the extravagant use of the word 'outrage' in the 126 articles and leaders they published during the week of the crisis, the editors vied with each other in the employment of 'contumelious' adjectives; thus the 'outrage' was 'unparalleled', 'cruel', 'unprecedented', 'unpardonable', 'intolerable', 'unimaginable', 'inexplicable', 'murderous', and 'criminal'. The use of such vituperation, argued Stead, could only have been designed to intensify popular passion and 'to inflame and irritate the feelings of millions . . . both in England and in Russia'.

To Stead, the behaviour of these editors and their staffs was therefore far more 'inexcusable' than the conduct of those nervous, incompetent,

Russian naval officers who had fired on the trawlers. The worst offenders, said Stead, were the editors of *The Times*, the *Standard*, the *Star*, and the *Morning Post* who seemed to have 'lost their heads . . . and for a whole week kept up a continuous firing at phantoms which brought two . . . Empires to the verge of war'. And, added Stead, this irresponsible behaviour was 'by educated and highly placed editors who had ample time and opportunity . . . to ascertain the facts . . . [and] . . . succumbed to the . . . temptations . . . to shout with the largest mob, and to pander to the passions of ignorant and excited men' in order to boost the circulation of their papers. They professed to have the utmost confidence in the Balfour government, which they knew was doing everything possible to resolve the issue, and yet 'they went on . . . howling for vengeance'. If the daily press and its directors can behave so badly in a minor diplomatic incident, how will they react when a very real and serious international crisis and threat to peace occurs? Will the metropolitan dailies, as in the Dogger Bank affair, direct 'a tremendous fusillade . . . morning and evening upon . . . unoffending millions whom they are endeavouring to hound into war?' (Stead: 1904: 599–602).

Stead specifically indicted Alfred Harmsworth, as proprietor and director of the two most widely circulated morning and evening papers, the *Daily Mail* and the *Evening News*, and the lesser *Daily Mirror*, and George E. Buckle and Moberly Bell of *The Times* for having bombarded the public with 'false statements . . . hurtful to the safety and welfare of the realm'. He accused Harmsworth and his 'hirelings' of such prevarications as the allegation that Russia had absolutely refused to render satisfaction for the actions of its Baltic Fleet and for insisting that there must be 'no discussion, no negotiation about the cowardly brutes . . . of the North Sea', and that no inquiry into the facts was required because Russia must be made to eat humble pie. Similarly, Buckle and Moberly Bell, after initially displaying calm and self-restraint, 'spared no wounding word' in clamouring for instant war, should Russia refuse to comply with the government's demand for redress. 'Day after day', asserted Stead, 'they worked . . . to inflame the passions of the nation, to excite its pride . . . Considering the standing of *The Times* – which, despite its small circulation, has a thousandfold the influence in international politics of that wielded by all of the Harmsworth papers . . . – it is impossible to describe the turpitude of its conductors during the late crisis.' After the 'conductors' of *The Times*, Stead ranked the editors of the *Standard* and *Evening Standard*, the *Morning Post*, and the *Pall Mall Gazette* as 'guilty men' who not only desired war, and worked for war, but when peace was assured by the government which they support, 'openly expressed their disappointment . . . on how the issue was resolved'. He was, however, less severe on the editors of the *Daily Telegraph*, the *Daily Chronicle*, the *Star*, the *St. James's Gazette*, and the *Globe*, but, 'inasmuch as they knew better, [he viewed] . . . their sin . . . the more heinous'. While the *Daily Telegraph* deviated somewhat from 'the path of reasonableness', it generally kept its balance, but he regretted that the usually sensible *Daily Chronicle* had 'blustered and bullied with the worst of them'. The *Star*, however, was worse, becoming 'hysterical' and clamouring for immediate retribution against Russia without waiting for an explanation from St. Petersburg. The *St. James's Gazette* reacted slowly, but by mid-week had joined the other papers in alleging that the Russian 'outrage' was deliberate. As for the *Globe*, from the beginning of the week, it 'ludicrously' and 'characteristically' insisted that the Admiral of the Russian armada had deliberately attacked the trawlers to demonstrate his command competence (Stead 1904: 603–5).

Of the twenty-one editors he had studied, Stead held eleven guilty of having 'done everything they ought not to have done and to have left undone' and, unhappily, this included his protégé and close friend, Robert Donald of the *Daily Chronicle*. Stead accused these editors of 'wilful . . . culpable ignorance', having 'entirely misread the situation, woefully misled the public . . . [and] . . . Instead of allaying passions, . . . fomenting . . . anger and . . . [aggravating] . . . every difficulty with which the Government had to deal'. He warned that if these editors and their papers are 'to be allowed . . . to renew, at some fresh [international] crisis, their efforts to launch Britain into war, an all-ruling Providence may abandon us to our doom'. But while he was pleased that a few editors did not 'lose their heads' on the Dogger Bank affair, Stead deplored their lack of courage 'to adhere to what their first judgement showed some of them to be the truth, that there had been a most deplorable blunder'. He regretted that 'The absence of any vigorous and resolute opposition on their part led the war press to proclaim that the whole nation was unanimous in demanding the humiliation of Russia or instant war.' Nevertheless, Stead praised some of the editors for 'keeping their heads' and preeminent among the few he lauded were J.A. Spender of the *Westminster Gazette* for his 'sane, sober and rational' handling of the issue, F.W. Pethick Lawrence of the *Echo* for his honesty, A.G. Gardiner of the *Daily News* for his moderation, Ernest Parke of the *Morning Leader* for keeping his paper 'fairly sensible', C.A. Pearson of the *Daily Express* for his 'rationality' and resisting 'the severe temptation to scream with the loudest', Thomas Hamber of the *Morning Advertiser* for keeping his journal 'less intemperate' and warning its readers that Britain risked becoming involved in another 'gigantic war' as costly as the late Boer War, and the directors of the *Daily Graphic* for at least being 'not up to much one way or the other' (Stead 1904: 605–6).

Finally, Stead concluded his survey of the London daily press with an assessment on how the papers might react and conduct themselves in the event of a major international crisis during the current dangerous decade with the observation that 'The result is, to the last degree, disheartening' and the warning that 'The future, with such a . . . Press in being, is full of perils.' But, 'with all deference, as an old journalist', he offered the following two suggestions on how the press might be rendered less dangerous and more effective in national and international crises:

1   That 'in the case of another of these constantly recurring crises', the government should apprise the editors of 'the gravity and truth of things' by summoning them to 'private and confidential' interviews or briefings with the Prime Minister and/or the Foreign Secretary and thus avert 'the publication of . . . fiery and criminal incentives to war . . . which . . . [might] . . . endanger the peace of the world'.

2   That 'it . . . be declared contempt of court . . . for any journalist to attempt to prejudice the finding of . . . [an] . . . international [Arbitration] Commission by commenting on the case which has been relegated to an international tribunal' (Stead 1904: 606).

While the second suggestion was patently impossible to implement in the existing British parliamentary democracy, Stead's first suggestion was not quite implemented until the ministry of Lloyd George and then in a very limited form. During the last eight years of his life (he died on the *Titanic* in 1912), Stead continued to be concerned with the increasing irresponsible sensationalism and alarmism of the press not only in Britain, but on the Continent – especially in Germany. In cooperation with such editors as J.A. Spender and in the face of opposition from the Foreign Office and the Germanophobic press, Stead facilitated goodwill exchange visits between British and German editors during 1906 and 1907 in a vain attempt to eliminate misunderstandings and to halt the dangerous deterioration in Anglo-German relations. Thus in 1906 Stead warned that the British press is 'afflicted' with 'a pestilential school of Germanophobists . . . who take a pure delight in converting the German Emperor into the Devil of the British Empire. Everything that ingenuity and industry can do to poison the minds of the average Briton against Germany . . . is done by this clique.' Sadly, he had privately to acknowledge that such behaviour was, in a sense, the 'bastard' offspring of his 'New Journalism' and the 'Government by Journalism' which he had espoused in his heyday during the 1880s. After all, he had also utilised incendiary language and vituperative adjectives in condemning the Disraeli regime, and Turkey and its Sultan, during the Bulgarian 'horrors' agitation in 1876–77 and in some of his campaigns and agitations during the 1880s.[2]

Notes

1   On the life and career of W.T. Stead, see Baylen (1969, 1972, 1983, 1984, 1988, 1989, 1992); Robertson Scott (1952: 72–259); Whyte (1924); Jones (1988); Shults (1972).

2   On Stead's efforts to improve Anglo-German relations by promoting exchange visits of German and British editors and journalists during 1906–7, see Stead (1906, 1908); Stead to A.G. Gardiner, 4 July 1906, in Koss (1973: 102); Mackinnon (1907); Higginbotham (1934: 190–1);

Hughes (1918: 285); Low (1907); The *Advocate of Peace* (1906); Spender (1927: 202); see also Humble (1977); Morris (1984: 78); Wilson (1983: 407); Minute to Mr Eyre Crowe, Sir Eric Barrington, Sir Charles Hardinge, and Sir Edward Grey, 26 June 1906, in Gooch and Temperley (1926–38: 359–60); Hale (1964: 296–300); Salmon (1923: 335).

References

Advocate of Peace (1906), 68: 215.

Baylen, J.O. (1969) *The Tsar's 'Lecturer-General'. W.T. Stead and the Russian Revolution of 1905*, Atlanta, GA: Georgia State University, College of Arts and Sciences Research Paper No. 23.

Baylen, J.O. (1972) 'The New Journalism in Late Victorian Britain', *Australian Journal of Politics and History* 18: 367–85.

Baylen, J.O. (1983) 'William Thomas Stead', in W.F. Kuehl (ed.) *Biographical Dictionary of Internationalists*, Westport, CT: Greenwood Press.

Baylen, J.O. (1984) 'The Review of Reviews', in A. Sullivan (ed.) *British Literary Magazines. Vol. 3: The Victorian and Edwardian Age*, Westport, CT: Greenwood Press.

Baylen, J.O. (1988) 'William Thomas Stead (1849–1912)', in J.O. Baylen and N.J. Gossman (eds) *Biographical Dictionary of Modern British Radicals, 1770–1914. Vol. 3: 1870–1914. Part 2: L-Z*, New York and London: Harvester/Wheatsheaf.

Baylen, J.O. (1989) 'W.T. Stead', in J.P. McKerns (ed.) *Biographical Dictionary of American Journalism*, Westport, CT and London: Greenwood Press.

Baylen, J.O. (1992) 'W.T. Stead: A Christ in Chicago', *British Journalism Review* 3: 57–61.

Gooch, G.P. and Temperley, H. (1926–38) (eds) *British Documents on the Origins of the War, 1898–1914*, vol. 3, no. 410, London: HMSO.

Hale, O.J. (1964) *Publicity and Diplomacy with Special Reference to England and Germany, 1890–1914*, Gloucester, MA: Peter Smith.

Higginbotham, F.G. (1934) *The Vivid Life: A Journalist's Career*, London: Simpkin and Marshall.

Hughes, S.L. (1918) *Press, Platform and Parliament*, London: Nisbet.

Humble, M.E. (1977) 'The Breakdown of Consensus: British Writers and Anglo-German Relations, 1900–1920', *Journal of European Studies* 7: 41–68.

Jones, V.P. (1988) *Saint or Sinner? The Story of W.T. Stead*, East Wittering: Gooday Publishers.

Koss, S. (1973) *Fleet Street Radical: A.G. Gardiner and the Daily News*, London: Archon Books.

Koss, S. (1984) *The Rise and Fall of the Political Press in Britain. Vol. 2: The Twentieth Century Press*, London: Hamish Hamilton.

Low, S. (1907) 'The Journalistic Tour of Germany, 1', *Contemporary Review* 92:1–11.

Mackinnon, J. (1907) 'British Journalists in Germany, 1 and 2', *Aberdeen Free Press*, 12 and 13 June.

Morris, A.J.A. (1984) *The Scaremongers: The Advocacy of War and Rearmament, 1896–1914*, London: Routledge.

Neilson, K. (1989) 'A Dangerous Game of American Poker: The Russo-Japanese War and British Policy', *Journal of Strategic Studies*, 12: 63–87.

Robertson Scott, J.W. (1952) *Life and Death of a Newspaper. An Account . . . of John Morley, W.T. Stead, E.T. Cook, Harry Cust, J.L. Garvin and Three Other Editors of the Pall Mall Gazette*, London: Methuen.

Salmon, L.M. (1923) *The Newspaper and Authority*, London and New York: Oxford University Press.

Shults, R.L. (1972) *Crusader in Babylon: W.T. Stead and the Pall Mall Gazette*, Lincoln: University of Nebraska Press.

Spender, J.A. (1927) *Life, Journalism and Politics*, vol. 1, London: Cassell.

Stead, W.T. (1904) 'Character Sketch. His Majesty's Public Councillors: To Wit, The Editors of the London Daily Papers', *Review of Reviews* 30: 593–606.

Stead, W.T. (1906) 'The Anglo-German Press: A Suggestion', *The Anglo-German Courier* 1: 73–75.

Stead, W.T. (1908) 'An Active Policy of Peace', *The Independent* 65: 698–703.

Whyte, F. (1924) *The Life of W.T. Stead*, vol. 2, London and New York: Jonathan Cape,

Wilson, K. (1983) 'The Foreign Office and the "Education" of Public Opinion before the First World War', *Historical Journal* 26: 403–11.

Chapter 7

Edward Dicey

JOURNALISM OLD AND NEW

[M]Y OBJECT IN WRITING THIS ARTICLE IS . . . to point out the extraordinary development of British journalism within the last half century,[1] and to show how discoveries in science, improvements in machinery, alterations to social life, and changes in the character and tastes of the newspaper reader have transformed the old journalism into the new. Throughout the course of a long life I, whether as leader writer, foreign correspondent, contributor, editor, and proprietor, have always been more or less closely associated with journalism, and know probably better than most of my contemporaries its merits and demerits, its success and its failures, its strength and its weakness. The subject is far too wide a one to be adequately treated within the limits of a magazine article, but I hope to indicate a few of the changes and their causes which have, for bad or good, transformed the character of British journalism.

I suspect very few of our younger generation of newspaper writers and readers can realise the almost undisputed supremacy wielded by the *Times* in the world of journalism during the early fifties . . . It was about this period that a friend of mine, on asking the then Editor, Delane, how it was that some news of importance had not appeared in the *Times*, though it had been published in other papers, was told in reply that the omission was not of the slightest consequence, as nobody believed any news till it was given in the *Times* . . . to the best of my belief, there was no permanent addition to the ranks of metropolitan daily journalism from the passing of the great Reform Bill up to the outbreak of the Crimean war. The advertisement duties were abolished in 1853. About the same time the paper duties were also thrown overboard. Both these imposts were described by the Liberals of the

Cobdenian era as 'taxes upon knowledge'. Never was there a more absurd abuse of language. The taxes in question were levied not upon knowledge but upon the purveyors of knowledge. In those days we believed in mechanics' institutes, in penny cyclopaedias, in the British workman who passed his evenings at home studying the tomes of Mill and Adam Smith and Grote. In accordance with the ideas of philosophic statesmanship, we swept away the advertisement duties, root and branch. If we had simply reduced these duties so as to throw open the advertisement columns of our papers to small people with narrow means, and had made the charge commensurate with the length of the advertisement, we should not only have retained an important source of revenue, raised automatically without any perceptible loss to the payers of the tax, but we should have done much to benefit the interests of sound journalism. In the old days public opinion in England saw no reason why the trade of purveying information should not be taxed like any other honest and lucrative trade. As long as the paper and advertisement duties remained in force, it was difficult, if not impossible, for men of straw, without capital, to start fresh newspapers. The removal of the taxes upon knowledge, however beneficial in other respects, has facilitated the mushroom growth of a large number of newspapers, chiefly devoted to finance, which look for profit to other considerations than those of legitimate journalism.

Whatever may be thought as to my views about the 'taxes on knowledge', nobody can deny that the removal of these duties gave a great impetus to the newspaper trade in the early fifties. Amongst the many curious incidents of my life, not the least curious lies in the fact that I was one of the first writers on the journal which has done more than any other to convert the old journalism into the new. If my memory serves me correctly, I answered an advertisement asking for leader writers on a forthcoming daily newspaper, and received a reply requesting me to call at the office of the *Daily Telegraph* . . . My experiences as a journalist were then extremely limited, my recommendations were meagre, but the applicants were few in number, and I was engaged then and there to write a leader for the same day . . . the then proprietor was a retired Colonial officer . . . his two fellow proprietors [were] brother officers in the Guards, well-known in the fashionable world of their day . . . The story in the office was that the two Guardsmen had each subscribed a few hundred pounds towards the capital of the *Daily Telegraph*, and had backed a bill to like amount. If so, a sum between £1,000 and £2,000 formed the capital on which, probably, the greatest financial success of any paper in the world was started on its career . . .

My original connection with the *Daily Telegraph* at this period only lasted for a few weeks . . .

My brief preliminary connection with the *Telegraph* has, at any rate, this advantage: that it made me personally acquainted with a phase of journalism even then moribund. I mean that of the days of the Whittys, the St Johns, the Mayhews, the Broughs, and a host of less well-known names, who represented so-called Bohemian journalism. They were not men of high education, judged by a University standard, but they had the journalistic faculty of being able to write rapidly and lucidly, and to furnish a readable article on any given subject at the shortest notice. They did not belong to West End clubs; they had no social ambition, or, if they had such ambition, it remained ungratified. Their chief purveyors of political information were the reporters in the House of Commons, and their chief resorts after they had sent in their copy were certain taverns or convivial clubs, which were, in those days, kept open to abnormal hours for the convenience of the Press . . . For me, individually, the Bohemian Press of London had no special attraction. 'Shop' of all kind always bored me; and of all 'shop' the least interesting to me is the discussion of the merits or demerits of newspaper articles that are practically dead after they have appeared in print. I am not, therefore, an altogether fair judge of the Bohemian era of journalism, but I am bound to say it seems to me nowadays to have been of a rather more original character than that of the era by which it was succeeded.

After having spent many years abroad, chiefly in Italy, and having become more or less well-known as a writer, I was, on my return from the then dis-United States in 1862, offered a permanent engagement as a leader writer on the staff of the *Daily Telegraph*. The editor was then Thornton Hunt, a son of the better-known Leigh Hunt, but himself a man of high literary attainments, of very wide reading, and of refined taste. The real direction of the paper lay in the hands of the leading proprietor, Mr J.M. Levy. This pre-eminence was due not so much to the fact that he represented the financial interest of the proprietary as to his extraordinary journalistic instinct . . . I can truly say that I never met one whose judgment was so sound, whose appreciation was so keen as to what his readers would like to read . . . His ambition was not only to make the *Telegraph* an extraordinary financial success, but to make it the most influential newspaper in the country. With this object in view, he had, at the period of my resuming my connection with the *Daily Telegraph*, gradually got rid of the light brigade of journalism, and had enlisted the services of men who, in his opinion, could treat serious subjects seriously, without being dull. The staff, when I joined, were certainly entitled, as a body, to the appellation of scholars and gentlemen. My colleagues were my dear old school friend, the late Sir Edwin Arnold, the winner of the Newdigate, and a professor after leaving Oxford at Poonah College; the Hon. Frank Lawley, who had been MP for Beverly and Parliamentary private secretary to Mr Gladstone; Herbert Slack, who had taken high honours at Trinity College; Jeff Prouse, a writer of singular grace and charm, who, if he had lived, might, I think, have equalled the reputation of Praed; and last, but not least, George Augustus Sala, the one man amongst us all who was not only gifted with ability but with genius . . .

It was the rule of the office to have at least three, generally four, leaders a day. One of these leaders was reserved to be written in the evening, so as to deal with the latest foreign or Parliamentary news. The other three were given out before luncheon time, and were expected to be delivered at the office about seven o'clock. The alterations in the conditions of the newspaper trade have rendered this halcyon state of things an impossbility. But I do not hesitate to say the literary work of the paper benefited largely by the absence of hurry. Any journalist who knows what it is to write an article against time, when every ten minutes the printer's devils are coming down to ask for fresh copy, torn from the MS you have just written, will appreciate the advantages of having plenty of time to think over your article, to look up books of reference, and to be able to read the MS over carefully and make your own corrections before you sent the article to the printers.

Every experienced journalist will admit that it takes longer to write a light and bright article than a solid – and shall I say stolid? – one of the same length. I attribute the great success of the *Telegraph* leaders at the period of which I write quite as much to the conditions under which they were written as to the talent of the writers. We were given a free hand, and we knew that if we produced something the public would like to read we should not be blamed even if we diverged to some extent from the instructions given us at the morning meetings. We had no great respect for constituted authorities, we cared very little for preconceived opinion, and we were not troubled with too strict reverence for absolute accuracy. We were, if I may venture to say so, the pioneers of the Press of today. I do not claim for ourselves any monopoly in the process by which journalism was made less ponderous, more attractive to the new class of readers who were daily coming to the front. A similar transformation was, as I am well aware, going on in other papers, and conducted with no less ability. All I contend is that when Matthew Arnold described us as 'young lions on the prowl for prey', the description, whether complimentary or otherwise, was not altogether undeserved . . . I cannot doubt that we did a good deal to make journalism popular with the public. Up to the period of which I write, that is, up to the sixties of the Victorian era, it was an unwritten law of journalism that every leading article should consist of three paragraphs, and that whatever the subject matter might be, it was not to be less than a column and a quarter, or to exceed a column and a half . . . To Sala more than to any other single writer on the Press belongs the credit of having freed journalism from these conventional bonds. To others amongst us should be assigned the credit of having introduced the system of descriptive articles on legal trials which attracted public attention, of commenting on the demeanour and aspect of the witnesses, and of pointing out day by day the bearing of the evidence adduced upon the rights and wrongs of the case at issue. When the decision of the Court was not in accordance with our own opinion we appealed to the public, and not unfrequently with success. The practice may have been open to objections, but it had this advantage: that it established very friendly relations between the leading eminent counsel of the time and the journalists who wrote articles day after day on sensational cases.

It has often seemed to me astonishing how very slow the London Press were in availing themselves of the facilities of telegraphic communication . . . I was told to use the telegraph as little as possible, as the public preferred graphic description by letter to curt messages by wire. This reluctance to employ rapidity of transmission, if obtained at the cost of the intelligence transmitted, prevailed to my own knowledge up to the opening of the Suez Canal in 1869 . . . Thanks to Archibald Forbes, the *Daily News* gave the best, or, at any rate, the most rapid, war news during the whole of the war which ended with the entry of the Germany Army into Paris and the outbreak of the Commune. From that date it became obvious that the model war correspondent of the future must be the man who could get his news wired off the first, not the man who could put together the best reproduction of what he had seen and heard and learnt . . . Thus, if my opinion is correct, the employment of the telegraph has proved fatal, and will prove still more fatal, to the literary merits of the foreign correspondence of our newspapers. Personally, I regret this change the less because the principle on which war correspondents were allowed to accompany armies on active service and to telegraph home comments and criticisms on what they had observed had always seemed to me utterly false and untenable. The object of any nation going to war and sacrificing its soldiers in battle is not to provide good reading for the public at home . . . no man in his senses will contend that our armies should be accompanied into action by a swarm of newspaper correspondents, competing with one another who can get hold of the most sensational intelligence and who shall get it known most rapidly to friend and foe alike . . .

It is a curious, though, I think, an undesigned coincidence that the various improvements in the machinery, the endless sheet, the system of machining, not from the original type, but from stereotyped moulds, and the substitution of mechanical for manual agency in putting the letters into words and the words into sentences, have accidentally synchronised with an extraordinary increase in the demand for cheap literature, and with the rapid augmentation of the newspaper-reading public . . . The penny papers still represent the small trading classes, the shop keepers, the clerks, as distinguished from the working men proper. But I cannot doubt that the elector who earns his day's board and lodging for himself and his family by the labour of his own hands, is represented by the halfpenny Press, by such papers as the *Daily Mail*, the *Daily Express* and the *Morning Leader*. To me, as to every thinking man, it cannot but be gratifying to find that the class of newspapers which the new electorate select as their organs does not differ materially from that of its predecessors. It is only just to say that these papers which count, or, at any rate, profess to count, their readers by millions, are uniformly loyal towards the constituted authorities of the realm. They may have collectivist proclivities, but so far they have manifested no desire for carrying socialism into practice; they are very keenly interested in foreign politics, and are perhaps more ready to 'think Imperially' than the rural and small town electorates. It is all very well to decry the love of sport, but the papers which represent the 'horny-handed sons of toil' derive a very large portion of their profits from the cricket and football editions, which appeal to the masses who are ready to pay for sporting intelligence. So long as the new electorate desire a sound, wholesome article for the gratification of their journalistic appetites there can be nothing rotten in the state of our Press.

Note

1   This article appeared in the *Fortnightly Review* 83 (1905). Dicey was born into a newspaper family (owners of the *Northampton Mercury*), and entered journalism after leaving Cambridge. He covered the American civil war and then joined the *Daily Telegraph* as a leader writer. In the late 1860s he was briefly editor of the *Daily News* and was subsequently editor of the *Observer* for nineteen years.

Chapter 8

C.P. Scott

THE *MANCHESTER GUARDIAN'S* FIRST HUNDRED YEARS

A NEWSPAPER HAS TWO SIDES TO IT.[1] It is a business, like any other and has to pay in the material sense in order to live. But it is much more than a business; it is an institution . . . It may educate, stimulate, assist, or it may do the opposite. It has, therefore, a moral as well as a material existence, and its character and influence are in the main determined by the balance of these two factors . . .

Character is a subtle affair, and has many shades and sides to it . . . Fundamentally it implies honesty, cleanness, courage, fairness, a sense of duty to the reader and community. A newspaper is of necessity something of a monopoly, and its first duty is to shun the temptations of monopoly. Its primary office is the gathering of news. At the peril of its soul it must see that the supply is not tainted. Neither in what it gives, nor in what it does not give, nor in the mode of presentation must the unclouded face of truth suffer wrong. Comment is free, but facts are sacred. Propaganda, so called, by this means is hateful. The voice of opponents no less than that of friends has a right to be heard. Comment is also justly subject to a self-imposed restraint. It is well to be frank; it is even better to be fair. This is an ideal. Achievement in such matters is hardly given to man . . .

One of the virtues, perhaps almost the chief virtue, of a newspaper is its independence. Whatever its position or character, at least it should have a soul of its own . . . There are people who think you can run a newspaper about as easily as you can poke a fire, and that knowledge, training and aptitude are superfluous endowments. There have even been experiments on this assumption, and they have not met with much success . . . A newspaper, to be of value, should be a unity, and every part of it should equally understand and respond to the purposes and ideals which animate it . . . Editor and business manager should march hand in hand, the first, be it well understood, just an inch or two in advance . . .

And what work it is! How multiform, how responsive to every need and every incident of life! What illimitable possibilities of achievement and of excellence! People talk of 'journalese' as though a journalist were of necessity a pretentious and sloppy writer; he may be, on the contrary, and very often is, one of the best in the world. At least he should not be content to be much less. And then the developments. Every year, almost every day, may see growth and fresh accomplishment, and with a paper that is really alive, it not only may, but does. Let anyone take a file of this paper, or for that matter any one of half a dozen other papers, and compare its whole make-up and leading features today with what they were five years ago, ten years ago, twenty years ago, and he will realise how large has been the growth, how considerable the achievement. And this is what makes the work of a newspaper worthy and interesting. It has so many sides, it touches life at so many points, at every one there is such possibility of improvement and excellence. . .

Note

1   This article first appeared in the centenary number of the *Manchester Guardian* (5 May 1921). It was subsequently reprinted on a number of occasions. Scott was appointed the paper's editor in 1872 at the age of 25, a post he retained until 1929. He bought the title in 1905. He is widely regarded as one of the most influential figures in British journalism.

Chapter 9

Lord Riddell

THE PSYCHOLOGY OF THE JOURNALIST

THE PSYCHOLOGY OF JOURNALISTS is a subject of perennial interest to the public and, in particular, to politicians and public men.[1] Therefore it may be useful to investigate the mental processes that excite so much comment, criticism, occasional admiration, and, sometimes, more or less sincere praise.

To begin with, we must admit that the publicity itch – the desire to communicate news or views, the desire to make some sort of sensation – is the basis of all journalism. All true journalists have it. The itch may be intuitive or acquired. It develops by use, but in course of time becomes attenuated, except with fanatics or individuals endowed with unusual enthusiasm. Every journalist can recall the delight experienced when he saw his first scoop or first article in print, and most of us must sadly confess how this joyous feeling of realisation tends to wear off . . .

Improved technique and increased facility bring pleasures of their own, but they are subjective, rather than objective. The journalist enjoys writing, but his pleasure at seeing himself in print becomes less acute . . .

We must admit also that journalism is a commercial business, and that a newspaper lives by selling news and views. Of course, this aspect of journalism colours the journalist's mentality. Like any other trader or professional man, he is bound by certain traditions, conventions, and ideals. At the same time, he is a trader and, as such, if he is to be successful – and it is on his paper that he depends for remuneration – he must be keen to produce readable 'copy'. He is hedged round with difficulties. Many people are not anxious for publicity or want publicity that suits them – publicity which puts them or their concerns in a favourable light. Therefore, in seeking after the truth the journalist has to combat these proclivities on the part of the public.

Interviewing, like cross-examination, is an art, but the journalist, unlike the barrister, cannot exercise compulsion. The witness must answer relevant questions, whereas the interviewed is under no such obligation. Therefore, a journalist has to adapt himself to the situation in dealing with unwilling or untruthful individuals . . .

A newspaper office is a hard taskmaster. There is no putting off things till tomorrow. The paper has got to come out. The copy must be ready. These necessities produce punctuality, tireless industry, and ceaseless vigilance. It may be safely asserted that there are no sleuths like newspaper sleuths. One would think that this would betoken corresponding energy and punctuality in journalists in dealing with their private affairs. Such is not, however, the case. Many able, prompt and active members of the profession are singularly slack and negligent when dealing with matters that concern themselves in private life . . . Happily, the modern journalist is introducing his professional habits into his private life. He has learned that a certain amount of money and a certain amount of attention to his private affairs are the basis of independence . . .

There is one aspect of journalistic mentality that must not be overlooked. Journalists are not to be bribed or 'got at'. Nor are they prepared to be treated as inferiors. There was a time when journalists, called upon to report a public dinner, were fed in an ante-room. Now they feed on terms of equality . . . Indeed, the attitude of the public, and, in particular, the attitude of public men, to the press have entirely changed . . . Servility is a thing of the past. On the other hand, pressmen have learned that, when in pursuit of business, like lawyers, doctors, and accountants, they must show a certain measure of respect and consideration to their 'victims', and fully realise that in doing so they lose none of their self-respect . . .

Journalism produces a strange sense of mental detachment. The journalist proper is an observer and recorder of the scenes with which he deals. He is rarely one of the actors. Of course, there are exceptions . . . Being a recorder, naturally and properly the journalist's first thought is, what sort of a story will this event make? What does it mean for his particular public? What are its implications? What is it worth in space and how should it be dealt with? A reporter called upon to write an account of a railway accident or colliery explosion is shocked at the sights he sees and sympathetic with the sufferers, but his uppermost thought is to secure an authentic, dramatic story, write it up in an interesting fashion, and to transmit it with the utmost dispatch. This sense of detachment lays the journalist open to a charge of cynicism, and one must admit the charge is not without justification. No body of men see so much of the twistings and turnings of their fellow creatures. No wonder they incline towards a cynical view of life. But they are also tolerant and free from jealousy. Men and things are dealt with according to their news values. Being human, journalists have their favourites, but they do not allow their likes and dislikes to spoil good attractive 'copy' . . .

Like most other people, journalists are sentimental concerning their own environment. The great world outside goes on from day to day. It is their raw material. They record its doings great and small, apparently without sentiment. But if a colleague dies or is seriously ill, then journalists are just as sentimental as other people in similar circumstances. They also take a deep interest in their calling and all connected with it. In fact, journalism and all that it implies are a world within a world.

This brings me to the point that there are many different sorts of journalistic psychologies. The public talk of journalists as if all journalists were of the same class or pattern . . . They may fraternise socially on the basis of a common calling, they may combine concerning industrial questions, they may fight a joint battle for the privileges of the press, they may co-operate in charitable work; nevertheless, there are fundamental differences that are obscured or disregarded when a man or woman is dubbed merely a journalist. Roughly speaking, journalists may be divided into three classes – the academics, the technicians, and the popularists.

The academics are not necessarily university men. Academicism is mainly due to intuition and environment. In short, academics have a critical, informing, and often reforming diathesis – to use a medical term – coupled with considerable powers of exposition. They usually abhor sensation unless it takes a literary form. They are cultured and cultivated – much interested in literature. Concerning high politics, the major part of their raw material, they usually hold decided opinions. They also take a mild interest in foreign affairs, on which they write with more or less knowledge . . . With their watch-dog minds and reforming propagandist proclivities, they render valuable public service. As a rule, they represent the views of small, but influential, classes . . . Notwithstanding its value, journalism of this sort has its dangers. When one is continually lecturing other people, one is apt unconsciously to become somewhat self-righteous and to regard one's self as specially nominated by the Almighty to put the world right. One is apt to forget that, in truth, one is turning out criticism and advice for so much per thousand words! Most academics are saved from these dangers by a sense of humour, coupled with a professional attitude of mind . . . In other words, they regard themselves merely as instruments for the purpose of expressing their papers' views . . .

There is not much to be said for the vast army of technicians, male and female, the specialists who concentrate on finance, sport, racing, fashion, the drama, architecture, music, shipping, markets, law, medicine, gardening, pigeons, photography, motoring, engineering, coal, steel, cotton, woollens, and a host of other subjects. There are, indeed, no fewer than, roughly, five hundred trade and technical newspapers. The army also comprises regiments of journalists, including numerous women, who specialise in magazine or periodical work, or who write periodical fiction. All technologists concentrate keenly on their subjects, and rarely diverge into the region of journalism in general. Those who work on daily, evening or weekly newspapers are demons for space. Like Oliver Twist, they are always asking for more, and thus raising constant problems for much-harassed news-editors and sub-editors. Some are enthusiasts because they are passionately devoted to their subject for personal reasons; others because it is their particular professional province . . .

We now come to the popularists, who understand what will interest the general public. They understand the art of presentation. They know what to put on the bill. They have the gift of selection. If a dozen news-editors, sub-editors, and reporters are called upon to choose for publication, say, twenty items out of a hundred, they will almost invariably make the same choice. The same remark applies to speeches. With unerring skill reporters will pick out the only things that matter. The popularists pride themselves on accuracy. This leads them to observe the old journalistic maxim, 'When you don't know, leave it out!' Most of the charges of inaccuracy levelled against the press are due to omissions . . . This is often unavoidable, considering the rapidity with which newspapers have to be produced. The journalist writes what he knows to be correct, and omits what he regards as doubtful.

We have to recognise that journalism has a psychology of its own. Newspapers are not, and cannot be, complete presentations of life, inasmuch as they deal mostly with the abnormal and exceptional . . . That explains why gradual tendencies and subtle changes in manners and customs are rarely noticed by the press . . . The world is full of tendencies and movements that come to nothing. Consequently, the journalistic mind is prone to disregard, or perhaps even treat with contempt, movements that give no definite signs of reaching their goal.

Dr Johnson, himself a journalist of no mean order, remarked that tediousness was the worst of all literary vices. It is certainly the worst of all journalistic vices. In the journalist's struggle to avoid it, he is apt to develop disregard for realities and proportions. The newspaper reader buys his paper for several reasons. He wants the ordinary bread and butter news, such as markets, stock exchange intelligence, law reports, racing and sports results, and the outstanding news of the day, but he also wants interesting reading. He wants something startling and fresh presented in attractive form. Therefore, the journalist is compelled, hour by hour and day by day, to strain for what will interest the reader. Pundits who are not in the business say that the reader should be supplied with what they think is good for him, instead of with what he wants . . . [but] if the reader is not satisfied he will not buy the paper, and the journalist will probably get the sack because he is not turning out a successful publication. Experience shows that pundits, when they enter the trade and face actual necessities, take the same course as other people . . .

[T]he journalist is like a tight-rope dancer. His audience expect him to give several different kinds of exhibition – the straight, dignified walk, startling gymnastics, and attractive tricks. If he does not fill the bill, he is a failure. If he only does the dignified part of the business, he is regarded as dull, whereas if he only performs startling gymnastics and pretty tricks, he is regarded as purely sensational. In short, to be a success, he must give a full bill to meet all tastes and requirements. To continue the analogy, tight-rope walking produces a certain type of mentality, and so it is with journalists. This peculiarity is accentuated by the fact that journalists, like members of other professions, are more or less a class apart . . .

Note

1   One of a series of talks on 'the technique of modern journalism' organised by the Institute of Journalists in 1928 and 1929, Lord Riddell's speech was delivered on 9 January 1929, and published in *Journalism by Some Masters of the Craft* (1932). Riddell was not a journalist but a solicitor who entered newspaper management with the *Western Mail*. He become chairman of the *News of the World*, although he also regularly wrote articles on politics for the paper, and of the Newnes and Pearson publishing firms.

Chapter 10

Tom Clarke

WOMEN IN JOURNALISM

Monday, 15 May 1922

TODAY MY REPORTING STAFF is augmented by a pretty young peeress, the Baroness Clifton.[1] She has been sent to me by the Chief [Lord Northcliffe] to have 'six months' run at £20 a week'. He met her aboard ship on his return from his world tour, and she told him she would like to be a journalist. He has taken her at her word. 'She is a pretty young thing', he said, 'who is bored with doing nothing, and it will be a great asset to have a pretty young woman belonging to such an old family on your staff. She is fragile and very sensitive, and you will lose her if you don't treat her nicely. The ordinary drudgery of reporting would kill her.'

Having had amateur journalists turned loose on me before, oftener than not with very unsatisfactory results, I did not feel particularly gleeful when the good lady reported for duty this morning . . . she was twenty-two, was the youngest peeress in her own right, and the only daughter of the late seventh Earl of Darnley . . . I wondered to myself, 'Whatever can I do with the woman?' It was soon evident that she was thinking, 'Whatever can he do with me?' She told me, very quietly, that she was a little bored with London after eighteen months' embassy life in Peking . . . Obviously she would have been of rare value on the social staff, but she turned big, dark eyes on me when that was mentioned and said, 'I would rather not. I want to do real reporting.'

'Not murders and fires and that sort of thing?' I said in jest.

'Oh, I should love to report a murder or go to a big trial,' she said eagerly . . . 'And', she proceeded, 'I would like to go to places like Chinatown [the district of Limehouse in London] and write about them.' . . .

'Well, later on, perhaps,' I said, 'but in the meantime let's get you on to some brighter aspects of London life. What about a special article on the lure of the London shops, behind the scenes in Bond Street and Hanover Square, the debutantes choosing their frocks, the progress of the battle of the skirts [the debate over hemlines].' She grasped the idea with a woman's enthusiasm, and later in the day sent a messenger with a crisp, well-written story giving all the facts with an atmospheric dressing that was unlike anything else in the paper. I rang her up to tell her she had not signed the article. It needed no signature, of course, to add to its merits or justify its publication, but I had a feeling that what we were paying for was her name as much as anything else. However, she said that for the present she preferred not to reveal her identity, and she made it clear that she wanted to succeed as a writing woman on the merits of her work alone, not because, but maybe in spite, of her being a peeress . . .

Tuesday, 16 May 1922

There were many inquiries today as to the identity of the writer of the article on the Lure of the Shops which was headed 'BY THE WOMAN CORRESPONDENT'. Even such a practised man-of-the-world journalist as Charlie Hands said it was delightful and original stuff, and my disclosure to him of the writer's identity moved him to some very far-seeing remarks on the subject of women in journalism. 'In ten years,' he said, 'and maybe before, you will see a revolution . . . more women than ever in newspaper work, reporting, sub-editing, news-editing, even editing. It's bound to come. All the advantages are with women. Firstly, they don't drink. Secondly, they are more in touch with the realities of life . . . From infancy her education in dress is a never-ending school of taste. Women are better judges; they have more taste; they are more human . . . their outlook is really wider than that of men.' Which reminded me of a recent talk on the same subject with Northcliffe. He was not so sure that there would be an avalanche of women in journalism, but he did say that a great measure of the success of his papers was due to the interest they took in feminine affairs. 'The old-fashioned stodgy papers,' he said, 'were for men only. They ignored news of interest to women. Now we look out specially for it. Women are the greatest newspaper readers. There were no news stories about the crinoline, but there are the liveliest news stories about the short skirt. Don't forget the women when you are framing your daily schedule. And don't forget that they read every scrap of social news you can get, especially the names. They read serials too. Don't be bluffed by journalists with only a man's outlook. Read the woman's page every day. . . .'

But to get back to Lady Clifton. Northcliffe rang up today and said about her, 'We have found a winner. But why did you not use her name?' I told him. 'Try to persuade her to sign herself ELIZABETH CLIFTON,' he said, 'by which name most people will know her. Later she will probably sign her real name. But don't hurry her. She will come round in time. I understand women. Talk to her in a quiet way about the other one (Lady Diana Cooper, who has been writing signed articles for us on occasions recently). Just mention casually how the other one is getting her name in print. Women have more jealousy than men. . . . 'Lady Clifton scored another success today with her work, and she has captured the hearts of all the young and old bloods in the reporters' room. She is certainly the best young writer-reporter I have ever had to try out. Tonight I said to her, 'I don't think you quite like being called *the* woman correspondent.' 'No,' she laughed, 'it does sound rather biological, doesn't it?' So it has been altered to *our* woman correspondent.

Note

1   This extract is taken from *My Northcliffe Diary* (1931). Clarke was serving his last few months as news editor of the *Daily Mail*. He was in constant touch with the paper's proprietor, Lord Northcliffe, who died in August 1922. Afterwards Clarke moved to Australia. He returned to Britain to join the *Daily News* as managing editor and then to edit the *News Chronicle*.

Chapter 11

Henry Wickham Steed

THE IDEAL NEWSPAPER

LIKE MOST JOURNALISTS WHO DREAM DREAMS I wonder some-
times what kind of paper I should try to turn out if I had, say, £1 million
or more to play with, and could either start a paper of my own or take over
and transform an existing journal.[1] Would it be possible, under the present
conditions of the 'newspaper industry', for a paper to rise superior to those
conditions or to turn them to account in such fashion as to restore and to
safeguard the freedom of the press? It ought to be possible . . .

[A] newspaper-maker of genius would grasp and utilise the complicated
conditions of modern newspaper-making and would discomfit his industry-
bound rivals before they could guess how he had done it. His success would
depend on his power to read the minds of the rising generation, to express
their own thoughts for them, and to lead them whither they would fain go
if they only knew the way . . .

The newspaper I dream of would reflect the distractions of modern
life no less faithfully than existing papers reflect them, but it would treat
them as distractions, not as the things that matter. It would search out the
truths behind these appearances and proclaim them, sparing no shams,
respecting no conventions solely because they happened to be conventions,
giving honour where honour might be due, but calling cant and humbug by
their names.

It would be quite fearless. It would not 'hedge' in its treatment of thorny
subjects; and if, as would be inevitable, it made mistakes, it would avow
them. It would accept only such advertisements as it thought honest, so that
its acceptance of them would be a moral guarantee to advertisers and to
readers alike. Net sales certificates it would steadfastly refuse to publish, and

it would scorn to canvass for subscribers or to offer them free insurance
or other benefits. If advertisers or their agents should seek to bring it to
heel, it would publish their names; and it would ruthlessly expose all under-
hand 'business' practices that came to its knowledge. A good part of its
capital would be spent in winning the confidence of young and eager minds
who would soon learn to trust its judgment and to heed its counsel. From
its first 'editorial' column to the last it would be a militant journal, tied to
no 'interests', careless of hostility, sure that none would be able to ignore
it.

My newspaper would, of course, make every effort to get the news, and
would put its main news on the front page – where it ought to be. It would
not fear to print several consecutive columns of one good 'story'. It would
treat with contempt the time-wasting device of sending readers from one
page to another so as to put the beginning of a different 'story' at the top
of every column. Good and careful typography can help readers to see what
is in a paper without defrauding them of reading matter.

My ideal newspaper would give 'all the news that's fit to print' as vividly
as possible, whether the news suited its 'policy' or not. For its policy would
fit the facts; it would not suppress or gloss over facts to suit 'policy'. In
cases of doubt whether discretion might not be the better part of publicity
it would give publicity the benefit of the doubt. To no government, statesman
or person would it lend support for other than public reasons, publicly stated.
It would be the servant of the public, to whose welfare alone it would
acknowledge allegiance, albeit without the misguided sycophancy that flat-
ters an imaginary public and assumes that readers 'would not stand' plain
speaking. A faithful servant tells his master the truth.

My paper would be national, not nationalist. It would be liberal, not
Liberal. It would strive for peace, without pacifism. It would make clear the
vital things for which nations and men may fitly fight and fitly die, if there
be no other way of upholding them. Never would it fall into the grievous
error of thinking the avoidance of conflict the same thing as peace . . . My
newspaper would seek to link the nations not only against war but in defence
of individual freedom and human right, so as to open the way for constructive international helpfulness; just as, in matters national and social, it would
work to harness all classes of citizens to the task of constructive improvement in the edifice of society.

Could such a paper as this – technically well-made, trustworthy, news-
giving, hard-hitting, full of vim and drive – hope to gain a circulation sufficient
to command, not to solicit, enough advertisement revenue to balance its
budget? I think it could, provided it were rich enough to 'stand the racket'
until it had won its public.

One day, perchance, some newspaper-making genius with a soul of his
own will do something like this. Then our advertisement-courting, dividend-
seeking, circulation-mongers will rub their eyes and wonder how it has been
done. Till then my ideal newspaper may remain in the realm of the ideal,

and the British press – if, indeed, it escape totalitarian servitude – will plod along its pedestrian way far below the breezy heights whereunto the heart of every true journalist aspires.

Note

1   This is a personal manifesto appended to a survey of *The Press* (1938). Steed joined *The Times* as its Berlin correspondent in 1896. After postings to Rome and Vienna, he returned to London and was appointed foreign editor in 1914. He was made editor (the last under the proprietorship of Lord Northcliffe) in 1919, while simultaneously working for Northcliffe's other titles, the *Daily Mail*, *Evening News*, and *Weekly Dispatch*. He left soon after Northcliffe's death in 1922. He was later a regular broadcaster for the BBC.

PART THREE

1945–1970

Introduction to part three

■ Michael Bromley

AN UNPRECEDENTED POPULARITY of the press during the
Second World War — achieved against the background of an expanding
audience for radio — rapidly evaporated in the 1950s. Competition from television, especially Independent Television (ITV) after 1955, may have
accounted for some of the decline, and after 1940 broadcasting offered new
regular alternative outlets for journalism. Nevertheless, some sections of the
press, notably the 'quality' dailies, the *Sunday Times* and the *Daily Mirror*,
managed to increase their circulations or to enhance their reputations. Overall,
however, it appeared that the press was ripe for 'modernisation'. In the 1950s
a number of national newspapers changed hands, as a new type of proprietor moved into the sector. The leading figure was Roy (Lord) Thomson who
subsumed his newspapers in the United Kingdom within a multinational cross-
media and leisure conglomerate. As well as 'streamlining' newspapers, he
saw the ITV franchises as 'a licence to print money' (Bromley 1995: 21).
Thomson's business activities led directly to the formation of a second Royal
Commission on the Press in 1962. In the thirty years following the Second
World War the press in particular, but the media in general, became 'increasingly concentrated in fewer and richer hands' (Murdock and Golding 1978:
146–7).

The extent to which both this inquiry and the earlier Royal Commission
were circumscribed by the force of the nineteenth century liberal intellectual
and ideological inheritance is indicated by O'Malley. Although the first
Commission led directly to innovations, such as the establishment of the Press
Council and the National Council for the Training of Journalists, it failed

ultimately to get to grips with problematising the application of Millsian philosophy in a late twentieth century commercial environment. What concerned Orwell deeply, which he characterised as a willingness to accept self-deception and an intellectual indifference to press freedom exercised on a mass scale, may have been incomprehensible to James and J.S. Mill.

As Orwell pointed out, this exposed the myth of a shared belief in the journalist as a critical and oppositional writer. For much of this period journalists debated how they might be restored to this role. Francis Williams argued for reasserting the primacy of the 'independent' editor freed from commercial pressures through the process of professionalisation. Not all journalists were potential professionals, however. Furthermore, the two-tier structure which had been identified in journalism before the war, was beginning to sub-divide further as radio and television, as well as public relations, provided alternative employment opportunities. As a rule, foreign correspondents, who were likely to be graduates, were classified as members of the higher echelon of journalism, standing apart from 'the great mass of working journalists' (PEP 1938: 12), and therefore more likely to see themselves as professionals. Yet James Cameron, a highly distinguished correspondent who did not have a university education, rejected the insulation of professionalism as antithetical to the transparency and accountability necessary in journalism. Moreover, if the newspapers which employed him disagreed with his approach, he either moved on to another title, or eventually into television. Cameron was content to ply his trade wherever he could do so according to the precepts he believed a journalist had to obey.

Williams and Cameron shared a conviction that journalism, at whatever level, should not act as a service industry to the media. Yet widespread routinisation, often within large corporate organisations, was beginning by 1970 to lead to the devaluation of journalism (Whittam Smith 1989: 20). It is perhaps not surprising, then, that many saw journalism in mainly opportunist terms, or as a rather cosy club with life-time membership. This may have bred a level of cynicism which veiled an underlying insecurity. Intepretations of Tomalin's well-known list of qualities for success in journalism have varied. Some have considered it a rallying-cry to the standard of critical, oppositional journalism, and others as being cynically exploitative.

References

Bromley, M. (1995) *The Press in Twentieth Century Britain*, Huddersfield Pamphlets in History and Politics, 21, Huddersfield: University of Huddersfield.

Murdock, G. and Golding, P. (1978) 'The structure, ownership and control of the press, 1914–76', in G. Boyce, J. Curran and P. Wingate (eds) *Newspaper History: From the 17th Century to the Present Day*, London: Constable, 130–48.

Political and Economic Planning (1938) *The British Press*, London: PEP.
Whittam Smith, A. (1989) 'A new "Golden Age"?', *British Journalism Review* 1
    (1) 19–21.

Chapter 12

Tom O'Malley

LABOUR AND THE 1947–9
ROYAL COMMISSION ON THE PRESS

IN 1947 THE LABOUR PRIME MINISTER, Clement Attlee, announced the establishment of a Royal Commission to investigate the press. This initiative was denounced by opponents of the government as an attempt to interfere with press freedom. The Commission's report was published in 1949 and has since been attacked by historians. Its analysis has been judged inadequate and its long term influence, negligible.[1]

This chapter challenges the negative assessments which have been made about the Commission. It does so by arguing that an understanding of why the Commission was appointed and of the difficulties faced by the 1945–51 Labour Cabinet in establishing it, helps to explain both its analysis and recommendations. The chapter also argues that the establishment of the Commission set an important precedent in the field of relationships between the press and government.

Section one sets the scene by discussing the ideological context within which relations between the government and the press were framed from the nineteenth century, describes the events which led to the establishment of the Commission and lists some of its key recommendations. Section two reviews some of the main criticisms which have been made of the Commission by historians. Section three explores the long term factors which led, in the 1940s, to calls for an inquiry into the press. This involves reviewing general criticisms of the mass press after 1900, the attitude of journalists to press reform and aspects of the Labour movement's critique of the press. Section four explores the attitudes of Labour MPs and Cabinet members to the press after 1945 and also outlines the main themes which ran through political debates around the Commission between 1946 and 1949. All of this provides the context for an account, in Section five, of how the Attlee Cabinet established the Commission. Section six provides a more detailed exposition of the Commission's findings and of contemporary reactions to those findings. The conclusion then draws together the argument and makes the case for a reassessment of the nature and significance of the Commission.[2]

Press freedom and the Commission

Before 1695 successive English governments tried to control printing through the exercise of the Royal Prerogative – a power claimed and exercised by the Crown to grant privileges – and through a series of Acts of Parliament, or licensing Acts, which imposed pre-publication censorship on all printed material. In 1695 the last of these licensing Acts lapsed and was not renewed. Thereafter governments used a combination of methods to restrict the range and amount of material published, especially in pamphlet or newspaper form. Taxes on advertisements, on paper and on newspapers were passed in the eighteenth century. The reporting of Parliamentary debates was restricted until the 1770s, writers were prosecuted for seditious libel and successive governments continued to subsidise journalists and publications (Siebert 1965; Targett 1996).

The political and social upheavals which accompanied industrialisation after the 1780s and the Napoleonic wars after the 1790s led to the expansion of a radical, illegal and unstamped press, which by the 1830s was challenging both the economic and political basis of the legal, stamped press. A combination of political reformers, philosophers, educators and journalists campaigned to effect a reduction in the taxes in the 1830s and the repeal of advertising duty (1853), stamp duty (1855) and paper duties (1861). After this governments exercised pre-publication controls over official secrets and during war time, but there were no more attempts to re-introduce sustained direct government controls over the press (Curran and Seaton 1991).

These changes in the nature of relations between the press and the government were accompanied by the articulation of a set of ideas which became known as the Liberal theory of press freedom. These ideas were most forcefully expressed in the nineteenth century. At the centre of this theory was the idea that the press played a central, if unofficial, role in the constitution. A diverse press helped to inform the public of issues. It could, through the articulation of public opinion, guide, and act as a check on, government. The press stood alongside the Lords Spiritual (i.e. clerical peers), the Lords Temporal (i.e. secular peers) and the House of Commons as the Fourth Estate of the realm, representing public opinion in ways which the other three Estates were unable, or unwilling, to do. The press could only fulfil this function if it were free from pre-publication censorship and were independent of the government.

This theory had been so widely canvassed in the early years of the nineteenth century that when, in 1859, the philosopher John Stuart Mill wrote his essay 'On Liberty', he simply took its central tenets for granted:

> The time, it is hoped, is gone by when any defence would be necessary of the 'liberty of the press' as one of the securities against corrupt or tyrannical government. No argument, we may suppose, can now be needed, against permitting a legislature or an executive, not identified in interest with the people, to prescribe opinions to them, and determine what doctrines or what arguments they shall be allowed to hear.
>
> (Warnock 1973: 141)

The idea that the press should be independent of government control or interference remained a central part of arguments mounted in defence of the activities of the press. In this view independence could and did mean independence from pre-publication censorship; from manipulation by bribery, subsidy or covert purchase or from attempts to interfere with the work of journalists. It is clear, however, that throughout the nineteenth century newspapers and journalists remained linked to the political system by subsidy, purchase and patronage (Koss 1991). When, occasionally, the extent of the links became widely publicised there was a chorus of disapproval. For instance, in March 1918 there was an outcry when it emerged that the Prime Minister, David Lloyd George, had purchased the *Daily Chronicle*. This was because he had contradicted one of the central principles associated with the idea that the press was the Fourth Estate of the realm, that is that 'newspapers and political parties, newspapers and government should be separate and independent powers' (Boyce 1978: 33).

The Liberal theory of press freedom, then, provided the framework for political debate about the press when the Labour government set up the Commission in 1947. One consequence of the Liberal theory was that it could have the effect of equating all forms of government involvement in the press with actual or potential interference with press freedom. So, when the Labour government initiated the process of establishing the Commission its motives were called into question, in terms which implied it was interfering with press freedom.

After six years of war (1939–45), the first majority Labour government was elected in July 1945. Clement Attlee was the Prime Minister and his deputy, Herbert Morrison, was Lord President of the Council. The newly elected government faced the daunting task of engineering an economic recovery from the ravages of war. In addition it was committed to introducing far reaching reforms of welfare, health and education, as well as to nationalising key industries such as the mines and railways. Many of these reforms were very controversial and provoked intense criticism from the Conservative opposition and sections of the national press. There had been a tradition of public criticism of the press, both inside and outside of the

Labour movement, which predated the 1945 election. By 1946 there was, also, a strongly held view amongst Labour MPs, journalists, and Cabinet ministers that there were good reasons for subjecting the national press to a public inquiry of some sort. These reasons are explored later, in Section three. The combination of the first Labour government with a large majority, representing a movement and a wider body of opinion which was critical of the press, with the activities of members of the NUJ who were also Labour MPs, set in motion the chain of events which led to the Commission.

In April 1946 the Annual Delegate Meeting (ADM) of the National Union of Journalists (NUJ) passed a motion calling for an inquiry into the press (Koss 1991: 1076). On 30 April, the Labour MP and NUJ member Tom Driberg asked Attlee if the government intended to act on the motion. On Morrison's advice, Attlee said that no action was planned (422. H.C. Debs. 5.s. cols 28–9; Cab. 124, 1070, fo. 5). By 2 July 1946 Morrison had changed his mind. This may have been due to pressure from MPs who were also NUJ members and to the impact of a spate of particularly hostile press coverage of the government on his thinking; but the exact reasons for this change of heart remain unclear. With Attlee's agreement he met an NUJ delegation later in July (Cab. 124, 1070, fos 2–6). A period of Cabinet debate followed over whether an inquiry should be established and also what form it should take.

Finally the Cabinet allowed a Parliamentary debate on 29 October 1946 after which a majority of MPs voted in favour of establishing a Royal Commission on the Press. The government therefore announced its intention of so doing (428. H.C. Debs. 5.s. cols 452–578). There followed a five month delay before Attlee was able to announce members of the Commission on 26 March 1947 (435. H.C. Debs. 5.s. cols 1231–4). The Commission, chaired by Sir William Ross, was appointed:

> with the object of furthering the free expression of opinion through the Press and the greatest practicable accuracy in the presentation of news, to inquire into the control, management and ownership of the newspaper and periodical Press and the news agencies, including the financial structure and the monopolistic tendencies in control, and to make recommendations thereon.
>
> (Royal Commission 1949: iii)

The Commission reported in June 1949. The Commissioners recognised that there were, potentially, problems with concentration of ownership in the national press and with the spread of chain ownership. They did not consider that these problems affected the press at the time, but that if tendencies towards concentration were to intensify then the Commission would consider this a worrying development. They felt that bias did exist in the press, especially in the popular dailies, and that this was the fault of the owners and managers of the press. Nonetheless, they considered that a free market press was the best way of ensuring diversity. The Commission proposed the establishment of a General Council of the Press to promote voluntary reform. Its object would be to safeguard the freedom of the press, to encourage a sense of public responsibility amongst journalists and to encourage measures that would improve efficiency in the industry. This body would review any tendencies likely to restrict the supply of information to the public – a catch-all idea which could include both government action and further concentration of ownership. The Council would censure undesirable journalistic practices and promote a code of professional conduct. It would publish reports on the state of the industry.

The Commission's Report was debated in the Commons on 28 July 1949. The government accepted the Report and endorsed the central recommendation that a General Council of the Press be established, voluntarily, by the industry to promote professional standards (467. H.C. Debs. 5.s. cols 2683–794). The newspaper proprietors were extremely reluctant to act and it was not until they were faced with the threat of a statutory Press Council in 1952 that they finally established a Press Council in 1953, albeit with a much narrower remit than recommended by the Commission (Levy 1967: 9–10). The Commission's comments on the general state of the press and its influence on press conduct have been heavily criticised. It is to these criticisms that we now turn.

Verdicts on the Commission

A total failure

Since the Commission reported its findings and recommendations have been heavily criticised by historians. These criticisms fall into two major categories. Firstly, that the Commission failed to diagnose accurately the state of the press in the 1940s and, therefore, to predict post-war developments in the industry. Secondly, that its recommendations have had no discernible impact upon the structure or conduct of the industry.

The press historian Stephen Koss has pointed to problems with the Commission's method of inquiry. The Commissioners were 'defeated by their own prodigious industry, which produced a mound of indigestible and sometimes contradictory material'. One consequence of this was that its analysis of the political dimensions of the press was weak, producing 'little more that a gloss on the subject' (Koss 1991: 1078–9). There was an equally dismal failure to analyse the question of ownership. In spite of examining evidence of the growth of local and regional press monopolies, the Commissioners responded with unjustified optimism to what they observed:

> Although the Commission was troubled by the large number of newspaper closures during the inter-war period, it took comfort in the belief that this had been only a temporary phenomenon caused mainly by

extravagance and lack of adaptability. 'In the provincial press as a whole', it concluded, 'there is nothing approaching monopoly.' The Commission's optimism was confounded by events. The total number of newspaper titles continued to decline.

(Curran and Seaton 1991: 280–82)

Not only was the Commission's analysis flawed, its recommendations have had little impact. Its proposals that mergers should be monitored 'had no discernible effect' and its view that press and broadcasting interests be kept separate was ignored when commercial television was introduced in 1954. Its proposal for broadly based training courses for journalists was also ignored by the industry which went about establishing vocational courses that 'encouraged uncritical acceptance of traditional values in the industry' (Curran and Seaton 1991: 285–6, 288). Even its key recommendation, the establishment of a General Council of the Press, produced, after nearly six years of delay, a mere 'complaints tribunal' which had 'no weapons beyond publicity and wounding criticism' (Seymour-Ure 1991: 236). The Council was an 'enfeebled' version of the Commission's proposal.

The Commission and its two post-war successors had 'very little influence on the press. Most of their proposals have been ignored' (Curran and Seaton 1991: 287–8). One underlying reason for the failure of the Commission was that it 'assumed that the modern press should measure up to some . . . of the supposed standards of its nineteenth-century counterpart'. As a result of being 'dominated by nineteenth century concepts of press independence' the Commission, and its successor in 1961–2, 'were largely exercises in frustration' (Boyce 1978: 39–40). These overwhelmingly negative assessments of the Commission are challenged in the rest of this chapter.

Criticising the press 1900–50

Criticisms of the mass press

The period after 1900 was marked by the rapid expansion of a cheap, national daily popular press, characterised by the *Daily Mail*, the *Daily Express* and the *Daily Mirror*. This expansion was accompanied by the emergence of powerful press barons and, by the 1920s, of chains of local and regional papers. By the 1930s, competition between rival national papers was fierce and resulted in the use of increasingly expensive marketing strategies to capture readership (Curran and Seaton 1991).

Contemporary commentators tried to account for, understand and interpret this phenomenon. There developed, after 1900, a set of criticisms, often from senior figures within the industry, of the nature and effects of this expansion which later underpinned demands for an inquiry into the press.

Writing in 1938 in his book on *The Press*, a former editor of *The Times*, Henry Wickham Steed, argued that the profit motive blunted the critical edge of the press:

> But the most serious symptom, and the most menacing to the health of what Socialists call 'capitalist society,' may well be the reluctance of newspapers which are themselves units in vast money-making concerns to examine searchingly the affairs of other money-making concerns and public companies that advertise reports of their annual meetings in the columns of those newspapers.
>
> (Wickham Steed 1938: 101)

In the same year the Political and Economic Planning Group (PEP) – a group of social researchers – reported on the press, deploring the fact that:

> economic accident which links the function of reporting, interpreting and commenting on news with the running of a large scale, highly capitalised industry, is having some unfortunate results, and we doubt whether a Press subject to these conditions can fully satisfy democratic needs.
>
> (cited in 428. H.C. Debs. 5.s. col. 460, 29/10/1946)

Both PEP and Wickham Steed were later recognised as preparing the way for the Commission by drawing attention to many of the issues which were to be central to that body's work (467. H.C. Debs. 5.s. col. 2734, 28/7/1949).

There was concern, also, about the concentration of ownership within the industry and the effects of this on the range of opinions expressed in the press. In 1918 the Independent MP N. Pemberton Billing asked:

> who elects the press? Any rogue with a million of money . . . can get control of the press, or a portion of it, at any minute; and so where is our democracy? Surely it is the duty of this House to stand between the capitalist press and the people?
>
> (Quoted in Boyce 1978: 36–7)

The editor of *The Spectator* and Independent MP Wilson Harris, writing in 1943, stressed how commercialisation and the growth of concentration (or combines) threatened diversity of opinion. He pointed out that the press:

> it is said, has become commercialized, the advertising side dominating the editorial in the interests of dividends; the creation of combines means that ostensibly independent organs are merely emitting views dictated by a single Rothermere or Kemsley or Beaverbrook.

He also worried about what would happen after the end of the Second World War:

> Whether the papers, with or without reduction in their numbers, will fall into even fewer hands than control them to-day is another, and highly important, question. Any move in that direction would be decidedly against the public interest.
>
> (Harris 1943: 70, 126)

During the war Michael Foot was concerned about issues of concentration in the film industry and the press. His knowledge of developments in the United States, where pressure was being applied to limit concentration of ownership, and his concern about concentration of ownership in the film industry informed his later involvement in the debates around the Royal Commission (Foot, interview).

To concerns about commercialisation, the profit motive, the growth of combines and the threat to diversity of option were added criticisms about the ethical standards of the industry. Harris was concerned about the way the press trivialised important issues. Others in the late 1940s echoed long standing concerns about how the press 'played up the sensation rather than the significant' and how individuals who felt maltreated by intrusive reporting had 'no recourse at all at the present time' (Harris 1943: 12–13; Hutt 1948: 15; 467. H.C. Debs. 5.s. col. 2731, 28/7/1949). In addition some commentators felt that poor ethical standards could be attributed to the malign influence of advertisers. Wickham Steed criticised advertisers who in 'a dozen ways . . . seek to influence the Press to their own advantage' (Wickham Steed 1938: 15; see Cockett 1989: 59–60, 126–7).

Fears about the lack of political independence of the press were current in the 1930s and 1940s. Writing in the 1930s Wickham Steed was critical of the political support that some proprietors gave to the Prime Minister, Neville Chamberlain, and his policy of appeasing the expansionist activities of Hitler's Germany, at the expense of presenting alternative perspectives. The Labour MP and journalist Ivor Thomas, writing five years later during the war, expressed fears about the political independence of the press in relation to the growing influence of government. He was worried that the growth of the government's public relations machine might mean that 'the independence of the Press may be sapped . . . It is only a small step from advice to instruction, but that step is all the way from a free to a totalitarian press' (Wickham Steed 1938: 61; Thomas 1943: 33).

These writers made proposals for change which focused on reforming the commercial press, not effecting a revolution in ownership. In so doing, they helped to frame the context within which the Commission viewed the issues and, ultimately, underpinned its preference for voluntary, not government imposed, statutory reform. Wickham Steed justified his discussion of the business side of the press on the grounds that scrutiny was important:

'A little light on dark places may perhaps be wholesome and help to check abuses that flourish in obscurity.' He suggested that manufacturers and advertisers might set aside 10 per cent of their annual spending on advertisements to sustain publications which sought to instruct rather than entertain (Wickham Steed 1938: 150–51, 154). Wilson Harris thought that proposals to limit dividend payments to shareholders and use the money to equip 'the paper to serve the public more efficiently . . . deserve more attention than they have yet received' (Harris 1943: 69).

Professional standards were seen as the solution to many of these problems. Wickham Steed argued that 'the gathering and selling of news and views is essentially a public trust'. Ivor Thomas's views followed on from this: 'The maintenance of professional standards in journalism is not less vital than in the other professions.' Wilson Harris considered that it was up to the industry, proprietors and journalists, who 'have it in their power . . . to set standards, honourable to the profession' (Wickham Steed 1938: 14; Thomas 1943: 22; Harris 1943: 91).

So, by the time the Commission sat there was a body of criticism from general commentators on the structure and conduct of the press. This criticism often came from people connected with the press, who did not want to see a wholesale breach with the traditional sets of property relations in the industry, but did see mild structural reform supplemented by the spread of professional, self-regulation within the industry as the way forward (see also Koss 1991: 1052–3; Williams 1959: 229).

Journalists' organisations and press criticism

Journalists were well aware of the criticisms of the mass press and, after 1920, inched towards adopting a policy on ethical standards. As early as 1917 the Central London Branch of the NUJ asked whether the Union should act 'as the guardian of the profession's honour'. In 1931 the NUJ's National Executive appealed to proprietors, editors and managers to limit the extent to which 'distressing' methods were employed in the collection of news, and to avoid intrusion into the private lives of private people. It offered moral and financial support to any member who suffered for refusing 'to carry out instructions repugnant to his sense of dignity'. In 1936, after some debate, the Union agreed a Code of Conduct. Clause 11 of the Code stressed the need for care:

> In obtaining news or pictures, reporters and Press photographers should do nothing that will cause pain or humiliation to innocent, bereaved or otherwise distressed persons. News, pictures and documents should be acquired by honest methods only.

In 1937 the Annual Delegate Meeting registered its disgust at intrusions into privacy and called on proprietors and government to co-operate in attempts to 'stamp out the malpractices of a small minority in the collection of news'. The NUJ preferred its Code of Conduct as a device to achieve this end, whilst its rival organisation, the Institute of Journalists (IOJ), promoted an ultimately unsuccessful bill to create a statutory register of journalists. In the 1940s the NUJ continued 'attempts to exert Union influence in the field of ethics and training' as a part of 'an effort to redress the balance against the overwhelming dominance of proprietors in the inter-war years' (Mansfield 1943: 521–9; Christian 1980: 279, 292).

By 1943 the Union was 'gathering information on the finance and economics of the newspaper industry, and . . . considering the post-war situation'. Its official historian noted, in the same year, that 'the Labour Party, the chief Socialist organisation in the country, has itself no definite plans for dealing with the Press, and indeed has made no serious inquiry . . . In all there is scope for constructive work by the Union'. (Mansfield 1943: 559). The debate leading up to the call for a Commission in April 1946 was underway within the Union before the 1945 General Election (428. H.C. Debs. 5.s. col. 454). The motion passed in 1946 called for an inquiry into the ownership, control and financing of national and provincial papers, news agencies and periodicals and drew particular attention to issues of monopoly and the suppression of facts.

Union officials stressed the political neutrality of the NUJ, highlighting its concern with the 'best supply of facts and news' and with press freedom (Bundock 1957: 185). They stressed their support for the free expression of opinion and the accurate presentation of news. They then raised questions, in their deputation to Morrison on 22 July 1946, about the effect of circulation wars on the growth of sensationalism; the disappearance of provincial papers; the growth of chain ownership and the effect of this on the independence of local papers; the suppression of news; the use of papers for propaganda purposes; the influence of financial interests on editorial; and the problems posed by monopoly. They called for 'A Royal Commission which would take evidence on oath, summon witnesses and order the production of documents, and report on ways and means of safeguarding and enlarging the freedom of the press' (Cab. 129.11. CP [46] 298, Annex).

In its 'constructive suggestions' to the Commission the Union proposed a whole host of measures for consideration: a law restraining monopolies; a reform of the libel laws; introduction of a right of reply; controls on the volume of advertisements; the encouragement of trust ownership in the press; restrictions on certain types of sales promotions; compulsory publication of who owned newspapers on each copy of a paper; a disclosure of financial and other interests held by the paper above leading articles; the prohibition of black lists; and the establishment of a Publishing Corporation to further the establishment of more independent papers. Its main recommendation was for:

> The creation of a professional body or a statutory body of inquiry set up by the government or the Lord Chancellor at fixed intervals, say of five years.

A British Press Board or Press Council is envisaged, something like the Arts Council or the Board of Governors of the BBC, or the General Medical Council, or the British Board of Film Censors. The Press Board or Council, of course, would not be identical with any one of these.

This Council should draw up and enforce a code of conduct; receive complaints about breaches of standards; supervise the space allotted to and the standards of advertising; work out rules governing the sale of properties; safeguard the status of editors; approve Trust deeds for tax allowances; publish an annual report on the state of the press and institute a range of journalistic and newspaper prizes. In addition the NUJ wanted reform to be carried out by the industry itself as voluntary self-regulation was 'the best line of approach' (NUJ 1947: 14–15).

In developing its stance towards press reform over the thirty years preceding the Commission, the NUJ was articulating many of the concerns and the stress on voluntary reform expressed by people outside the industry. Amongst those outside the industry with a direct interest in its affairs was the Labour Party and the wider trade union movement.

The Labour movement and the press 1900–45

Throughout the period under discussion, the Labour Party and the Trade Union movement were concerned about the nature and influence of the press. The ideas that developed over this period provided one important part of the context within which Labour MPs and Cabinet ministers viewed the press after 1945. In 1922 the Labour Research Department published a study of the press. It described the press as being used 'both for general capitalist propaganda and for direct attacks on the workers'. Ownership of the bulk of the London Press 'is in the hands of capitalist groups who are interested either in making direct profits out of the newspaper trade . . . or in using it as a means of maintaining the system with which profit-making is possible'. Advertisements were the key to profits and so 'directors and editors are particularly careful not to offend their advertising clients' (Labour Research Department 1922: 27, 44–5).

In 1928 Kingsley Martin, later the editor of the *New Statesman*, wrote an entry on the press in *The Encyclopaedia of the Labour Movement*. He attributed the monopoly of the modern press to the revolution in mass publishing associated with Lord Northcliffe. With few exceptions the press was run by 'a few autocrats' who decided what news went to the public and who, in the interests of circulation, cultivated 'the art of constantly exploiting sensational material without too far outraging the feelings of a large body of readers'. Labour had 'long ceased to look for a fair statement of its case in the Capitalist Press'. The influence of this anti-Labour press was countered by Liberal papers such as the *Manchester Guardian*, Labour's own *Daily Herald* and some socialist papers, such as *Socialist Review* (Kingsley Martin 1928: 56–60).

In 1929 Herbert Tracey, the Labour Party's publicity officer, argued that the monopoly exercised by the main press groups had been at the expense of independent newspapers and opinion. Only through the careful extension of an impartial broadcasting system could 'the dangerous consequences of monopoly . . . be counteracted'. On the brink of the 1931 election Stanley Hirst, the Labour Party President, told Conference that:

> a minority Labour Government is . . . subject to continuous attack through a network of daily, evening and weekly newspapers, politically hostile to Labour, which exaggerate its shortcomings, belittle its diffi-culties, and misrepresent or ignore its achievements.

This critical attitude was sustained throughout the immediate pre-war years. In 1936 the Labour Party produced a pamphlet, *The Power of the Press*, which attacked the links between the press and the wider economic struc-ture of society, links which ensured a pro-Tory, pro-business, anti-Labour position amongst the major newspaper groups. Nine years later, in its mani-festo for the 1945 election, Labour attacked the '"hard faced men" and their political friends', who in the recent past had controlled government, 'the banks, the mines, the big industries, largely the press and the cinema. They controlled the means whereby people got their living. They controlled the ways by which most of the people learned about the world outside.'

Labour's critique was not that far removed from aspects of the general criticisms outlined above. Its remedies were, likewise, reformist in their implications. Labour politicians believed strongly in the power of education to release and develop the rational side of people's personality. Ramsay McDonald, writing in 1919, stressed how Labour strove 'to transform through education . . . through the acceptance of programmes by reason of their justice rationality and wisdom' (Ryan 1986: 38, 40, 103, 124; Dickinson and Street 1985: 151). This involved supporting the Labour and alternative press and producing research under the auspices of the research departments of the Party and the TUC. In 1938 alone, Labour sold two million copies of its books and pamphlets. There was also a strong faith in the spread of general education, although as the socialist academic G.D.H. Cole recog-nised in 1948, this could be double edged, creating a 'mass reading public vulnerable to the influence of the millionaire press' (Fielding *et al.* 1995: 7; Cole 1948: 475–6). Kingsley Martin had summarised this faith in education and propaganda in 1928: 'Labour's remedy, therefore, against the capitalist Press lies first of all in the increase of knowledge about the methods, organ-isation, and objects of the Press and the growth of scepticism about its propaganda.' By trade unionists buying Labour papers, thereby building a strong Labour press, and by journalists standing up to proprietors, 'Socialists will be able to combat the political influence of the capitalist Press by the simple method of stating the truth about present-day industrialism' (Kingsley Martin 1928: 60–61).

Labour movement criticism of the press was therefore well established by the 1940s. But it was accompanied by a strong belief in education and voluntary activity by Labour movement supporters and journalists. It was not characterised by a systematic argument in favour of abolishing private owner-ship in the press. The Labour movement therefore operated within a wider climate of opinion on the press which stressed the need for predominately voluntary remedies to problems of press conduct and bias. The Labour Cabinet, after 1945, was influenced by these long standing criticisms, in its belief in the importance of educating people about the true nature of the press and in preferring voluntary to statutory remedies.

Labour, the press and the Commission

Labour and the press after 1945

The Labour government of 1945 was elected in spite of the fact that the majority of the national press was hostile to its programme. It was elected not least because of the strength of its vision of a society based on full employ-ment and adequate welfare services (Fielding *et al.* 1995). At the 1945 election Conservative supporting papers had 52 per cent of circulation and Labour 35 per cent. In contrast Conservatives gained 40 per cent of the popular vote and Labour 48 per cent (Seymour-Ure 1975: 166–7). Labour had the support of two commercially owned papers, the *Daily Mirror* and the *Sunday Pictorial*, and of the left inclined press, such as the *Daily Herald*, *Reynolds News* and the *Daily Worker* (Curran 1980: 87). There was no neat fit between elec-toral success and press support. This may be linked to the evidence which suggests that during the term of the Labour government the bulk of the newspaper reading public 'took little notice of editorial lines, be they Labour- or Conservative-inclined' (Fielding *et al.* 1995: 67).

Some contemporary politicians were aware of this mismatch, but this did not blunt the edge of concern amongst leading figures in both main parties about the importance and alleged influence of the press on the polit-ical process (454. H.C. Debs. 5.s. col. 861, 23/7/1948; 467. H.C. Debs. 5.s. cols 2729–30, 2738, 28/7/1949). Indeed the presence amongst MPs elected in 1945 of a large number of journalists or people connected with the press, put by one contemporary at around 40, of whom, according to the Labour MP Haydn Davies, 23 were NUJ members, may have gone a long way to creating a keen sensitivity to press issues in that Parliament (Koss 1991: 105; 428. H.C. Debs. 5.s. col. 453, 29/10/1946).

Many Labour MPs and Cabinet Ministers considered that the press was particularly hostile to the government. In the summer of 1946 the Attorney General, Hartley Shawcross, responded to press attacks on government rationing policy by attacking 'the proprietors of the gutter press', naming Kelmsley and Beaverbrook, and asserting that: 'They distort the facts; they suppress the news upon which free opinions can be freely formed.' After Kelmsley issued a libel writ, Shawcross, having consulted Morrison and Attlee, apologised (Chisholm and Davie 1993: 459–60; 428. H.C. Debs. 5.s. col. 474; Cab. 124, 1070, fo. 43; Margach 1978: 91–3; Shawcross 1995: 146–8).

Press hostility and Labour responses continued whilst the Commission sat. During the fuel crisis of 1947 the government suspended newsprint supplies to periodicals to save power. This was represented 'by most newspapers, as an interference with the right of free discussion' (Harris 1995: 336). In May 1948 Aneurin Bevan, the Minister of Health, attacked the press:

> Why should we who are responsible for clearing up the muddle of a century of capitalism allow ourselves to be scared by headlines in the capitalist Press, the most prostituted Press in the world?

The opposition-inspired debate on Bevan's comments prompted further complaints from Labour MPs about the press. Tom Driberg asserted that 'the greater part of the Press is in fact controlled by forces hostile to the Government' and George Jeger complained about the local press in his Winchester constituency:

> The local papers in my constituency . . . week by week contain letters attacking the local Labour Member of Parliament, letters attacking the proceedings which go on in this House and letters attacking individual Ministers by name, and . . . our letters of correction are rarely published.
>
> (Koss 1991: 16; 454. H.C. Debs. 5.s. cols 854, 867, 881, 23/7/1948)

Later in the year the press supported Tory opposition to the iron and steel nationalisation bill. In January 1949 Bevan had to make a Parliamentary statement repudiating unsubstantiated allegations of fraud in his Ministry which were made in the *Daily Graphic*. During the national emergency brought on by the Dock strike later in that year the press was 'extremely critical' of the government, and, in 1950, Morrison accused the press of conspiring with the Tory opposition to 'sabotage the steel industry in the interests of Conservative propaganda' (Harris 1995: 426, 432, 458–9; 460. H.C. Debs. 5.s. cols 338–42, 21/1/1949).

Whilst Labour MPs and some ministers waged a public campaign against the perceived hostility of the Tory press, the Cabinet had to deal with the press in terms of hostile leaks, information management and censorship. The leakage of secret information to the media was a recurrent theme in Cabinet meetings, reflecting strong feelings about the damaging effects of hostile coverage. Leaks occurred about the Health Service, November 1945; economic policy, December 1945; iron and steel and atomic energy,

April 1946; and foreign policy, May 1946, to name but a few (Cab. 128.2. CM 51 [45] 2, 8/11/1945; Cab. 128.2. CM 58 [45] 2, 3/12/1945; Cab. 128.5. CM 30 [46] 2, 4/4/1946; Cab. 128.5. CM 38 [46] 4, 29/4/1946; Cab. 128.5. CM 50 [46] 1, 20/5/1946).

Faced with a hostile press the Cabinet was very sensitive to the question of press censorship. In July 1946 it granted supplies of paper to a known publisher of Fascist books on the grounds that

> it would be indefensible to impose a political censorship by the use of economic controls which had been granted by Parliament for entirely different purposes. If it was wrong that Fascist books should be published, the proper course was to take specific power to prohibit them.
> (Cab. 128.6. CM 69 [46] 5, 18/7/1946)

Morrison, as Lord President, was in control of official information. The government established a Central Office of Information and a system of official and ministerial committees for co-ordinating and controlling information services: 'a complex system of indirect control' of the information services 'was established that allowed Ministers, specifically Herbert Morrison, a wide degree of control over information services'. The government was sensitive to allegations about the improper use of this machinery. As the Financial Secretary to the Treasury, Glanvil Hall, put it in 1947:

> The Government's job is not, in my view . . . to use the machine at their disposal to put over their own purely party point of view. They should use what facilities they have in order to get to the public the facts of any given situation, so that the public can be fully informed.
> (Wildy 1985: 2, 377; 435. H.C. Debs. 5.s. col. 1630)

Indeed contemporaries, and historians of the period, have noted how relatively ineffective the government was at using the machine at its disposal to present its case (435. H.C. Debs. 5.s. col. 1623–4; Fielding 1991: 115, 118).

So to suggest, as some did in 1946, that the government established the Commission to interfere with press freedom is to misunderstand the range of relationships that the government had with the press. It also had a complex set of relationships with the BBC and the film industry. When it set up the Commission it did so acutely aware of the problems that Labour faced from a hostile press, conscious of its desire to maintain an effective public information service and deeply concerned not to interfere, and not to be seen to be interfering, with press freedom. But this did not mean that it was not prepared to respond to long standing concerns about the press and to review its role in society, just as it reviewed government information services, aspects of the film industry and the BBC (Briggs 1979; Dickinson and Street 1985). Morrison, Attlee, other Ministers and the wider Labour movement were therefore critically aware of the problems posed for Labour by the press and this awareness underlay their willingness to initiate the inquiry in 1946.[3] But their critique was directed not at overturning private property in the press, but towards trying to reform the industry.

Arguments over the Royal Commission 1946–9

The decisions taken by the Cabinet were taken in the context of sharp political disagreements between Labour and the Tory opposition about the purpose and value of the inquiry. These debates influenced the climate in which the Commission's remit was framed, its members chosen and its work conducted, and also rehearsed arguments about chain ownership, advertising, and ethics which had been the staple of public discussion about the press for many years.

The issues were debated in the press and in a series of publications including those by Lord Camrose, Aylmer Vallance, Kingsley Martin and Wilson Harris during 1946 and 1947 (Koss 1991: 1077–8). Opponents of the inquiry used a variety of devices to attack it and set the tone which the supporters had to counter. At the core of the attack was the idea that the inquiry was, in some sense, an attempt to curtail press freedom by undue government interference.

Lord Camrose suggested that the grounds for appointing the Commission were 'more than flimsy, resting mainly on suggestions of a nebulous character made in the heat of a political debate and by the National Union of Journalists' (Camrose 1947: 10). Beaverbrook believed that the Commission was 'one of the Government Agencies in the persecution of newspapers' and T.E. Naylor reminded Morrison on 30 July 1946 that not all NUJ or Labour MPs members supported the idea of an inquiry, as it was against modern ideas of press freedom (Taylor 1972: 584; Cab. 124, 1070, fo. 34).

The Tory MP and ex-Minister of Information Brendan Bracken attacked Morrison, as soon as he suggested there might be a case for an inquiry, on 16 July 1946:

> I believe that the Right Hon. Gentleman has no respect whatsoever for the freedom of the Press or for the freedom of any one who ventures to criticise the Government or his august self.
>
> (425. H.C. Debs. 5.s. col. 1098)

The Tories continued to attack the inquiry on the grounds that the accusations made by its supporters were untrue. According to Sir David Maxwell Fyfe the only limitation to entry into the market was the price of newsprint; there was real choice in the range of national and provincial papers; and the left were well represented in the industry, in particular by the *Daily Herald*. He also considered the accusation of monopoly 'an abuse of words in connection with a subject where you have this variety of choice' (428. H.C. Debs. 5.s. cols 471–8, 29/10/1946). Tories accused the government of political bias in the appointment of the Commissioners (435. H.C. Debs. 5.s. 1653–4, 31/3/1947). They took advantage of the Commission's decision to take oral evidence in camera and, in 1948, of Bevan's attack on the press to discredit the inquiry and the government's involvement with it (439. H.C. Debs. 5.s. cols 202–4, 24/11/1947; 453. H.C. Debs. 5.s. col. 1010, 13/7/1948). Yet the Report, when published, was sufficiently ambiguous for both sides to claim it as a victory. This allowed the Tories, in this case Beverley Baxter MP, to impugn the government's motives whilst at the same time claiming the Report vindicated their position:

> The more we examine the situation the clearer it becomes that this was a political move to disparage and muzzle the Press ... Nevertheless, the Report is a brilliantly compiled document, and has proclaimed the character and the quality of the newspapers and the British Press beyond any further challenge.
>
> (467. H.C. Debs. 5.s. col. 2752, 28/7/1949)

But the view that there was no charge to answer and that the inquiry was motivated by desires to muzzle the press was not shared by supporters of the Commission. It was issues such as the tendency to monopoly in chain ownership and the influence of advertising and financial interests which exercised Tom Driberg in April 1946, and this he justified by pointing to the 'danger in the continued sabotage of national recovery by such enemies of the people as Lord Kelmsley' (422. H.C. Debs. 5.s. cols 28–9, 30/4/1946). In *Tribune* Hannen Swaffer supported the call for an inquiry. He alluded to fears about the influence of advertisers on editorial policy, of the prejudice towards 'Big Business' in the press, of monopoly control in some towns and to the linked fear that 'leading articles written in London are sent over the Creed machines to chain-store editors in provincial towns who are no longer allowed to have a printed opinion of their own unless some millionaire in far-away London gives his OK' (Hill 1977: 34).

Michael Foot MP expressed his concern about centralised control over local papers in the *Daily Herald* on 31 May 1946: 'London ownership has invaded the provinces and there is a steady growth of the syndicated leading article' (Jones 1995: 150–1). Foot repeated this concern in the October debate:

> No one can really imagine it is by choice of the people of South Wales that they read the 'Western Mail' if they want local news. No one can imagine it is by the democratic choice of the people of Plymouth that they can only buy, morning and evening, a Harmsworth paper.

He believed that the 'process of monopoly is not receding. It is getting worse.' Newspapers had made huge profits during the war and 'these financial resources are going to be unloosed on the newspaper market, and the people who will suffer are going to be all those independent newspapers that cannot stand the blast'. It was a problem exacerbated by the decline of editorial autonomy caused by the actions of aggressive proprietors. Legal changes to prevent chain ownership and the consequent distortion of news should be the main purpose of the Commission. In making these arguments he was echoing the debates of the 1920s and 1930s in the Labour movement, but also drew explicitly on the example of the Hutchins Commission on the press in the United States of America to justify the need for an inquiry. He asserted, confidently, the right of Ministers to criticise the press, pointing out that it was a form of hypocrisy for the press to attack Ministers and not to expect criticism in return. Like Morrison he asserted that the Commission was a blow for freedom of expression:

> So far from this being any attempt to interfere with the rights of free expression, it is a plan, or an effort, to protect the rights of free expression from the ravages of monopoly and financial privilege.
> (428. H.C. Debs. 5.s. cols 463–70, 28/10/1946)

Haydn Davies, who proposed the motion for the Commission in the October 1946 debate, felt the need to dispel negative arguments about the initiative so as to make space for legitimate discussion of the press which did not get bogged down in accusations of government interference in press freedom:

> This Motion was not put on the Order Paper at the behest of the Lord President of the Council, nor was it put down with the idea of muzzling the Press. It was not put on the Order Paper to curtail the freedom of the Press; it was not because we want to nationalise the Press so as to have State organs only . . . It is, therefore, untrue to say that we resent criticism of the government by the newspapers and therefore want to control them and curtail their freedom.

Davies therefore had to clear the ground of allegations which equated any government sponsored inquiry with interference in press freedom. He queried whether chain ownership was compatible with press freedom if powerful proprietors could buy up and then close down long established titles, and repeated allegations about centralised proprietorial direction over local papers. He repeated the point, previously made by PEP, about the difficulty of getting evidence 'upon which to frame a newspaper policy' by suggesting that 'only a Royal Commission, with power to send for persons and papers could get that evidence' (428. H.C. Debs. 5.s. cols 453–60, 29/10/1946).

So, at the core of the critique mounted by the public supporters of the inquiry were concerns about how the economic structure of the press influenced freedom of expression and the conduct of journalism. In proceeding along these lines critics were drawing on the arguments made in the 1920s and 1930s. They also had to add to these arguments by asserting that it was legitimate for a government to sponsor an inquiry into the press. In so doing they had to make an important distinction, which their opponents tried to blur. This was between, on the one hand, accepting the traditional, general idea, that government interference in the press was undesirable, whilst, on the other, advocating that it was possible for a government to promote inquiry and debate about the press in the interests of press freedom and democracy. This position, which balanced the orthodox position on press government relations with the desire to make a politically effective response to the widely held criticisms of the industry, framed the way Cabinet ministers dealt with the issue.

The Cabinet and the Commission

The Cabinet and the Commission: motives

The influences on Cabinet debate over the Commission included concerns about the political impact on Labour policies of a hostile press; pressure generated from the party and the NUJ; the sense of the need for the press to be subject to the same form of periodic inquiry as the BBC; a view about how the press should function in society; and the idea that an inquiry would help to educate public opinion about, and stimulate voluntary reform within, the industry.

Morrison made it clear on 3 October 1946 that one reason for the inquiry was that the large newspaper combines were 'using their influence to create a mood of discouragement and depression in the country' (Cab. 128.6 CM 84 [46] 2). He also invoked external pressures on the Cabinet to justify the move. On 27 September 1946, in a memo to Cabinet colleagues, he argued that the proposal:

> has strong backing from Government supporters and otherwise, and I think that we should be rightly exposed to the charge of weakness in the face of interested opposition if we turned down the powerfully supported representations of the National Union of Journalists and the Labour Members of Parliament whose Motion is on the Order Paper.
>
> (Cab. 129.13. CP [46] 360)

Asa Briggs has pointed out that 'few people before 1955 and 1956 considered the media comprehensively or related the Beveridge Report on Broadcasting to the Report of the Royal Commission on the Press' (Briggs 1979: 17). Morrison was an exception. He saw the links between inquiries into broadcasting and the press. Having gained Cabinet approval on

15 July to announce that the government thought that there was a case for considering whether an enquiry should be set up (Cab. 128.6. CM 68 [46] 6), on the next day he deliberately linked broadcasting and press policy:

> I must make it clear in all quarters of the House that the Government do not object in principle to subjecting the BBC from time to time to a searching inquiry by an independent body. All great channels for the dissemination of information to the public would, the Government believe, benefit from having their state of health examined by an independent inquiry from time to time, and we do not exclude the Press from that consideration.
>
> (425. H.C. Debs. 5.s. col. 1083)

He reasserted this link in the debate on the Commission's Report on 28 July 1949:

> We feel that the case for an inquiry of this kind from time to time has been vindicated. It has been accepted in principle for the BBC, which, quite rightly, is subjected to independent inquiry from time to time.
>
> (467. H.C. Debs. 5.s. col. 2698)

In making this point Morrison was expressing awareness of, and Cabinet support for, the idea that the press, for all its special quasi-constitutional status, was no more immune to inquiry than broadcasting. In a memo to the Cabinet on 25 July 1946 Morrison argued:

> I am inclined to think that, with all its faults, our press is still the best in the world, certainly in the larger countries, but I am sure that it will benefit from a thorough and impartial inquiry. The quasi-constitutional position which it occupies as what used to be called the Fourth Estate is, in itself, a reason for reviewing from time to time the way in which it is discharging its responsibilities to the public.

Opposition to this exercise stemmed, he asserted, from self interest and was 'partly due to the mistaken impression that the freedom of the Press is in some way threatened' (Cab. 129.11. CP [46] 298).

In articulating the demand for an inquiry Morrison developed the quasi-constitutional aspects of the initiative, by stressing the need both for a clarification of the role of the press in society and for periodic inquiries into the industry. Underpinning all of these ideas was the Labour movement's belief in the power of knowledge and education to act as a force for good. Morrison put this point to Cabinet on 30 July 1946 after Cripps, President of the Board of Trade, and Jowitt, the Lord Chancellor, had raised reservations about the proposal:

> The Lord President said that he had in mind that an enquiry would serve a useful purpose in bringing to light undesirable practices which would cease as soon as the light of publicity had been directed to them. He had not contemplated that the enquiry would lead to legislation.
>
> (Cab. 128.6. CM 75 [46] 2)

In September, when Cabinet discussion on the issue reopened after the summer recess, he reiterated and developed this point:

> As I told the Cabinet, I had not contemplated that the inquiry would necessarily lead to legislation, though it might do so. An authoritative account of the existing position, laying down general principles, which should govern the conduct and management of the Press would, however, be valuable in itself. There are certain dangerous tendencies which the mere institution of an inquiry should help to check, and in any case the Press is so important an influence for good or ill in a modern community that in my opinion a review such as I have suggested is overdue.
>
> (Cab 128.13. CP [46] 360, 27/9/1946)

Cabinet discussion then echoed the wider debate about the nature of the press in society and concerns about press freedom. But Morrison developed a rationale for the inquiry which asserted the need for a new regime of scrutiny over the press, and for a new era of social responsibility by the industry. He invoked the *de facto* practice of the periodic review of broadcasting as well as the notion that an institution claiming an important role in the constitution should not be immune from scrutiny. He was also asserting the fundamental point that government review did not, of itself, breach any dominant conceptions of the proper relationship between the government and the press.

The Cabinet and the setting up of the Commission

Morrison faced difficulties in Cabinet whilst establishing such a novel exercise. He faced opposition in Cabinet and then had to deal with the sensitive question of who should Chair and sit on the Commission. Once Cabinet was persuaded to act it was important that it be seen to act in a way which produced positive results and which did not justify accusations that it was trying to muzzle the press. From Morrison's perspective it required patience and persistence to achieve the goal. In this process he took advice from one of his Permanent Secretaries, Max Nicholson.

Attlee had agreed to Morrison's reopening of the question of an inquiry in early July 1946 (Cab. 124, 1070, fos 5–6). On 15 July Cabinet agreed that Morrison could announce that the government thought that there might be a case for an inquiry (Cab. 128.6. CM 68 [46] 6). Morrison's staff prepared a memo for the Cabinet on the subject which was circulated on 26 July (Cab. 129.11. CP [46] 298). At Chequers that weekend Attlee told Morrison that the next Cabinet meeting could decide on the issue but should hold back on an announcement until after the August recess (Cab. 124, 1070, fo. 31). At the meeting on 30 July, Stafford Cripps objected that a Commission would need legal powers to enforce the production of evidence and that the 'nature of the relation between the editor or the journalist and the proprietor of a newspaper would make it very difficult to get satisfactory evidence'. He also felt that before embarking on an enquiry some idea of whether the government would legislate or not was required. Jowitt, the Lord Chancellor, 'doubted whether it would be possible to secure the services of a judge for an enquiry of this kind'. As a result of these interventions the decision on whether to hold an inquiry, contrary to the view expressed at Chequers by Attlee, was deferred until after the summer recess, to allow the objections to be considered (Cab. 128.6. CM 75 [46] 2).

Morrison considered the question over the summer and on 27 September issued a memo to Cabinet arguing that judicial powers were not necessary and that legislation was not, necessarily, the object of the exercise. He retained the hope that a judge might be found to Chair the inquiry. At the Cabinet meeting on 3 October:

> doubts were expressed about the wisdom of initiating such an enquiry. There would be very great difficulty in obtaining evidence of the alleged abuses, and there was a real risk of a white-washing report. Even if the enquiry did bring to light abuses, its report would be an embarrassment unless adequate means of checking abuses could be devised. Would it in fact be practicable, without undue interference with the freedom of the press, to restrict the growth of large newspaper combines or to prevent the selective presentation of news? And was it not dangerous to launch an enquiry until the Government could see some way of doing this? Was it not preferable to seek a practical remedy for the present state of affairs by improving the presentation of the Government's case?

Jowitt repeated his objection to the appointment of a judge. A further delay ensued because Cabinet agreed that Morrison, Cripps and Jowitt should consult on the terms of reference, membership and the powers of the Commission to obtain evidence (Cab. 128.6. CM 84 [46] 2).

Morrison then mobilised some allies to support him. On 5 October he got Attlee's agreement to involving Aneurin Bevan and the Minister of Labour, George Issacs, in the *ad hoc* group consulting on the Commission. Bevan brought with him his experience with *Tribune* and his trenchant critique of the press, and Issacs had a background in the printing trade unions (Cab. 124, 1070, fos 55, 57; Mansfield 1943: 540). By 14 October Morrison and this *ad hoc* group had consulted and he produced a memo for Cabinet. The idea of a judge as Chair was dropped, and there was now an agreed form of words for the terms of reference which did not allude to the use of legal powers to enforce the collection of evidence (Cab. 129.13. CP [46] 379).

At the Cabinet meeting on 17 October, on 'the question of an inquiry on the lines proposed, opinion in the Cabinet remained divided'. It was agreed that 'it would be easier for the Government to institute such an inquiry in response to a demand supported after debate, by a substantial weight of opinion in the House of Commons.' This decision indicates both the importance of Parliamentary opinion in the Cabinet discussions and the desire of the Cabinet to be seen to be acting with substantial external backing in such a sensitive matter. Attlee stated that he would be involved in considering the composition of the Commission as he wanted 'a smaller body including a larger proportion of well-known names which would command public confidence. He also thought it would be preferable to include one or two people who had in the past been professionally engaged in newspaper management or journalism' (Cab. 128.6. CM 87 [46] 4).

After the debate on 29 October there followed a lengthy process of deciding on the membership and the Chair of the Commission. In this Attlee and members of the *ad hoc* group worked with Morrison. By late November, Sir Hector Hetherington had been approached as Chair, but he declined pleading volume of work. In January 1947 Sir Phillip Morris was approached and declined for similar reasons. The difficulty in finding an acceptable, high profile, Chair was confounded by the problem of arriving at a list of names acceptable to all of the members of the *ad hoc* group. This was, in itself, a function of the need to involve a group of people who would be perceived as representative and impartial to bolster the authoritative standing of the Commission. The final choice of Sir William Ross, of Oriel College Oxford, and an experienced member of Whitehall inquiries and committees, reflected this caution about the membership.[4]

During this process Morrison received advice, both solicited and unsolicited, from a range of people. Perhaps the most influential advice came from one of his Permanent Secretaries, Max Nicholson, who was consulted closely throughout the build up to the Commission and whose imprint can be detected on the decisions taken. Nicholson commented on Morrison's Cabinet memo which had been prepared for the meeting on 30 July. He endorsed the view that a free press was not a press free from public scrutiny:

> Newspaper proprietors would no longer be able to persist in the attitude that the freedom of the Press is something which exists and can be taken for granted irrespective of their activities. They would in future have to reckon with defending their actions before public opinion and this alone would go some way to restrain them from abuses.

He thought that the Commission could make recommendations 'without any question of interference with the Freedom of the Press'. He also stressed the issue of professionalism, which had figured so prominently in public debates about the press:

> The need for a strong unified organisation of the journalistic profession could for instance be brought home and something could be done to reinforce the somewhat questionable claims of journalism to be regarded as a profession at all by setting up standards and creating means of enforcing them.

He considered 'the main value' of a Commission would be in turning the spotlight on the press and 'helping to push through reforms that the press itself should have made if it had been professionally more vigorous' (Cab. 124, 1070, fo. 30a, 27/7/1946).

On 2 November 1946 Nicholson wrote to Morrison, referring to issues that had been raised in the October debate, especially the attacks on the proposed Commission as an attempt to muzzle the press:

> I am deeply concerned at the risk that the Commission may be prejudiced by the absence of any member who is publicly known to understand and to be a stout defender of the historical role played by the 'Freedom of the Press' in the British Constitution . . . G.M. Young . . . a writer and historian of great distinction, would do it excellently.
> (Cab. 124, 1070, fo. 103)

Young was appointed to the Commission, carrying with him expectations that he would represent, and be seen to represent, the long standing orthodox views about the proper relationship between press and government.

Recommendations and assessments

The Report

The Commission's Report and recommendations reflected the dominant nineteenth century view about the need to protect press freedom, whilst at the same time urging the by now well established demand for voluntary reform. The Commission denied that there was anything approaching a monopoly in the press or that there would be an increase in concentration of chain ownership. It concluded that: 'Local monopoly is in some areas inevitable but it has certain inherent dangers and where it is not inevitable it is clearly to be deprecated', and that a 'further decrease in the number of national newspapers would be a matter for anxiety, and a decrease in the provincial morning newspapers would be a serious loss'. It therefore endorsed concerns about the likely detrimental effect of concentrated ownership, without accepting that these effects were apparent at the time it reported.

On bias it found that all popular papers and some quality ones were guilty of 'excessive bias'. Whilst considering that there was a variety of political opinion in the press, there was too big an intellectual gap between the popular and quality papers. In recognising that the press had shortcomings it identified these as being not the fault of government, advertisers, outside financial interests or forms of ownership but the 'policy of those who own and conduct the Press'. Although the press was, in part, driven to produce material its public would accept, it did 'not do all it might to encourage its public to accept or demand material of higher quality'.

In rejecting immediate restraints on ownership and asserting that 'Free enterprise is a pre-requisite of a free press' it was reiterating dominant contemporary assumptions about the nature of the press. The critics we have examined attacked aspects of the free enterprise press, and recommended controls, mild or otherwise, on aspects of the industry, but they did not break with the idea that free enterprise was the framework within which the majority of the press would operate. There was no strong, indigenous tradition that stood out against free enterprise in the press. Consequently it was only credible for the Commission to deal with problems of ownership and standards by mild reform, both statutory and voluntary. It opted for vigilance and very mild reform on matters of ownership by recommending that steps might be taken to allow the Monopolies Commission to investigate local monopolies in order to publicise abuses.

It was tapping into a much wider consensus when it recommended self-regulated, voluntary reform, a consensus which included almost all of the critics of the press, and which mirrored Morrison's hope that the Commission would act as a catalyst for voluntary change. Its proposal for a General Council of the press fell into this category. The Council would represent proprietors, journalists, editors and the public and would be appointed, in part, by a senior judge. Its central remit linked the Millian doctrine with a voluntarist ethic:

> The objects of the General Council should be to safeguard the freedom of the Press; to encourage the growth of a sense of public responsibility and public service amongst all engaged in the profession of journalism – that is, in the editorial production of newspapers – whether as directors, editors or other journalists; and to further the efficiency of the profession and the well being of those who practise it.

To achieve these objectives the Council needed to take action:

(1) to keep under review any developments likely to restrict the supply of information of public interest and importance;
(2) to improve the methods of recruitment, education, and training for the profession;

(3) to promote a proper functional relation among all sections of the profession;

(4) by censuring undesirable types of journalistic conduct, and by all other possible means, to build up a code in accordance with the highest professional standards. In this connection it should have the right to consider any complaints which it may receive about the conduct of the Press or of any persons towards the Press, to deal with these complaints in whatever manner may seem to it practicable and appropriate, and to include in its annual report any action under this heading;

(5) to examine the practicability of a comprehensive pension scheme;

(6) to promote the establishment of such common services as may from time to time appear desirable;

(7) to promote technical and other research;

(8) to study developments in the Press which may tend towards greater concentration or monopoly;

(9) to represent the Press on appropriate occasions in its relations with the Government, with the organs of the United Nations, and with similar Press organisations abroad;

(10) to publish periodical reports recording its own work and reviewing from time to time the various developments in the Press and the factors affecting them.

(Royal Commission 1949: paras 664–84)

Items 1 and 8, assumed the need for ongoing vigilance over measures which might restrict press freedom, including the adverse affects of monopoly. Items 2 and 4 echoed long standing concerns about training and standards and accepted that these problems needed attention. Items 3, 5, 6 and 7 were about seeking to make the press work as an industry towards increasing co-operation and improving the conditions of its workers.

So, within the framework of voluntary regulation, the Council would deal with issues of monopoly, standards and competition, thereby minimising the role for direct government intervention. But this voluntary solution had been articulated, authoritatively, by a government-appointed Commission. The existence of the Commission had marked an assertion of the government's claim to intervene over the way in which the press conducted itself. The proposals for voluntary regulation, which had been canvassed well before the Commission sat, now had an authority, conferred by a Royal Commission and Parliamentary vote, and were the product of a process which showed how a government could intervene in the affairs of the press without threatening press freedom.

Some contemporary responses to the Report

Although *Tribune* condemned the Report as 'a tepid and unimaginative document' it welcomed the proposal for a General Council and asserted that the existence of the Commission had done some good as the 'press lords have been compelled . . . to introduce an element of apparent fairness into their political reporting' (Jones 1995: 164). The General Secretary of the NUJ, C.J. Bundock, later considered that the Report contained an 'immense amount of useful information' (Bundock 1957: 187). Others must have felt this too, because the Report sold 5,000 copies almost immediately, and within a few weeks another 4,000 were reprinted (467. H.C. Debs. 5.s. Written Answers, col. 51, 18/7/1949).

Morrison prepared a response to the Report for Cabinet and circulated it on 9 July 1949. He considered it a success as a constitutional initiative:

> It seems to me that the Royal Commission has fully justified its appointment by the first-rate survey of the British Press which it has produced; this has the additional merit of being extremely readable, and it is to be hoped that it will be as widely studied as possible. There is much indeed to be said for the view that it would be in the public interest that there should be periodical inquiries into the Press, say at ten yearly intervals; we have come to take it for granted that the BBC should be the subject of such inquiries, and, if the BBC is a monopoly, the Press is unique among our great institutions in enjoying a virtual monopoly of freedom from outside public criticism.

He argued that most newspapers had seriously misrepresented the findings of the Report to suit their ends, but that: 'No impartial reader could deny that, on balance, the report is distinctly critical of large sections of the Press on important aspects of their activities.' All the same he did have criticisms of the document:

> I think personally that the Commission has let the Press down lightly, that some of its criticisms might have been sharper, and that its approach to some of the major problems of newspaper ownership and control is unduly timid. I think it would have been justified by the evidence in making more positive recommendations, but its analysis of the present state of affairs seems to me on the whole balanced and sound, and we can hardly come forward with alternative proposals. In all the circumstances, therefore, I think that the report is one which the Government should in general accept.

He argued that the Cabinet should support the proposal for a General Council established on a voluntary basis. The government could not commit a judge to be involved in the selection of Council members, and government should not fund the Council as this would 'be represented as evidence of a desire for Governmental interference'. On recommendations requiring legislation he suggested that the government should not commit itself but 'be sympathetically disposed to legislation to give effect to the Commission's recommendations at a convenient opportunity' (Cab. 129.35. CP [49] 147). The Cabinet met on 18 July and endorsed Morrison's suggestions (Cab. 128.16. CM [46] 4).

In the debate on 28 July all sides laid claim to the idea that the Report vindicated their perspective, and there was strong support for the motion accepting the Report and its recommendations, including the one for the General Council. The Tory opposition spokesman, Oliver Stanley, welcomed the Report, asserted that the main charges levelled by critics of the press had been refuted therein, but agreed that a voluntary Press Council would help to deal with the problems of fairness in news presentation and sensationalism which were identified by the Commission. Haydn Davies, who criticised aspects of the Report's discussion of ownership, said: 'I support them 100 per cent in the proposal for the establishment of a Press Council which I believe will do more for the British Press and creative journalism than any other single thing.' Michael Foot was unhappy with the Commission's views on ownership which seemed a 'strange conclusion to reach from the facts which they assembled'. He directed his criticism firmly at the Commission's failure to consider the continuing dangers of current tendencies in patterns of ownership (467. H.C. Debs. 5.s. cols 2699–716, 2748, 2761–9, 2783).

From then on the government adopted a position of waiting while encouraging the industry to act. It believed strongly in the Report's potential as an educational document which would stimulate voluntary reform.

Conclusion

There are two key conclusions which need to be stressed. Firstly, the Commission was a product of the political circumstances of its day. These circumstances helped to frame the kind of analysis and recommendations that it made, and it should therefore be judged in this context. Secondly, the Commission was intended to set, and did set, an important constitutional precedent which broke with nineteenth century conceptions about the relationship between the press and government. It was this precedent which allowed future governments to initiate inquiries into the press and for arguments for government sponsored reform of the press to gain public standing.

The context of the Commission

The political context from which the Commission emerged helps to explain its analysis and recommendations. The assumption which informed its approach was a desire to reconcile the idea of independence from the government with the widespread desire for reform of the press. In 1900 the dominant conception of relations between the press and government included the idea that any form of government interference in the press was undesirable. The fact that governments and politicians had close, manipulative links with the press did not challenge the dominance of this conception. With the rise of a cheap, national, commercial press and its accompanying features of sensationalism, political bias and concentration of ownership, there emerged a growing chorus of criticism of the industry. Critics extended from senior journalists through academics, independent MPs, the Trade Union movement, the NUJ and the Labour Party. These critics challenged the worst manifestations of private ownership, but did not, generally, mount a sustained attempt to abolish private ownership of the press. At best they argued for some restraints on concentration. The dominant view, by the 1940s, was that there needed to be extensive voluntary reform of the industry. Yet critics of the press differed from opponents of the Commission in that they considered that an inquiry did not constitute interference with press freedom by the government, but, on the contrary, allowed the government to sponsor reform without interfering.

Later critics of the Commission have paid too little regard to the way in which it articulated a consensus that had developed since 1900. The Commission's findings and recommendations did not depart dramatically from what was, by 1949, an established set of perspectives on press reform. Thus, Morrison would have liked more positive recommendations, but it was never part of his thinking or of the Cabinet's to challenge seriously property relations in the press or to seek to impose statutory reform on the industry.

For Morrison the strength of the exercise lay, in part, in the way in which the Commission exposed the shortcomings of the industry and provided the impetus, and the mechanisms, for voluntary reform. This, perhaps, exhibited a misplaced belief in the power of exposure to stimulate reform and in the willingness of proprietors to initiate reform. However, these views were held by other reformers then and had yet to be disproved by the test of time. It is therefore important to temper criticism of the Commission for its analysis and weak recommendations by recognising that it drew the fundamentals of both from a widespread contemporary consensus about the industry and how to change it.

A constitutional precedent

The Commission also marked a break with previous attitudes of government to the press. Morrison justified the establishment of the Commission by placing it within the wider context of communications policy. He argued that the press was, like the BBC, an important part of the communications system in the country and that, therefore, it should be subjected to the same kind of periodic review as the BBC. In so doing, he was providing a new gloss on the concept of the Fourth Estate, turning the idea to his advantage by insisting that the 'quasi-constitutional position' of the press 'as what used to be called the Fourth Estate is, in itself, a reason for reviewing from time to time the way it is discharging its responsibilities to the public' (Cab.

129.11. CP [46] 298). This provided an important rationale for breaking with the long standing idea that government intervention in the press was likely to be government interference with press freedom.

There were no major inquiries into the press between the mid-nineteenth century and the Royal Commission. Once a precedent and a form of inquiry had been set there followed a series of inquiries into the press. The Royal Commission on the Press of 1961–2 was followed by another Royal Commission between 1974 and 1977. Although there was no institutional framework, such as that provided by the government's control over the BBC's Charter, to force periodic reviews of the press, in the thirty years after 1949 the two press Commissions coincided with the publication of the reports of two major government-initiated inquiries into broadcasting, the Pilkington Commission, 1962, and the Annan Report, 1977. During the 1980s a series of Private Members Bills, designed to give a statutory Right of Reply to citizens and to protect their privacy from unjustified intrusions by the press led, in 1989, to the establishment of the first of two government sponsored reports by David Calcutt into the press which, in turn, provoked a bout of voluntary reform of the system of self-regulation (McNair 1994:150–159, 191). The first Royal Commission had set a precedent which later governments were eager to follow. It therefore marked a turning point in the evolution of press–government relations.

The Labour government did not deal as vigorously with the press as some at the time and many since have felt that it should. The Commission's report did not break away from the idea that ownership of the press was a property right and that reform should be voluntary, by recommending statutory reform of ownership and regulation. Its specific recommendations were both attacked and ignored. Yet these points need to be set against the achievement of the exercise. The Labour government marshalled a tradition of press criticism and initiated a process which challenged dominant ideas about the government's not intervening in the conduct of the press, in the teeth of some fierce opposition. In so doing, it was able to demonstrate that intervention did not constitute damaging interference with press freedom. In achieving this the Labour government helped to develop a public discourse around press freedom which was no longer confined to the boundaries set by the orthodoxy so eloquently expressed by John Stuart Mill in the 1850s.

Notes

1   I would like to thank Diane Hardman and Richard O'Malley who helped to make the research for this chapter possible; Michael Foot for his time and courtesy; the staff at the PRO in Kew for their assistance, and Stuart Allan, Michael Bromley and Tim White who read and commented on earlier drafts.

2   The Royal Commission concentrated on the national and provincial newspapers, the principal newsagencies based in London, and the leading

journals commenting on news and current affairs. It excluded the publications of learned societies and also newsletters. It made no extensive inquiries into the religious, trade and technical press (1949: para. 20). This chapter follows this broad definition of the press.

3   Morrison was very conscious of the importance of the press. See: Donoughue and Jones 1973: 297–300, 359; Taylor 1972: 574, 601; Hubback 1985: 197–8; Curran and Seaton 1991: 73–6; 297–300; interview with Michael Foot. The received view is that Attlee did not bother too much about the press (Margach 1978: 87; Hennessey 1993: 328). Yet Attlee was very much aware of the importance of the press and this provided the context for his support of the Commission see: Harris 1995: 170, 194, 256, 341, 439–40, 472, 534–5; Cab. 128.1. CM 60 [45] 6, 6/12/1945; Cab. 129.11. CP [46] 298, 25/7/46; Cab. 128.6. CM 87 [46] 4, 17/10/46.

4   Details of this lengthy process can be traced in Cab. 124, 1070, 1071, 1072.

Sources

Interview with Michael Foot.

Manuscript sources and Parliamentary debates

Public Record Office

Cabinet Minutes: Cab. 128 (references are to Class Mark i.e. Cab. 128, file number, i.e. 6, Cabinet Meeting Number, i.e. CM 60, year of meeting, i.e. [45], and minute, i.e. 6, plus date where appropriate).

Cabinet Memoranda: Cab 129 (references are to Class Mark, i.e. Cab 129, file number, i.e. 11, paper's year and number, i.e. CP [46] 298, plus date where appropriate).

Lord President's Office Files: Cab. 124, 1070 (references are to Class Mark, i.e. Cab. 124, file number, i.e. 1070, and where possible page number, i.e. fo. 5).

Parliamentary debates

House of Commons Debates (references are given to the volume number, i.e. 422, the title, i.e. H.C. Debs. 5.s, the columns, i.e. cols 424–8, and the date).

References

Boyce, G. (1978) 'The Fourth Estate: the reappraisal of a concept', in G. Boyce, J. Curran and P. Wingate (eds) *Newspaper History: From the 17th Century to the Present Day*, London: Sage/Constable.

Brendon, P. (1982) *The Life and Death of the Press Barons*, London: Secker & Warburg.

Briggs, A. (1979) *The History of Broadcasting in the United Kingdom. Volume 4. Sound and Vision*, Oxford: Oxford University Press.

Bundock, C.J. (1957) *The National Union of Journalists: A Jubilee History 1907–1957*, London: Oxford University Press.

Camrose, V. (1947) *British Newspapers and their Controllers*, London: Cassell.

Chisholm, A. and Davie, M. (1993) *Beaverbrook: A Life*, London: Pimlico.

Christian, H. (1980) 'Journalists' Occupational Ideologies and Press Commercialisation', in H. Christian (ed.) *The Sociology of Journalism and the Press*, Sociological Review Monograph 29, University of Keele, Staffordshire.

Cockett, R. (1989) *Twighlight of the Truth: Chamberlain, Appeasement and the Manipulation of the Press*, London: Weidenfeld & Nicolson.

Cole, G.D.H. (1948) *A Short History of The British Working-Class Movement 1789–1947*, (3rd edn, rev.) London: Allen & Unwin.

Curran, J. (1980) 'Advertising as a Patronage System', in H. Christian (ed.) *The Sociology of Journalism and the Press*, Sociological Review Monograph 29, University of Keele, Staffordshire.

Curran, J. and Seaton, J. (1991) *Power Without Responsibility* (4th edn) London: Routledge.

Dickinson, M. and Street, S. (1985) *Cinema and State: The Film Industry and the British Government 1927–84*, London: British Film Institute.

Donoughue, B. and Jones, G. (1973) *Herbert Morrison*, London: Weidenfeld & Nicolson.

Elliott, P. (1978) 'Professional ideology and organisational change: the journalist since 1800', in G. Boyce, J. Curran and P. Wingate (eds) *Newspaper History: From the 17th Century to the Present Day*, London: Sage/Constable.

Fielding, S. (1991) '"Don't know and don't care": popular political attitudes in Labour's Britain, 1945–51', in N. Tiratsoo (ed.) *The Attlee Years*, London: Pinter.

Fielding, S., Thompson, P. and Tiratsoo, N. (1995) *"England Arise!" The Labour Party and Popular Politics in 1940s Britain*, Manchester: Manchester University Press.

Harris, K. (1995) *Attlee* (rev. edn), London: Weidenfeld & Nicolson.

Harris, W. (1943) *The Daily Press*, Cambridge: Cambridge University Press.

Hennessey, P. (1993) *Never Again: Post War Britain, 1946–51*, London: Vintage.

Hill, D. (ed.) (1977) *Tribune 40: The First Forty Years of a Socialist Newspaper*, London: Quartet.

Hubback, D. (1985) *No Ordinary Press Baron: A Life of Walter Layton*, London: Weidenfeld & Nicolson.

Hutt, A. (1948) 'Organisation of the British Press' in A. Kenyon and E. Jay (eds) *Entry Into Journalism*, London: Medallion Press.

Jones, M. (1995) *Michael Foot*, London: Gollancz.

Keane, J. (1991) *The Media and Democracy*, London: Polity.

Kingsley Martin, B. (1928) 'The Press', in H.B. Lees-Smith (ed.) *The Encyclopaedia of the Labour Movement Vol. 3* London: Caxton Publishing.

Koss, S. (1991) *The Rise and Fall of the Political Press in Britain*, London: Fontana.

Labour Research Department (1922) *The Press*, London: Labour Publishing

Levy, H. (1967) *The Press Council: History, Procedure and Cases*, London: Macmillan.

McNair, B. (1994) *News and Journalism in the UK*, London: Routledge.

Mansfield, F.J. (1943) *Gentlemen. The Press! Chronicles of a Crusade. Official History of the National Union of Journalists*, London: W.H. Allen.

Margach, J. (1978) *The Abuse of Power: The War Between Downing Street and the Media from Lloyd George to Callaghan*, London: W.H. Allen.

Negrine, N. (1994) *Politics and the Mass Media in Britain* (2nd edn) London: Routledge.

NUJ (1947) *Written Evidence Submitted By the National Union of Journalists*, London: Royal Commission on the Press, HMSO.

Royal Commission on the Press 1947–1949 Report (1949) Cmd 7700, London: HMSO.

Ryan, T. (1986) 'Labour and the media in Britain 1929–1939. A study of the attitudes of the Labour movement towards the new media, film and radio and of its attempts to use them for political purposes', unpublished Ph.D. thesis, University of Leeds.

Seaton, J. (1978) 'Government Policy and the Mass Media', in J. Curran (ed.) *The British Press: a Manifesto*, London: Macmillan.

Seymour-Ure, C. (1975) *The Political Impact of the Mass Media*, London: Constable.

Seymour-Ure, C. (1991) *The British Press and Broadcasting since 1945*, Oxford: Basil Blackwell.

Shawcross, H. (1995) *Life Sentence*, London: Constable.

Siebert, F.S. (1965) *Freedom of the Press in England 1476–1776*, Urbana: University of Illinois Press.

Targett, S. (1996) ' "The Premier Scribbler Himself": Sir Robert Walpole and the Management of Political Opinion', in M. Harris and T. O'Malley (eds) *Studies in Newspaper and Periodical History 1994 Annual*, Westport, CT: Greenwood.

Taylor, A.J.P. (1972) *Beaverbrook*, London: Hamish Hamilton.

Thomas, I. (1943) *The Newspaper*, London: Oxford University Press.

Warnock, M. (ed.) (1973) *Utilitarianism*, London: Collins.

Wickham Steed, H. (1938) *The Press*, Harmondsworth: Penguin.

Wildy, T. (1985) 'Propaganda and Social Policy in Britain, 1945–51; Publicity For the Social Legislation of the Labour Movement', unpublished Ph.D. thesis, University of Leeds.

Williams, F. (1959) *Dangerous Estate: The Anatomy of Newspapers*, London: Arrow.

Chapter 13

George Orwell

THE PREVENTION OF LITERATURE

ABOUT A YEAR AGO I ATTENDED A MEETING of the PEN Club[1], the occasion being the tercentenary of Milton's *Areopagitica* – a pamphlet, it may be remembered, in defence of freedom of the press. Milton's famous phrase about the sin of 'killing' a book was printed on the leaflets advertising the meeting which had been circulated beforehand.

There were four speakers on the platform. One of them delivered a speech which did deal with the freedom of the press, but only in relation to India; another said, hesitantly, and in very general terms, that liberty was a good thing; a third delivered an attack on the laws relating to obscenity in literature. The fourth devoted most of his speech to a defence of the Russian purges . . . Moral liberty – the liberty to discuss sex questions frankly in print – seemed to be generally approved, but political liberty was not mentioned. Out of this concourse of several hundred people, perhaps half of whom were directly connected with the writing trade, there was not a single one who could point out that freedom of the press, if it means anything at all, means the freedom to criticize and oppose. Significantly, no speaker quoted from the pamphlet which was ostensibly being commemorated. Nor was there any mention of the various books that have been 'killed' in this country and the United States during the war. In its net effect the meeting was a demonstration in favour of censorship.[2]

There was nothing particularly surprising in this. In our age, the idea of intellectual liberty is under attack from two directions. On the one side are its theoretical enemies, the apologists of totalitarianism, and on the other side its immediate practical enemies, monopoly and bureaucracy. Any writer or journalist who wants to retain his integrity finds himself thwarted by the general drift of society rather than by active persecution. The sort of things that are working against him are the concentration of the press in the hands of a few rich men, the grip of monopoly on radio and the films, the unwillingness of the public to spend money on books, making it necessary for nearly every writer to earn part of his living by hackwork, the encroachment of official bodies like the MOI and the British Council, which help the writer to keep alive but also waste his time and dictate his opinions, and the continuous war atmosphere of the past ten years, whose distorting effects no one has been able to escape. Everything in our age conspires to turn the writer, and every other kind of artist as well, into a minor official, working on themes handed to him from above and never telling what seems to him the whole of the truth. But in struggling against this fate he gets no help from his own side: that is, there is no large body of opinion which will assure him that he is in the right. In the past, at any rate throughout the Protestant centuries, the idea of rebellion and the idea of intellectual integrity were mixed up. A heretic – political, moral, religious, or aesthetic – was one who refused to outrage his own conscience . . . it is the peculiarity of our age that the rebels against the existing order, at any rate the most numerous and characteristic of them, are also rebelling against the idea of individual integrity. 'Daring to stand alone' is ideologically criminal as well as practically dangerous. The independence of the writer and the artist is eaten away by vague economic forces, and at the same time it is undermined by those who should be its defenders. It is with the second process that I am concerned here.

Freedom of thought and of the press are usually attacked by arguments which are not worth bothering about. Anyone who has experience of lecturing and debating knows them off backwards. Here I am not trying to deal with the familiar claim that freedom is an illusion, or with the claim that there is more freedom in totalitarian countries than in democratic ones, but with the much more tenable and dangerous proposition that freedom is *undesirable* and that intellectual honesty is a form of anti-social selfishness. Although other aspects of the question are usually in the foreground, the controversy over freedom of speech and of the press is at bottom a controversy over the desirability, or otherwise, of telling lies. What is really at issue is the right to report contemporary events truthfully, or as truthfully as is consistent with the ignorance, bias and self-deception from which every observer necessarily suffers. In saying this I may seem to be saying that straighforward 'reportage' is the only branch of literature that matters: but . . . at every literary level, and probably in every one of the arts, the same issue arises in more or less subtilized forms. Meanwhile, it is necessary to strip away the irrelevancies in which this controversy is usually wrapped up.

The enemies of intellectual liberty always try to present their case as a plea for discipline versus individualism. The issue of truth-versus-untruth is as far as possible kept in the background. Although the point of emphasis may vary, the writer who refuses to sell his opinions is always branded as a mere *egoist*. He is accused, either of wanting to shut himself up in an ivory tower, or of making an exhibitionist display of his own personality, or of resisting the inevitable current of history in an attempt to cling to unjustified privileges . . . Freedom of the intellect means the freedom to report what one has seen, heard, and felt, and not to be obliged to fabricate imaginary facts and feelings. The familiar tirades against 'escapism', and 'individualism', 'romanticism' and so forth, are merely a forensic device, the aim of which is to make the perversion of history seem respectable. .

[L]et me repeat what I said at the beginning of this essay: that in England the *immediate* enemies of truthfulness, and hence freedom of thought, are the press lords, the film magnates, and the bureaucrats, but that on a long view the weakening of the desire for liberty among the intellectuals themselves is the most serious symptom of all . . .

[It is assumed] that a writer is either a mere entertainer of else a venal hack who can switch from one line of propaganda to another as easily as an organ grinder changing tunes. But, after all, how is it that books ever come to be written? Above a quite low level, literature is an attempt to influence the viewpoint of one's contemporaries by recording experience. And so far as freedom of expression is concerned, there is not much difference between a mere journalist and the most 'unpolitical' imaginative writer. The journalist is unfree, and is conscious of unfreedom, when he is forced to write lies or suppress what seems to him important news: the imaginative writer is unfree when he has to falsify his subjective feelings, which from his point of view are facts. He may distort and caricature reality in order to make his meaning clearer, but he cannot misrepresent the scenery of his own mind: he cannot say with any conviction that he likes what he dislikes, or believes what he disbelieves. If he is forced to do so, the only result is that his creative faculties dry up. Nor can he solve the problem by keeping away from controversial topics. There is no such thing as genuinely non-political literature . . .

Literature has sometimes flourished under despotic regimes, but, as has often been pointed out, the despotisms of the past were not totalitarian. Their repressive apparatus was always inefficient, their ruling classes were usually either corrupt or apathetic or half-liberal in outlook, and their prevailing religious doctrines usually worked against perfectionism and the notion of human infallibility. Even so it is broadly true that prose literature has reached its highest levels in periods of democracy and free speculation . . .

Political writing in our time consists almost entirely of prefabricated phrases bolted together like the pieces of a child's Meccano set. It is the unavoidable result of self-censorship. To write in plain, vigorous language one has to think fearlessly, and if one thinks fearlessly one cannot be politically orthodox. It might be otherwise in an 'age of faith', when the prevailing orthodoxy has been long established and is not taken too seriously. In that case it would be possible, or might be possible, for large areas of one's mind to remain unaffected by what one officially believed. Throughout the whole of the Middle Ages there was almost no imaginative prose literature and very little in the way of historical writing: and the intellectual leaders of society expressed their most serious thoughts in a dead language which barely altered during a thousand years . . .

There mere prevalence of ideas can spread a kind of poison that makes one subject after another impossible for literary purposes. Wherever there is an enforced orthodoxy — or even two orthodoxies, as often happens — good writing stops. This was well illustrated by the Spanish civil war. To many English intellectuals the war was a deeply moving experience, but not an experience about which they could write sincerely. There were only two things that you were allowed to say, and both of them were palpable lies: as a result, the war produced acres of print but almost nothing worth reading . . .

The fact is that certain themes cannot be celebrated in words, and tyranny is one of them. No one ever wrote a good book in praise of the Inquisition. Poetry *might* survive in a totalitarian age, and certain arts or half-arts, such as architecture, might even find tyranny beneficial, but the prose writer would have no choice between silence and death. Prose literature as we know it is the product of rationalism, of the Protestant centuries, of the autonomous individual. And the destruction of intellectual liberty cripples the journalist, the sociological writer, the historian, the novelist, the critic, and the poet, in that order. In the future it is possible that a new kind of literature, not involving individual feeling or truthful observation, may arise, but no such thing is at present imaginable. It seems much likelier that if the liberal culture that we have lived in since the Renaissance actually comes to an end, the literary art will perish with it.

Of course, print will continue to be used, and it is interesting to speculate what kinds of reading matter would survive in a rigidly totalitarian society. Newspapers will presumably continue until television technique reaches a higher level, but apart from newspapers it is doubtful even now whether the great mass of people in the industrialized countries feel the need for any kind of literature . . . Probably novels and stories will be completely superseded by film and radio productions. Or perhaps some kind of low-grade sensational fiction will survive, produced by a sort of conveyor-belt process that reduces human initiative to the minimum.

It would probably not be beyond human ingenuity to write books by machinery. But a sort of mechanizing process can already be seen at work in the film and radio, in publicity and propaganda, and in the lower reaches of journalism. The Disney films, for instance, are produced by what is essentially a factory process, the work being done partly mechanically and partly by teams of artists who have to subordinate their individual style. Radio features are commonly written by tired hacks to whom the subject and the manner of treatment are dictated beforehand; even so, what they write is merely a kind of raw material to be chopped into shape by producers and censors. So also with the innumerable books and pamphlets commissioned by government departments. Even more machine-like is the production of short stories, serials and poems for the very cheap magazines . . .

Meanwhile totalitarianism has not fully triumphed anywhere. Our own society is still, broadly speaking, liberal. To exercise your right of free speech you have to fight against economic pressure and against strong sections of public opinion, but not, as yet, against a secret police force. You can say or print almost anything so long as you are willing to do it in a hole-and-corner way. But what is sinister, as I said at the beginning of this essay, is that the conscious enemies of liberty are those to whom liberty ought to mean most. The big public do not care about the matter one way or the other. They are not in favour of persecuting the heretic, and they will not exert themselves to defend him. They are at once too sane and too stupid to acquire the totalitarian outlook. The direct, conscious attack on intellectual decency comes from the intellectuals themselves.

It is possible that the Russophile intelligentsia, if they had not succumbed to that particular myth, would have succumbed to another of much the same kind. But at any rate the Russian myth is there, and the corruption it causes stinks. When one sees highly educated men looking on indifferently at oppression and persecution, one wonders which to despise more, their cynicism or their shortsightedness . . . any attack on intellectual liberty, and on the concept of objective truth, threatens in the long run every department of thought . . .

[L]iterature is doomed if liberty of thought perishes. Not only is it doomed in any country which retains a totalitarian structure; but any writer who adopts the totalitarian outlook, who finds excuses for persecution and the falsification of reality, thereby destroys himself as a writer. There is no way out of this. No tirades against 'individualism' and 'the ivory tower', no pious platitudes to the effect that 'true individuality is only attained through identification with the community', can get over the fact that a bought mind is a spoiled mind. Unless spontaneity enters at some point or another, literary creation is impossible, and language itself becomes ossified. At some time in the future, if the human mind becomes something totally different from what it is now, we may learn to separate literary creation from intellectual honesty. At present we know only that the imagination, like certain wild animals, will not breed in captivity. Any writer or journalist who denies that fact . . . is, in effect, demanding his own destruction.

Notes

1   This article appeared originally in the magazine *Polemic* (1946). Although obviously best known as a novelist, Orwell began writing for the London *Evening Standard* in 1941, joining a group of left-wing contributors including the paper's future editor, Michael Foot. During this period Orwell also wrote for the *Observer* and the *New Statesman* and was literary editor of *Tribune*.

2   At this point Orwell inserted the following footnote:

It is fair to say that the PEN Club celebrations, which lasted a week or more, did not always stick at quite the same level. I happened to strike a bad day. But an examination of the speeches (printed under the title *Freedom of Expression*) shows that almost nobody in our own day is able to speak out as roundly in favour of intellectual liberty as Milton could do 300 years ago – and this in spite of the fact that Milton was writing in a period of civil war.

Chapter 14

Francis Williams

WHAT KIND OF FREEDOM?

T HE INFLUENCE EXERCISED BY A NEWSPAPER derives from the nature of the medium[1] – from the fact that it arrives daily before its readers as an ambassador from the outside world conveying to them news of events as seen through the eyes of its staff, docketed and assessed in importance and interest by men working daily at high speed, interpreted and commented on by men required by the nature of their task to make immediate judgments. The character of a newspaper may be set in a certain mould by its proprietor . . . But even with such a newspaper the selection of news and features, the twist and turn given to the reporting of events, the total flavour of the daily dish put before the public, reflect, and cannot help but reflect to a very large degree, the personality and judgment of the man who does the daily job of producing it – the editor. The proprietor may inspire the big political campaigns. They seldom, experience indicates, have much influence anyway. It is the editor who makes each daily issue what it is.

It is curiously the case indeed – although some newspaper proprietors and managers do not even yet appear to have got around to the fact – that the commercialisation and popularising of the press so far from diminishing the importance of the editor has in many ways enhanced it – even by the standards of commercial success themselves. That great newspapers are made by great editors the whole of newspaper history shows. But it is also the case that popular papers depend for their success upon their editors to a degree not always sufficiently appreciated for their own good by those who profit from them . . .

There is indeed nothing like a good editor for a newspaper. Whatever may be the level of journalistic success to which they aspire, only those newspapers that hold their editors seem to succeed. The correlation between stability of tenure in the editor's room and a newspaper's success, whether in prestige or circulation, is so close, in fact, as almost to provide the basis for a mathematical formula for the guidance of ambitious newspaper proprietors.

This is obviously so in the case of the more serious newspapers: no one has ever disputed the importance of its editor to *The Times* or the *Manchester Guardian*. Similarly, the *Observer* has been made by two editors, the first that great journalist J.L. Garvin who created serious Sunday journalism, and the second David Astor . . .

It is, however, when one turns to popular journalism where the unimportance of the editor compared with the proprietor is now sometimes accepted as a proven fact that the principle demonstrates itself in the most surprising way . . .

In fact although the industrialisation, commercialisation and popularisation of the press have done a good deal to alter the face of journalism they have done nothing to impair the basic journalistic fact that newspapers are made by journalists . . . It is the daily impress of an editor's personality that gives a newspaper character whether the character be grave or gay, austere or scandalous.

Moreover, the importance of the editor which seemed at one stage in the commercialisation of the press to be in so much danger of being diminished seems likely to become not smaller but larger as time passes. The age of the strongly individualist newspaper proprietor who himself impressed an editorial personality on his paper is almost over: we are moving into the era of the administrators . . .

The substitution of ownership by public corporations for ownership by individuals does not of course mean, any more than it does in other industries, that effective managerial control is not in fact vested in the hands of very few people . . . But it does make it less likely now than in the past that newspapers will become the personal vehicles of dynamic personalities and more likely that their commercial control will pass increasingly into the hands of high-grade salaried executives. The managerial revolution came to Fleet Street somewhat later than most other places but it is by now firmly entrenched there . . .

The real danger facing a good deal of journalism today, in fact, is not, as it seemed to be a generation or two ago, that much of its historic duty of public information may be twisted to serve the propaganda purposes of powerful individuals but that it will be pressed into a pattern that denies it all purpose other than the purely commercial one of attracting the largest number of paying customers by whatever means comes most readily to hand.

The responsibility of journalists, and especially of those in editorial authority, will become especially great if this should prove to be the case. The defence of journalism as more than a trade and greater than an entertainment technique — although a trade it is and entertaining it must be — is properly the journalists' and no one else's. It is they who are the legatees of history in this respect. They have both a professional and a public duty to look after their inheritance.

That is not, of course, to suggest that the interests of editor and publisher are necessarily antagonistic. They are far from having proved so in many famous partnerships of the past: they are very far from being so in many instances today, indeed it is difficult to see how any newspaper can succeed at the highest level except when they are identical. Nor is it to suggest that the proprietor and publisher is necessarily likely to be less concerned with the truest interests of the press than is the journalist . . . Nevertheless the guardianship of journalistic values rests primarily with the journalist: *c'est son métier*. He cannot disassociate himself from this responsibility without ceasing, in a fundamental sense, to be a journalist. Nor is there any final excuse for him in the claim that he is, after all, simply a hired man who must do as he is bid. He must be ready, as must all men when issues of principle arise, to stand up and be counted.

The relationship between editor and publisher can never be simple — unless it is so simple as to make the editor no more than a paid servant . . . to do so is, in fact, to set aside a good deal of what is most important in the history of the press and to overlook the fact that the freedom of the journalist – freedom not only from censorship or intimidation by the State but from censorship or intimidation by anyone including his own employer – is an essential part of press freedom.

This freedom involves the right of individual reporters to report facts honestly even if they prove inconvenient to the fancies or prejudices of editors or news editors, it involves the freedom of foreign and political correspondents to report and interpret the evidence before them according to their independent judgments and journalistic conscience, even if to do so is awkward for the policy of the paper that employs them, and it most certainly involves the degree of independence possessed by an editor in his relations with his publisher. Such independence clearly cannot be absolute. Whether a newspaper is owned by an individual, a joint stock company or a trust the right to decide the kind of newspaper it is to be, the sort of public it is to aim for, and the policies it will in general support must rest mainly with those who own it.

Mainly but not entirely, for a newspaper is more than a piece of property, it is a living personality with a character and tradition deriving not only from those who own it or edit it but from its readers, from the interests it has historically served, and from the community of which it is a part, a fact . . . recognised by some proprietors through the formal instrument of trust deeds and articles of association. This double responsibility is especially true of those newspapers that serve a specific local community, nourished, as C.P. Scott said of them, 'by its resources, reflecting in a thousand ways its spirit and its interests', so that they 'in a real sense belong to it'. To alter the character of such a paper for reasons solely of increased profit, or to buy and sell it as though it were no more than a piece of merchandise without regard to the purposes and policies that have won for it its special place in the community, is an abrogation of the true responsibilities of newspaper ownership, although one which some of those who have made large profits out of newspapers have found by no means uncongenial.

Free enterprise is a valuable bulwark of a free press. But the freedom of the press differs from, and ought always to be recognised as greater than, the simple freedom of an entrepreneur to do what he pleases with his own property. A journalist has commitments to the commercial interests of those who employ him. But he has other loyalties also and these embrace the whole relationship of a newspaper to its public.

This is equally so whether the character of a paper derives from the authoritative discussion of public affairs or from its power to interest and entertain a wide variety of readers whose concern with public affairs is limited and intermittent. The influence of a newspaper on its readers derives not only from its expressed opinions but from its daily selection of news, the honesty of its reporting, the weight of its headlines, the values it emphasises in its features, the whole picture of the world and what is important in it that it daily presents to those who read it. By the very nature of daily newspaper production these depend more upon the editor and his staff than on anyone else. The editor is legally responsible for all that appears in the paper he edits; his moral responsibility is not less. He ought not to be allowed to escape it. But he ought also to be put in a position to sustain it in the public interest no less than his own.

The correct working relationship between a newspaper editor and his proprietor or publisher is not easy to define. It has been much discussed, although less so in Britain than in some other countries. In Norway the leading journalists' associations have defined the correct relationship as one that, within the broad framework of policy laid down for a paper by its owners and mandatory on it by reason of its traditions, gives the editor 'complete freedom to maintain his own opinions even though they may not in some cases be shared by the publisher or management' and that places upon him 'the entire responsibility for the editorial content of the paper' . . .

Much the same is true in Sweden . . . A number of Dutch papers have similar provisions in their company statutes requiring that so long as he holds office the editor shall have absolute independence in his decisions on the editorial contents of the paper.

In Britain independence in the control of editorial policy is similarly guaranteed to the editor of the *Manchester Guardian* under the Scott Trust . . .

Such independence is far from belonging to the editors of most great commercial newspaper enterprises. Nor, since their purpose and the relations they have with their readers are so different, would it be wholly appropriate. Yet . . . the diminution in the status of the editor to no more than a paid servant of proprietorial interests, the mere tool of other men's whims and financial appetites, that has accompanied a good deal of the commercialisation of the last half century or so runs dangerously counter to the public interest and is contrary to the traditional role of journalism in public life.

The journalist is at once freer and more vulnerable than the barrister, the solicitor, the doctor. Freer because he belongs to a more open profession that recruits men and women of diverse experience through many different doors and must be able to do so if it is to maintain its true character; more vulnerable because he is a wage-earner dependent for the most part on one employer. Yet his professional responsibilities to the public are not less than theirs . . . the preservation of the strictest ethical and professional standards in the press is no less important to society than in their case. And because he is dependent, to an extent they are not, upon the goodwill of a single employer, the journalist may find himself less able than they to resist pressures that would reduce them.

The journalist ought to accept and ought to be required to accept standards of professional integrity morally not less mandatory than those of the barrister, the solicitor or the doctor. But what is required in their case to safeguard the public against professional malpractice is required in his case not only for this reason, important though it is, but also to provide the journalist himself with a safeguard against those pressures to which one who is dependent upon a single master may find himself vulnerable: a professional power to set against, and if necessary act as a counter-balance to, the immense and growing power of financial control in the newspaper industry.

Note

1   This extract is taken from *Dangerous Estate: The Anatomy of Newspapers* (1957). Williams became a journalist at the age of 17, rising to the post of city editor on the *Sunday Express*. He joined the *Daily Herald* in 1929, becoming editor in 1936. He was also a broadcaster with the BBC during this period. He disagreed with the *Herald*'s proprietor, Lord Southwood, over the paper's approach to the fierce circulation 'wars' of the 1930s, and he left the editorship in 1940. After working first for the Ministry of Information and later as public relations adviser to the prime minister, Clement Attlee, he returned to journalism with the *Observer*, *News Chronicle* and *New Statesman* and to broadcasting.

Chapter 15

James Cameron

JOURNALISM
A trade

I HAD WRITTEN HUNDREDS OF THOUSANDS, probably millions, of words of this kind or that, and broadcast probably even more[1] . . . I was being paid quite a lot of money; about half of what was being attributed to me. I found it very difficult to understand why. I did not subscribe to the notion that it was the function of a newspaper man to traffic wholly in the eternal verities and to change the world by the impact of divine enlightenment; nevertheless it seemed to me that I was skidding about rather aimlessly on the surface of something that ought to be doing a trifle more than it did. My father in his solemn moments had spoken often about the implications of the profession of journalism; I knew what he meant but realised the fallacy of the phrase.

This was one of the many misunderstandings that are brought about by talking about the profession of journalism. Journalism is not and never has been a profession; it is a trade, or a calling, that can be practised in many ways, but it can never be a profession since its practice has neither standards nor sanctions. There are no minimum requirements of scholarship nor credentials before a man can call himself a journalist (very fortunately for me); there is no formal body to discipline those in breach of its non-existent code of rules . . . there is no cohesion of intention nor association of purpose. This may well be a good thing, since while this flexibility and permissiveness gives entry to a number of dubious oddballs it equally does not exclude many valuable and original people. It is fatuous, however, to compensate for our insecurity by calling ourselves members of a profession; it is both pretentious and disabling; we are at out best craftsmen, and that is by no means an ignoble thing to be.

I am no great propagandist of the virtues or values of the press; nevertheless I hold its functions in the most jealous of consideration. It is certainly the case that most politicians and even more officials forget that in a democratic society the theoretical master of events is the people. This is indeed a great illusion, nevertheless it is possible to argue that the reporter engaged in serious affairs must be the people's eyes and ears; he must be the instrument associating people's government with people's opinion. Not even the most articulate and charismatic political leader can make an impact on democratic opinion without communication; he can do no more than invoke a special public attitude towards facts already made known to the public. Opinion is made, even created, by the continual pressure of a wild variety of facts, or semi-facts, which vary between the banal and the cosmic, all of which bear in some way on the human situation. How this charivaria of information is transmuted into public opinion is a most mysterious thing, since every newspaper accepts that while many of its subscribers never read the sports pages, for instance, great numbers never look at anything else. It can only be explained in terms of certain atomic experiments in physical laboratories, where effects are wrought by the effect on the mass of a constant exposure to particles, in this case facts. I have rarely heard a more elaborate and pompous definition of journalism than this, but for some reason it seems to work.

It is also the case that in what is called the American democracy the role of the reporter is significantly different from that of, say, the British. In Britain, both executive and legislative responsibility is vested in parliament. It is accepted that the Opposition has exercised responsibility in the past and may in the future; they have on the whole access to the relevant data of affairs; their debates are carried out in a fairly public dialogue. It is the business of the British press to reflect and communicate this, but not necessarily to initiate it.

In the United States, on the other hand, there is no framework for national debate within the government . . . This alone has created a situation in which the only form of national debate is the press – not wholly by editorialising, but by the continual presentation of information and argument from all angles of every issue. The system is without shape or direction, and is on the whole in my view very casually performed; it is nevertheless the American newspaper man's extremely important share in the process of what, for want of a more precise word, we call democracy. I doubt whether more than a handful of American journalists so define or recognise that function, any more than most British journalists accept their peripheral role in society. British journalism at its best is literate and lightweight and fundamentally ineffectual; American journalism at its best is ponderous and excellent and occasionally anaesthetic. After working a great deal in both areas it seems to me that Britain cannot match America's best but incomparably transcends America's norm . . . The *New York Times* is the best and worst newspaper on earth, a daily monument to the sloppy and extravagant simplification of the overdone: the *Daily Mirror* is the worst and best newspaper, a gymnastic in the dedicated technical expertise of the persuasive non-think. I have worked for them both, but I cannot yet determine which I like least.

I myself have always felt myself a passing indifferent reporter, since it has never interested me to write about anything in which I did not feel myself somehow engaged, however academically; I was always deeply bored at having to define occasions that involved values I did not understand . . . latterly I concluded that the only advantage of maturity and a fairly high price was to indulge one's prejudices. I cannot remember how often I have been challenged, and especially in America, for disregarding the fundamental tenet of honest journalism, which is objectivity. This argument has arisen over the years, but of course it reached a fortissimo – long years after this – when I had been to Hanoi, and returned obsessed with the notion that I had no professional justification left if I did not at least try to make the point that North Viet Nam, despite all official Washington arguments to the contrary, was inhabited by human beings . . . and that to destroy their country and their lives with high explosive and petroleum jelly was no way to cure them of their defects . . . This conclusion, when expressed in printed or television journalism, was generally held to be, if not downright mischievous, then certainly 'non-objective', within the terms of reference of a newspaper man, on the grounds that it was proclaimed as a point of view . . . To this of course there could be no answer whatever, except that objectivity in some circumstances is both meaningless and impossible. I still do not see how a reporter attempting to define a situation involving some sort of ethical conflict can do it with sufficient demonstrable neutrality to fulfil some arbitrary concept of 'objectivity'. It never occurred to me, in such a situation, to be other than subjective, and as obviously so as I could manage to be. I may not always have been satisfactorily balanced; I always tended to argue that objectivity was of less importance than the truth, and that the reporter whose technique was informed by no opinion lacked a very serious dimension. It can easily be misrepresented. Yet as I see it – and it seems to me the simplest of disciplines – the journalist is obliged to present his attitude as vigorously and persuasively as he can, insisting that it *is* his attitude, to be examined and criticised in the light of every contrary argument, which he need not accept but must reveal. There is a way of being scrupulous about this which every thinking journalist understands. He has at least the resources to present his liberal principles for consideration and debate, and to argue the basic importance of moral independence – which includes, to be sure, the need to question *him*. Surely the useful end is somehow to encourage an attitude of mind that will challenge and criticise automatically, thus to destroy or weaken the built-in advantages of all propaganda and special pleading – even the journalist's own. The energetic argument for liberal thought must by definition, I should imagine, embody that machinery for its own conquest, since it presents itself as equally vulnerable.

This was a matter of consideration for me for a long time; I have to say that while it brought about some interludes of great doubt and uneasiness, it disadvantaged me much less than I had expected. It would have reinforced several theories and prejudices if I could have recorded a long history of professional persecution; in general the contrary was the case. I knew no other way of doing the work I had to do; if the newspaper trade had objected I would doubtless have starved. I did indeed go hungry from time to time, but thereafter I prospered greatly, at least intermittently. And since this was on my terms, I have to reason that this argued a greater flexibility in the industry than in me.

At the same time I have struggled for years against the conviction that my whole intellectual position was, if not false, then ambiguous. I am aware of the world in which I live, and of the character of my own life. I am immensely and continually conscious of a world of nuclear bombs, of vast hunger, of curable injustice, of a meretricious press and cheapjack television, of perilous and apparently endless international division, of unreasonable cruelty and suffering for which almost nobody cares, and of my own silly efforts to make money to provide me with irrelevant comforts or necessities like drink and to ensure some measure of security for my family.

Note

1   This extract is from *Point of Departure: Experiment in Biography* (1967). Shortly after the period he is writing about, when he had been appointed 'the first roving correspondent of the *Daily Express*', Cameron resigned from the paper over an attack on a Labour minister in the *Evening Standard*, and the following year he left *Picture Post* after its editor, Tom Hopkinson, was sacked over the handling of Cameron's reporting of the Korean war. Cameron then spent nearly ten years as a roving reporter with the *News Chronicle*. In all, he wrote for more than a dozen publications, and later contributed a weekly column to the *Guardian*. He was also a regular broadcaster, and in the 1970s became something of a television celebrity.

Chapter 16

Nicholas Tomalin

STOP THE PRESS I WANT TO GET ON

THE ONLY QUALITIES ESSENTIAL for real success in journalism are ratlike cunning, a plausible manner, and a little literary ability.[1] If you look at the jewels of the profession, you will see that this must be so . . . Some are more literary and less cunning than others; some certainly are more plausible; but it is these three shared qualifications that make all of them recognisably of the same breed.

The ratlike cunning is needed to ferret out and publish things that people don't want to be known (which is – and always will be – the best definition of news). The plausible manner is useful for surviving while this is going on, helpful with the entertaining presentation of it, and even more useful in later life when the successful journalist may have to become a successful executive on his newspaper. The literary ability is of obvious use.

Other qualities are helpful, but not diagnostic. These include a knack with telephones, trains and petty officials; a good digestion and a steady head; total recall; enough idealism to inspire indignant prose (but not enough to inhibit detached professionalism); a paranoid temperament; an ability to believe passionately in second-rate projects; well-placed relatives; good luck; the willingness to betray, if not friends, acquaintances; a reluctance to understand too much too well (because *tout comprendre c'est tout pardonner* and *tout pardonner* makes dull copy); an implacable hatred of spokesmen, administrators, lawyers, public relations men and all those who would rather purvey words than policies; and the strength of character to lead a disrupted life without going absolutely haywire. The capacity to steal other people's ideas and phrases – that one about ratlike cunning was invented by my colleague Murray Sayle – is also invaluable.

None of these things makes the difference between a good journalist and a bad one. Goodness and badness in journalism are difficult to define, and depend roughly on the same qualities as they do anywhere else.

It is more difficult to get into journalism proper (by which, I'm afraid, I mean metropolitan national journalism) than it is to succeed once you are there. Once in (given the ratlike, plausible and literary knacks), things are reasonably easy. But to get in, at the right level and the right time to display your talents, is extraordinarily difficult. This explains the widespread resentment and bewilderment felt by non-journalists who feel — frequently quite justifiably — that they could do as well, if not better, than those within the charmed circle.

Anyone who has got into the club, however, has no right to complain. His talents are constantly and publicly on display to his colleagues and his customers. He needs no formal system of grading, no office politics, to demonstrate how good, or bad, he is . . .

There are three reasons why the club is so difficult to join. Firstly, it is because journalism (or 'the communications industry' as aspirants like to call it) is now the fashionable profession in this country . . . it is obvious that the old prestige careers like the civil service, Foreign Office and even politics offer no glamorous prospects. The only enjoyable job is to stand back and earn a living describing our [the UK's] predicament.

Secondly, it is because there are surprisingly few good journalistic jobs available. Thirdly, it is because journalism is so complex and various that editors and publishers usually don't really know what they want . . .

Your greatest test, therefore, will be getting your first good job. Persistence is probably the most valuable quality here. If you read the industry's brochures you may imagine employers are searching for new talent, winnowing out contenders, and selecting the finest. In an intermittent undisciplined way this does go on occasionally, but the best editors are far too busy editing to bother with it. In practice what happens is that a constant stream of applicants are interviewed and forgotten, and no one thinks about hiring until a gap or a sacking occurs. Then the first plausible candidate to turn up gets the job.

Friends can help. The best Fleet Street newspapers are not the open-ended institutions they like to appear, but feudal fiefdoms all bound up in intimate friendships and shared values. All good publications are communities essentially cliquish and inward-looking; the best editors are good because they have the most talented friends. Therefore you need to cultivate like-mindedness, and pals at court . . .

An even more powerful help is a famous mother or father. Journalism, being fashionable, is a privilege profession. In its present state it shows many of the aspects of the aristocracy, and lineal descent is one of them . . .

However, the best — and more honest — way of all to get into the club is to offer a unique selling proposition. You can get a really good, exclusive story. Discover something that no one else could discover, write it down well, and take it to the correct man. If he wants it, he will subsequently want you, provided you don't sell yourself short.

If this is an unsatisfactory situation, it is because journalists are always better at describing than doing, at telling others what is wrong than in practising what we preach. We are also oddly incompetent at examining ourselves. We are like Englishmen with our tender – and false – stereotype of ourselves as rough-hewn, cynical, full of endearing faults, incomprehensible to outsiders, but at heart absolutely splendid. We are like Jews in our love of telling long, lugubrious and insulting stories about ourselves, and our fierce resentment of anyone else doing so. We are like doctors: we make the worst, most touchy and litigious subjects of other people's journalism (which is strange, because we are forever writing, fascinatedly, about ourselves in the fond pretence that others are as interested in our parochial problems as we are). We are obsessed with our professionalism, and convinced that there is not only a mystery to our craft, but a whole spectrum of laboriously learned techniques. We demand an apprenticeship, examination results, and years of drudgery before we allow entrants a proper chance to show their talents, and yet virtually all the really successful (and really good) journalists have somehow or other managed to escape such a cumbrous ordeal.

There are, of course, difficult techniques to master. An apprenticeship is essential. But one year, or even six months' hard work, should be enough for anyone to learn all the practical techniques necessary. And this, in a just world, should be done by being in contact with the brightest minds and best institutions in journalism, that is to say, in Fleet Street . . .

A man who has served his apprenticeship on the *Frensham Clarion* is, according to orthodox teachings, meant to have had a far better training. He knows in his bones the correct form of address for a mayor, the legal intricacies of probate courts . . . and always to get the number of dead into his first subordinate clause. With such a superb start, he won't *necessarily* spend his life in Frensham, but he is in terrible danger of doing so unless he unlearns it all in favour of the totally different, and no doubt disreputable, disciplines demanded by Fleet Street newspapers. Officially he is imbibing that precious indefinable thing 'a news sense' at the grass roots. But he may not immediately realise that local news like weddings, funerals, road-widening schemes, magistrates' courts, and aldermanic elections isn't really news at all. It's information, vitally necessary to that local society and to sell the local newspaper, but in real terms frivolous and trivial, properly fit only to be transmitted in some data-processing fashion, by computer.

While trotting round the flower shows the apprentice will have it continuously drummed into his head that the journalist's job is to transmit something called 'facts'. C.P. Scott's antique motto 'Comment is free, facts are sacred' will be inscribed in pokerwork above his apprentice desk.

This idea is adequate only at the data-processing level of journalism. For anyone more talented than a news agency man, the idea of a 'fact' is so simplistic it is a lie. Facts are not sacred; the moment any reporter begins to write his story he has selected some and not others, and has distorted the situation. The moment he composes the 'facts' into a narrative form he has commented on the situation. The idea of 'facts', to be shoved at readers like little lumps, is best forgotten very swiftly.

To say a journalist's job is to record facts is like saying an architect's job is to lay bricks – true, but missing the point. A journalist's real function, at any rate his required talent, is the *creation of interest*. A good journalist takes a dull, or specialist, or esoteric situation, and makes newspaper readers want to know about it. By doing so he both sells newspapers and educates people. It is a noble, dignified and useful calling. (All this is not, of course, to say that a journalist should ever be inaccurate, or false to the truth as he sees it. He must create interest while being truthful . . .)

The most valuable lesson a small local newspaper can teach an apprentice is that its most interesting contents, which sell the paper, are the classified advertisements. Even less real journalism can be gathered from schools of journalism, or from some academic course.

The only good teaching institutions in journalism are, I repeat, good newspapers . . .

To attack the idea of a comprehensive training scheme in journalism, and to assert that really good reporters and editors are born and not made, is difficult and dangerous. It appears to derogate a lot of brilliant people. It also smacks of arrogance, dilettantism, and a kind of whimsical disregard of honest craftsmanship . . .

The trouble is that journalism in Britain is crucially divided. Half, or three-quarters, or perhaps even seven-eighths of it, is a service industry, shovelling out perishable facts and names just as the United Dairies deliver milk. The other half, or fragment, is a collection of wayward anarchistic talents responding to, and usually opposing, the society which they are supposed to report.

It serves no purpose to pretend that these two traditions aren't in many ways opposed to each other. No one denies life is tougher, and more *real*, for foot soldiers and general practitioners than it is for generals and specialists. No one denies this is so for the yearly batch of . . . trainees. But it really is a nonsense, born of a vague egalitarian urge to improve the public relations image of an unjust world, to pretend that they are cleverer, or even man for man more valuable, than the men who try to be brilliant on their wits alone.

Note

1   This article appeared in the *Sunday Times Magazine* (26 October 1969). Tomalin's first jobs in journalism after leaving Cambridge in the 1950s were as a gossip columnist and diary writer on the *Daily Express*, *Evening Standard* and *Sunday Times*. In 1967 he became literary editor of the *New*

Statesman. He also established himself as a special correspondent, particularly covering the Viet Nam war for the *Sunday Times*. He went to Israel to cover the Yom Kippur war for the paper in 1973 and was killed in a rocket attack.

PART FOUR

1970 and after

Introduction to part four

■   Tom O'Malley

T HIS SECTION CONTAINS READINGS from, or about, the period after 1970. Although not apparent in 1970, the next three decades ushered in new developments in technology which, when combined with changes in the political and economic context of the media industries, helped to reshape journalism and to intensify debates about ownership, standards and ethics (McNair 1994).

The details of these developments have been mapped by a number of writers (Curran and Seaton 1991; Tunstall 1996). In 1970 the long economic boom which had powered consumer spending, industrial growth and a growing sense of cultural and political confidence amongst workers was about to end. By the middle of the decade the NUJ was lobbying the Labour government (1974–9) to introduce a post-entry closed shop in the industry, a move which was fiercely opposed by managers and proprietors. The appointment of a Royal Commission on the Press (1974–7) in one sense reflected the strength of pressures for reform, from within the Labour movement, on the Labour government. At the same time proprietors were demanding changes in working practices and technology to restore profitability, a view they expressed forcefully to the Royal Commission which reported in 1977. The intensity of the mid-decade recession, and the gradual, forced, retreat of the Labour government from its key social policies after 1976, was accompanied by a sustained ideological assault on the Left and trade unionism from the national press.

The election, in May 1979, of a Conservative government, under Margaret Thatcher, marked a turning point. Thatcher led her Party to three consecutive victories, in 1979, 1983 and 1987, before her mishandling of the economy, of local taxation and of the question of policy on Europe, plus her widely disliked authoritarian style, precipitated a coup in the Parliamentary Conservative party in 1990. From 1990 until 1997 her legacy was sustained by John Major, who managed to secure a fourth election victory for the Party in 1992.

These Conservative governments pursued a policy of encouraging private ownership in the media and other industries, as well as legislating to restrict the autonomy and power of trade unions. They were also characterised by an authoritarian attitude on questions of official secrecy, using the law to ban trade unions at government communications facilities, to seek the imprisonment of civil servants who leaked information and to justify police raids on the BBC.

There were a number of developments in these years that merit attention. The pattern of concentration of ownership in the national and local press, already established by 1970, continued (Williams 1996). In the 1980s the government's failure to deploy its powers under the 1974 Fair Trading Act allowed a series of take-overs of national papers by Rupert Murdoch, a stalwart supporter of Mrs Thatcher. In the same period the government introduced new policies which restructured public service broadcasting along more commercial lines, by forcing change within the BBC and by passing the 1990 Broadcasting Act (O'Malley 1994). During the 1990s newspaper and broadcasting companies lobbied the government successfully, to allow greater opportunities to take each other over. A set of more liberal ownership rules were enshrined in the 1996 Broadcasting Act (Williams 1996).

One of the most important things affecting journalists in this period was technological change. In 1970 all national newspapers were using nineteenth century, hot metal, technology to print papers. This involved employing large numbers of printers and compositors. By the late 1990s all national papers used computer technology in news gathering, data base compilation, page make up, printing and distribution. In broadcasting the diffusion of cable, video, internet, and satellite technologies raised, as Bromley discusses in this volume, new questions about what a journalist was. For printers the introduction of new technology, marked by the disputes at Warrington (1983) and Wapping (1986), meant the loss of jobs and industrial power within the national press.

The mid-1980s was a period when some on the Left and many on the Right predicted that the spread of new media technologies would lead to a new information utopia, with the flowering of a range of new newspapers and forms of mass communication. But, in the press, the power of the main companies which were established by the mid-1980s was consolidated and little evidence has emerged to suggest that the diffusion of new technologies in the electronic media has led to the development of new, challenging, diverse forms of journalism and mass communications. It has led to the spread of more commercial media services, in satellite, cable and computer based technologies, which in turn have posed new sets of problems for regulators (Collins and Murroni 1996).

It was control over the implementation of new technologies which allowed them to be used as a tool of industrial restructuring in the UK print industry. The Wapping dispute was followed by an assault on unionisation within the industry. Casualisation developed within the broadcast media, as new technologies were deployed to restructure production around commissioning and outsourcing rather than in-house production. This, in turn, had implications for the development of journalism, in so far as the critical tradition of mass broadcast journalism in the UK was based, in part, upon continuity of employment. Equally, it had implications for equal opportunities policies which became harder to implement in a casualised, underpaid workforce.

Journalism, across print and the electronic media, was restructured in the 1980s and 1990s, in ways hardly foreseen during the 1950s and 1960s. Yet, in the area of standards, there was some continuity. Just as questions of standards occupied the Royal Commission in 1947, so they occupied politicians and journalists in the 1980s and 1990s. The problems of inaccuracy, misrepresentation and intrusion into privacy, epitomised by the aggressive, cynical, populism of Rupert Murdoch's *Sun*, stimulated backbench MPs to introduce measures designed to protect privacy and to grant a Right of Reply to individuals on matters of factual inaccuracy (McNair 1994). The gulf between the popular and serious journalism in the press has arguably become more pronounced in these years (Sparks 1991). In broadcasting there has been a tendency towards redefining journalism as personalised, infotainment programming. The tension, so apparent since the nineteenth century between commerce and ethics, between the moral high ground and the gutter, remained a potent source of disruption within journalism in the period after 1970.

Doig's article maps the interaction between journalistic practice, ownership and government after the 1970s. He raises the question of how much investigative journalism was possible after the changes of the 1980s and 1990s and, in so doing, touches on a central tenet of liberal press theory. The concept of the press as watchdog, so close to the heart of nineteenth century theorists of the Fourth Estate, underpins investigative journalism; the decline of this kind of journalism is therefore a matter of some concern. Equally, Gall's study of the micro politics of industrial relations at the *Mirror* in the early 1990s is critical of both managers and trade unions and raises questions about the social purpose of newspapers – profit or public good? – and of the crucial link between strong trade unionism within the industry and the sustenance of a critical, investigative edge in journalism. More studies of these issues would be illuminating.

The sense of crisis in journalism in the 1980s is expressed in the founding editorial of the *British Journalism Review*. In summarising concerns over ownership, ethics, press freedom, the lack of an analytical culture in journalism, the inability of journalism to act like a profession and the malign influence of advertising, the editorial echoes well established themes, but with a sense of urgency which stemmed from the rapid changes of the previous decade. Its stress on the need for a reinvigoration of journalistic efforts to raise standards echoes the strong preference for voluntary reform which has dominated journalism in this century.

One commonly held view amongst academics and commentators is that Rupert Murdoch's *Sun* has contributed most to the decline in standards of journalism in the last third of the century. Its overt support for right wing populist politics on matters of defence, industrial relations, foreign policy, gender, race and broadcasting has been widely criticised. (Hollingsworth 1986; Searle 1989; O'Malley 1994). The extract from Grose is, in many ways, a standard defence of the paper. Grose stresses its popular appeal and illustrates its closeness to its readers by describing the use of phone-in hotlines. Her breezy prose, which offers no explanations and expects few queries, describes the *Sun*'s obsession with Royalty in the 1980s and 1990s, as if the paper were engaged in a public service. The populism and cynicism of this type of journalism is not unique and is a central part of the long history of journalism. The *Sun* still awaits a major study.

One area of journalism which changed rapidly after 1970 was local and regional journalism. Franklin and Murphy, pointing to a trend established by the mid-1970s, outline the decline in the number of published titles and the impact of new technology and concentration on the numbers and style of publication. This decline in the presence of local news in the diet of information consumed by the public has interesting implications, and should refocus attention on the increasing centralisation of news production and the relative importance of the national rather than the local media as sources of news and information.

Petley argues in his article on columnists that the national press is profoundly conservative in its content. His study shows how columnists in the 1990s articulated conservative social and political values. Columnists pronounced on a great deal of topics, often with the flimsiest of qualifications. He shows how they used the idea of commonsense to define issues according to their right of centre, often ill informed, perspectives. In a sense Petley's piece illustrates, in detail, the texture of the dominant conservative voice in national print journalism in the 1990s.

The question of what voices might succeed in a world influenced by the internet is explored by Doull. He points to the problems posed by the net for journalists, not least of all the fact that it consists of lists within lists, and that it is very difficult to conceive of what kind of an audience is out there ready to read their work. He celebrates the net's potential as a research tool, and insists that practitioners will have to take account of this technology in the next century. Doull provides a useful starting point for debate about the utopianism and superficiality which dominates many public discussions about the impact of technological change on work and culture, and can be read with profit in association with Williams (1974), Winston (1986) and Forester (1990).

References

Collins, R. and Murroni, C. (1996) *New Media New Policies*, Cambridge: Polity.

Curran, J. and Seaton, J. (1991) *Power Without Responsibility* (4th edn), London: Routledge.

Forester, T. (ed.) (1990) *Computers in the Human Context*, Oxford: Basil Blackwell.

Hollingsworth, M. (1986) *The Press and Political Dissent*, London: Pluto.

McNair, B. (1994) *News and Journalism in the UK*, London: Routledge.

O'Malley, T. (1994) *Closedown? The BBC and Government Broadcasting Policy 1979–1992*, London: Pluto.

Searle, C. (1989) *Your Daily Dose: Racism and The Sun*, London: Campaign For Press and Broadcasting Freedom.

Sparks, C. (1991) 'Goodbye, Hildy Johnson: the vanishing "serious press"', in P. Dahlgren and C. Sparks (eds) (1991) *Communication and Citizenship*, London: Routledge.

Tunstall, J. (1996) *Newspaper Power: The New National Press in Britain*, Oxford: Clarendon Press.

Williams, G. (1996) *Britain's Media – How they are Related* (2nd edn), London: Campaign For Press and Broadcasting Freedom.

Williams, R. (1974) *Television, Technology and Cultural Form*, London: Fontana.

Winston, B (1986) *Misunderstanding Media*, London: Routledge & Kegan Paul.

Chapter 17

Arnold Wesker

JOURNEY INTO JOURNALISM

T HE JOURNALIST KNOWS HIS WORLD is among the least perfect of
all imperfect worlds.[1] Most are raring to get out and write books – the
best of them do, frustrated by small canvases and the butterfly life of their
hard earned thoughts and words. 'Conveyor belt work, harsh, destructive,
written in a hurry. I'm increasingly irritated by the necessary approxima-
tions of journalism.' They can't really be called callous just because they
need the relief of their own humour. 'Jesus! What a background I had! Were
you born in a ghetto? You were? Really? That's true? God, how I resent my
father for being so rich. All the best people were born in a ghetto; look at
Wesker, that's why he was born with a silver typewriter in his mouth. If
only my father had bought us a ghetto, one we could go to for weekends,
now that would have been something!'

Yet, despite such disarming wit I can't rid myself of the suspicion that
they seem to *relish* the process of what they expose more than they *care* about
what is exposed. A very dubious mechanism is at work when such a large
number of people assume for themselves the self-righteous responsibility of
interfering to protect society against others whom *they* have decided are interfering and self-righteous. Especially when their own definition of their duty
to investigate 'secret and well protected misbehaviour' is such a boomerang.
Journalism may not be a secret activity but it is certainly one of the most
'well protected'. Which editor would allow an investigatory profile of his
newspaper to appear in his own columns? Certainly a gentleman's agreement
prevents them printing damaging information about each other. The sports
department once printed two stories about how *the Sun* manufactured a sports
story. The editor of *the Sun* wrote to his counterpart on *the Sunday Times* and
said 'lay off'.

All motives, even for the serious journalist, are suspect except his own. (I'm not referring to the anonymous little Farts of Fleet Street which every newspaper seems obliged to produce in gossip or comment columns all over the world.) And this makes him like the vicious prison officer whom society also justifies because he appears to be guarding society against its 'undesirables'. Yet, though someone must guard prisons, one is constantly tempted to wonder what kind of mentality opts for the job of ensuring men are deprived of their freedom. Similarly, though someone must guard society from charlatans, exploiters and political fraudulence, yet, one wonders, how carefully are those guards chosen for their wise ability to distinguish between honesty and dishonesty? How 'pure' can the soul be that traffics in human blemishes? And, further, are the pressures of journalism, profit-motivated as they must finally be, conducive to the exercise of perspicacious judgments? Like gladiatorial arenas, newspapers claim to know their audience's taste for blood. Hence little is celebrated, there is no conflict in that act; crucifixion is more dramatic. Although one famous columnist points out how journalism is a flat communicator: 'you can't see the face of the man writing the print. Television is much more alive. You can measure what's being said by the manner and face that's saying it. That's *real* conflict – vivid.'

But the soul, however insensitive, wearies of destruction; carnage must as well as 'love itself have rest'. An individual, an organisation, a society has a tone of voice, through it you can guess at its nature. What sort of nature lives in the arid, hollow tone of a hunter's horn behind which a smile leers? Society may wish to have its watchdogs, but continuous barking is a noise which, like the drip of a tap, can drive out all feeling with its bleak monotony; and sometimes innocent children are savaged.

But if we look at the difference between literature and journalism it becomes even more complicated. Fact may not be truth, and truth, if it has any chance of emerging, may rest in the need to interpret those facts, and both processes, the fictional and the journalistic, are human and thus imperfect; therefore I must concede as a playwright that art, like journalism, is presumptuous. But has journalism's infinitely smaller canvas the wrong kind of discipline to allow any but a superficial exploration of the complex subjects it chooses to handle? You feel you can argue with literature, temper its vicarious experience with your own. Journalism intimidates because its currency appears to be irrefutable fact and the great myth about himself and his profession to which the journalist succumbs is that he is engaged mainly in the communication of objective fact. But if we view journalism as a chemical compound and break it down we would find the ingredient 'fact' existed in only small quantities and even then lumbered by human impurities.

| Journalism | = | Investigation or Information or Comment. |
| Investigation | = | 'Facts' conveniently or maliciously leaked + (maybe) the evidence of documents – both selected and interpreted by journalists. |

Information	=	Selected 'facts' + description, vivid or feeble depending upon individual powers of perception.
Comment	=	Personal opinions in leaders, reviews, features and gossip columns.

Yet even at the level of fact, which is not a discovery to be sneered at, the manner and amount of research done is questionable; the newspaper's library of old clippings is still the journalist's incestuous bed of primary knowledge; myths, prejudices, distortions and inaccuracies are perpetuated through his continual recourse to that brown-papered past of old copy. The cigarette packet warns that smoking can be a danger to health; no newspaper carries the warning, daily, that 'selective attention to data herein contained can be a danger to your view of the world'.

Still, someone who is not a journalist should be worried about writing a play with such a setting; it could end up contrived. And yet, there is a special part of the artist's experience which is not contrived: he or she has been the journalist's subject, frequently – as have been many public figures, and it is said of the sadist that only his victim truly understands him. In the end, the journalist, as recipient in a very special way of human experience, is the magnified personality in which drama deals. Though only engaged in handing on fragments of information he or she does so under the apparent omnipotence of daily print, which exaggerates his importance and tempts him to exaggerate pronouncements. The dilemma begins when he finds he can only inform without revealing, which leads him to simplify what is complex and confuse it for clarification; in the process he erodes ardours and enthusiasms, deflates egos so that not vanity but self-confidence cracks, and distorts our image of the world. His tragedy begins when each 'god' he self-righteously topples chips away at his own self respect; the damage he does to others destroys a part of himself, and that's a very familiar state; no writer could find himself alien in that sad territory.

Note

1   This extract is from *Journey into Journalism: A Very Personal Account in Four Parts* (1977). This was published five years after Wesker spent some weeks at the *Sunday Times* researching for his *The Journalists, A Triptych* (1979). The delay in publication was due to a dispute between Wesker and a number of *Sunday Times* journalists over the veracity of the account. Wesker, the author of seven volumes of plays (Penguin), has recently published his autobiography, *As Much as I Dare* (Century).

Chapter 18

Alan Doig

THE DECLINE OF INVESTIGATORY JOURNALISM

Introduction

IN BRITAIN THE 1970S APPEARED TO BE the peak of the power of the media in investigating political and administrative corruption. The Poulson scandal – a major case of contract corruption that involved MPs, civil servants and dozens of local politicians – was pushed into public prominence by a range of publications and programmes and created an atmosphere of public concern – Harold Wilson, the Labour Opposition leader, was calling for 'nothing less than a full and open inquiry' as early as 1972 – during extensive police, parliamentary and official inquiries. Local newspapers and radio stations as well as national television companies and newspapers undertook investigations in the face of official secrecy, hostility and ignorance. Investigatory journalism became seen, certainly within the media industry, as a flagship activity.

From the advent of the Conservative Government in 1979 this activity has, with few exceptions, been in decline for a number of reasons, including significant structural changes in the ownership and organisation of the media industry, conflict with governments, and the use of the law and other means to discourage reporting. Since the 'back-to-basics' campaign and the subsequent media criticism of the performance of the Major government, from cash-for-questions and the Scott inquiry, however, the media may be regaining its taste for investigatory journalism but, in the light of the reasons for its decline during the 1980s, however, it is debatable whether investigatory journalism will continue at the level and with the prominence that it did in its heyday.

From exposé to investigatory journalism

The coincidence of changes in societal attitudes – a questioning of the values and interests of the political system, the growth of self-expression and individual rights – with the collapse of the Conservative government in 1964 had several important consequences. The clash with the government over the Vassall spy affair resulted in two journalists being jailed for refusing to reveal their sources by a tribunal which most editors were convinced had been established as a device to punish their investigations into the 'erosion of democracy' and the 'predatoriness of officialdom' (Doig 1990: 61–72). The subsequent enthusiasm of the press in their pursuit of the Profumo case shortly after the Vassall affair revealed their capacity for relentless inquiries into what had been the private world of politicians and the impact of newspaper reporting on public opinion and political events. Despite the Denning inquiry's conclusion that 'scandalous information about well-known people has become a marketable commodity' and that (in an early reference to cheque-book journalism) newspapers were 'trafficking in scandal for reward' (Denning 1963), newspapers were quick to learn that exposé journalism, particularly sex-and-politics stories, was an exploitable market with a receptive audience.

Exposé journalism is as old as newspapers themselves. What was new was its use from the 1960s at a national level, often by newspapers traditionally not used to such journalistic methods, and its role in being both a symptom of and a consequence of public concern at the activities and conduct in the political world. The overtly political and partisan press of the Victorian period had been steadily replaced by close ties between newspaper proprietors and senior politicians who shamelessly used each other to influence events and control the flow of information. At editorial level the development of the Lobby system (the provision of unattributable official information) and ministry briefings provided a necessary flow of stories at regular intervals. At one level, therefore, public or political issues could be presented or interpreted to reflect the wishes of the government of the day. At another, journalists and newspapers became increasingly dependent on official sources for news and increasingly disinclined to challenge those sources or seek alternative information.

One Victorian lesson – that sex, reputation and scandal sold newspapers (detailed reporting of divorce cases was a staple) – did not, however, fade away. The popular press always sustained that tradition, supposedly justified by societal values of respectability and propriety which governed the behaviour of those with public standing and professional responsibility. Thus, just as blackmailers found their victims among doctors, priests, school teachers, and magistrates (Hepworth 1975), so the popular press published stories on the indiscretions and misconduct of such people for the same reasons. One obvious example, and a traditional popular newspaper story, was any story involving the police and prostitutes. As the world of prostitution in London became more controlled by organised crime gangs and the protection of their activities became more institutionalised through bribery of the police (and the payments to the police spread up and through the ranks) so popular press crime journalists were expected to have a detailed knowledge of their field and to produce dramatic results ('crusading' journalists as they were termed). Given their readerships, however, their stories invariably focused on prostitutes and pimps, rather than on the police, and played up the sex and scandal aspects rather than the environment of corruption that tolerated their activities. While aware of the corruption, such journalists were also aware, as one Sunday paper reporter later said, that 'it would completely destroy my role to have my byline on a story knocking the police' (Chibnall 1977).

Real changes came during the 1960s when the serious newspapers began looking at the scandals *and* their contexts. Thus in 1963 the techniques of news-magazine reporting (such as more space and descriptive material) were employed on major stories such as the Rachman scandal to explain the background and structure of a ramshackle housing empire that employed dubious letting methods and accounting practices – a story that, with its sex-and-violence aspects and the social deprivation involved, attracted, for the first time, both serious as well as popular attention across the media. In 1969 two young journalists from *The Times* went one stage further and employed popular press techniques, using bugging devices, total secrecy and whole-page reporting, to allege that Metropolitan detectives were taking bribes and that there was evidence of widespread and institutionalised police corruption (Tompkinson 1982; Cox *et al.* 1977). The impact of articles in *The Times* sparked off concerted efforts to tackle police corruption among the CID, including the appointment of Sir Robert Mark as the Chief Commissioner who accepted the newspaper's decision to publish without prior warning – because its editor feared that the allegations would not be 'properly investigated' – to be 'at the time and in hindsight . . . absolutely right' (Mark 1979).

The growing awareness of the pervasiveness of corruption at a local and national level, and the impact of serious journalism devoted to investigations, thus brought together two complementary ingredients to encourage the growth of investigatory journalism – 'the vital combination for anything to happen was evidence of criminal activity and widespread publicity for the scandal', says *World In Action*'s former executive producer Ray Fitzwalter.

The golden days of investigatory journalism

In 1976 a member of the Royal Commission into Standards of Public Life stated that

> almost all the investigations that have led to prosecution have been sparked off either by *Private Eye* or by commercial television or by other branches of the media or by other unofficial bodies or individuals. They have not been initiated from any official source. Furthermore . . . the

police (not surprisingly) take the view that it is no part of their duties to seek out evidence of malpractice but only to start inquiries after information indicating corruption has been provided to them.

(Royal Commission 1976)

The Royal Commission was set up in December 1974 by the Labour government in response to the rising number of cases of corruption in the public sector and, especially, to the ramifications of the Poulson affair (Tomkinson and Gillard 1980; Fitzwalter and Taylor 1981). John Poulson was an architect who exploited contacts from every area in public life – contacts made through his political activities, his work, his masonic activities and social occasions – to obtain contracts for which he used any resource of his architectural firm to provide both rewards and incentives. The success of his firm and its emergence as a national organisation followed his recruitment of public relations companies run by T. Dan Smith, an energetic and ambitious former local Labour politician. Their campaign, organised and mapped out, was to seek building and design contracts for their various companies from local councils who had access to substantial capital and revenue funds for urban redevelopment during the 1960s and early 1970s.

Local politics in the 1960s and early 1970s was not an area of high public interest or participation, despite extensive powers and growing expenditure. Many local councils had been dominated by one party for a long period of time and run by a handful of members (and sometimes senior officers) who were also locked into other local power-bases – such as regional public bodies, trade union organisations, the magistracy – and who mixed with local business leaders, union organisers, newspaper editors, and senior police officers at official, social and recreational level. This integration of the local élites often led to the development of local cultures where influence-peddling, deal-making and bribery were the currency of a 'complex network of informal occupational codes of conduct and ambiguous professional relationships reflecting the subterranean values of that culture' (Chibnall and Saunders 1977: 51). Such practices were, in turn, reinforced and protected from outside scrutiny. Despite formal or notional national links or relationships – for example, trade union organisations, national supervision of police forces, combined ownership of national and local newspapers – territorial jealousy and collusive self-interest saw little information flowing vertically out of the locality or upwards within organisational structures (Murphy 1976).

Such apparent normality, compounded by a lack of information, a disinterest in the activities of local government and assumptions about its lack of political significance (in financial or decision-making terms), explains why, at the beginning of the affair, both the media and the Director of Public Prosecutions (DPP) were unaware of the longevity and pervasiveness of Poulson's network. The DPP later told the Royal Commission in 1976 that what gave 'cause for serious concern arising out of the Poulson–Dan Smith cases is the fact that corruption in particular areas can evidently be so widespread without discovery' (Doig 1984: 25). The *Sunday Times* wrote in 1972 that 'revelations at the bankruptcy hearing . . . have followed a simple journalistic rule: "scandals" in public life, once scented, grow in complexity according to the number of journalists investigating them. Yet the Poulson affair is, in fact, straightforward' (Doig 1983: 76).

The genesis of what turned out to be the somewhat complex Poulson affair lay in his bankruptcy which, until he appeared in court in 1972 to explain where the money had gone, had only attracted media interest first in the *Bradford Telegraph and Argus* and then in *Private Eye*, in articles written by Ray Fitzwalter (Fitzwalter 1973) and Paul Foot. The latter presciently noted that some people were 'praying that whatever happens to the Poulson empire its affairs will be conducted with the minimum of publicity, and that, if Mr Poulson goes down, he goes down alone', an eventuality that rapidly evaporated with the unravelling of the payments to, and the names of, prominent public figures – especially that of Reginald Maudling, unsuccessful runner-up to Ted Heath for leadership of the Conservative Party and, at the time, the Home Secretary.

For the inquisitive journalist there were, in addition to the activities of John Poulson, many similar stories around in local and national politics. In local government, the traditional patterns of politics in the North-East and South Wales – long-standing political party domination, entrenched autocratic political leadership, quiescent media – were repeated throughout the United Kingdom at a time when governments provided the legislative and financial framework for infrastructure development in, for example, housing and shopping centres. With no strategic regional or area plans, no overall coordinating policy, no firm controls on borrowing and expenditure, and no effective means of accountability or scrutiny, mismanagement, waste, fraud and corruption flourished. At a national level the TV programme *This Week* had already highlighted the growing issue of MP-consultants, an area now brought back to public prominence by the Poulson affair. Earlier described by MP Francis Noel-Baker as opening the door 'for a new form of political corruption' (Noel-Baker 1961: 91) and the subject of two parliamentary inquiries in 1969 and 1974 (Williams 1985), the issue was forced by Adam Raphael of the *Observer* who singlehandedly prompted a very reluctant Parliament to act in 1976 upon three MPs who had allegedly been paid by Poulson (Raphael 1989: 130). There had already been in the *Times* the 'firm-within-a-firm' exposé of corruption in the Metropolitan police which, together with later tabloid investigations into the relations between the police and pornographers, led to a number of high-profile corruption cases. Other cases were to be found across the public and private sectors, from obscure areas such as the Royal Navy's catering supplies department to the Crown Agents, from cities in north Scotland to public servants' sharedealings in suppliers and the payment of business commissions in the private sector, many first revealed by the media investigations and leading to major inquiries as well as prosecutions (Doig 1984).

The range of cases, the likelihood of some form of official response and the willingness of the media to publish stories, at a time when political activism and interest was relatively high, made journalism an increasingly attractive profession; 'they all came in', says Mark Hollingsworth, the former *World In Action* journalist, 'because they had a moral and political fervour about them and they didn't want to get involved in politics, I suppose. Journalism was the next best thing.' David Leigh, who worked on the *Observer* and Thames TV's *This Week*, also saw his role, as he entered journalism in the 'golden age', to call governments to account, not to service those in power.

The attractions of investigatory journalism accelerated the traditional way to a position in the national media – learning the trade in the local media and getting promotion through a mix of luck, a good portfolio of stories and perseverance – by their taking on younger journalists sooner and thus in turn increasing their experience and expertise of investigative journalism early in their careers. While Michael Gillard of the *Observer* is less convinced of a golden age he thinks that the coincidental combination of motivated, liberal graduates and 'good' stories did provide many of today's investigative journalists by giving them the time and experience of learning the 'how' and 'why' of events at an early stage in their careers.

At the same time these journalists were finding an increasing number of media outlets that encouraged the focus of their work as well as catering to a growing audience, often university-educated and having lived through the counter-culture climate of the 1960s. That culture was itself successful in developing cheap and marketable publications that spread the accessibility of do-it-yourself journalism. Thus, in addition to TV's *World in Action*, *Panorama*, *TV Eye*, *Man Alive*, *The London Programme*, the press's *Observer*, *Sunday Times* and *Guardian*, and more radical magazines such as the *Leveller*, *New Statesman* and *Private Eye*, there were an increasing number of sporadic publications such as *Counter Information Services*, *Up Against the Law* and *Community Action* and various investigative publications at a local level such as *Rebecca*, *Liverpool Free Press* and the *West Highland Free Press* (Minority Press Group 1980; Whittaker 1981).

The point about the variety of publications and the high profile of investigatory journalism was that there was almost a self-fulfilling perception of investigatory journalism as a public interest, core media function. On mainstream outlets such as the *Sunday Times* and *World in Action* senior figures such as owner Roy Thomson or executive producer David Plowright were prepared to underwrite such a function with the appropriate support, time and resources to pursue stories, an approach identifiable in newspapers with the promotion of specific teams – 'Insight' in the *Sunday Times* or 'Close-Up' in the *Telegraph* – or individuals such as Richard Norton-Taylor or David Leigh and Peter Chippindale in *The Guardian*, or Adam Raphael at the *Observer*. The *Sunday Times*' 'Insight' was the great role model, according to David Leigh, with huge investigations, sufficient time, large budgets and a strongly supportive editorial approach. He himself came to the *Observer* at the start of the 1980s to do the same – establish an investigative team, with enough time for research, no editorial interference and a budget which also paid for freelance assistance.

In television IBA mandated key peak-time slots for current affairs and the wish to match the status of quality newspapers ensured the development of investigatory programmes; Ray Fitzwalter says that 'there was a period there when people were prepared to spend more resources for depth coverage. It began to grow up in TV, to a certain extent, emulating that, and there was a transfer of resources and people across into TV.' He himself was integral to the success of the leader – *World In Action* – although it was closely matched in timing and focus by the BBC's *Panorama*. Both reflected the team approach and the journalist free from routine duties with the resources, time and editorial commitment to detailed, authoritative, insider explanations of what was happening behind the public decisions and pronouncements. All tended to reflect the collective sense of purpose and commitment described by *Sunday Times* editor Harry Evans for his own newspaper, as 'that remarkable unity of purpose, varying in its expression but unshakeable in its conviction . . . and all the benevolences that flow from a community where individuals, in all the fractious moments and rivalries, hold each other accountable to certain ideals' (Evans 1983: 378).

Ends and means

Around the mid-1970s, however, the purposes and *esprit de corps* of investigatory journalism were beginning to provoke adverse reactions, ranging from Prime Minister Harold Wilson's bitter complaints about 'cohorts of distinguished journalists' combing the country for information with which to damage the Labour Party to a reader of the radical magazine *Leveller* who wrote of his concern about journalists who 'compete for corruption stories just like scientists compete to be published . . . using the élite techniques and rituals of investigative journalism which of course only a very few mortals are competent to do' (*Leveller* 1978). Editors were concerned at the tensions in the news rooms between the orthodox journalists who had to complete regular copy and the investigatory journalists free to pursue their interests. Peter Preston, the former *Guardian* editor, suggests that journalists designated as investigative journalists could lose the rhythm and news flow of a newsroom, tending to become focused on their own agendas. Such designations put pressure on journalists to deliver but loosened an editor's control over their activities. Regular journalists were also sceptical of the impact of one-off investigative stories. Crime reporters who relied on daily contact with the police admitted that they would avoid such stories; 'we burnt our fingers bad over the bribery case. We don't want to do more stories like that, we want to live it down,' said a crime reporter on *The Times* after the 1969 story on police corruption. Investigative journalists have, said Adam Raphael, formerly executive editor of the *Observer*, to 'keep on week after week if they want to make changes' but such singlemindedness could bring with it newsroom 'boredom' toward over-long concentration on one subject without developing the readers' interest, as well as editorial wariness over the pursuit of stories which the investigative journalist alone decided to follow.

At the same time there was an increasing institutional concern at the investigations into politicians' behaviour: there was an awareness within the political world that the anathematisation of a few individuals (Clarke 1981) was an unwelcome but sometimes necessary means of exposing the alleged 'rotten apples' but wariness that partisan reporting, circulation boosting competition and 'the thrill of the chase', rather than investigations in the public interest, could motivate journalists and have longer-term implications for the credibility of, and the public's confidence in, politicians and the political system. Journalists Barry Penrose and Roger Courtiour were warned by their bosses at the BBC over their inquiries into the extraordinary circumstances surrounding the Thorpe affair (where the former leader of the Liberal Party was charged and later acquitted of the incitement to murder a male model who had made allegations of homosexuality against him) because of what they were finding and because their target was a well-connected politician. They were told that the inquiries 'involved too many difficult factors. The truth isn't necessarily the overwhelming consideration' (Doig 1990: 232; Penrose and Courtiour 1978). John Whale also wrote in the *Sunday Times* of concern that the stimuli of sex and cover-ups in the Thorpe affair were the cause of the intense competition among journalists for the 'scoop' rather than the public interest aspects of the story. The general newspaper probing into the private business interests of Prime Minister Harold Wilson's inner circle from 1974 to 1976 was partly a result of competition between the *Daily Mail* and *Daily Express* to be the first to unearth revelations of land transactions involving his staff. His (largely ignored) complaints of press harassment for political ends were to find an echo a year later when the *Daily Mail* attacked British Leyland over allegations of bribery. The government-funded motor vehicle empire was accused of operating a multi-million pound slush fund to pay overseas bribes and commissions. It was not the alleged details of the fund that caused the subsequent row but the publication by the newspaper of a forged letter linking the payments to government ministers and government-appointed public figures. The *Daily Mail* was sued and lost while the forger, a British Leyland employee, was jailed. The rest of Fleet Street turned on the *Daily Mail*, accusing it of irresponsibility and political bias, and being 'blinded by lust for a scoop'. The 1977 Royal Commission on the Press warned:

> it is certainly the case that some newspapers of the right persistently seek for discreditable material which can be used to damage the reputation of Labour Ministers or those connected with the Party or with

trade unions . . . it is not new evidence that the *Daily Mail* is a polemical and politically partisan newspaper, for it has been that for a long time. What is new is the extreme lengths to which the newspaper was prepared to go in an attack on the Government based on inadequately checked information.

(Royal Commission 1977: addendum, para. 7)

The cost of printing and the price of ownership

Notwithstanding the high public profile of investigatory journalism during the 1970s, that profile was not translated, with the exception of the *Sunday Times*, into sustained increased sales. As inflation began to spiral so the print costs and wages followed suit, driven by the inter-union competition among the largest group of newspaper employees – the production staff. These were distributed between four competing unions whose strength varied according to function but who each dominated one of the four areas of news production. Shift working, multiple employment and function monopoly combined with tight union organisation, competitive wage demands and union control over job recruitment to provide high wages, production domination and a sense of technological security (Martin 1981) which was seen as a stranglehold that was a source of bitter but privately-expressed concern among managers and editors. Bob Edwards, once a *Mirror* editor, talks of the late 1970s when union leaders had enormous and irresponsible power, where 'restrictive practices and rackets were rampant' (Edwards 1988: 212) while Harold Evans, when editor of the *Sunday Times*, remembers 'industrial chaos', 'guerilla warfare', and inter-union disputes that meant that 'week after week, month after month, the work of hundreds of people in all departments was thrown away' (Evans 1983: 79). At the *Sunday Express* John Junor was complaining that

> economic troubles were mounting around us. Newspapers were increasing in size and price and so people were buying fewer of them. Commercial television meant that there was vastly more competition for advertising, revenue costs were soaring, we were seriously over-manned and the mechanical unions had their ignorant Luddite hands firmly and permanently round our windpipe.
>
> (Junor 1990: 159–60)

Most owners avoided any direct involvement in the management or structures of their newspapers; Lord Astor watched *The Times* slide into financial difficulties from his Mediterranean home while the owners of the highly-profitable *News of the World* treated it as a means of funding their pastimes such as 'champagne, a company stud farm and private golf courses' (Jenkins

1986: 52 and 57). There were, however, businessmen who saw profit and potential in the newspaper industry and were prepared to buy in. Between 1961 and 1975 the increasing financial deficits, the inexorable confrontation with the unions and the willingness of existing owners to wash their hands of their rapidly-dwindling assets for a suitable price led to Murdoch picking up the *News of the World*, Thomson *The Times*, and ARCO the *Observer*. By the mid-1980s, Robert Maxwell had picked up the *Mirror* empire (*Sunday Mirror, Mirror, People*), Murdoch had added *The Times* and *Sunday Times*, and Lonhro the *Observer*. The *Daily Express* and *Sunday Express* fell to Trafalgar House, a construction conglomerate, in 1977. Trafalgar later floated off its newspapers in Fleet Holdings which was taken over in 1985 by United Newspapers. In the meantime the *Daily* and *Sunday Telegraph* were taken over by Argus run by the Canadian Conrad Black. Within twenty-five years, therefore, only the *Guardian, Financial Times* and the two *Mails* retained their 1961 proprietorial structures.

The struggle for profitability began in the early 1980s with circulation-boosting activities, price cutting and more aggressive popular journalism – the beginnings of the bimbo-and-bingo tabloid journalism – helped by the cash from the Reuters flotation and the de-manning activities begun by United Newspapers and Maxwell at the *Mirror*. Management and editors, supported by the new owners, used the threat of cuts and closure (Jenkins 1986: 177; Bower 1988: 398) to try to curtail costs and union demands. The break-through came with the attempts of Eddie Shah, a regional freesheet publisher, to break into Fleet Street with *Today*. Shah's earlier defeat of the unions, using new Conservative legislation, new technology and a single-union agreement with the EETPU, persuaded Murdoch, whose efforts to intro-duce new working plant and practices were stalemated with the unions, to relocate in Wapping. (Murdoch later took over and then closed *Today*.) In the process Murdoch deployed 'every legal weapon in the labour law created by the Thatcher governments' and exploited the production tech-nology that had long been available in the USA and elsewhere. The other newspapers soon followed his example, with most fleeing the physical restric-tions of Fleet Street, dismantling or radically renegotiating the restrictive practices of the unions and drastically cutting their workforces (Melvern 1986).

Such was the attraction of the benefits of the new technology and arrange-ments that several attempts were made to set up new newspapers, of which only the *Independent* and *Independent on Sunday* survive (Chippindale and Horrie 1988), while money was pumped into new developments in communica-tions, including cable and satellite TV. The new owners, according to journalist Simon Jenkins, wanted to make their newspapers public monu-ments to their entrepreneurial skills, as their predecessors wanted monuments to their political power. But it seemed that, for once, the market for glory and the market for newspapers were on converging courses. Not just Rupert Murdoch but David Stevens at the *Daily Express* and Robert Maxwell at the *Daily Mirror* (despite his support for Labour) seemed tailor-made for Mrs Thatcher's new Britain. Their 'initial declarations were business-like, their chapel confrontation spectacular and their attack on production costs obsessive. Less demonstrative proprietors followed where they had led' (Jenkins 1986: 217).

Owners, editors and influence

Such owners and editors also realised the value of a government whose efforts provided the legislative and policing framework within which to achieve their goals. They were commercially-minded predators with a tremendous reservoir of influence: in 1986, out of a total issue circulation of over 31 million for each occasion (weekday or Sunday), Murdoch controlled over 10.5 million, Maxwell 9.16 million and United 5.6 million. Murdoch, with three daily newspapers, was in the most important position. Unlike Matthews at the *Express* who saw 'himself as striving for Britain's greatness and revelled in the resulting comparison with Beaverbrook' (Jenkins 1986: 215), or Maxwell who saw himself as the great communicator and problem-resolver and used the Mirror Group Newspapers as a covert slush fund to underpin his other financial deals (Bower 1988; Thompson and Delano 1991), Murdoch was a 'consummate opportunist'.

Not interested in becoming a 'newspaper baron' or using his newspapers as 'an extension of a political party', he was more experienced in 'using politicians to further his own interest rather than theirs' (Chippindale and Horrie 1990: 50). Thus his support of the Conservatives in 1979 was allegedly reflected in the new government's decision not to refer Murdoch's takeover of *The Times* and *Sunday Times* to the Monopolies and Mergers Commission, subject to Murdoch's acceptance of certain guarantees of editorial independence. The *Sun* moved from endorsing Wilson in 1970 to supporting Thatcher in 1979, a relationship nurtured by her and her political advisers. The support for Mrs Thatcher was widespread through the rest of the Conservative press but Murdoch's support was important for its effect on the young working-class voter whose switch was necessary in many Labour marginals. The revival of nationalism after the Falklands War, and the retreat of the Labour Party to leftwing purity (as a reaction to its defeat in 1979), persuaded large sections of the press to run an anti-red, smear-tactic campaign at the next general election in 1983 (Doig 1990; Hollingsworth 1986). By then the impact of the anti-union legislation and the defeat of the print unions ensured solid owner and editorial support, a distinct contrast from the more fluid support of twenty and forty years ago. As the *Sunday Times'* Brian MacArthur pointed out, although papers such as the *Daily Mail* and *Daily Express* preached to the converted, merely confirming their political prejudices, and 48 per cent of *Sun* readers still voted Labour and probably read it for its 'entertainment', the popular papers, however, have never been quite so biased as they are today, nor so potent a threat to standards of political debate . . . if three newspapers read by nearly 20 million readers present politics in such simplistic terms, is it any wonder that serious issues deserving serious consideration do not get a serious hearing?

(*Sunday Times* 1992(a))

The proprietors stamped their influence on the newspapers through their choice of editors. Harry Evans' move from the *Sunday Times* to *The Times*, to have 'six opportunities for excellence to every one the *Sunday Times* had', was short-lived, following complaints from the Murdoch-appointed managing director of Times Newspapers that the newspaper's economic content was reinforcing 'the impression that the editorial policy of *The Times* in this matter is to criticise the Government and to consider its economic policies mistaken' (Evans 1983: 287). Not long after, Evans was forced out by Murdoch for apparently lacking a clear editorial policy and creating upheaval among the staff of *The Times*. Murdoch's replacement, Charles Douglas-Home, told Evans 'I would do anything to edit *The Times*' while Murdoch's choices for the *Sun* and, later, the *News of the World* reflected his preference for editorially loyal, market-aware, hard-working and production-competent editors (Chippindale and Horrie 1990: 328–9).

Such editorial direction soon percolated to journalists, either overtly as it was at the *Sun* or it might be atmospheric, as at the *Sunday Times*; in 1992 its news editor, Michael Williams, noted the influence of a strong editor on a newspaper, arguing that

all newspapers have a culture and all successful journalists adapt to the culture of their newspapers . . . the value-system is defined by the editor and I produce Andrew Neil's newspaper. Newspapers are hierarchical organisations so it works all the way down the line.

It was a short step from firm editorial control to interference as editors and proprietors were prepared to interfere to use editorial policy as a useful tool to pursue, as in the case of Maxwell, the proprietor's enthusiasm for public attention (Thompson and Delano 1991) or, as in the case of Lonhro, when there was an issue involving the group's other interests. One such occasion was described as 'a watershed for the paper and Rowland's proprietorship' and another was the cause of resignations and public comment (Hall 1987: 230–1; *The Times* 1991; Select Committee on Members' Interests 1989). In December 1991, Mike Durham, former social affairs correspondent at the *Sunday Times*, was scathing about claims that redundancies at the newspaper offered a chance to bring in 'new blood':

let me set the record straight. Mr Neil does not want fresh talent. He needs more trusties – compliant hacks who will turn out the usual fare of insulting trivia, apply the necessary spin, inject political bias to order, write to a lifeless formula, work all hours and, along the way, put up uncomplainingly with a regular dose of ritual humiliation. I am sure there will be plenty of candidates. Personally, as one of those given 'voluntary severance', I couldn't get out fast enough.

(*UK Press Gazette* 1991)

Anthony Bevins, for nine years a political correspondent for the *Sun* and *Daily Mail*, said of the insidious nature of the process: 'to survive and rise in, or on, the "game", you pander to the political prejudices of your paymasters, giving them the stories that you know will make them salivate.' This has been accepted by an editor of the *Daily Express*, Sir Nick Lloyd, who said that

the culture of the newspaper actually does, up to a point, have an enormous effect on the reporters and on the specialists so that they know what is likely to go in. Now the danger, and I accept that there is an enormous danger in this, is that they spend all their time looking at the stories that are not really stories in the first place, and stories which are not as good as stories they might get if they were less blinkered.

(*Independent* 1992(a))

Cautions and auctions: television

For several investigatory journalists TV in the 1980s appeared a more committed, better-resourced and more independent medium (*The Listener* 1984) where, against the totality of the cost of programme production, TV investigatory journalism was relatively cheap, involving primarily staff costs, and was attractive to companies as evidence of a commitment to the public interest and 'serious' TV. Furthermore such programmes were paced in terms of a mix of light and deep analysis, studio debate and field research, to allow time for the latter approach to come to fruition. The two prime-time slots mandated by the IBA were matched by similar prime-time slots on the BBC while both BBC2 and Channel 4 developed their own investigative/current affairs programmes. There seemed, therefore, to be the range and support of investigatory programmes on TV in the 1980s as there were in newspapers in the 1970s.

TV, however, was one area where the influence of the Conservative culture could not initially be easily imposed on the corporatist culture of the BBC or the independence of the ITV companies. Mrs Thatcher and her advisers saw themselves as radical reformers for whom corporatism and consensus were largely responsible for the country's economic and social decline. She had the support of the Cabinet which was dominated by radical Tories who questioned the workings of the establishment and the consensus politics that sustained it. The BBC exemplified much of what they distrusted about the system – an unwieldy, self-sustaining, self-satisfied institution that by its nature could hold no clear, decisive views on contentious issues but was devoted to fudge, compromise and endless tolerance.

(Leapman 1986: 183)

The 'bludgeoning' of the BBC, as the then director-general put it, was heralded early when a *Tonight* report on the INLA, a Northern Ireland terrorist group, was accused by the new Prime Minister in 1979 of 'reflecting gravely on the judgement of the BBC and those who were responsible for that decision' (Cockerell 1988: 254). It continued over the BBC's even-handed approach to the Falklands War, in particular a *Panorama* programme at the outbreak of hostilities which convinced the government that programmes that challenged government and its policies were to be criticised at every opportunity. Thus the *Real Lives* programme in 1986 was withdrawn, the BBC's reporting of the US bombing of Libya in 1986 attracted open hostility and the *Secret Society* programme on the Zircon satellite in 1987 was preceded by police raids before being banned on 'national security' grounds. Alasdair Milne, the director-general, was sacked shortly after by the politically-appointed board of governors (Milne 1988) who had increasingly begun to exert their authority over editorial independence to the point where they became involved in executive decisions, including that to settle out of court with a number of Conservative MPs who issued libel writs over *Panorama*'s 'Maggie's Militant Tendency' programme in 1986. Says Adam Raphael, the programme

has gone down in BBC folklore as the film that scuppered not only the Director General but also a whole generation of current affairs television . . . Investigative reporting whether on television or in newspapers inevitably carries risks. If there is a lesson to be drawn from one of the most searing episodes in the Corporation's history, it is that bad management rather than bad journalism let the BBC down.

(Raphael 1989: 209–210)

By the time the Conservatives were facing the 1987 general election, the BBC was short of funds, was regularly criticised in the press for its expenditure and programmes, was subject to the Peacock Commission on alternative sources of funding, and its new senior management were directed by a director-general 'who had never made a programme in his life and his deputy who many people . . . believed had never made an interesting programme in his life. Overnight life changed in the BBC' (Cockerell 1988: 316). Former *Guardian* editor Alastair Hetherington said in 1989 that the malaise in the BBC — because of the belief that the Governors will not support critical or inquisitive journalism — has done much damage. 'Play safe' has too often become the rule, not least in news and current affairs . . . I encountered in the ITV newsrooms people who had left the BBC not so much because of the higher pay offered by YTV or Central or others, but because of sadness and disillusion with what was happening to the BBC.

(Hetherington 1989)

The impact of investigatory journalism at the BBC became diluted, in terms not so much of the quality of some of the programmes or the journalists involved but of managerial prevarication over attracting political criticism or an apparent unwillingness to lend full support to the investigation of some subjects. As with some print journalists, some BBC journalists took themselves and their stories across to what seemed at the time the more supportive ITV environment.

In 1987, after her third general election victory, Margaret Thatcher told a meeting of ITV and BBC chiefs that television was 'the last bastion of restrictive practices in British industries'. She was also keen to deregulate and revamp the ITV franchise structure, to allow more competition and open the door for new entrepreneurs. An aside in the Peacock report, the possible auctioning of franchises, was seized upon as the vehicle for reform — a process that also appealed to the Chancellor of the Exchequer as a more reliable source of funds from the ITV companies (Davidson 1993). The pace was accelerated by the Thames TV *This Week* investigation into the shooting by the SAS of three IRA terrorists in Gibraltar which challenged the government's claim that the terrorists were armed and about to detonate a huge car bomb. The programme also produced witnesses who contradicted the official circumstances of the actual shooting. There was, said the IBA chairman, unprecedented government pressure to stop the programme — and similar pressure on the programme makers later — as Mrs Thatcher's reactions went 'beyond anger'. The government's newspaper supporters attacked the programme, led by the *Sunday Times'* 'Insight' whose 'statements' from the witnesses claiming that *This Week* had mis-reported them were later refuted by those witnesses who told Roger Bolton that they were 'outraged at the way their comments had been misused by the paper' (Bolton 1990). Three *Sunday Times* reporters complained about the editorial addition of 'spin' to the 'Insight' story, one suggesting that 'my copy was used to discredit another piece of investigative journalism' and another that 'I expressed strong reservations about our coverage . . . I wanted nothing to do with what you were preparing.'

The government itself responded by publicly accusing the programme of 'trial by television' and 'contaminating' the evidence before the inquest was held. Since there was no trial and the inquest was being held in an overseas jurisdiction, this was held to be somewhat disingenuous. Nevertheless, the level of sustained government pressure forced Thames Television to set up its own inquiry into the impartiality of the programme under a former Tory Minister and a libel barrister whose report (Windlesham and Rampton 1989) effectively cleared the programme of bias and inaccuracy. The report was dismissed out of hand by the Conservative government, further strengthening Mrs Thatcher's determination to end ITV independence.

Under the 1990 Broadcasting Act the IBA, commercial TV's governing body, was converted into the ITC in January 1991. The ITC was given the mandate to oversee the auctioning of all ITV company franchises to the highest bidder, subject to all bidders having passed a quality threshold. This threshold, reportedly added later to the Bill by some Cabinet ministers alarmed at the crude accounting principle being applied to the shake-up of ownership, required evidence of 'sufficient time' being given to programmes on news and current affairs, the regional area where the company was based, education, religion and children's viewing. If the quality of a bid was exceptional, then it could be accepted in preference to the highest cash bid, as happened to Granada, but it was generally accepted that the economics of the marketplace, with a cursory nod toward a 'quality' threshold for eligibility, would push the winners toward the soft, tabloid-style entertainment necessary to attract the audiences and thus the advertisers whose money would be essential to cover the price of the franchise.

Amid the drive for such programmes, investigatory journalism (no longer with mandated slots) is not seen as a likely vehicle for peaktime profit in a climate where, as one former investigative journalist says,

> people are much more concerned about ratings, about the number of people who watch the programme. There are more criteria on whether a programme will get a big audience. This is bad news, because there are very important stories which will never get big audiences.

Another journalist believes that the Act was the 'last fling of Mrs Thatcher's scorpion tail', a conscious act to open up another lucrative market to her supporters in the private sector and to end a monopoly that was providing 'fertile grounds for the vile enemies of the state to do troublesome current affairs broadcasting'. He argues that the changes now place ITV firmly in the entertainment business, 'run by entertainment business characters and accountants . . . they are not in their hearts journalists and, therefore, when you do investigatory stuff which is troublemaking by its nature you're dealing with a lot of people who don't like you.'

Conclusion: last chance saloon for whom?

The changes during the 1980s have, it has been argued, left the BBC digesting the 'mission to explain', and a 'laborious' referral process 'fraught with uncertainty and of itself a disincentive to embarking on difficult projects' (*Guardian*

Weekend 1992) rather than an unfettered commitment to investigate. There have, for example, been claims that the pursuit of stories or the broadcast of *Panorama* programmes have been affected where 'an issue that might embarrass the Conservative Party, or otherwise damage the core interests of the political establishment' appeared to provoke a climb down (Horrie and Clarke 1994). Inside the BBC the view is that

> what Birt has done is to denude the BBC of its investigative powers, its ability to cause trouble. It's hard to make an investigative documentary anyway. With Birt's checking system, it's twice as hard. If there's any spicy material in it at all, it takes you all your time getting past the internal censors.
>
> (*Independent on Sunday* 1992(a)).

On the other hand, the BBC senior executive who argued that ITV could not adhere to traditional programme scheduling – 'the idea that there will be a *World in Action* or *This Week* at 8.30 p.m. on ITV . . . is a fantasy . . . It will be a schedule of comedy, drama and entertainment' – may yet be proved right. In 1992 Granada's chairman, David Plowright, was ousted, warning that the old-style current affairs approach was unlikely to survive: 'the schedule used to be led by programmes but now ITV is moving towards the US system of a market-led schedule whose sole purpose is to sell goods to consumers' (*Independent* 1992(b)). *World In Action* was dropped for two weeks in 1994 in a ratings war with the BBC (who had extended *Eastenders*), while the director of programmes for one of the new franchise holders has warned that size of audience and not purpose of programme dictates air-time; 'it isn't part of the function of the ITV system to get people out of prison. Its function is to make programmes that people want to watch'; with the competition for advertising revenue and the implications that had for economic survival, 'ITV could not afford to take a dive in ratings, even for half an hour in prime time' (*Independent on Sunday* 1992(b); *Independent* 1992(c)).

In 1992 David Leigh argued that newspapers have avoided many of the regulatory restraints on television and may remain freer to pursue investigatory stories:

> even the most debased newspaper is ultimately run by journalists who know a story when they see one. Even the *Daily Mail* will put in a story discreditable to the Tory Party if it's good enough. They may put it at the bottom of page 5 but they can't resist it because it's a story and, basically, journalists, shown a story, can't not print it in some form or other.

Certainly there has been an increase in interest in print investigative journalism. The *Spectator* wrote in 1989 of the arrival of Andrew Neil and his ambition to fashion a paper in his own image with 'Insight' high on Neil's hit list when he took over. It was founded in the Sixties, not one of Neil's favourite decades, and went on steadily winning awards through the Seventies. Neil bizarrely regarded it as 'a state within a state' and a vehicle for the 'hard Left', yet the enterprise, if not the personnel, survived.

(Marsden-Smedley 1989)

Now the *Sunday Times* has revived 'Insight' because, Michael Williams suggested, newspapers have to be more of a package, including entertainment, to compete with TV. A brandname such as 'Insight' and the kudos of an investigative facility, albeit with a much smaller team of reporters, means that it has an editorial value so long as the stories are a good read and, if possible, offer the 'split story' – a news item on the front page and a much more detailed feature story on the inside pages – but Williams stressed that such hard news should only be a minority part of a newspaper's mix of features, news and 'a good read'.

Any revival of investigatory journalism, therefore, must work within a very different environment than that which promoted investigative journalism in earlier decades. The new rules on cross-ownership between newspapers and TV companies are developing large commercial companies where regularity and accessibility of material is a more likely guarantee of audiences, and thus income, and where upfront investigative journalism becomes lost in the corporate activity which will be judged by ratings and profit rather than performance and the public interest. The TV companies and their newspaper colleagues may begin to resemble each other – 'more bland and consumer-led than in the past, sacrificing revelatory stories for those with an immediate, less analytical impact on their readers' and where investigations are seen as 'too costly, time-consuming and speculative and, more crucially, not saleable enough' (Browne 1996).

Any investigatory journalism that does take place must also do so against a background where the more traditional restraints on investigatory journalism, such as cost or the threat of legal action, now play a much more significant role in the world of a more conservative and cautious editorial approach, of management accountants and owners with profit margins and shareholders to satisfy. The downward pressure on costs cuts back on the time for the background work; one journalist on a quality daily says that

the news desk are not always sympathetic to that. I think in the recessionary climate they are particularly unsympathetic. For example, at the moment we can't take on casuals so if there's a reporter on something long term you can't say that journalist can go off and do it, and take on a casual if there's a big news story, because of the budget. There's a constant pressure and that sort of journalism can get cut out . . . it is the area that gets squeezed.

Peter Preston says that all editors must judge the cost of proceeding against the less quantifiable cost of ending a story but protecting a newspaper's finances. This has become especially true of the use of libel which reached extraordinary proportions in the mid-1980s; 'the perception', says Raymond Snoddy, the *Financial Times'* media correspondent, 'that juries were setting out to punish newspapers for their transgressions rather than to compensate the victim for any loss of reputation involved had a chilling effect on investigative reporting' (Snoddy 1992). Michael Gillard at the *Observer* has no doubts that the 'big legal stick' is a major threat to the investigatory journalist:

> when people make a decision – do you want to investigate this politician, this big businessman, this company – people say even if we are right, and I think we are right, how much is it going to cost. Not only is there the on-cost, the libel, the legal cost, first of all, to get it published and defend it afterwards but there is the cost of the journalist who is not able to do anything else but preparing briefs of lawyers – who needs all of this?

Peter Preston believes that the nature of investigatory journalism in newspapers has changed dramatically over the past ten years. Most journalists come into *The Guardian* with regional experience while the newspaper has encouraged the growth of area interest so that journalists can develop expertise from which investigative journalism will flow, providing a spread of coverage that ensures a more regular flow of good stories and avoids the threat of story boredom or obsession that can come from the free-range investigatory journalist. 'Purely in terms of the stories we got,' says Preston,

> I think we are much more effective now with a whole variety of specialists watching areas like the secret services or the criminal fraternity or Whitehall or the under-reported monitoring bodies on government than we ever were when there were two classes of office, one of investigative journalists who were supposed to investigate and other sorts of journalists who were not there to investigate anything . . . The best results came from having a lateral mind applied first to the rota of events to ask not what happened but what does it mean and who was involved, and why . . . If the thing that makes you leap up is a really good exclusive story that makes the shit hit the fan, that makes, rightly or wrongly, your week then it is important to think of the best means of getting it.

The answer, he suggests, is to nurture the specialist journalists, to develop the contacts and information and then 'not to worry':

> These things go in patches; with any newsgatherer of that sort you can go through six months or nine months of nothing coming out. That's

not because they're not trying but that things need luck and patience. Investigatory journalism is not a conveyor belt but casting your line on the pond and see who bites.

At the other end of the spectrum, down in Wapping, Michael Williams supported Preston's view of the likely future of investigatory journalism: 'if one can get scoops out of people who know their subjects it's better than having teams of investigatory journalists.' His view is that journalists who are diligent and careful, who are keen to piece together the whole picture and who have a sceptical approach to the governmental structures will carry out investigations in addition to their regular news input and should be encouraged to do so.

Over all of the media industry, however, linger the unprecedented and bruising battles with governments during the 1980s when there were repeated struggles over the arena that investigative journalism had made its own during the 1970s – the conduct of politicians and governments – and the increasing willingness of governments to use the courts and other means to warn the media from probing too deeply. The £2 million pursuit of *Spycatcher*'s author and various newspapers through numerous courts to uphold the (selective) right of governments to demand a lifelong agreement of confidentiality was unsuccessful only because so much of the information was already in the public domain. Governments were prepared to ignore evidence of malpractice in parts of GCHQ (as well as ban the book detailing the allegations [Hooper 1987]) and took the *Observer* to court (but lost) for allegedly bribing a civil servant (who had earlier been found guilty of being bribed by the newspaper) to reveal evidence of multi-million pound Whitehall wastage. Governments also made particular examples of such 'leakers' by pursuing Clive Ponting and Sarah Tisdall in the courts; the former was acquitted but the latter convicted – provoking a furious reaction from those who felt that the *Guardian* buckled under government pressure to return papers that identified the source (Hooper 1987: 123–35; Caute 1984).

The opportunity for government to even curb further the media's propensity to pry, and to teach it the importance of confidentiality and privacy, has also occurred at a time when the traditions of exposé journalism and the techniques of investigatory journalism have been combined to pursue the bimbo-and-bingo interests of the tabloid press in producing sensational stories involving a variety of people in the public eye. The era of what was to be colloquially termed 'bonk journalism' arrived, with the focus on

sex, preferably with a hint of scandal and involving celebrities. These could be of the major variety, such as members of the Royal Family, or the lesser stars of the music and media industries who came . . . to occupy increasing quantities of tabloid newsprint.

(McNair 1994)

On the basis that some of the relevance or public interest value in some of the stories might be doubtful, politicians and the government began looking for ways to impose a degree of restraint and responsibility on the press without appearing to regulate what was published.

The government instituted an inquiry by David Calcutt QC on the treatment of privacy by 'certain sectors' of the media. It recommended that the existing Press Council be replaced by a Press Complaints Commission (PCC) as the final opportunity for the press to demonstrate that it could effectively regulate itself without the imposition of any statutory policing (Calcutt 1990). The relevant government minister, David Mellor, warned that the eighteen-month trial for the PCC was, for the press, 'drinking in the last chance saloon'. Mellor himself was later to depart from ministerial office, in part because of his affair with an actress which was revealed by the *People* and in part because of free flights and a holiday which he accepted from the daughter of a leading figure in the PLO (Doig 1993). Calcutt himself later came back with recommendations that there should be a statutory tribunal to oversee the behaviour of the press, that invasion of privacy should be a suable offence and that the use of means of physical intrusion, such as bugging and tele-photo lenses, should be criminal offences (Calcutt 1993).

Nevertheless the exposure of Mellor by the *People* was seen in part as an attempt to underline the consequences of tighter restrictions on what the press could publish in terms of their effects beyond curbing the excesses of 'bonk' journalism. The PCC itself recognised that there might be a conflict between invasion of privacy and the expectation that holders of public office 'must always be subject to public scrutiny' and said within days of the Mellor story breaking that there was a public interest right to publish stories about private behaviour which affected or might affect the conduct of public business. Backbench support for Mellor focused particularly on the methods used to collect the information and on the question of privacy but the government was quick to suggest that legislation for the latter was unlikely, particularly after an unexpected source – the editor of the *Sun* – alleged that government ministers were prepared to offer stories which damaged the reputation of political opponents. The *Sunday Times*, reflecting the views of many newspapers, said that it was less a question of standards than the existence of double standards: politicians publicly pontificating about the behaviour of others while their 'private peccadilloes are left unreported', and the 'rank hypocrisy' of politicians who maintained that their lives were their own while not being 'above dishing the dirt on a fellow politician if it suits their own political or personal purposes'. The publication of the affair was 'a legitimate matter to bring into the public domain, especially in an age when politicians are eager to promote their "happy family" image to curry favour with voters' (*Sunday Times* 1992(b)).

This aspect of media investigations was particularly evident following the controversial attempt by the Conservative government at the 1993 Conservative Party conference in Blackpool to regain electoral support by announcing a campaign to get the country 'back to basics'. The underlying theme was that fundamental Conservative values – ranging from free trade to respect for law and order, from sound money policies to the sanctity of the family, from self-discipline to respect for the church and the monarchy – were at one with the core values of the nation. Inevitably it was also, despite later Conservative protests to the contrary, seen as a moral campaign, particularly when assessed in the context of other speeches which were made around that time by Cabinet ministers about social and family issues. The campaign proved disastrous for the Conservatives as, almost immediately, there unfolded a series of media stories which reinforced the initial scepticism of many that the Conservatives were singularly badly positioned to launch such a campaign, and which exposed the government to allegations of political expediency, of double standards and, ultimately, of sleaze as a number of junior Conservative ministers and MPs were purported to be involved in sexual or financial misconduct. The latter included allegations of MPs being paid to ask parliamentary questions, which led, in October 1994, to the establishment of the Nolan Committee (Ridley and Doig 1996).

Despite the House of Commons Privileges Committee's report on the cash-for-questions cases that accused the *Sunday Times* of standards that fell substantially below those expected of 'legitimate investigative journalism' (Committee of Privileges 1995: xxiii) – a somewhat premature stance in view of the subsequent activities of the *Guardian* and others in investigating allegations of payments for lobbying, the resurgence in investigative journalism is, as Nolan reported in May 1995, a necessary if sometimes unwelcome activity:

> a free press using fair techniques of investigative journalism is an indispensable asset to our democracy . . . they have a duty to enquire – coupled with a duty to do so responsibly – and in that way contribute to the preservation of standards in public life.
>
> (Nolan 1995)

It may be no surprise that in July 1995 the government announced that 'a free press is vital to a free country' and that there would be no attempt to control contents or to regulate the industry (*Government's Response* 1995).

In 1993 Magnus Linklater, once of 'Insight', reported on a thirtieth anniversary party with old and new members, noting that the gulf between 'what is now accepted as investigative reporting and what was understood then is a yawning one' (Linklater 1993). Nevertheless it was another 'Insight' story that took the lead in what, in February 1996, nearly led to the defeat of the government; in 1990 it published the first major article that was to lead to the Scott inquiry (Scott 1996: 2). Investigative journalism may no longer be in a golden era but it has not yet lost its Midas touch.

Acknowledgements

I should like to thank the following for interviews (the appointments are those held at that time). The presentation of their views, and the contexts in which they are placed, have been my responsibility:

Peter Preston, editor, *Guardian*
Ray Fitzwalter, executive producer, *World In Action*
David Leigh, journalist, *This Week*
Michael Williams, news editor, *Sunday Times*
Mark Hollingsworth, journalist, *World In Action*
Christian Wolmar, journalist, *Independent*
Rosie Waterhouse, journalist, *Independent*
Adam Raphael, executive editor, *Observer*
Michael Gillard, journalist, *Observer*
Nick Rufford, 'Insight' editor, *Sunday Times*

I should also like to thank the British Academy for funding research into UK public sector fraud and corruption, of which this paper is part of a survey of media investigations and official responses.

References

Bolton, R. (1990) *Death on the Rock and Other Stories*, London: W.H. Allen/Optomen Books.

Bower, T. (1988) *The Outsider*, London: Mandarin.

Browne, C. (1996) *The Prying Game*, London: Robson Books.

Caute, D. (1984), 'The *Guardian* and Sarah Tisdall', *Granta* 12.

Calcutt, D. (1990) *Report of the Committee on Privacy and Related Matters*, Cmnd 1102, London: HMSO.

Calcutt, D. (1993) *Review of Press Self-Regulation*, Cmnd 2135, London: HMSO.

Chibnall, S. (1977) *Law-and-Order News*, London: Tavistock.

Chibnall, S. and Saunders, P. (1977) 'Worlds Apart: Notes on the Social Reality of Corruption', *British Journal of Sociology* 28, 2.

Chippindale, P. and Horrie, C. (1988) *Disaster! The Rise and Fall of News on Sunday*, London: Sphere.

Chippindale, P. and Horrie, C. (1990) *Stick It Up Your Punter!*, London: Mandarin.

Clarke, M. (1981) *Fallen Idols*, London: Junction Books.

Cockerell, M. (1988) *Live from Number 10*, London: Faber & Faber.

Committee of Privileges (1995) *1st Report*, 1994–95, HC 351–i, London: HMSO.

Cox, B., Shirley, J. and Short, M. (1977) *The Fall of Scotland Yard*, Harmondsworth: Penguin.

Davidson, A. (1993) *Under The Hammer*, London: Mandarin.

Denning, Lord (1963) *Report*, Cmnd 2152, London: HMSO.

Doig, A. (1983) 'You Publish At Your Peril – The Restraints on Investigatory Journalism', in M. Clarke (ed.) *Corruption: Causes, Consequences and Control*, London: Frances Pinter.

Doig, A. (1984) *Corruption and Misconduct in Contemporary British Politics*, Harmondsworth: Penguin.

Doig, A. (1990) *Westminster Babylon*, London: Allison & Busby.

Doig, A. (1993) 'The Resignation of David Mellor', *Parliamentary Affairs* 46, 2.

Edwards, R. (1988) *Goodbye Fleet Street*, London: Jonathan Cape.

Evans, H. (1983) *Good Times, Bad Times*, London: Weidenfeld & Nicolson.

Fitzwalter, R. (1973). 'Breaking The Poulson Story', *New Statesman*, 4 May.

Fitzwalter, R. and Taylor, D. (1981) *Web of Corruption*, London: Granada.

The Government's Response (1995) 'Privacy and Media Intrusion', Cmnd 2918, London: HMSO.

Guardian Weekend (1992) 'Trust Me: I'm With *Panorama*' (D. Hill), 19 February.

Hall, R. (1987) *My Life With Tiny*, London: Faber & Faber.

Hepworth, M. (1975) *Blackmail: Publicity and Secrecy in Everyday Life*, London: Routledge & Kegan Paul.

Hetherington, A. (1989) *News in the Regions*, London: Macmillan.

Hollingsworth, M. (1986) *The Press and Political Dissent*, London: Pluto.

Hooper, D. (1987) *Official Secrets*, London: Secker & Warburg.

Horrie, C. and Clarke, S. (1994) *Fuzzy Monsters: Fear and Loathing at the BBC*, London: Heinemann.

The Independent (1992a) 'Cometh the Election, Cometh the Smear' (A. Bevins), 3 February: 19.

The Independent (1992b) 'The Difficult Man from Manchester' (S. Summers), 17 June: 15.

The Independent (1992c) 'ITV Likely to Move Current Affairs Out of Prime Time' (M. Brown), 1 September.

Independent on Sunday (1992a) 'What Makes John Birt Run' (W. Leith), 5 July: 3–40.

Independent on Sunday (1992b) 'The Importance of Being Earnest' (A. Pearson), 24 May: 21.

Jenkins, S. (1986) *The Market for Glory*, London: Faber & Faber.

Junor, J. (1990) *Listening for a Midnight Tram*, London: Chapman Publishers.

Leapman, M. (1986) *The Last Days of the Beeb*, London: Allen & Unwin.

[*The*] *Leveller* (1978) 'Letter to the Editor: "Don't Join the Professionals"', 5 August/September: 18.

Linklater, M. (1993) 'An insight into *Insight*', *British Journalism Review* 4, 2.

The Listener (1984) 'On the Trail of the Official Cover-Up' (B. Woolley), 4 October: 5–6.

Mark, R. (1979) *In the Office of Constable*, London: Fontana.

Marsden-Smedley, P. (ed.) (1989) *Britain in the Eighties*, London: Paladin/ Grafton.

Martin, R. (1981) *New Technology and Industrial Relations in Fleet Street*, Oxford: Oxford University Press.

McNair, B. (1994) *News and Journalism in the UK*, London: Routledge.

Melvern, L. (1986) *The End of the Street*, London: Methuen.

Milne, A. (1988) *The Memoirs of a British Broadcaster*, London: Coronet.

Minority Press Group (1980) *Here Is The Other News*, London: Minority Press Group.

Murphy, D. (1976) *The Silent Watchdog*, London: Constable.

Noel-Baker, P. (1961) 'The Grey Zone: The Problems of Business Affiliations of Members of Parliament', *Parliamentary Affairs* 15.

Nolan (1995) *First Report of the Committee on Standards in Public Life*, Cmnd 2850–I, London: HMSO.

Penrose, B. and Courtiour, R. (1978) *The Pencourt File*, London: Secker & Warburg.

Raphael, A. (1989) *My Learned Friends*, London: W. H. Allen.

Ridley, F.F. and Doig, A. (1996) *Sleaze: Politicians, Interests and Public Reactions*, Oxford: Oxford University Press.

Royal Commission on Standards of Conduct in Public Life (1976) *Report*, Cmnd 6524, London: HMSO.

Royal Commission on The Press (1977) *Final Report*, Cmnd 6810, London: HMSO.

Scott (1996) *Report of the Inquiry into the Export of Defence Equipment and Dual-Use Goods to Iraq and Related Prosecutions*, Vol 1, Cmnd 115, London: HMSO.

Select Committee on Members' Interests (1989) *Parliamentary Lobbying: Minutes of Evidence*, HC 44, London: HMSO.

Snoddy, R. (1992) *The Good, The Bad and The Unacceptable*, London: Faber & Faber.

Sunday Times (1992a) 'Paper Round: Press Ganged all the Way to the Ballot Box', 2 February.

Sunday Times (1992b) editorial, 'Press Politicians and Privacy', 26 July: 23.

The Times (1991) 'Letter to the Editor', 12 December: 21.

Thompson, P. and Delano, A. (1991) *Maxwell*, London: Corgi.

Tompkinson, M. (1982) *The Pornbrokers*, London: Virgin Books.

Tompkinson, M. and Gillard, M. (1980) *Nothing to Declare*, London: John Calder.

UK Press Gazette (1991) 'Letter to the Editor', 23/30 December: 20.

Whittaker, B. (1981) *News Ltd*, London: Minority Press Group.

Williams, S. (1985) *Conflict of Interest*, London: Gower.

Windlesham, Lord and Rampton, R. (1989) *The Windlesham/Rampton Report on 'Death on the Rock'*, London: Faber & Faber.

Chapter 19

Bob Franklin and David Murphy

THE LOCAL RAG IN TATTERS?
The decline of Britain's local newspapers

LOCAL AND REGIONAL NEWSPAPERS are in serious and probably irretrievable decline. The decline is quantitative as well as qualitative. Fewer local newspapers are published, sold and read and those which remain publish less news; especially less local news. 'Regional newspaper journalism' has been likened to 'a town centre after the construction of a new ring road. Every year more and more readers take the by-pass and rely on other information sources' (Prichard 1994: 55). Some of the factors which have been instrumental in prompting this decline can be listed:

1   The burgeoning growth of free newspapers with their editorial reliance on non-journalistic sources of news and their financial reliance on advertising revenues rather than copy sales.
2   The need for paid weekly papers to compete with free newspapers in local markets and, where possible, to adopt similar cost-cutting strategies.
3   Local newspapers' adoption of new technology which empowered proprietors against both production and editorial staffs.
4   The introduction of individual contracts for journalists with evident implications not only for the NUJ but also for the content of newspapers.
5   The declining circulations of the local press and the intensified competition for constantly dwindling markets of readers and advertisers.
6   The incorporation of local papers into multinational conglomerates with a consequent reduction of local editorial autonomy.

The declining news content of local papers is not only regrettable but also significant since traditionally they have proved influential in defining what is news, especially political news, in their circulation areas. A study in Leicester revealed that a local newspaper, rather like a well advertised lager, can reach parts of the local population which even big-selling tabloids cannot reach. On one Leicester council estate, 56 per cent of residents read the *Sun* and 25 per cent the *Mirror*, but 83 per cent read the *Leicester Mercury* and 94 per cent read the local municipal newspaper (Gray 1981).

But this decline of the local newspaper as a source of news is not, of course, a recent phenomenon. With the benefit of hindsight, the 1977 Royal Commission on the Press contained a number of omens to trigger alarm bells among even the most complacent of local hacks. The Commission's study of 'Attitudes to the Press', for example, asked readers to rank seventeen items of typical local/regional press coverage in order of preference. It was undoubtedly telling as well as portentous that the most favoured item of coverage in both evening and morning regional newspapers was 'Television and radio programmes' (Royal Commission 1977: 44).

The increasing irrelevance of news reporting in local newspapers also reflects developments in other media. Many observers believe, for example, that the new market driven broadcasting system introduced by the *Broadcasting Act 1990* will provide less news and current affairs programming for the majority of viewers, while obliging the chattering classes to subscribe to dedicated news channels such as CNN and SkyNews. The common news pasture of the public service tradition is becoming ever more enclosed by the market. Similarly the much heralded era of multimedia will witness people using media less and less as a source of news. The days when viewers switch on television or readers pick up a newspaper and expect to be presented with news are allegedly over. *The Economist* looks forward with enthusiasm to the

> dawning digital age in which the humble television will mutate into a two-way medium for a plethora of information and entertainment: movies on demand, video games, databases, educational programming, home shopping, telephone services, telebanking, teleconferencing, even the complex simulations of 'virtual reality'.
>
> (*The Economist* 1993: 21)

We wish to explore four aspects of the decline of local newspapers:

1 The decline in published titles and circulations.
2 The impact of new technology on the local press.
3 The growing concentration of ownership of the local press and the tendency towards local monopoly.
4 The emergence of the local tabloid and changes to the profession of journalism in the local setting.

Local newspapers in decline; dwindling markets for readers and advertisers

The number of local newspapers published has suffered an unrelenting post war decline. In 1948, a total number of 108 provincial daily newspapers were published in the UK, but this figure had reduced to 98 by 1961 and was reduced further to 89 by 1995 (*Royal Commission* 1977; ABC 1995). Paid weekly papers have suffered a similar decline from 1,306 titles published in 1948, to 1,228 in 1961, with a further reduction to 797 by 1988; a 32 per cent decline across the period (*Royal Commission* 1977; *Benns* 1988). Free local newspapers have expanded against this trend. Published titles have grown from 185 in 1975 to 325 in 1980, to 822 in 1987 and 1,156 titles in 1990 (Franklin and Murphy 1991: 85).

Circulation figures have mirrored the decline in the number of published titles. The cynical but essentially accurate answer to the question 'who reads newspapers?' is 'fewer and fewer people'. Some observers believe that the drop in sales is temporary, reflecting contingent factors such as the recession and high levels of unemployment, but ex-*Mirror* editor Roy Greenslade argues that the decline is long term and irretrievable (Greenslade 1992: 16). A number of reasons underlie declining newspaper sales. The most obvious can be stated in a single word: television! In the early 1980s, 58 per cent of those questioned regarded television as their main source of news against 27 per cent for newspapers. A decade later, the figures had changed to 80 per cent against 20 per cent; in short the gap had doubled (Goodman 1993: 4). Teletext, moreover, serves up a diet of news in a much more readily digestible form. Unemployment is a second factor. Unemployed people have less money to buy newspapers but, more significantly, reading a newspaper is a habit which is closely tied to work routines. Third, the cover price of newspapers has risen disproportionately to other goods; more than twice the average price inflation of other goods. Fourth, newspaper readership requires literacy as a basic skill, but a survey conducted by the Adult Literacy and Basic Skills Unit in 1990 discovered that 25 per cent of people in the 16–20 year age group had reading difficulties (Greenslade 1992: 16). Since 1993, two other factors have been significant although their impact has typically been discussed only in the context of the national press. The price war initiated by News International in July 1993 has had a devastating effect on local papers. The plummeting cover price of national newspapers has made them increasingly attractive to local newspaper readerships, prompting further circulation decline in local markets. Swingeing rises in the price of newsprint have also taken their toll. Increasing costs of newsprint were cited as one of the major causes for the closure of the editorially excellent *Yorkshire On Sunday* in July 1995.

Whatever the reasons, the evidence of long term post war circulation decline is unequivocal. So far as regional daily papers are concerned, the Royal Commission on the Press (1977) reported a sustained decline from aggregate sales of 11.1 millions in 1961 to 9.1 millions in 1976. The figure stood at 6.8 millions in 1987, a decline of 39 per cent across the period. By October 1995, the aggregate circulation of daily regional papers in England, Northern Ireland, Scotland and Wales was down to 5,310,323; a 53 per cent reduction in circulation in less than two decades (ABC 1995). Only 12 of the 89 regional morning/evening newspapers listed by ABC showed any circulation increases between January and June in 1995 compared with the same period in 1994; 75 newspapers reported a decline. Moreover, where increases were registered, these were typically slight. The *Carlisle Evening News and Star*, for example, improved its 1994 circulation of 27,998 by a mere 36 copies; the *Belfast Telegraph* added an average 44 sales to its daily 136,670 copies sold in 1994. Recorded decreases, however, were usually more substantial. *Kent Today*, for example, lost 11 per cent of its sales for the previous year, while the circulation of the *Bath and West Evening Chronicle* dropped by 8.1 per cent across the year. Some newspapers confront a very bleak future as annual circulation losses accumulate to alarming figures. The *Manchester Evening News*, which was selling 237,772 in 1992, saw daily sales reduced to 193,063 in 1995; a reduction of 44,709 (or 19 per cent) across three years (ABC 1995). This compares with a total daily sale of nearly 700,000 evening papers in Manchester in 1964. Circulations of paid weekly papers have suffered an equivalent post war decline but remain tolerably high at 7.7 million copies with an additional 2.45 million copies for regional Sunday newspapers. Sunday regionals enjoyed a considerable expansion in terms of published titles and circulations during the early 1990s; in the mid-1990s, the picture seems less certain. While Glasgow's *Sunday Mail* (+3.7 per cent) and Edinburgh's *Scotland On Sunday* (+1.3 per cent) have increased circulations, the *Sunday World* (-1 per cent), the *Sunday Post* (-5.6 per cent), *Wales on Sunday* (-3.4 per cent) and Plymouth's *Sunday Independent* (-3.2 per cent) have each suffered circulation decline; *Yorkshire On Sunday* has been obliged to close (ABC 1995). The growth of free newspaper distribution has been spectacular, achieving more than 43.5 million newspapers per week by 1991 (Franklin 1994: 34).

These trends in the local press – the declining sales of daily and weekly paid newspapers and the rapid expansion of free newspapers – signal two important consequences. The former trend has resulted in the elimination of competition and the creation of local press monopolies. McGregor's Commission (*Royal Commission* 1977) seemed untroubled by this situation, arguing that broadcast media would serve as a countervailing power. But the growth in cross media ownership, with single groups controlling both newspapers and a number of ILR stations, renders McGregor's argument anachronistic and unconvincing.

The growth of free newspapers, which typically possess fewer financial and journalistic resources, has resulted in more local newspapers featuring a smaller proportion of news in their editorial columns and becoming increasingly reliant on non-journalistic sources of news (see the discussion of the changing character of local journalism below). During the 1980s, regional newspapers shed large numbers of journalists; one large newspaper group managed 'to cut its editorial staff numbers in half' (Prichard1994: 56). Free newspapers have had a crucial impact on the news content of local newspapers. The economic logic of free newspaper production – which identifies readers rather than news as the 'commodity' to be sold – generates an ethos in which the editorial is necessarily subordinate to the requirements of advertising. Free distribution, moreover, places free newspapers beyond public accountability. Free newspapers do not have to win a circulation or earn the respect of their readers; loved or unwanted they are pushed through the letter box at regular intervals.

The decline in number of titles and circulations has had another significant effect. It has diminished local press advertising revenues which are a vital and significant element in the financial viability of all newspapers. In 1956, when commercial television was in its infancy, the British press (national and local) enjoyed 90 per cent of all news media advertising revenues which amounted to £103 millions. By the mid-1960s, advertising expenditure had trebled, but the total press share had fallen to 65 per cent and television (24 per cent) had overtaken the share of total advertising of the national press (20 per cent). By the late 1980s, television's share had risen to 31.4 per cent and national newspapers had enjoyed a remarkably steady 16 per cent for more than a decade, but the paid weekly share of total advertising had declined from 8.2 per cent to 4.7 per cent; regional dailies from 16.4 per cent to 10.3 per cent. Certain types of advertising have proved especially problematic. Jobs advertisements which account for approximately one-third of regional advertising, have recently fallen by as much as 50 per cent (MacArthur 1991: 6). By contrast, free newspapers had expanded their share of total advertising revenues to 7.7 per cent (AFN 1990: 14). By 1989, the total regional press share of 22.8 per cent of all advertising revenues was worth £1.7 billions although it was predicted that, by 1999, total regional press share would have fallen to 18 per cent. Advertising is a very unstable source of revenue which is particularly prone to cuts during a recession. 'When the economy sneezes', Baistow claims, 'Fleet Street catches a cold and the weaker papers tend to get pneumonia' (Baistow 1985: 33). The malaise is prolonged among regional and local newspapers and has already proved fatal for some free newspapers.

'Year zero': new technology and new contracts

The local press has undoubtedly been revolutionised by the introduction of new technologies of production during the 1980s, but the consequences of applying this new technology have not always been congruent with some observers' initial expectations. New technology, it was claimed, would lower the production costs of newspapers by reducing staffing levels and promoting multi-skilling. There would be a burgeoning of new titles and an unprecedented expansion of pluralism as different cultural and political groups, empowered by the new technology, established their own newspapers. New groups would emerge to challenge the dominance of established publishers in the newspaper market. To adopt the discourse of the cultural revolution, the new technology would 'let a hundred flowers blossom'. However, some observers were sceptical, claiming that the new technology would simply strengthen the market prominence of the already powerful newspaper monopolies, but these dissenting voices were barely audible above the enthusiastic clamour of advocates of the 'Fleet Street revolution'. Consider the following extract from a biography of Eddie Shah.

> [The year] 1986 has been billed as year zero of the Fleet Street revolution. It opened momentously. In the course of just one week at the end of January, Eddie Shah successfully concluded the first dummy run of his new colour daily *Today*; Robert Maxwell, having reduced the workforce at Mirror Group Newspapers by 2,000, told advertisers they could expect cuts of up to half in his newspapers' advertising rates . . . most dramatic of all, Rupert Murdoch's News International produced its four titles . . . from behind barbed wire at a new printing plant in Wapping while, in effect, locking out 5,000 members of the traditional print unions. It will also be a record year for new launches. In the past few months no less than six national titles have been planned in an industry which has become a by-word for stagnation.
>
> (Goodhart and Wintour 1986: xi)

It is difficult to imagine a more splendid lesson about the wisdom of offering hostages to fortune. The commentators are wrong in almost every particular. They were correct, however, to point up the inevitable losses of jobs which would be consequent on the introduction of the new technology.

Initially, the shedding of labour was achieved by signing 'new technology agreements' with the printing trades unions. Unions in the provincial and regional press never displayed the militancy which characterised Fleet Street industrial relations; nor did they possess the same industrial muscle as their counterparts on London national daily and Sunday papers. Having broken the traditional print union structure with new technology agreements, proprietors focused on journalists and began to impose individual contracts of employment; a twin process described as an 'employers' offensive' (Gall 1996: 2). The purpose of the offensive has been threefold. First, newspaper groups wished to end the system of collective bargaining and to impose wage settlements determined by market forces; essentially an economic goal. Second, companies wished to eradicate any basis for effective trade union practice by 'individualising' the employment relationship. Finally, newspaper groups wished to prevent the NUJ from using the new direct input technology as a lever to increase its bargaining power in relationship to management. From the company's perspective, there was little point in simply replacing the NGA with the NUJ (Gall 1996: 108). The introduction of the new contracts was achieved very rapidly; by 1989 more than half of the NUJ's provincial members no longer enjoyed collective bargaining agreements (Gall 1996: 93).

Journalists' new contracts typically involve the unilateral abrogation of existing agreements between the NUJ and the company and their replacement with a contract between the individual employee and the company. Franklin and Murphy (1991: 51) reproduce a letter from the Chorley Guardian Co. Ltd (part of United Newspapers) to its journalists which outlines the intended transition to an individual contract (Figure 19.1).

GMJ/MG   12 January 1990

Dear

Any contracts that still exist between non-management employees and the company are out of date and no longer relevant to today's circumstances in staff relations.

Most of you have never been invited to sign a contract and I feel that the time has come to take account of the changed situation and set down mutually beneficial terms that reflect the need for a better understanding that can only be in all our interests.

Please read the contract carefully. Feel free to come and see me to discuss any point that you feel unhappy about or may need clarification. You will note that the salary review date changes to June 1st, 1990.

You are reminded that although under the terms of contract salaries will not be the subject of collective bargaining, you remain free to be a member of a trade union and the contract does not affect your basic rights.

Yours sincerely

G.M. JOHNSTON
MANAGING EDITOR

Figure 19.1   Letter sent to journalist employees of the
Chorley Guardian Co. Ltd in 1990

The velvet glove tone of the letter, expressed in phrases such as 'mutually beneficial terms' barely conceals the iron fist policy which prescribes that the journalist is to lose all collective bargaining rights; the most basic means of redressing the inequality between the corporate strength of the employer and the individual weakness of the employee is eliminated. The journalist is allowed to be a member of a union   the employer would be breaking the law to deny such a right – but, in the individual contract offered to the Chorley Guardian journalists, he or she is specifically debarred from taking 'an active role in any such trade union'; a phrase undoubtedly constructed for its imprecise meaning (Franklin and Murphy 1991: 52). Journalists on local newspapers across the country are being 'forced' to sign such contracts. In February 1994 the United Newspaper management at the *Sheffield Star and Sheffield Telegraph* told the 96-strong NUJ chapel that it was derecognised and that the house agreement would end in three months. The consequences of such changes for levels of pay, staffing and conditions of service in the local and provincial press seem obvious; the knock-on effects of these latter changes for the range and quality of editorial content seem similarly self-evident.

Shaking up and shaking out

The trend of ownership since the war has been one of concentration into local monopolies controlled by large combines. By the early 1990s over 60 per cent of the British local press was owned by the largest ten companies (MMC 1991: 11; MMC 1992: 16) and over 80 per cent was in the hands of the top fifteen companies (MMC 1991: 11). This concentration was achieved not by large combines launching new publications but by their taking over existing titles. EMAP's 1992 Annual Report, for example, revealed that while £17m was spent in three years on launches, £65m was spent in one year on acquisitions (EMAP 1992). This is in the context of a total turnover of £269.4m and an operating profit of £33.9m. Such a high level of activity in takeovers is typical of all the combines.

A number of these acquisitions were brought about by the exchange of titles between conglomerates in order to establish local monopolies, a process which the Monopolies and Mergers Commission has never impeded. This inter-conglomerate exchange of titles is now a characteristic form of re-organisation in the industry. In 1991–2 Reed Regional Newspapers, the second largest publisher of local newspapers in the country, gave to Thomson Regional Newspapers, then the largest, a series of weekly titles in Tyneside in exchange for the *Blackburn Telegraph* and associated weeklies in Lancashire. This helped to consolidate Reed's strength in the North West while Thomson achieved the same consolidation in the North East (Reed 1992).

Similarly, United Newspapers and EMAP sold each other outliers from their empires and consolidated in their own areas of strength. EMAP bought the *Northampton Chronicle and Echo* and the *Cambridgeshire Town Crier* from

United and in turn sold them the *Western Telegraph*, the *South Wales Guardian* and the *Cardigan and Tivy-Side Advertiser*. There was a net inflow into United of £5.5m as a result of the deal (EMAP 1992; United Newspapers 1992; MMC 1992). Such deals may also involve agreements not to encroach on each other's circulation areas.

Not all acquisitions by the market leaders are the result of such exchanges. Well established independent local newspapers fall prey to the logic of the market and offer themselves for sale to firms with the financial reserves and the economies of scale to cope with the new market conditions and to weather the recession.

The Thomson empire, for instance, has been broken up and sold off in three large helpings. Late in 1995, the Barclay twins paid £90m and Northcliffe's Associated Newspapers £82m for their respective parts of the TRN Scottish titles, while Trinity Holdings acquired the TRN local titles for a further £24.5m. This represents both a re-assertion of the market position of Associated Newspapers and a continuing metamorphosis of Trinity from a medium sized company based on the ownership of the *Liverpool Echo and Post* to one of the biggest regional newspaper combines in the country, with an increasingly multinational character. During the period from 1992 until the end of 1995 they spent £62m on acquisitions of titles in England and Scotland. The company now controls about 13 per cent of the circulation of the UK regional and local press.

The Barclay twins' acquisitions in Scotland represent a move towards the acquisition of newspapers by conglomerate holding companies in order to compile a portfolio of assets. The twins' other holdings are based on their original property empire and include hotels, shipping, casinos and car dealing. They also own the *European* which they bought from Maxwell. Other major sales of local newspapers occurred in 1996. In June of that year, Johnston Press bought EMAP's 65 titles including four evening papers, 30 paid weeklies and 31 free newspapers. The new company will be the largest single newspaper publisher with 146 titles under its control (Sharpe 1996: 1). In late June 1996, Westminster Press placed 50 local titles including eight daily newspapers on the market for an anticipated £200 millions (Morgan and Sharpe 1996: 1). In November 1996 Newsquest bought Westminster Press for £305 millions.

The end of 1995 and the beginning of 1996 has been witness to two major changes in the pattern of ownership of the British local and regional press. The first was the sale of Reed Regional Newspapers by Reed Elsevier to a management buy out financed by Kohlberg Kravis Roberts. This represents the first foray by the American conglomerate into British media ownership. Its business is based on retailing in the USA, and its media arm is K-111 Communications whose chief executive is a former Macmillan President, William Reilly. K-111 owns a television news for schools channel as well as numerous educational and other specialist magazines in the USA. It was founded as an 'investment vehicle for KKR' (Tomkins 1995).

The consequence of this is likely to be a move towards the subsumption of the local and regional press into companies where they are part of a range of media enterprises which are all regarded as 'investment vehicles' and which are therefore likely to be disposed of when the returns are seen as less profitable than those that which might be achieved from other investments.

At the beginning of February 1996, however, a more profound change took place with the formation of a combine between MAI, the media company owned by the Labour Lord Hollick which controls the ITV franchises Meridian and Anglia, and United Newspapers which owns Express newspapers and a local and regional newspaper empire. This is the first merger of a major newspaper combine with a terrestrial commercial TV company since the relaxation of the ownership rules for broadcasters in the Autumn of 1995. This almost certainly represents a systemic change in the form of the corporate ownership of local papers towards their being part of a range of different communication technologies available to publishers rather than as the central focus of business activities.

Some of this momentum comes from the established mode of acquisitions, but some arises from the move by newspaper companies into new technology. Associated Newspapers are expanding their £30m cable TV company Channel One to provide a 24-hour a day local news service in the West Country. United Newspapers' regional evening paper, the *Yorkshire Post*, is already facing competition from the cable TV company Bell Cablemedia in Leeds, York and Harrogate. Now that United Newspapers are part of a company with major TV interests it seems likely that they will attempt to broaden the basis on which they compete in such areas. Local newspapers are already involved in local broadcasting. EMAP for instance owns Radio Aire (Snoddy 1995).

Newspapers are also experimenting in the use of the internet as a supplement or alternative to newsprint. Evening newspapers are already moving into the provision of online business information and advertisements and EMAP and Associated Newspapers are using the internet to distribute information in parts of the operations outside the local and regional press. If this proves commercially successful it is conceivable that they will extend their use of this technology into all of their outlets (Waldman 1995).

This concentration of ownership and technological change has taken place in the context of a general contraction in the industry, partly as a result of a long term secular trend towards lower rates of newspaper reading and partly because of the relentless tightening of labour market conditions which is a feature of modern capitalism. In a time of falling revenues Reed, for instance, have maintained profits by 'cost savings'. Overall they achieved staff reductions of 9 per cent in the year 1991–2. They lowered newsprint costs and closed eleven loss-making titles including the *Birmingham Daily News* (Reed 1992).

EMAP in the same period boasted of 'cost reductions' in all divisions which showed through 'into a 22 per cent increase in the second half year profits'. They have their own native Midlands euphemism for the process of staff reduction: 'Along the way, sadly, there had to be some goodbyes.' The *Luton Citizen* was closed. The *Nuneaton Tribune* was metamorphosed into a weekly free sheet and sold to Coventry Newspapers Ltd (EMAP 1992). United Provincial Newspapers faced a 2 per cent reduction in classified advertising volumes and 'most paid for titles showed declines in circulation. The closure of eight loss making free titles enable the free newspaper sector to increase profits substantially' (United Newspapers 1992: 12).

Survival and the maintenance or improvement of profit in the context of a declining market are thus achieved by the reduction in numbers of that most disposable of commodities: labour.

The local tabloid and a changing local journalism

There is a growing 'tabloidisation' of the local press. This is not to imply that local and regional newspapers are treading the same path as the *Sun* or *Mirror*, by publishing prurient stories about roadside fellatio or politicians' sex romps – nothing alas so interesting! But there has been a 'dumbing down' of the local press which has coincidentally been accompanied by a general move from broadsheet to tabloid format. This has involved the use of shorter, brighter stories, the increased use of stories about entertainment, shopping and 'human interest' stories; and lots more pictures.

This has been a deliberate policy reflecting editors' concern to create a newspaper appropriate for the local market. A Reed editor explained that his newspaper was 'precision' produced to meet the demands of readers as revealed in market research; the latter revealed readers' demand for this shorter, livelier material.

In the light of these developments it is perhaps not surprising that MMC analyses of weekly newspapers, but especially of the free newspapers, shows that the absolute amount of news may be less than 20 per cent of total newspaper content, while figures of around 30 per cent are common. But the constitution of even this impoverished news content is changing in two significant ways.

First, public relations handouts are increasingly a major source of news which are published with little, if any, editorial revision. These information subsidies are essential to a newspaper's well-being because the substantially reduced number of journalists must nonetheless continue to fill the editorial columns that remain. Simply reprocessing handouts which fall on to the journalist's desk along with the rest of the post is the most economically efficient way to minimise production costs. Little wonder that the general secretary of a major journalistic trade union commented that 'journalism's a desk job now. News used to be gathered on the hoof, now it's all telephone calls to press relations people and rent-a-quote MPs.' Such revised journalistic news gathering protocols mean that major news stories can be very inadequately reported. A study of the local press coverage of the 1992 general election, for example, revealed that four of the twelve newspapers in the study carried no election coverage across the four weeks of the campaign (Franklin 1994: 177). The same study also illustrated the extent of the reliance by the local press on public relations handouts even when reporting substantive news stories. More than half (55 per cent) of the reports featuring the Labour candidate, published by one local newspaper, were based on press releases issued by the local Labour Party and almost half (49.3 per cent) of those press releases were published virtually verbatim or with only a minimal editorial revision (Franklin 1994: 168). Local newspapers' coverage of local political news is similarly driven by the information subsidies emanating from townhall public relations departments and other communications conscious political interest groups (Franklin 1986: 28).

The news content of local papers is changing in a second way as it becomes increasingly difficult to distinguish editorial from advertising. This ever more frequent congress between advertising and editorial has been disparagingly dubbed by journalists as 'advertorial'. These 'Features' are designed specifically to attract advertising but also facilitate the general move from traditional 'news' articles to items with a consumerist bent. Their formats are highly stylised. Typically they feature a local company which is moving premises, celebrating a centenary or expanding its business in some way. A rather tedious formulaic article celebrates the history of the company in euphuistic tones while, on the strength of the article, the paper solicits adverts – usually in the form of best wishes messages – from the firm's suppliers and major customers. Gall has argued that the increased frequency of advertorial reflects not only the growing influence of advertisers, but the de-recognition of the NUJ which makes journalists less able to resist the management policy of 'currying favour with the advertisers in order to . . . guarantee future and hopefully increased business' (Gall 1993: 20). Journalists' lack of industrial muscle means that they are no longer able to serve as a bulwark of probity against such editorial banality.

Certain publishers, such as Thomson Regional Newspapers, seem particularly willing to subordinate 'hard news' to consumer stories. TRN's *Newcastle Chronicle*, for example, gave front page prominence to news of a price reduction drive at Tesco's even though this meant relegating a story about a double murder in the city to the inside pages of the newspaper. When TRN owned the *Scotsman* in Edinburgh, two pages were devoted to a story about a toy – International Rescue's Tracey Island – which parents were finding difficulty in buying in local shops. According to the editorial director of TRN, quoted in the *UK Press Gazette* of 18 March 1991, this constitutes, 'hard evidence that our newspapers are recognising real issues and that times have changed' (Gall 1993: 20). Certainly times have changed; the idea of newspapers without news is growing apace and enjoys the support of powerful backers!

These changes in editorial emphasis and in journalists' news gathering and reporting routines have eroded the idea of the journalist as a professional whose occupational legitimacy relies on the performance of an institutional role as an investigator who is central to the process of democracy and public life. The demands on a journalist to give primary loyalty to the corporation rather than the community are shown by the way in which individual contracts demand unqualified loyalty to corporate owners before all else, as the Chorley Guardian/United Newspapers' letter to employees indicates (see Figure 19.1).

In the case of EMAP, Bob Feltham, the managing director of their newspapers, enthuses about the recruitment of journalists into an army of sellers of the company's corporate image: 'there was successful collaboration with EMAP's magazine division resulting in *custom written specialist features appearing in our newspapers promoting our magazine titles and providing a basis for the advertising sales for the papers too*' (our emphasis; EMAP 1992). At the same time, a company training school has been set up in the rooms above the offices of the *Peterborough Evening Telegraph*. This means that EMAP journalists work, and are being trained, entirely in the ethos of the company and are not exposed to general professional ethics which traditionally would have regarded the blurring of the role of the reporter with a tub thumper for corporate promotion and a spieler for the advertising department as entirely unacceptable.

Summary

There has always been a central contradiction in what James Curran describes as the liberal theory of press freedom (Curran and Seaton 1991: 277–94). The contradiction inheres in the idea that the free market is supposed to be compatible with, if not the guarantor of, a free press. This press would service democracy by the provision of news – factual accounts about the functioning of the political system – and by giving voice to the alternative views about the way in which society's affairs might be conducted. Local newspapers in brief provided the information base for citizens who made policy choices via the democratic process. Newspapers should be documents of record in the local community recording the courts and the council, as well as providing a forum for debate. But the consummation of free market and free press has never been achieved, no matter how devoutly it might be wished. The costs of investments in plant and buildings combined with the pursuit of income through advertising and expansive readerships, in order to survive economically, results in the minimax philosophy and the constant search for material which costs least and earns most. No market could work in any other way.

This has produced a long term tendency in the popular and local press towards entertainment, trivia and sensationalism based on the lowest common denominator in terms of expectations of reader literacy and attention span. Similar trends can be identified in the quality market where more and more sections have to provide 'lifestyle' articles which appear to be aimed at making readers think about grotesque clothes, exotic holidays, expensive motor cars and intellectually demanding versions of the sexual act. Gresham's Law seems to operate in this context; bad material drives out the good. In this case the value judgement is that the material is bad for an informed democracy. The trivial drives out the serious. There are fewer and fewer places for investigative news; news is judged by its high earning, low cost quality. The constant downward pressure on the number of journalists, moreover, means that they simply do not have the time to carry out the traditional democratic function.

The idea of the professional journalist was of a worker whose commitment was to an idea of the story and its revelation to some community of people unified by belonging to a common political entity. The authority of the news narrative derived from the idea that the journalist was writing what he or she believed to be true. This is what distinguished editorial material from advertising, PR handouts or a publishing company beating its own drum. Our contention is that the collapse of the market for local newspapers is driving the industry to the erosion of that fundamental distinction. This is not because it is managed by people who seek the destruction of local democracy. On the contrary major examples of local newspaper investigation can be cited. The *Manchester Evening News* with the full backing of management led the investigative exposure of the Stalker affair (Murphy 1991); a clear example of corporate owners making editorial room for journalists to carry out their traditional role. But these endeavours were accompanied by the slow, long-term inexorable decline in readership. It is this manifestation of the market, and the normal market response to it, which is metamorphosing the butterfly into the grub.

References

Association of Free Newspapers (1991) *A-Z of Britain's Free Newspapers and Magazines 1990*, Gloucester: Association of Free Newspapers.

Audit Bureau of Circulation (1995) *Audit Bureau of Circulation: figures*, October, London: ABC.

Baistow, T. (1985) *Fourth Rate Estate*, London: Comedia.

Benns Media (1988) London: Benn Business Information Services.

Curran, J. and Seaton, J. (1991) *Power Without Responsibility* (4th edn), London: Routledge.

East Midlands Allied Press (1992) *Annual Report*, London EMAP.

The Economist (1993) 'Multimedia: the tangled webs they weave', 16 October.

Franklin, B. (1986) 'Public relations, the local press and the coverage of local government', *Local Government Studies*, July/August: 25–33.

Franklin, B. (1994) *Packaging Politics: Political Communication in Britain's Media Democracy*, London: Edward Arnold.

Franklin, B. and Murphy, D. (1991) *What News? The Market, Politics and the Local Press*, London: Routledge.

Gall, G. (1993) 'Journalism for changing times: the impact of new technology and industrial relations on the editorial content of the provincial press', Paper presented to the Annual Conference of the Political Studies Association, University of Leicester, 21 April.

Gall, G. (1996) 'Employment and Technological Change in The British Provincial Newspaper Industry', unpublished Ph.D. thesis, University of Manchester Institute of Science and Technology.

Goodhart, D. and Wintour, P. (1986) *Eddie Shah and the Newspaper Revolution*, London: Coronet.

Goodman, G. (1993) 'Too Much To Read?', *British Journalism Review* 4(1): 3–5.

Gray, P. (1981) *Communication Behaviour*, Leicester: Centre For Mass Communication Research.

Greenslade, R. (1992) 'Unpopular press', *Guardian*, 19 October.

MacArthur, B. (1991) 'Gloom, doom but no boom', *UK Press Gazette*, 17 June.

Monopolies and Mergers Commission (November 1991) *Cmnd 1992*, London: HMSO.

Monopolies and Mergers Commission (October 1992) *Cmnd 2057*, London: HMSO.

Morgan, J. and Sharpe, H. (1996) 'Westminster Press Up For Sale', *UK Press Gazette*, 28 June.

Murphy, D. (1991) *The Stalker Affair and The Press*, London: Unwin Hyman.

Prichard, C. (1994) 'The cuddlies and junkies wrestle for the regionals', *British Journalism Review* 4(4): 55–8.

Reed International (1992) *Annual Report*, London: Reed International.

Royal Commission on The Press (1977) *Final Report*, Vol. 3, Cmnd 6810, London: HMSO.

Sharpe, H. (1996) 'EMAP Sell Off Sparked By Heathrow Meeting', *UK Press Gazette*, 7 June.

Snoddy, R. (1995), 'Survey of Leeds and the North: Microcosm of media change – Yorkshire press, TV and radio', *Financial Times*, 20 June.

Tomkins, R. (1995) 'International Company News: KKR-owned media company plans IPO', *Financial Times*, 6 September.

United Newspapers (1992) *Annual Report*, London: United Newspapers.

Waldman, S. (1995) 'A year on the Net', *Guardian*, 17 November.

Chapter 20

Roslyn Grose

CALL THAT A NEWSPAPER?

*T*HE SUN PRIDES ITSELF ON ITS NEWS COVERAGE[1] . . .

It's ironic, therefore, that it is the paper that most regularly has to bear the jibe: 'Call that a newspaper! There's no news in that rag, just tits and bums.'

This is a familiar view, expressed by those who equate news with columns of grey type spread over broadsheet pages, rarely broken by a headline or a picture.

The Sun is full of news. It is just presented in a different way. An interesting exercise is to mark the day's major news stories in one of the so-called 'heavies' like *The Times*, the *Daily Telegraph* or *The Independent*. Then try to find those stories in *The Sun*. You will. The amount of space and prominence given to them will simply be different.

The paper has always faced up to the fact that most people's basic interests are not politics, philosophy or economics. They are more likely to be money, sex, crime, sport, food, drink and what's on telly.

News editor Tom Petrie has done that job for nine years and knows instinctively which stories to follow each day to give the readers what they want.

'We've always been an opportunist paper,' he says. That explains stories like the most talked-about front page of all time, the one bearing the headline 'Freddie Starr ate my hamster'. It met all the criteria for a *Sun* front page lead. It was exclusive, it had human interest, it was surprising, even shocking enough to make reader exclaim, 'Cor, did you see that!'

with

dealing with everyone

The Sun has a great rapport with its readers which results in many of its most outstanding news scoops. On the news desk they take literally hundreds of calls a day from readers. Tom Petrie says, 'They seem to like joining in.'

Of course, for every call that produces a front-page story there are dozens of false alarms or good-intentioned calls from people who think they have uncovered some hot news. All are dealt with sympathetically . . .

The Sun always wants to know, even if it means giving a little old lady advice on which social services department to contact to do something about the holes in her ceiling . . .

The Sun invented the readers' phone-in as a way of getting material for stories. The paper asks them to call and tell of their experiences in a particular situation. Almost every time, the phone lines are jammed. A very few are tricksters and hoaxers but overwhelmingly the calls, which have to be checked out individually before a word is published, are genuine.

The benefit of the system to both readers and journalists is enormous.

Another *Sun* innovation has been 'You the jury', where readers are asked to phone in their votes on a controversial issue or story. A record 195,000 calls were received within two days when a woman was gaoled for pouring boiling water on the genitals of a youth who raped her five-year-old daughter . . .

Some of the paper's greatest scoops have been stories about the royal family. Prince Edward's decision to depart from the marines in January 1987 was first announced by *The Sun*. And the information came yet again in an out-of-the-blue phone call. It was anonymous but news staff were able to stand it up.

Reporter John Kay checked out the tip-off that Prince Edward had decided to pack it in because he could not take the tough training . . .

'He told his father [Prince Philip] that he did not want a career in the marines,' Kay recalls. 'But in order to deflect public criticism of Edward, Buckingham Palace were preparing to put out an official announcement that Prince Edward was quitting because of a leg injury.'

That is the version that would have gone down in history but for . . . *The Sun* . . .

When that night's first edition hit the streets, all *The Sun*'s rivals were forced to pick up the story . . .

Intensive investigations by the police, the Ministry of Defence and the marines failed to uncover the source of *The Sun* story . . .

[M]ost of *The Sun*'s royal stories come from the reporters who regularly follow members of the royal family around – not only on royal tours but on day-to-day engagements.

This concentration on the royals started in earnest when Prince Charles came out of the navy. He was twenty-eight and had once expressed the view that thirty was a good age for a man to marry. *The Sun*'s editor of the time, Larry Lamb, was determined *The Sun* would win the race to announce that

Charles had met his match. He appointed the paper's first permanent royal roundsmen. Their brief: to follow the prince on a daily basis.

That is how *Sun* writer Harry Arnold and photographer Arthur Edwards came to the very early conclusion that Lady Diana Spencer might become the future queen.

What this means is that the royal reporters have been able to build up an amazing network of contacts and 'moles' over the years. Royal estate workers, footmen, detectives, they all pass on the tit-bits of information that enable reporters to work out what's going on behind palace walls.

Take Fergie's pregnancy. *The Sun*'s star royal photographer Arthur Edwards was told by a Sandringham estate worker that the Duchess of York had been heard to say: 'Can't stay. Got to go and rest. Doctor's orders.' Just afterwards, Arthur and royal writer Harry Arnold saw Fergie in Switzerland and, fathers both, spotted the sure signs of morning sickness.

'We broke the story,' says Arthur. 'And then we spent ten days on tenderhooks [*sic*] till Buckingham Palace finally announced it . . .'

Those are some of the big royal stories. But there have been loads of small ones, at which *The Sun* excels. Who would have thought, for instance, that the heir to the throne's thinning hair would make the front page? That is exactly what happened when Arthur spied the beginnings of a bald patch on the back of Prince Charles' head and took two snaps of it. 'Oops Charles there's a patch in your thatch' was the headline.

It was one of Edwards' first picture-stories about the prince and he was anxious not to offend His Royal Highness, so asked for his by-line to be left off the picture . . .

[T]here are a lot of other stories with what news editor Petrie feels are essential ingredients to tickle the palates of *Sun* readers — a sense of fun and the capacity to amaze.

Petrie cites an example: 'We ran a story about a couple who had won £40,000-odd at bingo. They only had one child and they blew [*sic*] the lot on microwaves, televisions, videos and such, then went back to the DHSS for a hand-out . . .

That sort of story is compulsive reading and it is the lifeblood of *The Sun*' . . .

A high point in the paper's popularity was reached during the Falklands War when *The Sun* gave itself the title 'The paper that supports our boys'. Headlines like 'Gotcha' (when the *Belgrano* was hit) and 'Up yours Galtieri' were not to everyone's taste but they obviously caught the mood of the moment . . .

The Sun has been accused of being jingoistic and its Falklands coverage obviously stirred its readers' patriotic feelings. It's [*sic*] arrival among our boys at war was not always greeted with pleasure, however. A young officer wounded in the hostilities told a *Sun* journalist afterwards: 'Your headlines often made us feel sick. There were ritual burnings of *The Sun* in some quarters.'

Note

1   This extract is taken from *The 'Sun'-sation: Behind the Scenes of Britain's Best-Selling Newspaper* (1989), published to coincide with the twentieth anniversary of the paper's re-launch under the proprietorship of Rupert Murdoch. The 1980s marked the hey-day of *the Sun*. It overtook the *Daily Mirror* as the national daily newspaper with the largest circulation in 1978 and for most of the following decade it averaged sales of more than four million.

Chapter 21

Gregor Gall

LOOKING IN THE *MIRROR*
A case study of industrial relations in a national newspaper

Introduction

THE YEARS 1992 TO 1994 WERE extremely eventful ones at Mirror Group Newspapers (MGN). Robert Maxwell, their widely despised owner, died in a mysterious boating accident; the *Daily Mirror* was at its (former) journalistic best, campaigning for and supporting the miners over the pit closures programme announced by Michael Heseltine; various board-room coups took place which ushered in the entry of Murdoch hatchetman David Montgomery; three editors and over 100 journalists were sacked; the workforce threatened strikes and held numerous occupations; and an internecine price war broke out with the *Sun* while the *Mirror*'s circulation continued to fall steeply. This chapter examines these tumultuous changes at MGN and the interrelation between them while focusing on two critical areas: the battle between management and the unions over the way the company is run, that is, their industrial relations; and the political direction of the papers. The first part will involve looking at what the management has done to increase the share value of the company to enable the owners to retrieve their loans from MGN. This will therefore focus on the sacking of journalists and attacks on the unions there in an attempt to reduce operating costs. The irony of a left-wing, pro-Labour paper read by a predominantly working class readership attacking the rights of its workers and their unions cannot be lost on many people. These attacks on the journalists and their union will be set in the wider context of the changing nature of industrial relations in the rest of the national newspapers. The second part will seek to consider what effect the new owners of the MGN have had on the political direction of the *Mirror* and what this may mean for Britain's 'free press' and political pluralism. Furthermore, the relationship between the strength and position of the National Union of Journalists (NUJ) and the political and editorial direction of MGN's papers, and in particular the *Mirror*, will be considered.

Before the chapter recounts the recent dramatic events at the *Mirror*, it begins by setting the chain of events in a historical context. The Maxwell period is briefly examined to reveal the nature of the industrial relations of this era and specifically the state of the *Mirror* chapel of the NUJ. The research for this paper is based primarily on secondary sources such as the *UK Press Gazette* (*UKPG*) and NUJ's *Journalist* but it has been supplemented by a small number of interviews with NUJ full-time and lay officials. Consequently, the main focus is on the journalists and the editorial area.

The Maxwell days

When Maxwell took over MGN in 1984 he engaged in a strategy of undermining the collective confidence and strength of the workers there, in particular the NUJ, through bullying, intimidation, threats, retreats and then counter-attacks. Over the years the introduction of merit pay and personal contracts undermined collective bargaining and compounded the NUJ's weakness. The chapel leadership was the other side of the industrial relations coin; it believed in making concessions rather than confronting Maxwell and his managers to defend its members' interests and ironically some of those journalists who opposed Maxwell's take-over soon became his greatest supporters. This cycle of NUJ demoralisation and retreat was broken by a revolt in May 1991 when Maxwell was forced to back down from implementing named compulsory redundancies. Initially the journalists were resigned to the cuts but the mood changed when a number of activists said enough was enough. The journalists held a worktime meeting to oppose the cuts which did not break up until the redundancies were withdrawn; Maxwell caved in because if the meeting had continued it would have prevented the production of the paper that night. This juncture showed the potential power of the journalists to stop production under direct input but it also emphasised the need for the collective exercise of this power by a well-organised, confident chapel. The successful rebellion injected new life into the NUJ chapel such that it became more assertive.

From the death of Maxwell to the appointment of Montgomery

Following the death of Maxwell in November 1991 MGN was put into the hands of the administrators on behalf of the other shareholders and those to whom Maxwell was in debt. According to *Mirror* columnist Paul Foot (*Socialist*

Worker, 31 October 1992), the journalists had a much greater sense of freedom in what they could write because there was no despotic proprietor strolling the corridors and dictating editorial policy. However this period of freedom was to last for less than a year. 'Black Friday' — 23 October 1992 — saw the start of what was to become a process of huge upheaval in terms of personnel and editorial policy at MGN and the *Mirror*. Over 300 journalists, clerical and advertising workers, telephonists and security guards occupied the *Mirror* newsroom for seven hours in response to the appointment of David Montgomery, ex-Murdoch man and ex-*Today* and *News of the World* editor, as chief executive of MGN. The occupation overwhelmingly (278: 4) voted to tell management that they refused to work with Montgomery and were unimpressed by promises from the editor, Richard Stott, about job security and protecting the paper's political line. One journalist said:

> People were outraged over management threatening to impose a Thatcherite bastard on us. We voted overwhelmingly to stop the paper unless we received written assurances.
>
> (*Socialist Worker*, 31 October 1992)

With ten minutes to go before final deadlines for that night's paper Stott returned with another letter of assurance of editorial independence, a continuation of the MGN's pro-Labour line, a no redundancies pledge, and continued union recognition. A much depleted occupation narrowly voted (57: 41) to accept these assurances and to produce the late editions of the paper. Many had already left, presuming that the paper would not come out, and the vote was swung by 'management toadies', as one journalist put it.

On 11 November Bill Hagerty, editor of the *People*, was sacked, or, as the company said, 'vacated the editorship'. This provoked a three-hour mandatory union meeting by journalists from all three titles (the *Mirror*, *Sunday Mirror* and *People*) because Montgomery had gone back on one of the pledges. He refused to meet the union representatives. On the same day seven compositors were compulsorily sacked. On Monday 16 November, under Montgomery's reorganisation which aimed to create, in his words, a 'tight and efficient operation' (*Financial Times*, 17 November 1992), over 100 *Mirror* freelance journalists were sacked by MGN and prevented from entering the building. These 'casuals' consistently formed 25 per cent of the *Mirror* staff and were *de facto* permanent staff working five days a week, most having been there for between two and five years but without employment contracts. Staff journalists on the *Mirror* refused to do work for the *Mirror*'s sister Sunday papers and a picket line of sacked journalists turned away many journalists turning up to do shifts for the Sunday papers. At the same time Stott was sacked, to be replaced by David Banks from Murdoch's *Telegraph-Mirror* in Australia. The company pledged that it would remain a pro-Labour paper but that it would seek, in the company's words, 'a more modern approach' with less 'ranting [Labour] propaganda' (*Financial Times*, 17 November 1992).

A week later journalists voted 101: 69 in a 'consultative ballot' in favour of industrial action over the job losses and the changes and they planned to hold a legal ballot for industrial action. This forced Banks to agree to meet the NUJ to discuss both the sackings and journalists being moved to different departments without consultation. However, at the same time, some casual journalists on the Sunday papers were issued with personal contracts, which the NUJ advised them not to sign, and the assistant managing director of the well known anti-union company, TV-am, was appointed company secretary and legal director for MGN.

Soon after, Banks sacked the Northern Ireland correspondent, whereupon the journalists voted a motion of 'no confidence' in him and called for the sacking of Montgomery. The journalists stopped work for four hours over this and were then promised a meeting with Banks on the sacking. He then reneged on this and sent letters to all staff threatening dismissal if they took industrial action and giving them five days to pledge their support for him or leave. He said:

> I would not expect you to continue to serve under an editor whom you felt was unfit to hold office. If I have not heard from you within five days I will assume you support the motion and we can arrange to have a chat.
>
> (*UKPG*, 21 December 1992)

Banks then promised to meet to discuss, but not negotiate over, his plans for using no further casuals and for work flexibility among the remaining staff. He also stated that he would not negotiate on the (personal) contracts issued to part-time Sunday staff or to newly appointed full-time staff which excluded them from current and future union house agreements.

Since January 1993, there has been a further catalogue of notable events: fifty or more journalists were sacked upon the arrival of many *Today* staff; an MGN journalist was disciplined for criticising the sackings in a letter to a newspaper; the political editor was forced to leave; a key NUJ activist was moved into a non-journalistic area; and the deputy editor of *Today* was appointed as group managing editor with a remit to 'look at the quality of journalists' which led to forty-four further sackings. These journalists were, to quote MGN, 'not the kind of people the *Mirror* wants' (*UKPG*, 8 February 1993). Ann Robinson left in March for *Today*, saying:

> I don't feel at home at the *Mirror* any more . . . I don't like the atmosphere [and] I don't think journalists ought to be motivated by fear.
>
> (*UKPG*, 8 March 1993)

In journalese, these events could be characterised as 'a revolution from above', but this revolution was not only one from above but also a continuing 'permanent revolution'.

MGN was then taken to court by the NUJ in February 1993 over its unilateral change of journalists' terms of conditions, that is, breach of contract. MGN had imposed a five-day week on its sub-editors who currently worked their thirty-five hours over a four-day week. The company was found to have acted unlawfully since it failed to consult those affected and threatened them with the sack if they failed to comply with the company's requests. The NUJ subsequently had to take MGN back to court for contempt as it failed to comply with the ruling. The company avoided contempt by forcing the subs to sign new contracts which stipulated five-day working, or else face the sack. Several did sign, while both the NUJ father of the chapel (FoC) and deputy FoC were sacked along with two other subs for not signing. The two NUJ officials were also told that their chapel positions were incompatible with their jobs. The chapel responded to this by holding first an immediate worktime meeting and then a disruptive meeting in early March against management's refusal to discuss union recognition and the sacking of staff. The company replied by threatening summary dismissal if any journalists held an 'unlawful' chapel meeting without permission, saying, 'This was the latest in a series of eight meetings which have disrupted the *Mirror* and lost thousands of copies' (*UKPG*, 15 March 1993).

Throughout this period Banks refused to meet the NUJ, even though it remained formally recognised, despite letters and pleas from the NUJ's general secretary. The NUJ chapel voted 60/40 per cent in favour of strike action and 79/21 per cent in favour of industrial action short of a strike to force genuine recognition and negotiation. However, this vote in early February was never put into action and the forced departure of Paul Foot in early April marked the end of any possible union opposition for the foreseeable future. Subsequent attempts to force MGN to enter into negotiations with the NUJ have focused on lobbying the Labour Party and TUC to use their influence (without success).

Since this period flexible work hours for no extra pay, multi-skilling and a clampdown on expenses have been introduced. In addition, further attacks on journalists' conditions and trade union rights have been mounted. MGN's move to Canary Wharf contravened health and safety regulations over VDUs, and the NUJ's representative on the company's health and safety committee has been prevented from attending its meetings even though she had a legal right to do so under the 1974 Health and Safety Act (*Journalist*, April/May 1995). Journalists on the *Sporting Life* have been forced to work on twelve Sundays a year, with no extra pay and only time off in lieu, in response to the deregulation of the racing industry. When the pay review date came in 1993, across-the-board rises topped up by merit pay were abolished in favour of full performance related pay, paid at either a 3 per cent, for 'good performer', or a 0 per cent increase for 'under performers'. Thus by the summer of 1993 some 150 journalists, the so-called 'defiant element' according to Montgomery, had been sacked along with 450 workers in other areas of the business. The workforce now stands at just below 3,000. The unions (the GPMU and NUJ) have been *de facto* fully derecognised. What is particularly ironic is that 'the paper that fights for a fairer Britain' has taken part in a campaign with the Labour Party and the TUC for part-timers' rights and for workers' rights such as maternity leave.

Before moving on to look at the reasons underlying these attacks on the journalists and their union, it is worth noting that a similar process has been experienced by the journalists and NUJ after MGN led a consortium in 1994 to take over Newspaper Publishing, owners of the *Independent* and *Independent on Sunday*. Initially some twenty journalists were issued with personal contracts, whose terms and conditions were considerably poorer than those negotiated between the union and the company. Indeed, to issue such personal contracts was in contravention of the house (collective bargaining) agreement between the union and the company and this clearly raised the prospect that the management wanted to derecognise the NUJ chapel. In 1995 the company sacked forty-eight journalists, followed by another forty-four in 1996, and derecognised the NUJ. These measures come on top of redundancies, pay freezes and increases in the working week which took place prior to the take-over.

The battle between management and the journalists

There can be no doubt about Montgomery's role in MGN. The banks, having rejected bids and management buyouts through fear that they would be forced to sell at too low a price, put him in charge with one aim. This was to cut labour costs, increase profits, pay off debts and raise the share price of MGN, in order to get it to a position where it could be sold off and thus allow the banks to recoup their money and make a profit on the sale. The word 'banks' is used because, led by NatWest (30 per cent) and Goldman Sachs (10 per cent), they own 54.8 per cent of MGN. This is their collateral for the huge sums that they lent Maxwell, after he had proved himself a good businessman and socialist by sacking thousands of workers and increasing the profits of the British Printing Corporation (in 1981).

Labour costs were targeted by Montgomery as not only the largest single component of operating costs but also the mostly easily cut. He has cut manning levels to those of MGN's main competitor, News International (NI), in order to carry out the banks' wishes to increase the value of MGN. City analysts suggested that this would mean sacking 30 per cent of the work-force (4,000 in mid-1992) while James Capel, stockbrokers, reported, using 1991 figures, that this entailed raising the turnover per worker by 58 per cent; in 1991 MGN workers accounted for £113,332 turnover per worker per annum while those at NI accounted for £178,883 per worker per annum. This meant increasing the operating profit per worker by 43 per cent at MGN, since in 1991 each MGN worker contributed £20,626 while each worker at NI contributed £29,564. A media analyst put it bluntly, saying,

'Murdoch started the process, Maxwell took it forward and Montgomery must complete it' (*Sunday Times*, 22 November 1992). Montgomery has indeed pleased the bankers; when he took over shares were at 50p; by early March 1993 they had risen to nearly 100p, by January 1994 they had reached 170p, and thereafter moved to around the 200p mark – well past 120p, the price at which the banks put in their money.

Thus it should be clear that MGN was not fighting for economic survival, as some managers and commentators alleged. The company was in fact highly profitable and the banks sought to make it even more so. This did not stop MGN from saying that it was in 'a fragile state', to try to convince the workers that they needed to make sacrifices to save their jobs. The banks wanted to turn MGN into an NI. It should come as no surprise to find that NI is more profitable than MGN. This is not just because Murdoch sacked 5,500 printers and established a non-union printing operation. It needs to be remembered that Maxwell carried out his own massive but less publicised programme of redundancies, wage cuts and flexible work practices on the printers in 1985. The main difference concerns the NUJ; it has been completely broken at NI. Those journalists and NUJ members who moved to Wapping to ensure that Murdoch got his papers out incalculably weak-ened their own union organisation by strike-breaking. By early 1990 all NI journalists had signed personal contracts and the NUJ was therefore no longer recognised for collective bargaining or any other matters. Today it is still completely marginalised. This was not entirely inevitable, because NUJ members there voted clearly several times to take strike action to resist de-recognition but these mandates for action were frittered away as negotiating chips. That they produced no concessions was said by the union leadership to mean that strike action would not make any difference. This has allowed Murdoch to impose low pay rises and pay freezes and to sack innumerable staff. For example, in September 1992 twenty-six long serving journalists on *The Times*, including the NUJ FoC who led the journalists to Wapping, were sacked to be replaced by younger and cheaper staff.

Montgomery's task of cutting labour costs necessarily meant attacking the journalists and the NUJ. This meant marginalisation and derecognition as many other companies have successfully done in the national press (see p. 242). Derecognition and personal contracts allow MGN not only to sack journalists with minimum compensation but also to make them work harder for less money. Derecognition means that the union has no role in deciding terms and conditions; across-the-board pay rises will be ended; only those performing exceptionally will get rises; and bonuses will be scrapped and hours lengthened.

For this task Montgomery has an exemplary record as a hatchetman and ruthless manager. As editor of the *News of the World* he helped to persuade NUJ members there to strike-break at Wapping. As editor and chief exec-utive of *Today* he ran a non-union shop, the NUJ having been derecognised in 1986, and when Murdoch's debts became too threatening in 1990 he implemented large staff cuts at *Today*. Montgomery is suitably ruthless; he guaranteed in person Stott's job to him, used him to prevent the journalists from going on strike, and then sacked him a week later as well as sacking the 100-plus journalists without warning or explanation. Two other ex-NI executives have also been appointed, including Charles Wilson, one of the masterminds of Wapping.

In attacking the journalists and the NUJ, Montgomery will have been well aware of the potential power of this group of workers. The introduction of direct input was used to get rid of the well organised NGA compositors. Journalists now do the compositors' job of inputting material, setting and sub-editing it on screen. They are now central to production and this gives them the potential to slow down and halt production through a work-to-rule or strike/occupation to win their demands. He will have been concerned to decollectivise, individualise and atomise the journalists, through derecognition and personal contracts, to prevent them from using this potential as the *Mirror* journalists had shown in 1991. For the journalists it is, however, a potential that is double edged because the new technology means that fewer journalists are required, with the help of agency copy, to produce a paper. This means that, in the absence of support from the printing workers in refusing to run the presses, only well supported lightning strike action amongst the journalists can halt production and beat back the employers.

Thus as soon as Montgomery was appointed, he set up an alternative production system using the equipment of the *Sporting Life* and Sunday magazine supplements. He obviously considered that industrial action by the journalists was possible and was determined to beat them and keep production going using this system as part of his overall plan. He stated:

> I [am] determined to safeguard production. The guiding principle is to implement change without losing papers.
>
> (*Sunday Times*, 22 November 1992)

The task of the journalists successfully to resist the management was difficult, given the demoralisation inside the union due to the wave of derecognitions and personal contracts suffered and the (internal) crisis of the NUJ arising from the sacking of the General Secretary (Gall 1992, Smith and Morton 1990). Moreover, there were divisions amongst the journalists at MGN: there was the NUJ chapel, the British Association of Journalists (BAJ) chapel and also the *Mirror* journalists chapel (i.e., the non-NUJ/BAJ chapel). However, the greatest immediate problem facing the journalists was how to take such action as could stop Montgomery before the initial anger slipped away and the momentum was lost, whereby demoralisation and pessimism set in and the plans for maintaining production were perfected. The task was difficult but not impossible given the success of the 1991 sit-in and the preparedness of the journalists to hold disruptive but not production halting meetings. Even these disruptive meetings had worried management; they banned union meetings in the newsroom unless permission was given and none were allowed beyond 3p.m. But what made the task particularly difficult was that the leadership of the NUJ insisted upon following the well-worn but failed strategy of trying to obtain legal injunctions in British and European courts and seeking the support of Labour MPs to stop the management and their imposed changes.

The wider context: the employers' offensive in the national papers sector

Since 1989 the NUJ has suffered a number of major defeats at the hands of the employers in the national and provincial press and in the book and magazine industry in regard to both the ending of union rights, that is, collective bargaining and recognition, and attacks on journalists' terms and conditions of employment. The same broad strategy and tactics which the employers have used to marginalise and derecognise the NUJ at MGN have been used by newspaper, magazine and book employers. This is particularly apparent if we look at the recent industrial relations developments in the rest of the national press. Thus the NUJ has been derecognised for all trade union purposes (recognition, consultation and collective bargaining) by Express Newspapers, Associated Newspapers, NI and the *Telegraph* group (see Table 21.1). To replace union recognition personal contracts have been introduced through bribes and intimidation. The position of the NUJ at the *Guardian/Observer* and the *Financial Times* is precarious, where the chapels have been marginalised within the maintenance of the framework of collective bargaining and union recognition. Here fairly major changes have been forced through without negotiation, much less proper consultation, with regard to work patterns, pay and conditions, and staff levels (see Table 21.2).

The most striking aspect of the process of union derecognition and marginalisation has been that the employers all engaged in introducing the change at the same time. The *Express* group was first to initiate the process, followed by Associated, NI and then the *Telegraph* group. This suggests not that the employers were acting in concert with each other but that some awaited the response of the journalists, that is, the degree and nature of resistance of the NUJ chapels, before moving to introduce derecognition and personal contracts for their own journalists. The basis of this was trying to limit the risk of successful opposition: if, say, the Express Newspapers NUJ chapels knocked back their employers it would, other things being equal, increase the likelihood of NUJ chapels at Associated Newspapers having the confidence to resist their employers effectively. As part of the process, journalists on different titles within different groups were targeted before others in a gradual fashion; thus in NI journalists on *The Times* and *Sunday Times* were not targeted until resistance from the *Sun* and *News of the World* journalists had collapsed. Another quite apparent feature in the national

Table 21.1 NUJ derecognition in national newspapers

Group	Date of derecognition & personal contracts	Nature of resistance by NUJ	Tactics used by employer	Type of derecognition	Results of derecognition
Express Newspapers	1989–93	Refusal to sign; worktime meeting; legal remedy.	Pay rise.	Partial then full.	Loss of 9-day fortnight; pay freezes.
Telegraph	1989–91	Refusal to sign; strike vote.	Pay rise; threat of sack; sackings; negotiations.	Partial then full.	Loss of 9-day fortnight; job losses.
Associated Newspapers	1989–90	Refusal to sign; strike votes; worktime meeting; legal remedy.	Pay rise; new recruits; negotiations.	Partial then full.	N/A
News International	1989–90	Refusal to sign; strike vote.	Pay rise; cash bonus; negotiations	Full.	Redundancies; pay freezes.

Note: 'Negotiations' denotes the tactic of giving the standard (three month) notice of termination of the house agreement, in order to give the impression that negotiations over the following three months could resolve the issue.

Table 21.2 NUJ marginalisation in national newspapers

Group	Details of marginalisation
Guardian/Observer	From 1989 executives on personal contracts; end of closed shop; pay freezes and below RPI rises; increasing use of merit pay; threat to end collective bargaining; below inflation pay rises.
Financial Times	From 1991 threat of derecognition; pay freeze and below RPI rises; increasing use of merit pay; failure to compensate adequately for RSI.

newspaper sector has been the length of time taken to introduce derecognition and personal contracts and its measured nature; partial derecognition at first, followed by full derecognition. These tendencies towards a gradual approach are probably indicative of the relatively high levels of union membership density and organisation.

Common to all of these defeats and setbacks for the NUJ (as at the *Mirror*) has been the policy of the NUJ leadership of using strike ballots and token strikes as negotiating chips to reach a compromise rather than using the potential of the journalists' power through indefinite strikes to force a full retreat on the part of the employers. When the ballots and token strikes (24 to 36 hours) failed to budge the employers, the NUJ leadership, instead of arguing for an escalation of action and lobbying the other workers and unions for their support, moved away from confrontation and either tried to reach a settlement that was much less favourable to its members or instigated legal and other means against the employers such as court cases, industrial tribunals, lobbying MPs, and the Press for Union Rights Campaign. This signal of weakness sent to the employers by the NUJ served only to increase the confidence of the employers. The alternative strategy of striking immediately without a ballot, mass picketing and secondary action from print workers was rejected out of hand by the leadership because it breached the current employment legislation (for a fuller exposition of this argument see Gall 1992).

The future political direction of the 'Mirror'

Given the changes in editors and personnel, the future of MGN newspapers' traditional pro-Labour political direction must be in serious doubt. This is of obvious importance to the political life in Britain today as the *Mirror/Daily Record* is the only non-Tory mass circulation daily paper. It sells over three million copies per day which is roughly the same as its right-wing rival, the *Sun*.

Before the implications of the changes are drawn out, two important caveats need to be made. First, the degree of 'left-wingness' and campaigning journalism of the *Mirror* of the 1980s should not be exaggerated. As Diamond (*Guardian*, 22 February 1993) argues, the *Mirror* of the pre-Maxwell era, with editors such as Cudlipp and King and with a critical faculty, was a vastly superior paper. Therefore, to lament the left-wing *Mirror* is to remember another bygone era, not the 1980s. Second, some doubt must be cast on the extent of influence of the Tory press and the *Mirror* as a counter-balance on political life in Britain. For example, the Tory press and the *Sun* ('what won it') is commonly believed by many, including the Labour Party, to have been instrumental in returning the Tories to power in the 1992 general election. A basic failure to put forward a credible, coherent and sustained political alternative to the Tories offers a more convincing explanation for Labour's defeat. The importance of the removal of the *Mirror* from its traditional pro-Labour stance should thus not be over-estimated. Indeed, that the *Mirror* has made a rightward shift in the last decade is symptomatic of the wider rightward shift in the Labour Party and the trade union movement. The Labour Party, ignoring its large long-standing and core working class support in its craven search for a small number of middle class voters, the support of business and parliamentary power, has moved away from a fairly right-wing form of social democracy and some minimal regulation of the market to a form of politics where the market is to be left to operate freely and where any concerns of social justice are minimised.

However, given that three million people buy the *Mirror* because of a concrete identification with Labour, which cannot be said of the *Sun* (both Labour and Tory voters buy the *Sun*), the change in political line of the *Mirror* is still important. It is probable that in the near future it will cease to be any sort of left-wing paper and its consistent support for Labour may wane. This is not such a big step given the moves it has made recently. Some indication of this potential projection can be gained from two events. The first is the concern of even the most right-wing Labour MPs, the late John Smith and ex-leaders, about the political changes in the form of letters to the MGN board, motions in parliament condemning Montgomery and their presence on NUJ *Mirror* demonstrations. The second is that even the *Sun*, in its recent populist anti-Tory period, has started accusing the *Mirror* of being a Tory paper run by Tories. We shall now look at the editorial and management changes of the papers.

MGN has been filled up with the henchmen of Murdoch, a well known right-winger and reactionary. Montgomery himself is also a well known right-winger and Orangeman. In addition to Montgomery senior staff from right-wing papers such as the *Evening Standard*, *Today* and *The Sunday Times* have been appointed to very senior editorial positions. For those journalists that remain and those that join MGN, the continuing use of performance related pay and the *de facto* derecognition of the NUJ will, under the new editors, mean that the only way to keep their jobs, ensure pay rises and hope for promotion will be to produce exactly what the editors want. Without a strong(ish) trade union to act as a counter-balance and to provide collective strength and protection for the journalists they will have no option but to comply and conform to what Montgomery described the new *Mirror* would be: 'more balanced . . . intelligent . . . [and] in depth as opposed to strident and abusive' (*UKPG*, 20 September 1993). The statements by the editors that they 'will not be puppets' of Montgomery and that they themselves will both manage their newspapers and set the editorial policy while Montgomery pledges he will not interfere (*UKPG*, 21 December 1992) ring rather hollow. Montgomery does not need to interfere with the editors and editorial policy, say on a day-to-day basis as Maxwell did, because the editors that he has appointed are already 'his men'. Thus Banks wanted to stare facts in the face and ignore them, talking in upbeat fashion about the recession, unemployment and poverty as well as trivialising the more serious parts of the papers. He wanted to bring back 'fun, laughter and cheekiness' and get away from 'a culture of whinge and cringe'. He continued:

> we have to get away from a depressing diatribe about what we believe is wrong in this country and start to put forward positive visions and

attitudes. The great challenge of being at the *Mirror* is that if you help to restore the *Mirror*, you help to restore Britain.

(*UKPG*, 21 December 1992)

This is the same as Montgomery when he criticised 'the tunnel vision of the *Daily Mirror*, which grinds on supporting the Labour Party'.

The result of this trajectory has been the dominant focus on royalty, celebrities, advertising promotions and trivia as well as a sparser and more superficial coverage of 'hard' news and events. All of this contrasts very sharply with the year after Maxwell died. Without an interfering, bullying proprietor the editors and journalists were themselves able to decide much more about what went into the papers, without the fear of the sack. This temporary 'freedom' was most graphically shown by the *Mirror*'s coverage of the miners' dispute in October 1992 when it swung totally behind them; the paper asked people to go on the miners' two great demonstrations and to go to meetings about the miners and it published posters for them, and so on. This showed what the *Mirror* could be like, a compassionate, radical and campaigning paper.

Another area highlights the likely political projection. The *Mirror* is the only national daily newspaper with a 'troops out' position on Northern Ireland. This is likely to be dropped because Montgomery is an Ulster Protestant and Orangeman. As editor of *Today* in 1988 he attacked the *Mirror* for running a front page editorial calling for the withdrawal of British troops from Northern Ireland and he put the news of the Guildford Four's release in one column on an inside page while other national newspapers made this front-page news. The *Mirror* has already down-graded the importance that it attaches to Northern Ireland by sacking its Northern Ireland staff reporter and relying now on news agencies for copy about Northern Ireland.

What is meant, then by the *Mirror*'s remaining 'left-of-centre' as the MGN board stated? The likely direction of the *Mirror* is two-pronged. It is likely to compete with the *Sun* on its ground of undiluted trivia, sensationalist reporting and sleaze. It is likely to become more of an entertainment paper rather than a newspaper. On the other track it is likely to continue to support the Labour Party as opposed to the Tories but this may be done in a less prominent form, supporting Labour only in general elections but telling the Labour Party what to do and being increasingly right wing in this. Under this projection the loyalty of readers and Labour voters may be retained but at the same time the new editorial direction can be pursued.

Conclusion

So what, then, is the future for the *Mirror*? With the arrival of the new management and editors, the departure of the 'defiant element' of journalists, the removal of union influence and the increased and renewed emphasis on making as much profit out of the papers as possible, not very bright must be the reply. Any ability that the *Mirror* had to expose, scrutinise and explain will be severely diminished. The quality of the paper in terms of its providing a counter-balance to the Tory press and in particular the *Sun*, and providing thorough, competent news reporting has been eroded and curtailed to a very great degree as a result of the reduction in the number of journalists and the type of (new) journalists employed within the new management and ownership structures. The only circumstances under which the *Mirror* could be envisaged to fulfil some of these functions in the future would be in a populist period such as that of the *Sun*'s anti-Major crusade. But as is evident from the *Sun*'s coverage this was neither permanent nor an about-turn of face or politics; it remains vicious in its alternatives to the crisis in Britain and cries not for the removal of the Tories but for better, stronger and more stable Tory governments. There is no reason to think that the *Mirror* would not be any less fickle and untruthful. Here the *Sun* had to run to some extent with the anger of its readership against the government but only to save its circulation. For the *Mirror*, only its pro-Labour readership may exert a little 'control' or 'pull' in this respect, but again for commercial reasons.

The workforce has been made to pay the price of Maxwell's thieving and corruption, of saving the banks' money and of financing the takeover of the *Independent* and its Sunday sister paper. To be 'fair' to the management of MGN it has to a greater or lesser degree deliberately undermined the NUJ and eroded the journalists' terms and conditions of employment just as other national newspaper companies have done to their journalists and the NUJ chapels there. The significance of the actions of MGN is that perhaps, rather naively, one might have expected something better from a Labour-supporting paper, that is, that MGN would be a 'good' or 'model' employer. That MGN has done what it has done shows that the company is driven by the same over-riding objective as other newspapers, namely, to increase its profits, no matter what and no matter how. Until the journalists rebuild their union organisation there will be little room for opposition to the management on any issues, whether editorial or remunerative. The blame for the failure of union opposition to the new regime and the destruction of the renewed strength of the *Mirror* NUJ chapel must in large part lie with the leadership of the NUJ. Only a recognition of its disastrous strategy can help it to build successful union resistance in the future and provide the prospect of decent newspapers within our 'free press'.

References

Gall, G. (1992) 'The NUJ: a union in crisis', *Capital and Class* 48 (Autumn): 7–15.

Smith, P and Morton, G. (1990) 'A change of heart: union exclusion in the provincial newspaper sector', *Work, Employment and Society* 4, 1: 105–24.

Chapter 22

British Journalism Review

WHY WE ARE HERE

WE ARE PLEASED TO HAVE ARRIVED AT THIS POINT.[1]

Sad, perhaps, that it has become necessary to raise the flag of insurrection against the advance of those poisonous weeds that are now choking the life-blood out of British journalism. But, more optimistically, rejoicing that there is still plenty of excellence and even outstanding journalism in our midst which we can celebrate.

We are convinced that the best will triumph, though not without effort . . .

Anyone who thinks seriously about the media in 1989 must notice a great discrepancy between general statements and the actual world to which they are supposed to apply. Freedom of the press is uttered as a cliché, and perhaps honoured as an aspiration, but does not appear to be a condition which the nation as a whole fights tigerishly to defend. Journalists and editors, in any medium, are rarely if ever respected as heroes of the people. Newspapers and television companies feel themselves to be getting less not more free. The famous axiom continues to be intoned, but the activity it describes is dominated by interlocking crises: a crisis of standards, a crisis of credibility, a crisis of freedom itself.

It's an odd business we are in, to be sure. James Cameron used to call it 'our trade'; Henry Louis Mencken dismissed the notion that journalism was 'an art' – he saw himself as a critic of life, of things and ideas and, above all, a craftsman. Hugh Cudlipp used to suggest that we were all walking a kind of tightrope somewhere between reality and dreamland. An outstanding editor of the *News Chronicle*, the late Robin J. Cruikshank, once called the business a great mix between a dedicated public service by people who wanted to report, and maybe change, the world and a mass entertainment operation run by a corps of jazz singers. Whatever one's definition, the business is now subject to a contagious outbreak of squalid, banal, lazy and cowardly journalism whose only qualification is that it helps to make newspaper publishers (and some journalists) rich. Perhaps the greatest weakness of British journalism, when we compare it with the journalism of many other European countries, as well as with some of the best of American journalism, has been its lack of a reflective and analytical culture . . .

Conflicting interests

The malaise is not solely the fault of journalists and proprietors. On several fronts, newspaper and television journalism have had their opportunities and rights narrowed, in the last few years, by government decision. Many of these erosions have occurred in the field of national security, which has been given a broad definition. But this does not diminish their importance. On the contrary, it is at the interface between the interest of the State and the interest of the media   acting, it should always be remembered, on behalf of their audience – that national attitudes are put most crucially to the test. What the recent record of government reveals is a state of mind which, given these conflicting interests, is never prepared to put freedom of expression first. Its actions tend to suggest not only tactical resistance to pieces of journalism it does not like but a strategic desire to weaken journalistic enterprise.

The telling examples here come from television. The 1988 Thames Television documentary, *Death on the Rock*, was subjected to an unprecedented campaign of official pressure before, during and long after its transmission. Not only did ministers, as was arguably their right, press for it not to be shown. They pursued their efforts to blacken the programme and its makers, by fair means and foul, for many months.

But perhaps this is not surprising, given the government's overall approach to the future of television. If there is one pattern visible here it is of the weakening of self-confidence in each of the television networks . . . What is perhaps less well perceived is the benign consequence for government of television companies which are deprived of the interest and confidence and sheer sense of their own permanence which has, on occasion, made their journalism a mighty scourge . . .

But what of journalists themselves? Journalists are *drawn* into the business rather than systematically trained and recruited. They don't even require the basic training provided they are quick and street-wise. They take no oath of fidelity to a moral or ethical code as doctors do. Nor is there any objective measure of skill as there would be for a bricklayer or carpenter. It is mainly down to chance and opportunity, luck or habit. Journalism is something you DO, as an individual, for money or a career, maybe in the hope of stardom on this or that newspaper, magazine, radio or TV programme. Nobody actually encourages the young journalist to aim at some distant summit of higher purpose, or some set of social or moral values. There is no fundamental credo set in stone which inspires the newcomer towards serving his or her fellow citizens with the facts of life, straight, true, with decency, and even amusement. All of which means that perfectly good journalists can be found sneering at such a catalogue of high moral objectives . . .

Pimps or pimpernels?

Well, we might wonder, what are we here to do? To enhance the coffers of proprietors and publishers? To dance in the street busking our way into the gutter? To revile, sneer, giggle, titillate and fawn as the levels of civilised behaviour slide still further down the voluptuous drain? To collaborate in the process of ever-declining standards in social mores so long as the banknotes float in? Maybe the time has come to ask whether journalists wish to choose between a role in society as pimps or pimpernels?

In print journalism it seems to us that two major complaints can be made about the present state of affairs:

1   Contrary to most predictions the concentration of ownership has grown more intensive as a result of new technology rather than less so, and it is a concentration which now envelops not only the printed word in newspapers, magazines and books; but also radio, TV and film, in a world-wide commercial network.

2   The virtually unchecked downward spiral in standards of journalism – with the trivialisation of material, vulgarisation, invasion of privacy, squalid behaviour by certain groups of publishers and journalists, and ultimately the pure invention of stories and material.

One could add a third problem – one of long standing – which is the enormous growth and power of the advertising industry.

There is another side to the balance sheet. The *Independent* is the first quality national daily newspaper launched for over 130 years. Most other quality papers have plainly benefited from the revolution in production costs . . . There is some superb journalism in some of the national press and there is excellence around in radio and TV and some magazines. It is not all bad by any means and much of what is good is genuinely outstanding by any standards of journalism anywhere in the world.

But as with all things journalism cannot escape the driving force of Gresham's law: the bad will drive out the good . . . or at least reduce it to the margin of life, if the only objective is commercial profit.

Compared with the United States, where the First Amendement guarantees press freedom and is taken with the utmost seriousness, the British tradition assigns less importance to embarrassing the government than to letting government govern. British law grants the press no privileges, and the press has never asked for them. This no doubt reflects the ambivalent place the press has always occupied in the estimation of the British public. It may explain why the present government has been able to move with impunity against the media. But there is another possibility: that the press now does not deserve respect, because it does not do what it should as well as it could. The crisis of freedom, in other words, originates in the crisis of credibility – which in turn arises from a crisis of standard.

More than twenty years ago Cecil Harmsworth King, then head of the *Mirror* group, predicted a great polarisation in the British press . . . King glimpsed into a future where there would be only a handful of quality newspapers serving a minority of the population at one end of the social spectrum (inevitably an elitist minority); and, at the other end, the mass of the population being offered varying forms of pap. In terms of effective journalism that means disenfranchisement for more than 80 per cent of the newspaper buying public.

Downhill for TV?

It is no longer a defence of the state of affairs to argue (as many still do) that the electronic media have filled the gap. The truth is that they have not. Indeed there are now disturbing signs that the electronic media are likely to follow the same path as the printed word . . . downhill. Nor is it any longer sufficient to go on blaming Rupert Murdoch . . . or the rest of the oligopoly moguls who increasingly control the system. They don't write the stuff. They pay the expenses, to be sure, and write the pay cheques. But it is the journalist who performs. And it is journalists who are becoming increasingly worried and in many cases deeply dejected at what they are called on to do.

Of course, not all of them feel depressed. Some will defend the status quo with great passion and strong bank balances. Nothing we can, or will, say now or in future will persuade them that they are wrong. Yet the army of journalists who know in their bones that there is something rotten about today's business . . . that army is growing . . .

Note

1   The *British Journalism Review* first appeared in 1989: this extract is from the editorial in the first edition.

Chapter 23

Julian Petley

FACES FOR SPACES

Journalists write because they have nothing to say,
and have something to say because they write.

(Karl Kraus 1986)

I was brought up by parents who smacked me if I was naughty.
I owned a golliwog, yawned through religious instruction,
read every adventure of the Famous Five and joined the
Shakespeare Reading Society because it was a great place
to meet boys.

(Anne Diamond, in Coles 1994)

When Charles Moore took over as editor of the *Sunday Telegraph* the place
where he really made his mark was in the paper's five (yes, that's five)
comment pages. And when he succeeded Max Hastings at *The Daily Telegraph*
it was again the comment columns to which he turned his, and his readers',
attentions. This is how, on 15 January 1996, the new editorial order made
its presence felt, under the headline: 'Britain's sharpest newspaper brings
you the cutting edge of comment':

> Tomorrow the comment pages of the *Daily Telegraph* will be even better.
> We will be introducing our new team of columnists, who will bring
> you the best writing in Fleet Street on current affairs. On Mondays,
> Anne McElvoy, the talented young writer who made her reputation
> commentating on foreign affairs, will illuminate events abroad and at

home. Janet Daley, the voice of sanity on the BBC's *Moral Maze*, will be writing about social affairs on Tuesdays from tomorrow. On Wednesday, Boris Johnson, Britain's sharpest political commentator, will cast his caustic eye over the political scene, during what could be an election year. On Thursdays, the controversial columnist Barbara Amiel will speak her brilliant mind. Fridays will feature a column from the rapier pen of Steven Glover, the most fearless moralist in modern journalism. And the funniest satirist of his generation, Craig Brown, will be appearing on Saturdays. There will be more room for your letters and for your favourite *Telegraph* writers such as W.F. Deedes, Frank Johnson, Robert Hardman and Claudia Fitzherbert. The *Daily Telegraph* is the epicentre of national debate.

Now, whilst one might well want to question the objectivity and impartiality of a political commentator, even the 'sharpest', who just happens to be a Conservative candidate at the next election, the probity of employing the proprietor's wife (Amiel), and the kind of 'sanity' which Daley is supposed to represent, Moore could hardly be accused by the rest of Fleet Street of over-hyping his 'star' columnists. At around the same time, the *Sunday Telegraph* was boasting of 'Britain's brightest political commentator', Matthew d'Ancona; the *People* of Carol Sarler, 'love her or hate her . . . read Britain's sassiest columnist'; and the *News of the World* was still breaching the Trade Descriptions Act by billing Woodrow Wyatt as 'the voice of reason'. Meanwhile the *Daily Mirror* puffed its line-up of Brian Reade, 'Britain's wittiest TV columnist'; Marje Proops, 'the world's greatest advice columnist'; and Tony Parsons, '*the* column, *the* writer'. It might also be remembered that Parsons featured strongly, when he was the *Telegraph*'s rock critic, in that paper's television advertisements aimed at younger readers. Even more star-studded is the *Sun*, with Norman Tebbit, 'telling it like it is'; Deidre Sanders, 'the world's no.1 agony aunt'; Garry Bushell, 'the column that runs on pure beef'; and finally, Anne Robinson, 'Britain's no.1 writer . . . Britain's no.1 columnist in Britain's no.1 paper . . . She's write out in front'. In the middle market tabloids, the *Daily Mail* offers Simon Heffer, 'the pundit the politicians dread'; Baz Bamigboye, 'Britain's brightest guide to all that's best in entertainment'; Andrew Neil, 'the voice of controversy'; and William Oddie (not to be confused with birder and former Goodie Bill Oddie), 'one of Britain's most outspoken theologians'. The *Mail* also pushes its top columnists in its promotional literature, such as the brochure which boasts that 'our writers are unmatched for their brilliance and include such stars as Lynda Lee-Potter, Nigel Dempster, Richard Littlejohn, Keith Waterhouse and Baz Bamigboye'. And naturally the *Daily Express*'s new editor, Richard Addis, was quick to play the star card in his paper's endless war with its only remaining mid-market competitor. Thus on 2 January 1996 he announced that

the brilliant columnists for which the *Daily Express* is justly renowned, such as Peter Tory in today's paper, have a bigger and better home on

Page Eleven. This is the showcase where you will be able to read some marvellous new writers who are joining the *Express* over the next few weeks.

These turned out to include Mary Kenny, 'one of Britain's wisest and wittiest columnists'; Ross Benson, 'Britain's top diarist' now returning to his previous role as 'a brilliant and highly-acclaimed feature writer'; Chris Buckland, 'this is REALLY the column that politicians dread'; Paul Henderson, 'one of Fleet Street's most formidable reporters'; Roy Hattersley who, as the new television critic, 'brings a fresh and intelligent eye to the nations's premier entertainment medium. He will be the icing on the cake of our new-look, easier-to-read television pages'; and finally, Philip Norman, 'one of Britian's outstanding journalists' who will 'apply his wit to all aspects of the world we live in'.

Well, we've certainly come a long way from the days when large tracts of newsprint, especially in the 'quality' press, were wholly anonymous. Indeed, the phenomenon of the star column has now become so pronounced that one of its most stellar practitioners, Keith Waterhouse, has actually written about it. As he puts it:

> In much the same spirit as the Emperor Caligula appointed his horse consul, Northcliffe is said to have made one of his commissionaires an editor. Nowadays he would have made him a columnist.
>
> Column writing has always been the one journalistic assignment that everybody believes they could do given the chance. But now everybody's actually getting the chance. Television personalities, politicians, retired judges, superannuated editors, comedians, novelists, dons, plus short-lived holiday reliefs, are all getting into the act. How oh how (to coin a variation on their favourite why oh why) do they get the work?
>
> Bigger and ever-bigger papers is the answer to that rhetorical question. More pages mean more regular features. In production terms, an opinion column, provided it is filled on time and at approximately the right length, is a safe space-filler – the story isn't going to fall down.
>
> (Waterhouse 1995: 12)

However, the rapid growth in the number of press pundits since the mid-eighties cannot be explained only in terms of the increase in pages to be filled. As Nimmo and Combs have argued: 'punditry has become a form of entertainment, both shaping and adjusting to popular expectations regarding how to keep up with and understand "what's happening" ' (Nimmo and Combs 1992: 12). The phenomenon therefore has also to be seen as part of the response of the press to a situation in which the vast majority of people regard television as their prime and most reliable source of news.

Newspapers, whose overall readership is in steady decline and which are desperate to attract younger readers in particular, are thus tempted to go where broadcasters, because of regulation or audience expectation or a mix of both, cannot – into the realm of opinion and comment, something of which they have never been exactly shy anyway. The rise of press punditry also has to be seen as part of the growth of a media-wide star system: not for nothing are papers keen to attract columnists who also have well-developed TV personae such as Anne Diamond, Anne Robinson, Jeremy Paxman and Robert Kilroy Silk (although the traffic flows the other way too, of course). This in turn is linked with the accelerating metamorphosis of newspapers – tabloid and broadsheet alike – into primarily entertainment-led media. As Anthony Sampson has noted in a seminal piece, whilst serious journalism of all kinds has been in headlong retreat there has been a contemporaneous

> explosion of columns providing comment without facts, discussing friends, parties, or other journalists. Newspapers are much less about history, more about conversation of the most basic kind: 'What did you do today?' 'I've been worrying this week about knick-knacks. Why don't I have any?', we were asked recently by Joan Smith in the *Independent on Sunday*. Scores of other columnists tell us what happened to them on the way to Sainsbury's, what their children did at school, how they enjoyed their holidays. One wonders what there is left for these people to talk about at home.
>
> (Sampson 1996: 45)

That star columnists are no mere space fillers, and perform an important commercial function for newspapers, is proved by examining how much they're prepared to pay for them. For a breed only too happy to enquire into others' financial affairs, journalists are notoriously coy about their own remuneration; however, according to Tunstall:

> The columnist transfer market became more and more active in the late 1980s and early 1990s. Several columnists made several moves, with the *Sunday Times* (under Andrew Neil) being the publication most determined to corner column talent from both the other upmarket and midmarket papers. By the early and mid-1990s an average fee was probably about £1,000 per column, fees of between £25,000 and £75,000 being the standard range for one column per week. Two and three columns a week were paid more. William Rees-Mogg was paid £60,000 for one column by the *Independent* and £120,000 for two columns a week by *The Times*. Editors can also offer other frills – display on the page, travel expenses, and the right to do occasional pieces for competing papers.
>
> (Tunstall 1996: 179–180).

And according to Cal McCrystal in the *Independent on Sunday*, 22 March 1992, political columnists can expect to earn not less than £40,000 and, if they're Joe Haines at the *Mirror*, more than £80,000. Over at *The Times*, meanwhile, another star of the columnar firmament, Bernard Levin, makes £100,000 by McCrystal's reckoning. As far as female columnists go, according to Joanna Coles in the *Guardian*, 18 February 1994, Lynda Lee-Potter at the *Mail* and Anne Diamond at the *Mirror* both get £100,000, but the record holder appears to be Anne Robinson at *Today* with £200,000 (and that's before she moved to the *Sun*!). This even beats Julie Burchill, who was known whilst at the *Mail on Sunday* to squeak that 'I get £120,000 for two hours work a week', although the only real surprise here is that her column took her that long.

It should by now be apparent that there are two distinct types of star columnist. The first is the star who has made it outside press journalism and, on the basis of their fame elsewhere, is called in to write the occasional – or even regular – column: for example, Pat Kane or Armando Iannucci at the *Guardian*. The second are those columnists who are famous simply for being columnists. And here, of course, one needs to distinguish between political columnists, such as Hugo Young at the *Guardian* and Simon Heffer at the *Mail*, star reviewers such as Alexander Walker at the *Evening Standard* and Garry Bushell at the *Sun*, agony aunts such as the *Sun*'s Deidre Sanders and the *Mirror*'s Marje Proops, and all-purpose pundits such as Lynda Lee-Potter and Keith Waterhouse at the *Mail*. It is on this last group that I want mainly to concentrate in this chapter.

Now there is, of course, nothing wrong in principle in importing the occasional star as a columnist – indeed, if they're informed and can write well they can be a welcome breath of fresh air into Fleet Street's notoriously self-enclosed little world. The problem arises when stars are employed simply because they're stars. An area long prone to this tendency has been television reviewing although, unfortunately, it has now spread into other parts of the papers too. As Michael Poole has pointed out, the archetype of this kind of writing was Clive James' television column at the *Observer*, 'playful, top-heavy with foregrounded personality, aggressively non-specialist' (Poole 1984: 54). The real subject of the column was not television but James himself, who was employed primarily to be funny and chose to be funny about television. Since Poole wrote his seminal piece, things have gone from bad to worse. In 1996, Sean Day-Lewis, the television critic of the *Telegraph* and, along with Chris Dunkley of the *Financial Times*, one of the very few television critics who knows anything at all about the medium, was replaced by Christina Odone, the former editor of the *Catholic Herald* and very much an up and coming cross-media star. However, she marked her appointment by telling the *Guardian* that radio is 'much my favourite medium' and that she regarded television 'as a medium for information rather than entertainment. Watch rarely – investigative documentaries and newsy slots'. Worse was to come however, as Day-Lewis explained in the *Guardian*, 19 August:

A few days after my farewell review column I was rung by a friendly listings editor. Would I like to become a regular on her paper's panel of previewers? I accepted. Next day came an embarrassed second call: 'There is nothing against you or your writing but the trouble is you are known as a writer about TV and we are really looking for the unexpected', she explained. So there it was. Absolute proof that previous experience of having written about TV is now a disqualification for writing about TV.

With the execrable A.A. Gill at *The Sunday Times*, Roy Hattersley at the *Express*, and sundry forays by the likes of Terry Wogan, Paul McKenna, David Aaronovich and Ulrike Jonsson it's indeed hard to disagree with Day-Lewis, or with Elaine Showalter who complained in the *Guardian*, 20 September 1996, that 'the chief qualification for writing about TV seems to be a sneering, dandyish contempt for the medium and its proletarian audience, and an overweening self-regard'.

What is even more problematic, however, is when a star television critic uses his regular column as a space for blatant political propagandising. I'm referring, of course, to Garry Bushell in the *Sun*, whose television column frequently reads more like a political one. Thus, for example, the BBC's refusal to put on any special programmes for St. George's Day elicits the comment: 'what mugs we must be, paying the BBC to insult our intelligence, our heritage and our religion' (22 April 1992). A *This Week* programme on the judicial system causes Bushell to opine that: 'there is little wrong with British justice that wouldn't be put right by tougher laws, including the death penalty – televised if need be. It's what the voters want, but TV never puts the majority view' (29 April 1992). BBC coverage of misdeeds by the British army triggers off charges that the Corporation is 'anti-Western, anti-British' and that 'for telly trendies it seems to be an article of faith to take the enemy side' (21 May 1992). Even an ITV series, *Before Columbus*, about America before it was colonised by Europeans, somehow becomes an excuse for a rant about how 'many middle class trendies are so full of loathing and self-guilt that they back any side except ours, from Stalin to Saddam' (23 September 1992). Meanwhile a BBC documentary on racism becomes the pretext for a 'review' which tells us that 'TV bosses have always mollycoddled non-Europeans . . . They have also suppressed all discussion of immigration' (1 July 1992). And so on, and on . . .

It could, of course, be argued that we shouldn't take too much notice of Bushell, that he's a one-off, or, like the baby in *Alice in Wonderland*, 'he only does it to annoy, because he knows it teases'. However, it is my contention that Bushell's column is but an extreme example of a marked and long-term tendency in the British press as a whole to blur, and indeed at times to abolish, the distinction between the political and 'non-political'. In fact, long before Mrs Thatcher's wholesale politicisation of British society the Conservative press had fully assimilated the old left-wing dictum about the personal being political and had set about applying it in its own way. That is why the much-discussed decline in the amount of 'hard' news and comment in the British press has done absolutely nothing to weaken its profoundly Conservative (and conservative) orientation – indeed, quite the opposite. As Seaton and Pimlott have put it: 'it might be argued that non-political media coverage is politically more important in the long run than overtly political material because of the role of the media in establishing or modifying acceptable values' (Seaton and Pimlott 1987: x). The only word which I would quarrel with here is 'more', replacing it with 'as' because, as Colin Sparks has observed, it would be a serious error to 'celebrate the politicisation of the apolitical at the expense of the depoliticisation of the political' (Sparks 1988: 215). It is an equally serious error, however, to ignore the political and ideological dimensions of apparently 'soft' news and features; sadly, it is one committed by far too many commentators on and critics of the British press. The Right has never had such problems, however, and that master propagandist Joseph Goebbels would have found his dreams come true in present day Fleet Street:

> This is the really great art – to educate without revealing the purpose of the education, so that one fulfils an educational function without the object of that education being in any way aware that it is being educated, which is also indeed the real purpose of propaganda. The best propaganda is not that which is always openly revealing itself; the best propaganda is that which as it were works invisibly, penetrates the whole of life without the public having any knowledge at all of the propagandist initiative.
>
> (Goebbels, quoted in Leiser 1974: 124)

Or as the second Lord Rothermere put it, the *Daily Mail* supports the Conservatives 'not only in the leading article but throughout'.

There have, however, been a few attempts to mine the political and ideological riches of the 'soft' seams of the British press, amongst them Curran *et al.* (1980) and Sparks (1988, 1992), and these have a direct relevance to the study of press punditry.

In their exploration of the 'human interest' story Curran *et al.* note that there is a 'rejection of any attempt to explain events as having a relation to social, economic or political forces'. Life appears as fragmented, atomised, a series of discrete events stemming from the actions of individuals who are severed from any kind of social context. The world is represented as a panorama of separate human dramas, and the causes of the events which take place in it are portrayed as random and unpredictable; luck, fate and chance play a key role here, as do 'eternal' human drives such as fear, love, hate and greed. As in Mrs Thatcher's infamous dictum, here there really is 'no such thing as society': human interest stories 'represent the world of experience, the world of individuals, as opposed to the impersonal abstractions of institutions . . . Social structure is concealed. The world merely forms a fixed, given background' (Curran *et al.* 1980: 308, 311). Or as Sparks puts it:

> The popular press embeds a form of immediacy and totality in its handling of public issues. In particular, this immediacy of explanation is achieved by means of a direct appeal to personal experience. The popular conception of the personal becomes the explanatory framework within which the social order is presented as transparent.

Thus, as Sparks concludes about the *Sun*, (although his remarks could apply to any tabloid paper, and even to parts of certain broadsheets too):

> It is not simply that the substantive contents of this paper are politically reactionary: that they certainly are in language, tone, general ideology and concrete policies. The central problem is rather that they offer the experiences of the individual as the direct and unmediated key to the understanding of the social totality.
>
> (Sparks 1992: 41)

No wonder, then, that such papers are so bitterly hostile to all 'ologies' and 'isms', and especially to sociology and socialism!

If, however, 'society' is denied, it is replaced by a sense of community (of a kind). To quote Curran *et al.*:

> This varied, diverse, multifaceted panorama of individuals is reunited in the form of a community that shares common universal experiences: birth, love, death, accident, illness, and, crucially, the experience of consuming. Individuals are symbolically reunited within a 'passive community of consumers'.
>
> (Curran *et al.* 1980: 306)

Since these words were written, of course, consumption has come to play an even greater role in social life, and indeed its promotion was central to the Thatcherite project.

Another way in which the atomised, randomised world of the human interest story is given coherence and brought together in an imaginary unity is via the promotion of the idea of the nation (and again we should note the crucial importance of nationalism, and specifically English nationalism, to Thatcherite discourse). Thus identification is invited with symbols of national unity, prestige and 'heritage', which are presented as above narrow, party-political differences. As Curran *et al.* put it: 'these symbols are clearly distinct from the world of politics and are offered with an assumption of universal approval'. Examples here could include the Queen Mother, 'Our Boys', British beef, and so on (for an extended discussion of this topic see Billig 1995).

Human interest stories, then, exaggerate and mythologise the common-
alities between people and 'magic away' real structural divisions, inequalities
and conflicts. But (although this is not discussed by Curran *et al.*) even
this most populist form of culture cannot entirely deny the visible evidence
of social problems of one kind or another – crime, homelessness, drug
abuse and the like. So what it does is to construct a whole series of 'out
groups' – travellers, ravers, social security 'scroungers', single mothers,
foreigners, 'benefit tourists', persistent young offenders, 'bail bandits', for
example – on whom all these problems can be blamed. And, of course, the
construction of these demonised 'others', these deviant 'thems', is a crucial
means by which 'we' affirm our membership of 'us'. Hence the central
importance of crime stories to the populist press. As Steve Chibnall has
pointed out:

> Sociologists from Durkheim onwards have frequently noted [that] crime
> and the processing of offenders offers an opportunity for the celebra-
> tion of conformity and respectability by redefining the moral boundaries
> of communities and drawing their members together against the threat
> of chaos . . . Crime news may serve as a focus for the articulation of
> shared morality and communal sentiments. A chance not simply to
> speak *to* the community but *for* the community, against all that the
> criminal outsider represents, to delineate the shape of the threat, to
> advocate a response, to eulogise on conformity to established norms
> and values, and to warn of the consequences of deviance.
>
> (Chibnall 1977: x–xi).

Needless to say, xenophobic stories of the kind of which the British press
has made such a speciality perform exactly the same kind of function *vis-à-
vis* the construction and maintenance of a sense of national identity.

What distinguishes so much British newspaper journalism, especially (but
by no means solely) in the popular press, and especially (but by no means
solely) in 'soft' features and news stories, is a bluff, no-nonsense, 'common
sense', John Bull-ish populism. Of these ingredients, 'common sense' is the
most crucial, as has been noted by numerous commentators. William
Hardcastle, a former editor of the *Daily Mail*, called it 'the popular paper
for sensible people', and Dave Hill, writing in the *Guardian* on 9 March 1992
in the run-up to the general election in which the *Mail* was, as usual, to
perform as a mere adjunct to Conservative Central Office, stated that:

> The great gift of the *Daily Mail* is for persuading its 4.3 million readers
> that they know exactly who they are. Though far from sheep-like, the
> *Daily Mail* assures them, they are the type of people who instinctively
> know that certain things are right; people for whom particular plain
> truths are self-evident except to the mischievous and the mad. This
> catalogue of common sense permeates every page of every edition of

the *Daily Mail* with a subtle but remorseless ubiquity that makes it just about the most ideologically-refined vehicle for right-wing propaganda in the whole of newspaperland.

And Andrew Marr in the *Independent*, 24 August 1993, made a very similar point about its most famous pundit, Paul Johnson, arguing that 'part of his trick is the assumption of sturdy omniscience, the pose of the plain-speaking man forever proven right in his homespun predictions'. Much the same, of course, could be said of Richard Littlejohn, Woodrow Wyatt, Lynda Lee-Potter and others, just as Hill's remarks could almost equally as well apply to the *Sun* and the *Telegraph* (especially under the editorship of Charles Moore). Indeed, when Moore was building up his mammoth five pages of comment columns in the *Sunday Telegraph* his proudest addition was apparently Andrew Gimson's 'At the Bar of World Opinion', in which the pundit based his column on his conversations in a different pub each week. According to Moore, interviewed in the *Guardian*, 14 February 1994:

> The point is to try to present how things *are* rather than how you expect them to be. There's a sort of rhetoric about everything these days. If you ring up a spokesman for a union or pressure group they say the same clichéd things in the same clichéd way. We try to get behind that and convey what people are really saying.

In any other country the idea that the function of journalism is to reinforce and pander to what people think they already know would be regarded as grotesque, perverse and irresponsible, an abject surrender of journalistic values and integrity to populist commercialism of the worst possible kind. In England, however, we have become so accustomed to newspapers doing just that that Moore's remarkable admission passed entirely without comment. In such circumstances, the *Independent on Sunday*'s redoubtable Wallace Arnold is only *just* a joke:

> Despite the envious barbs of nations less reliable than our own, we British have long excelled at thought. We are to be congratulated on our avoidance of the fashionable 'isms' that so beset the thinking patterns of our European counterparts. One can have too much of the abstract. Personally, I prefer real life. I sometimes wonder whether Monsieur Michel Tournier ever popped into his local butcher for a string of sausages, and if so what on earth he did with them when he got them back home. Eschewing such obvious Continental time-wasters as 'post-modernism', 'quantum mechanics', 'existentialism' and 'trans-vestism', we British have been content to light our pipes, set our caps at a thoughtful angle, put our feet up in front of a freshly lit fire, take a refreshing swig from a glass of halfway-decent claret, and treat ourselves to a jolly good snooze. More so than Monsieur Tournier and

his ilk, we realise the immense benefit of treating the brain to a jolly good rest. For then – and only then – can common sense begin to flourish. 'Common sense': that's an expression which won't get you very far in the smoke-filled bars and cafes of Paris, hampered as they are by the Union of French Intellectuals and Allied Eggheads (!).

And just in case you think I'm being a little po-faced about Wallace, is this him again, or A.A. Gill?:

> *Talking Liberties* (Channel 4) promised enlightenment via a conversation with Jacques Derrida screened at midnight. Your critic tuned in, took one look at the great man and fell immediately into a deep sleep. Like Alan Whicker, M. Derrida is a tonic and should be available on the National Health.

Well actually it's neither. Proving that 'common sense' is not the prerogative of the pundits of the popular press it's John Naughton in the *Observer*, 14 June 1992, now elevated into one of its star columnists. And so is this:

> *The Late Show* (BBC2) came last week from Paris, France. This was made clear on Monday night, when Brains Dunant was shown standing in front of the Eiffel Tower. The purpose of the jaunt, it transpired, was to enable those of us living in the provinces to bring ourselves up to speed on 'the state of French culture – the preoccupations of its cinema, the latest in television, visual arts and music and what's happening in the world of ideas'. And all in a week. A case of: If it's Wednesday then it must be Althusser.
>
> On Wednesday, it was indeed Althusser but the season opened – as these things must – with a solemn piece on Jack Lang, the thinking woman's culture vulture. He is Mitterrand's glamorous Minister of Culture: think of him as Melvyn Bragg with an annual budget of £1 billion and you will get the picture. Wednesday's piece on Althusser was actually rather good and shed compassionate light on the philosopher's mental illness, though it was overly reverential towards the incoherent Marxist flapdoodle which constituted his *oeuvre*. Indeed, the abiding fault of the entire week's programming was its tendency to take French culture at its own inflated face value.
>
> (John Naughton, *Observer*, 18 October 1992)

That populist and 'common sensical' attitudes characterise significant parts of *all* of the British press could be demonstrated by looking at its coverage of any number of subjects, issues and stories. For the sake of brevity and clarity, however, I have decided to concentrate on how the pundits responded to the murder of the Liverpool toddler James Bulger in 1993. (For discussion of press coverage as a whole see Petley 1994 and Franklin and Petley 1996.)

Take, for example, the alleged effects of horror videos, and specifically the video *Child's Play 3*, on the killers of James Bulger — Jon Venables and Bobby Thompson. On the basis of an extraordinarily unwise remark by the trial judge, Mr Justice Morland, to the effect that 'it is not for me to pass judgement on their upbringing but I suspect that exposure to violent video films may be in part an explanation', the fact that the father of one of the boys had rented horror videos, and a highly tendentious document (the so-called 'Newson Report') from a group of child experts which purported to show a link between on-screen and real life violence but turned out to be part of MP David Alton's lobbying campaign for stricter video censorship, the press constructed an utterly absurd and dangerously misleading fantasy in which *Child's Play 3* had 'caused' the murder of James Bulger. And this in spite of the fact that the police officer in charge of the case, and the forensic psychiatrist appointed by the Home Office to interview Thompson and Venables, categorically denied that videos — including *Child's Play 3* — played any part whatsoever in the case! Furthermore, however selectively the press may interpret the evidence about media 'effects', there is a vast amount of hard evidence which suggests that their crude, behaviourist, 'hypo-dermic' model is entirely inadequate for understanding the relationship between the media and their audiences (Cumberbatch and Howitt 1989; Gauntlett 1995; Barker and Petley 1997).

Nothing daunted, however, the pundits passed judgement. Thus Anne Diamond in the *Mirror*, 1 December 1993:

> our gut tells us they *must* have seen the evil doll Chucky [from *Child's Play 3*]. They *must* have loved the film. And they *must* have seen it over and over again because some of the things they did are almost exact copies of the screenplay.

In fact they aren't in the very slightest, but never mind that because I'm a sociologist and therefore quite unfitted to comment; as Diamond concludes: 'God protect us from the "ologists" — because their hackneyed perception is dangerous. I sometimes think that a degree in some sort of "ology" blinds you to common sense. We all know that violence begets violence.' However, Diamond was very far from alone in her woefully misplaced certainties. Thus Roy Hattersley in the *Mail*, 2 April 1994: 'now it is hard to believe that anyone honestly doubted it. For the effect that video nasties have on impressionable minds is so obvious that common sense alone confirms the damage that they do'; and similarly Minette Marin in the *Sunday Telegraph*, 3 April 1994: 'common sense suggests more and more powerfully as time goes by that the youthful mind can be brutalised, and that violent videos should be restricted.' Perversely, the apparent volte-face by the child experts was used as a stick with which to beat the penitent 'ologists'. Thus the comedienne Dillie Keane in the *Mail on Sunday*, 3 April 1994:

at last – 26 top child psychologists have admitted they were wrong about the effect video nasties have on children. You can't help wondering where they studied, just in case you mistakenly applied to the same colleges . . . To us less qualified mortals, the link was inescapable. If only these 'experts' had got their act together sooner.

A similar line was adopted by Peter McKay in the same day's *Sunday Times*:

we didn't need 25 'top psychologists' to admit to Michael Howard, the home secretary, that video nasties affect children. Nor are many of us likely to be surprised to hear them now say that they'd put 'liberal ideas of freedom' before common sense . . . The idea that we possess 25 'top' psychologists is black comedy. You might as well talk about 25 top three-card-trick operators.

It was of course inevitable that Lynda Lee-Potter should join the fray in the *Mail*, 6 April 1994:

this is not some new finding that has struck the sensible rest of us like a thunder bolt. This is not wondrous enlightenment from experts. Anybody with any nous or basic understanding of themselves, let alone the rest of human nature, has always known that video nasties are corruptive, destructive and evil, for adults as well as children.

Meanwhile in the *Sunday Telegraph*, 10 April 1994, Mary Kenny hailed the Newson document as 'a historical landmark in recognising something we know instinctively to be true, but which has been institutionally denied ever since the Lady Chatterley trial in 1960: that what we read and look at influences us'.

In the *Guardian*, 16 April 1994, Edward Pearce accused sceptics of waiting upon 'that factitious, impossible proof which is the last stronghold of smirking complacency'; in the *News of the World*, 17 April 1994, 'Voice of Reason' Woodrow Wyatt stated that 'we all know [violent nasties] breed horrific rapes and other brutal crimes'; and finally, vaguely left-wing moralist turned decidedly right-wing moralist, Melanie Phillips, in the *Observer*, 17 April 1994, painted those sceptical of crude 'effects' theories as 'ivory tower academics in thrall to an abstract ideology which rubbishes those who report the real experience of real children as naive'.

My earlier remarks about the construction of 'out groups' by the press are also amply borne out by newspaper coverage of the Bulger case since, entirely predictably, Conservative papers were keen to interpret the Bulger murder as evidence of the emergence of a lawless, anti-social 'underclass' in Britain. However, it's interesting that the first pundit to attempt to make this link was writing not for a Conservative, or tabloid, paper, but for the *Independent*; this was Brian Appleyard, on 1 December 1993, who asked rhetorically: 'Would you allow an ill-educated, culturally deprived, unemployable underclass unlimited access to violent pornography?' Ignoring the inconvenient fact that *no one* in Britain has unlimited access to such material anyway, he blithely continues that if you abolish censorship (which most certainly has *not* happened in the UK) 'you don't just get Mapplethorpe for the connoisseur, you also get vicious drivel for the masses. More painfully, you also get unarguably fine films such as *Taxi Driver* and *Goodfellas*, which, if you are honest, you would rather were not watched by certain types of people.' *Reservoir Dogs* is also singled out as a 'brilliant, bloody film that I would prefer not to be seen by the criminal classes or the mentally unstable or by inadequately supervised children with little else in their lives'. Meanwhile, in the *Telegraph*, 20 February 1984, the inner-city GP and Fleet Street regular Theodore Dalrymple also bemoaned the condition of a section of the population, although not with any direct reference to the 'underclass'. However, it is clear to whom he is referring. This is a terrible sphere in which 'children are growing up without any spiritual or cultural framework whatever', a world of 'degraded rootlesssness and desolate isolation', in which mothers appear not to know that parental control is either 'desirable or necessary' and 'fathers, except in the biological sense, are generally unknown or, if known, are violent, arbitrary, abusive and uncouth'. In this void of 'quotidian savagery' 'there are no positive moral influences [but] there are plenty of negative ones, chief among which are those of television and worse still, of video'. Whilst 'liberals in Hampstead' and the 'intellectual classes' pooh-pooh the effects of video, from which they are anyway immune, 'the effect on minds which are entirely empty of a moral framework' is likely to be devastating. And no review of the pundits on this topic would be complete without Lynda Lee-Potter displaying, in her column in the *Mail*, 13 April 1994, all the sympathy for her gender for which she is so renowned:

> There are thousands of children in this country with fathers they never see and mothers who are lazy sluts. They are allowed to do what they want, when they want. They sniff glue on building sites, scavenge for food and, until now, they were free to watch increasingly horrific videos. By 16 they are disturbed and dangerous.

One final example of how the Bulger murder allowed the massed ranks of pundits to give full rein to their 'common sense' views will have to suffice. This was provided by the publication of a report, *Children and Violence*, by the Gulbenkian Foundation in 1995. This had been commissioned in the wake of the murder 'to provide as accurate a picture as possible of the level of all kinds of violence to and by children and young people' and to 'propose ways of challenging social and legal endorsement of any form of inter-personal violence and policies and practices which tend to increase violence involving children and young people' (Gulbenkian Foundation 1995: 4). The seventeen members of the commission included representatives of the National

Society for the Prevention of Cruelty to Children, Save the Children, the National Children's Bureau, Young Minds, the Council for Disabled Children, and the writers Penelope Leach and Claire Rayner. The report itself was an extremely wide-ranging document which looked at the question of children and violence in a broad social context; however, nine of the report's 300 pages were given over to the question of smacking, which it viewed with disapproval and recommended should be banned. Inevitably, this was pounced on with barely suppressed glee by Fleet Street's finest, and the vast majority of the papers, broadsheet as well as tabloid, covered the report in such a way as to suggest that this was the *only* topic with which it was concerned. Needless to say, the tone of the coverage (and not only in the editorial and comment columns) was bitterly hostile. Here, however, I want to concentrate solely on what the pundits had to say.

First off was Janet Daley in *The Times*, 26 October 1995, who fumed that the report's recommendation that smacking should be banned gives us

> a fairly clear hint that the permissive lobby has learnt nothing from the disastrous consequences of its own ideology . . . The present genera-tion of abusive, feckless parents are themselves the product of a child-rearing (and schooling) philosophy that refused to teach them self-control.

(Incidentally, Daley's response at the end of the Bulger murder trial to those who had the temerity to suggest that the background of Thompson and Venables might have had something to do with their actions was to rail against the 'social science platitudes of the age' as 'offensive nonsense' [*The Times*, 25 November 1993]). *The Times*, in fact, refused to devote *any* news columns at all to the report; instead, it followed Daley, on 11 November 1995, with an asinine piece from Libby Purves headed 'Beware the smacking police'. The commission is referred to as 'well meaning and wrinkled, the Great and the Good: safely past early parenthood', and the author avers: 'oh, how the palm itches to deliver a smart clip across its backside'. In the *Sunday Express*, 12 November 1995, the columnist Carole Malone (who she?) berates the Gulbenkian Foundation as 'a liberal little body of perfection seekers' and argues that 'perhaps someone should tell Saint Penny that while in theory smacking may well beget smacking and violence in later life, in the real world loony liberalism is likely to lead to a lot worse. Children need discipline, and sometimes punishment.' (Curiously, discipline is the subject of another item in the column, which shows a PVC-clad Mary Tyler-Moore brandishing a riding crop astride Dick Van Dyke. Is Ms Malone trying to tell us some-thing here?)

Even those columnists who had some sympathy with the report's recom-mendations on smacking couldn't help but use it as a stirrup with which to mount their favourite hobby horses. Thus Minette Marin in the *Sunday Telegraph*, 12 November 1995:

the sort of people who strongly oppose corporal punishment are the very people who usually incite me to violence. They are the wet progressives of every stripe – the nicey-nicey, feelly-touchy, anti-authority, anti-discipline, egalitarian guilt-ridden liberals, who can be relied upon for the wrong response to every social evil.

Similarly in the *Mail*, 13 November 1995, Keith Waterhouse, whilst attacking some of the report's most vociferous critics (such as the Chief Rabbi Lord Jakobovits in, er, the *Mail*), still used it as a battering ram against one of his favourite targets – overweening authority and heartless bureaucracy:

Into the mind floats a sinister though all-too-familiar montage of images. The dawn raid by social workers. The six policemen at the door. The remorseless interrogation of the bewildered child. The council care order, made in a closed court. The parents refused all information as to their offspring's whereabouts or current welfare. The breaking-up of the family, possibly for years.

What I have tried to suggest in this chapter is that, in the case of the British press at least, it is extremely misleading to divide newspapers into 'hard' and 'soft' sections, and to regard only the former as being worthy of political and ideological analysis, the latter belonging solely to the realms of entertainment. In order to further my argument I have concentrated here not on party political columnists such as Simon Heffer and Boris Johnson but, rather, on what I have called all-purpose columnists (and ignored weaselly appellations such as 'social affairs columnist' – after all, unless you're unfortunate enough to be Mrs Thatcher, what *isn't* social?). For the same reason I have tried to avoid quoting columnists on specifically *party*-political issues. It is, however, extremely hard to avoid the conclusion that columnists taken as a whole are a remarkably conservative – and indeed largely Conservative – bunch. Just consider the following list, all of whom appear regularly in the British press: John Junor, Auberon Waugh, Peregrine Worsthorne, W.F. Deedes, William Rees-Mogg, Bernard Levin, Roger Scruton, Richard Littlejohn, Simon Jenkins, Bruce Anderson, Peter Hitchens, Woodrow Wyatt, Bernard Ingham, Christopher Booker, Judge Pickles, Paul Johnson, Robert Kilroy Silk, William Oddie, Norman Stone, Norman Tebbit, Boris Johnson, Simon Heffer, Matthew Parris, Edward Pearce, Peter McKay, Lynda Lee-Potter, Ann Leslie, Minette Marin, Mary Kenny, Barbara Amiel, Janet Daley, Melanie Phillips . . . The list seems endless. Of course, it could be argued that there are important differences between some of these columnists – for example, between traditionalist and libertarian Conservatives. However, I would want to argue firmly that what unites these columnists is far more significant than what might appear to divide them, and that one of the key uniting factors is the kind of 'common sense' populism which I delineated earlier. Anyway, it cannot be exactly controversial to suggest that an overwhelmingly Conservative press employs an overwhelming number of Conservative (and conservative) pundits of one kind or another!

As Simon Frith and Jon Savage have pointed out in a piece which deserves far more attention than it has so far received, one of the key effects of the Thatcher era

> was not simply to widen the intellectual gap between journalists and academics, but, more importantly, to increase the importance of journalists as cultural ideologues while undermining the cultural authority of educators . . . The press was particularly significant for Margaret Thatcher's radical ambitions, as her intellectuals (and hers was a determinedly cultural project: she wanted to change how British people *thought*) were operating in right-wing think tanks that lay outside the intellectual establishment . . . Thatcherism was thus defined, to a large extent, not in specialist journals or elite forums but in newspaper columns and in well-publicised reports and position papers; it represented a well thought-out (and effective) strategic use of the media by intellectuals.
>
> (Frith and Savage 1993: 110–11)

Frith and Savage are entirely correct; indeed one of the main reasons why the university sector was treated with such hostility and contempt by Conservative governments since 1979 was because of the principled refusal by all but a few eccentric and deviant academics to bang the Thatcherite drum (on this matter see also Young 1991: 401–26). Some even had the temerity to criticise Thatcherite ideology, and this was regarded as tantamount to high treason, witness the witch hunts against the former SSRC, sociology courses (especially those at the Open University), and the Department of Peace Studies at Bradford University. Indeed, the Thatcher regime made its attitude to dissident and independent academics crystal clear early on in its existence when government ministers suggested in all seriousness that the 364 economists who publicly protested at the monetarist madness of 1980–1 should be forced to apologise publicly for their 'sins'! As Hugo Young noted in a seminal piece in the *Guardian* during the coal dispute:

> Thatcherites presume that anyone who is not plainly with them is secretly against them: an enemy of the state . . . One of Thatcherism's most startling gifts to British society is to have thoroughly politicised it. Little now occurs, in large reaches of public and sometimes private life, which does not have political importance and is not subjected to a test of its relevance to the prevailing ideology. This may be a condition more normally associated with Marxist socialism. But it has happened.

Perhaps the best example of the gap between Thatcherite ideologues in the press and what they love to refer to as 'the chattering classes' (a label unthinkable anywhere but in England, it has to be said) was provided by a more than usually bizarre campaign by *The Sunday Times* in 1987/8. According to an editorial of 20 September 1987, entitled 'Britain's breed apart':

> Britain's intelligentsia has become the lost tribe of the 1980s . . . It has become increasingly divorced from the land it lives in. It hates everything the Thatcher government stands for, but realises that the nation is not listening. So it has retreated to its own left-wing laager, where erudite moaning is taken for wise critique . . . Rarely have the ideals of the country's intellectual elite been so out of kilter with the aspirations of plain folk.

Battle was joined again by the pundit Brian Walden in his column on 29 November 1995. According to him: 'the preoccupations of many intellectuals in our society are divorced from popular sentiment . . . Eventually the bulk of the population will be confronted by an elitist culture which shares few of its values.' Further on we discover that 'the frightening truth is that any anti-capitalist, anti-Western, anti-Israeli material is meat and drink to many intellectuals. They swallow it uncritically.' As a consequence

> there is already a widespread view, faithfully reflected in the tabloid press, that our cultural and intellectual elites are inherently treacherous. They are seen as the enemies of what most people want and the friends of those who want to destroy Western values.

The end result of this 'treachery' is 'a severance of much of the intellectual community from the rest of society'. (Incidentally, a comparison of these sentiments with those of Garry Bushell, quoted on p. 256, reveals that the gap between the tabloid and 'quality' press is a good deal less wide than many commentators have suggested.)

Matters reached something of a head on 10 January 1988 with the infamous article by Norman Stone on contemporary British cinema entitled 'Through a Lens Darkly'. According to Stone, films such as *The Last of England*, *My Beautiful Launderette* and *Sammy and Rosie Get Laid* offer a grim vision of Thatcher's England that 'has nothing to offer an overwhelming majority of the potential audience' and 'present a public view of [the] country which everyone·else sees as childish caricature'. What has allowed the creation of such 'disgusting' films, we are informed, is the unholy alliance of an 'alienated intelligentsia' with 'supposedly enlightened semi-public bodies with a certain amount of money to spend on "open culture"'. What these films really express, then, is not so much a valid criticism of Thatcherite Britain but simply a 'paranoia bred of isolation from the market'.

Fortunately Stone's diatribe was so grotesquely tendentious and so riddled with the most elementary errors that it rather put an end to the paper's squalid, philistine, McCarthyite little campaign (for further discussion of this topic see Petley 1988). It was left to Neal Ascherson in the *Observer* to draw the moral of all this, identifying the sentiments expressed by the *Sunday Times* and its pundits as 'populist imbecility nourished on the porridge of resentful prejudice' and an appeal to 'England's equivalent to the Nazi "gesundes Volksempfinden" – healthy folk instinct'. Ascherson concluded that:

> the intention is to 'denationalise' the intellectual Left, by contrasting its discontent with the happy, dynamic Golden Age which the mass of the nation is alleged to be entering . . . Anyone who has ever sampled the language of the Soviet media towards dissidents and the recalcitrant young, especially in the Brezhnev period, will recognise this stuff at once. It's the old call to get your hair cut, stop listening to foreign broadcasts, and start writing positively about life in new towns or the personal conflicts of factory managers. It's the voice of the populist boor through the ages.
>
> (Ascherson 1988: 37–8)

Unfortunately this slime of imbecility still covers vast tracts of the British press and, as I have illustrated, lies particularly thickly over the columns of its pundits. One doesn't have to be Antonio Gramsci to realise that 'common sense' is not the same as good sense, and that it is fundamentally ideological and deeply reactionary. Its ideological nature is, of course, masked by the fact that the ideas which it embodies are so taken for granted that it feels like a kind of 'natural' wisdom. But as Stuart Hall has pointed out:

> It is precisely its 'spontaneous' quality, its transparency, its 'naturalness', its refusal to be made to examine the premises on which it is founded, its resistance to change or to correction, its effect of instant recognition, and the closed circle in which it moves which makes common sense, at one and the same time, 'spontaneous', ideological *and unconscious*. You cannot learn, through common sense, *how things are*: you can only discover *where they fit* into the existing scheme of things.
>
> (Hall 1977: 325)

That newspaper columns veritably saturated with 'common sense' can call themselves 'the voice of reason' and the like is, of course, all part of the trick. Similarly, newspapers' habits of labelling their pundits 'controversial', 'refreshing' or 'courageous' depends on the paranoid and utterly nonsensical fantasy that these are somehow or other doughty lone voices holding out boldly against an inrushing tide of 'political correctness'. As Jeremy Hardy put it in the *Guardian*, 2 November 1996:

> if those who claim they are rolling back the frontiers of political correctness have interpreted history accurately, at an unspecified date in the 1980s, the Left took over the world. Reagan and Thatcher were firmly

in power, the arms trade was booming, mass unemployment became the main tool of government, and yet, insidiously, black lesbian Trotskyists were filling every position of authority.

Unfortunately this is not a caricature of a certain kind of paranoid, enraged position, witness Richard Littlejohn's remarks to the effect that 'already it is impossible to get work in the health service or with the local authorities unless you are a non-smoking, disabled, ethnic lesbian' and that the 'the country is now run by limp-wristed *Guardian* readers' (Littlejohn 1995: 57, 27). It goes without saying, of course, that the *Mail*'s reviewer, cited on the book's dustjacket, found this drivel 'irreverent'.

This is as preposterous as Andrew Neil's claims, endlessly repeated in his autobiography, to be an arch-enemy of the Establishment. They reach such a pitch in the chapter entitled 'Manifesto of a Modern Meritocrat' that one wonders just whom he is trying to fool. For example, of his days at the Conservative Research Department he tells us that:

> I was on the fast track for a political career and, with vowels a little more Anglicised and some pinstripe suits, no doubt membership of the Establishment beckoned, as one of the up-and-coming outsiders they periodically allowed in. But the more I saw of the Establishment, the less I wanted to joint it.
>
> (Neil 1996: 367)

Whether this and endless other such examples represent bitterness and resentment at being 'left out' or, conversely, guilt and bad faith for having abandoned his much-vaunted Paisley roots, is a matter between Neil and his analyst. However, the absurdity of the former editor of *The Economist* and *The Sunday Times* (to name but two of Neil's many media jobs) setting himself up as an 'anti-Establishment' figure was seized on with glee by virtually every review of the book. As Polly Toynbee noted in the *New Statesman*, 1 November 1996:

> he concocts a self-aggrandising farrago about himself as the loner who rocked the foundation of the ruling classes. Here is a man name-dropping the great and not-so-good, dining in the best restaurants, picking up the best-looking girls in Tramp's, spinning about the globe interviewing Madonna or dropping in on Downing Street. And we are supposed to believe he is some kind of outsider? Please.

The fact that the post-*Sunday Times* editor slipped quickly and comfortably into the role of a pundit for the *Mail* – under the inevitable banner, 'the voice of controversy' – is yet one more proof, as if it were needed, that Neil's pique at being excluded from the Establishment, if that is indeed what's troubling him so, is misplaced in the extreme.

Of course, all this nonsense about supposedly 'controversial' pundits is linked not simply to paranoid delusions about the immanent, all-engulfing presence of 'political correctness', but to the even more bizarre and freakish illusion (from which Andrew Neil suffers in spades) that Thatcherism represented some kind of 'radical' social force (as opposed to a perverse and anachronistic throw-back to discredited Manchester liberalism). In this respect the pundits are at one with the rest of the journalism that surrounds them in their papers, merely bawling from the roof tops the values expressed rather less stridently (well sometimes, anyway) on other pages. If, for all its alleged 'courageousness', most punditry is abjectly craven and conformist, it's in perfectly good company. If it turns the standards of decent liberal journalism on their heads who, quite frankly, would notice, since those standards are so conspicuous by their absence in vast tracts of the British press?

In short, punditry simply magnifies the shortcomings of the popular press as a whole: it doesn't attempt to inform or educate the public – rather, it tells them what it thinks they want to hear and simply stokes the fires of popular prejudices and mythologies: bigotry over the breakfast table. Indeed, if we define 'political correctness' as an unthinking, adherence to ideological tramlines then large sections of the British press come a perilously close second to the old-style Pravda in the 'political correctness' stakes.

References

Ascherson, N. (1988) *Games With Shadows*, London: Radius.

Barker, M. and Petley, J. (eds) (1997) *Ill Effects*, London: Routledge.

Billig, M. (1995), *Banal Nationalism*, London: Sage.

Chibnall, C. (1977) *Law-And-Order News*, London: Tavistock.

Coles, J.(1994) 'Queens of the Street', *Guardian*, 18 February.

Cumberbatch, G. and Howitt, D. (1989) *A Measure of Uncertainty*, London: John Libby.

Curran, J., Douglas, A. and Whannel, G. (1980) 'The political economy of the human-interest story', in A. Smith (ed) *Newspapers and Democracy*, Cambridge, Massachusetts: MIT Press.

Franklin, B. and Petley, J. (1996) 'Killing the age of innocence', in J. Pilcher and S. Wagg (eds) *Thatcher's Children?*, London: Falmer Press.

Frith, S. and Savage, J. (1993) 'Pearls and swine', *New Left Review* 198, March/April: 107–116.

Gauntlett, D. (1995) *Moving Experiences*, London: John Libby.

Gulbenkian Foundation (1995) *Children and Violence*, London: Calouste Gulbenkian Foundation.

Hall, S. (1977) 'Culture, the media and the "ideological effect"', in J. Curran, M Gurevitch and J. Woollacott (eds) *Mass Communication and Society*, London: Edward Arnold.

Kraus, K. (1986) *Half-Truths and One-and-a-Half Truths*, Manchester: Carcanet.

Leiser, E. (1974) *Nazi Cinema*, London: Secker & Warburg.

Littlejohn, R. (1995) *You Couldn't Make it Up*, London: William Heinemann Ltd.

Neil, A. (1996) *Full Disclosure*, London: Macmillan.

Nimmo, D. and Combs, J. (1992) *Political Pundits*, New York: Praeger.

Petley, J. (1988) 'The price of portraying a less than perfect Britain', *The Listener*, 21 January.

Petley, J. (1994) 'In defence of "video nasties" ', *British Journalism Review* 5,3: 52–7.

Poole, M. (1984) 'The cult of the generalist', *Screen* 25,2: 41–61.

Sampson, A. (1996) 'The crisis at the heart of our media', in *British Journalism Review*, 7,3: 42–5.

Seaton, J. and Pimlott, B. (1987) 'Introduction', in J. Seaton and B. Pimlott (eds) *The Media in British Politics*, Aldershot: Avebury.

Sparks, C. (1988) 'The popular press and political democracy', *Media Culture and Society* 10,2: 209–23.

Sparks, C. (1992) 'Popular journalism: theories and practice', in Dahlgren, P. and Sparks, C. (eds) *Journalism and Popular Culture*, London: Sage.

Tunstall, J. (1996) *Newspaper Power*, Oxford: Clarendon Press.

Waterhouse, K. 'Climbing the column', *British Journalism Review*, 6,3: 12–15.

Young, H. (1991) *One of Us*, London: Macmillan.

Chapter 24

Matthew Doull

JOURNALISM INTO THE TWENTY-FIRST CENTURY

ONE OF THE THINGS THAT OFTEN GETS SAID about the digital revolution in general and the Internet in particular is that they give EVERYONE the power to be a publisher. Technology has enabled us to produce our own newsletters, magazines, video documentaries and web sites. So now everyone is a content provider as well as being a content consumer. It's no longer a one-to-many broadcasting model, but a many-to-many, or point-to-point, medium.

This is, in theory, very exciting. A.J. Liebling said that the power of the press belongs to those who own one, and suddenly those of us who have computers and net connections all own one. In addition to shifting the balance of power in our society, this opens up incredible new opportunities for individual creativity.

But, so far, what has it really produced on the web? A bunch of homepages that turn out to be lists of lists, or lists of links, or links to other links. At the current growth rate of web servers and new homepages, we will soon have billions of such web sites. Lots of writing and lots of new writers. And no publishers.

But just because you have a copy of Microsoft Word that doesn't make you a writer. Knowing Quark Xpress doesn't make you a designer. Knowing HTML, the formatting language of the worldwide web, doesn't make you an interactive designer. Technology is a tool: do not confuse it with talent or the will of the market.

And this isn't the first time a new medium has come along, promising to transform radically the way we relate to each other. Consider this quote:

> Let us not forget the value of this great system does not lie primarily in its extent or even its efficiency. Its worth depends on the use that is made of it . . . For the first time in human history we have available to us the ability to communicate simultaneously with millions of our fellow men, to furnish the entertainment, instruction, and widening vision of national problems and national events. An obligation rests on us to see that it is devoted to real service and to develop the material that is transmitted into that which is really worthwhile.

You may be thinking that this was written by Al Gore or Newt Gingrich or some other cyber-personality. In fact, it was Herbert Hoover, speaking in 1924 as the American Secretary of Commerce about the radical, fast-moving new medium of that age – radio. Radio started out in the 1920s as a many-to-many medium, just like citizens' band radio (CB) and, in some ways, just like the web today. Everyone was their own broadcaster.

Radio was totally user dominated and user controlled, because in the beginning the airwaves were wide open. All you needed in order to secure a licence to broadcast was proficiency in Morse code, which is about as simple as HTML is today. In 1995 an issue of *Wired* had an article by staff writer Todd Lappin on the parallels. He wrote that radio 'was a wireless community that operated according to its own set of rules, protocols, customs, and taboos. Creative experimentation was encouraged, monopolising bandwidth was considered bad form, and blatant commercialism was completely uncool.'

As the airwaves became more popular that interactivity was lost. Professional broadcasters began to appear, and newcomers to radio didn't want to hear radio geeks blathering on in Morse code. Like the newbies now flocking online, these new listeners wanted their information in professional, wrapped packages.

What are newcomers to the net looking for? It's certainly not a billion of anything, whether quirky homepages, brands of beer, or content-sources. In addition, most people aren't going to want to turn around after a hard day at the home-office and begin work on their own web site, any more than most of them return home from their office-commute now and sit down and write novels.

What most people want from the media is either information, or an experience they can't create for themselves. And the information they want is not just the right to search a billion databases – they want some point-of-view that is congruent with their own; they want some source that is reliable and trustworthy. As for experience, they want to connect with some imagination they feel comfortable with; that can carry them away from the mundane or even horrible reality of their everyday lives; that can expand their minds, scare the shit out of them, soothe their souls . . .

Kevin Kelly, *Wired*'s executive editor, has written: 'The web is a building – a great big universal library, but in case no one noticed, nobody spends their Friday nights at the library. I believe libraries are almost holy, but people visit them as often as churches.' The problem with the web – as it exists so far – is that it is a woven cloth of information, when what people want is a woven cloth of experience. There are only two kinds of experience you can have on the web so far: browsing and publishing. Browsing is good for about twenty minutes before you get bored or frustrated. Publishing is good for a lifetime – if you have an audience, and that's the problem. The item in shortest supply on the web, and probably on the web of the future, is an attentive audience. Nobody is paying attention because they are busy click-browsing, or because they're busy having their say as publishers.

Think about the stories you hear about the web: almost without exception they are stories about publishing, and not about experiencing, or sharing, or learning, or having your mind changed. They are stories about publishing pornography, or the secrets of the Church of Scientology, or an up-to-the-minute picture of your coffee-maker. The web is a nation of publishers, and in a world of spoon-fed media consumers that is something of a breath of fresh air. But the web will not really flourish until it incorporates some of the sense of common audience that broadcasting has. In other words, until it can move beyond serving as a gigantic global library to create communities, it is not going to fulfil its promise.

Should people stop putting up a billion web sites? Of course not – and, anyway, nothing will stop them.

Once the novelty of net surfing has worn off, once people have figured out what interactivity really means, consumers are going to want something very different from what they currently get on the web, however. After a long day of work, they're going to want the same things they get now. They want to let themselves get carried away by other people's imagination, and participate in that experience. People want to consume media and connect with others through experiences they couldn't create themselves.

What a publisher or entertainer provides is context and point-of-view. Editors help you to make sense of the boundless information and opportunities that exist. What counts are personality and perspective, and hearing someone's opinion on why something matters, or what's really important in that spew of data flow we get every day. That's what media professionals provide.

In a world of hyperabundant information, the greatest luxury is point-of-view. Put another way, context is more important than content. Perhaps that does not sound very radical – after all, that is what Tom Wolfe's 'new journalism' that emerged in the 1970s was all about. As the cover price 'war' between broadsheet newspapers in Britain in the mid-1990s demonstrated, information tends to become a commodity. The only way to give it value is to add point-of-view or context. With the web, the opportunities to create context are exponentially greater than they are in print or broadcast journalism. Context on the web consists not just in the point-of-view taken by the writer, but in the hyperlinks and multimedia he or she chooses to open, connected to his or her work. That means seeing your work as part of a larger conversation, rather than as a perfectly-formed *oeuvre* in isolation.

There is also a further way to add context that is unique to this medium, and is perhaps the thing that will most frighten people who romanticise the image of journalists as ink-stained wretches. That is software. Digital technology has created the ability to manipulate information in real time and perform all sorts of fancy tricks on it that will make it more personal and more relevant. The software behind a web site can remember what I like, and tailor the information it serves to me next time to reflect that. It can also automatically put me in touch with people who share my tastes – or, indeed, with people who do not, if I want to pick a fight.

The work of journalists will never be performed by intelligent agents and software robots that mechanistically create my *Daily Me*. Software can do a lot of things but it cannot yet seek out and then elegantly speak the truth – and if you are not motivated by a desire to speak the truth, then call me old-fashioned, but I don't think you should be a journalist. Software will be an invaluable tool, however, in the arsenals of journalists who know how to use it to add further value to the experience they are creating for their users/viewers/consumers.

The power of microprocessors creates a fundamentally different relationship between a consumer and his or her media than any other technology. Computers allow people to manipulate information with a speed and efficiency that has never before been possible. Journalists who ignore this and cling to the belief that they are the keepers of the Word will find that they are themselves ignored. So, while the web desperately needs the talents of journalists and editors, it will also require them to develop some new talents and abandon some old habits. They must accept that communication is no longer going to be entirely one-way.

Today's journalism students must have a very different relationship with technology than the one that I had when we were taught to use computers as little more than glorified typewriters. Today's journalists must be able to use the web as a research tool – and, indeed, to weave it into the very fabric of their craft by participating in online communities and by embracing the technologies that are creating a new medium.

The most important thing to know about good journalism in the twenty-first century is that technology will only increase the demand for it. Russell Neuman, who by reputation is not given to hype, wrote recently:

> Take it as given that within five years, networked computers in the workplace and the home will compete on an equal footing with the existing news media as a routine source of news for over half the public in the industrialised world. Sceptical? OK, then make it ten years. We're not discussing the end-point anymore, just the shape of the diffusion curve.
>
> (Quoted in Fulton 1996)

If you don't like computers, get used to them. One in three British homes has one, and they are being shipped into British homes at the rate of over 30,000 per month. Every single eight-year-old child in the land is computer literate. They will need to be served by a journalistic profession that understands their new realities.

Last year I was told a wonderful story by a man who had been given $500 million by the Canadian telephone companies to develop interactive media; a story that explains why existing communications and media companies are so worried about the digital future. He told me the true story – recounted by Stan Davis and Jim Botkin (1995) – of a five-year-old girl who was afraid that there was a monster under her bed. So, like any normal girl of her age, she decided to write a story about the monster moving from under her bed to under her brother's bed. She powered up her computer, opened up her word processor and wrote the narrative. Then, just for fun, she opened up her graphics application and drew some pictures of the monster. Then she took some digital video of her and her brother and respective beds, and inserted it into her story, which was now a complete multimedia piece. Then, as you do when you are five, she uploaded it to a web site where people from all over the world started coming across it.

At the age of five she was the writer, the director, the camera operator and the distributor of her own movie. The moral of the story is that WE had better figure out how to serve her media needs when she is twenty – or we're toast.

References

Davis, S. and Botkin, J. (1995) *The Monster Under the Bed: How Business is Mastering the Opportunity of Knowledge for Profit*, New York: Touchstone Books.

Fulton, K. (1996) 'A tour of our uncertain future', *Columbia Journalism Review* (March/April), located at www.cjr.columbia.edu

Practice and Image
1700–2000

Introduction to part five

■   Tom O'Malley

THIS SECTION BRINGS TOGETHER four essays spanning changes in the history of journalism which extend beyond forty years. Michael Harris explores the ways in which the practice of national journalism in the UK became fused with a physical space in London, Fleet Street, to produce the idea of Fleet Street as a metaphor for all things to do with the national press and, in so doing, draws on discussions about the public sphere and the invention of tradition. The changes of the 1980s, which saw most national papers leave Fleet Street, may have broken the physical link between place and function, but the cultural resonance of the metaphor remains intact.

Allan also uses the concept of the public sphere to analyse aspects of the history of the concepts of objectivity and impartiality in the print and broadcast journalism of the nineteenth and twentieth centuries. The context which shaped the development of these concepts and their application has shifted over time. New developments in ownership, technology and practice are, arguably, pushing these concepts to the edge of news production. In order to understand what is happening to them, and to act to reassert anew the concepts of objectivity and impartiality as components of a contemporary public sphere, we need, he argues, to pay attention to their history.

Craft or profession? Bromley's article revisits the issue of the uncertainty of what constitutes a journalist in the period after 1945. By tracing debates about status and training he pinpoints the recurring uncertainty amongst journalists about whether they are a craft or profession. He shows how technological change in the 1980s, and the emergence of multi-skilling as a strategy by employers to improve productivity, has intensified questions of what is, was, or will be a journalist.

Bailey and Williams explore the memoirs of journalists, mainly those relating to the period after 1945. They argue that these much neglected sources can reveal valuable material about the ideas and working conditions and practices of journalists. The bulk of this material is anecdotal and unreflective, and most does not reach the levels of analysis and reflection exhibited by writers such as James Cameron or John Pilger. Yet any history of the press in this period will have to take full and critical account of all the different types of journalists' memoirs.

The history of press and broadcasting journalism has been interwoven with debates about the function of the industry, its status and the responsibilities of its practitioners. These questions have remained areas of conflict and redefinition. If, now, at the end of a century of mass communications, we can begin to see these issues in longer term perspective, moving from the particular issues of today to the patterns and complexities of the past, in order to grasp more fully the dynamics of the present, then this is to be welcomed. Our collection is intended to aid readers in this process.

Chapter 25

Michael Harris

FAREWELL TO FLEET STREET?

WHERE THINGS HAPPEN (THE PLACE) and what happens there (the process) can become fused within a cultural identity. A building, a street, a town can assume a composite character in which an activity of a highly visible and public kind supersedes, without entirely submerging, the more conventional geographical usage. This happened to Fleet Street. Through a set of historical circumstances this short stretch of urban roadway became the focus for a national newspaper industry and, from the later nineteenth century, the place and the process became interchangeable in a sometimes confusing way. The overlap in usage began to break up in the 1980s as the entire apparatus of the London press was removed from Fleet Street and relocated in unexpected parts of the London region. This abrupt shift was accompanied by a long sequence of 'goodbyes' and 'farewells' in which various forms of nostalgia and foreboding were mingled (for example, see Barson and Saint 1988; Powell 1987; Rook 1989; cf. Lewis 1986). The rupture of Fleet Street and the newspaper business seemed to fit the picture of a more comprehensive ending in which the entire superstructure of the print culture was being dismantled. Gutenberg and his moveable type was already being identified as the representative of an obsolete process overtaken by new and more powerful forces (Smith 1980). The hard-copy newspaper with its unwieldy systems of production and distribution had, it was suggested, finally hit the buffers, leaving news and information to flow through the electronic circuits of the new technology to be assembled and dispersed by the finally liberated consumer. In the event, the printed news serial remains afloat, demonstrating a level of durability and resistance to change which might have been predicted. The content of the news serials, pumped out through the computerised offices of the familiar Fleet Street titles, continues to follow the priorities and adopt the formulas established in the seventeenth century. Print remains the medium of transmission and the giant production plants with associated street-based distribution still fits a pattern of commercial activity that is profoundly familiar. Massive shifts have occurred in the technology, internal organisation and in the scale and character of consumption. However, the individual issue in the hands of the reader remains an irreducibly traditional product. Locked into a nexus of commercial and political interests and relying, as ever, on a multiplicity of small financial transactions continuously renewed, the texts carry an indelible impression of the historical process. Fleet Street was the setting for the construction of the English newspaper and what follows will suggest ways in which the place and the process came to be locked together.

The development of the printed serial as a mechanism in the flow of news through London was organised from the seventeenth century around the main centres of public information and ritual which were strung out along the east/west axis of the metropolis. In Westminster parliament and the principal civil law courts, located within the same cluster of riverside buildings, formed a primary news centre at the west end of town. Towards the eastern edge of the City, whose boundary was marked off by Temple Bar, was a second nuclear centre for news. This was made up of the sessions house in the Old Bailey, where criminal trials for the London region were on regular public display, and Newgate prison from which the condemned, equally regularly, began their westward procession to execution at Tyburn. A third focal point in the linear flow of information was provided in the heart of the City by the Royal Exchange, the location for a substantial concentration of national and international commerce as well as of wholesale and retail trading. Stretched out along the river, London contained within its constituent parts a massive concentration of people whose lives were increasingly geared to the lines of serial print woven between the nuclear centres of news.

The east/west flow of information through the built-up areas of London ran in tandem with the movement of traffic and people pouring along the thoroughfares which linked Westminster and the City. In this configuration Fleet Street formed a crucial, 400-yard stretch running parallel to the River Thames and leading through the congested City ward of Farringdon Without towards Ludgate Hill. It was marked off at its western end by Temple Bar, adjacent to the sprawling complex of the Inns of Court, and at the east by the River Fleet crossed by the Fleet Bridge. By 1750 the lower reaches of the massively polluted river had been covered by a stretch of roadway later identified as Farringdon and New Bridge Streets linked at the east end of Fleet Street by Ludgate Circus. As well as the physical presence of the law, emphasised by the nearby streets and buildings which made up the precincts of the Fleet Prison for debtors, the street was also marked off by the structures of the church. At the west end St. Dunstan's and at the east St. Bride's constituted the focal point of separate parochial organisations.

The street itself was therefore located in a complex and tightly focused network of interests whose physical presence in this central part of the built up area drew in large numbers of people to supplement the endless torrent of those passing through. The continuous movement of traffic and people into and through the area, obstructed by Temple Bar and jammed into a narrow roadway, was creating local difficulty by 1700. In his serialised perambulation the London Spy, Ned Ward, described how he and his companion emerged from the ramshackle Whitefriars area to the south

> into the Common Road, Fleet-Street, where the Rattling of Coaches, loud as the Cataracts of the Nile, Robb'd me of my Hearing . . . however, when we had waited with Patience for a seasonable Minute, to perform the dangerous service [the hazard of crossing the Kennel] we at last ventur'd to Shoot our selves thro' a Vacancy between two Coaches.
>
> (Ward, 1924: 157–8)

Such manoeuvres, more or less successfully completed, remained the daily experience of the users of Fleet Street and the issue of traffic congestion has yet to be resolved.

Lining Fleet Street through the seventeenth and eighteenth centuries were the densely packed urban terraces of shops and houses within which a conventionally miscellaneous range of commercial and social activities were represented. No single trade or interest dominated the area. Even so, within Fleet Street and its immediate environs, some indications of a local relationship to the flow of news and information began to assume a heightened visibility from 1700. As a public space, the street itself became the location for forms of business in which social and cultural exchange were integral elements. Between Temple Bar and the Fleet valley public houses of all kinds formed satellite news centres. Supplying customers with cross-sections of printed news serials, the coffee houses, taverns and beer shops provided a link in the chain of news supply.[1] Coffee houses such as Anderton's, Dick's, Nando's, Peele's and the Rainbow remained in place in Fleet Street long enough to become repositories for the collection and storage of news serials for public reference. In the mid-nineteenth century the proprietors of Peele's Coffee House were trying, unsuccessfully, to find a repository for six tons of accumulated newspapers (Harris, 1989: 45–6). At the same time, the main public houses became the meeting point for the shareholding proprietors of the eighteenth-century London newspapers (Harris, 1987: 74–5). This form of use, in which the elements of business, sociability and the exchange of information were involved, suggests the way in which individuals and groups were constructing what has been described as a bourgeois 'public sphere'.[2] The process can also be identified in the erratic ramblings of Samuel Johnson as, arm-in-arm with James Boswell, he roamed Fleet Street at all hours of the day and night. His sphere of influence was consolidated in the Mitre Tavern (also, perhaps, in the Cheshire Cheese) while his ideas, literary, social and philosophical, received their fullest public expression through lines of serial print.[3]

Part of the public life of Fleet Street, which overlapped with the commercial, news-related activity of the public house system, involved public displays. Coffee houses and taverns were themselves involved with this kind of cultural/commercial activity as they were with a broad spectrum of business enterprises including sales by auction. At the same time, Fleet Street became the base for permanent shows packaged to cater for a more generalised form of public curiosity. Mrs Salmon's Waxworks, at what became number 189, emphasised the presence in wax of the current royal family and their attendents.[4] Down the street towards Temple Bar, at 197 Fleet Street, was Mr. Rackstraw's museum. Founded in about 1740 and still in business at the end of the century, the Rackstraw displays seem to have had a more scientific steer. A handbill of the 1780s announced that just added to the regular anatomical exhibition was a 'figure moulded from a woman, dissected after execution'.[5] Waxworks were still part of the Fleet Street scene in the 1850s, presumably, to some extent, keying in their displays to the coverage of events in the rapidly expanding newspaper press.

Alongside the public houses and displays which honeycombed the street before 1800 were shops run by what in London would have appeared a routine miscellany of retailers and manufacturers. Cashing in on the massive presence of the public and using print to develop their market, barbers, cork-cutters, lottery-ticket sellers, cabinet makers and druggists identified themselves through handbills passed about in the neighbourhood.[6] However, if there can be said to have been a dominant presence in this sector of the Fleet Street community it was provided by members of the London book trades. Print as a product had been manufactured in and around Fleet Street since the sixteenth century when the printer Wynkin de Worde moved eastward from Westminster into the City. This was not to become the primary geographical location for the high-flying dealers in, or publishers of, books. The streets around St. Paul's Cathedral remained the focal point for the 'respectable' booksellers and stationers whose social, political and, to some extent, economic interests were worked out through Stationers' Hall located nearby in Ave Maria Lane.[7]

None the less, trade clusters came to be identified with landmarks at either end of the street: the first around Temple Bar at addresses in both Fleet Street and the Strand, and the second, and substantially less respectable, around Fleet Bridge. One of the explanations for the early linkage between the newspaper and Fleet Street may be found in the presence of a dynamic and entrepreneurial sector of the London book trade which was pushed by market forces towards the publication of serial print. A similar kind of association, between mixed publishing and an active news centre, was involved in the appearance of the first English news serials which were kick-started at the Royal Exchange early in the seventeenth century.[8] In Fleet Street, it was in the modest neighbourhood of the Fleet Bridge that the first English daily newspaper, the *Daily Courant* (1702–35), was published. It initially formed part of the output of Elizabeth Mallet whose production schedules were constructed around various forms of ephemeral material.[9] Her association with the *Courant* seems to have been short-lived and the paper was almost immediately taken over by one of the earliest groups of shareholding booksellers to be associated with this form of publication. The general development by which the newspaper became locked into the upper levels of the London book trade was not specifically a Fleet Street phenomenon. Even so, members of the Fleet Street trade were well represented among the self-selecting groups of proprietors, and the meetings organised to discuss management tended to gravitate to the coffee houses and taverns along the main east/west thoroughfare made up of Fleet Street and the Strand. In this way there gradually emerged the structure of what I have called elsewhere the first newspaper establishment and it was in and around Fleet Street that elements of the newspaper business began to take on a shadowy form.[10]

The stages by which Fleet Street, the Strand and the streets and alleys running north and south of the main thoroughfare became saturated by the newspaper business has yet to be charted. In the 1790s elements of the earlier pattern of dispersed production remained in place. London newspapers were still published from locations extending from Covent Garden to St. Paul's. However, during the first decades of the next century the print-driven newspaper, and by extension Fleet Street itself, began to experience accelerating change. Prior to 1800 the processes of newspaper production and distribution could be contained within the framework of conventional bookselling. But as the forces of industrialisation were applied to print the existing arrangements were blown apart. The need for, and benefit of, a concentration of manufacture in larger units, the harnessing of new power sources, particularly steam, and the build-up in specialist staff on the editorial side combined to create an entirely new industry which was held by a sort of centrifugal force within Fleet Street and its environs.

In the street the refronting of houses and the introduction of gas lighting, as part of a piecemeal attempt at improvement, had done little to alleviate the disintegrating character of the neighbourhood.[11] The association of the area with manufacturing, in the form of print, and the inescapable traffic problems made Fleet Street a difficult location for local government intervention. News reports involving Fleet Street continued in the nineteenth century to emphasise the presence of an active trade in prostitution, street robberies and fires as well as traffic accidents.[12] At the same time, economic forces were operating within the unstable environment. The first purpose-built printing office opened in 1825 in Bouverie Street, which had been cut through an existing clutter of lanes and alleys to the south of Fleet Street in the 1790s (Barson and Saint 1988: 17). This combination of redevelopment and the application of new industrial strategies was to have a special significance for the newspaper business. By the 1820s a heavy concentration of the London daily and evening papers were published from addresses identified with either Fleet Street or the Strand. The physical impact of this presence is not easy to follow in detail but seems to have imposed an increasing pressure on the local housing stock. As the scale of the newspaper business increased, the existing buildings, which were narrow fronted, three or four storey houses used for modest commercial purposes, began to be subjected to a long process of modification, renewal and replacement. Two circumstances accelerated this interchange between environment and industry. In 1855 the tax on newsprint was abolished and shortly afterwards the associated taxes on advertising and paper were also removed. In the same year the Metropolitan Board of Works was set up in an attempt to bring some element of coordination to the interventions of London's local government. Although Fleet Street fell within the jurisdiction of the City, reconstruction was brought directly on to the agenda in all parts of the metropolis.

Some sense of the local pressure created by the tax repeals can be identified in relation to the first national paper to be sold for 1d., the *Daily Telegraph*. Set up in 1856, its circulation had within ten years overtaken *The Times* (Barson and Saint 1988: 21–2; Griffith 1992: '*Daily Telegraph*'). The paper was established in the Strand but by the mid-1860s had moved to premises abutting Peterborough Court at number 135 on the north side of Fleet Street. The move involved extensive rebuilding though the physical constraints of the new site were intractable. In 1866 the paper employed about 200 people, organised in departments and linked directly into the telegraph system. This proved particularly useful when the premises were set on fire by an arsonist.[13] Behind the Fleet Street offices was a large, two-storey warehouse with the roof and walls on the upper floor made of glass and metal. Here, an enormous quantity of paper was stored, tightly packed in bales and supervised by employees. On the ground floor and in the basement was the new gas-powered, multi-feed printing machinery under the control of the paper's gas manager and a staff of fitters. The warehouse belonging to the *Telegraph* backed on to the premises used for printing two other large-scale London papers, the *Morning Herald* and the *Standard*. Such a massive concentration of newspaper activity on the north side of Fleet Street crammed into the limited spaces between the urban terraces led remorselessly towards the construction of purpose-built newspaper offices. The first of these to appear in Fleet Street itself was the *Daily Telegraph* building opened in 1882. It was a grandiose and ornate structure rising to five storeys and completely engulfing Peterborough Court (Barson and Saint 1988: 24–5; Boston 1990: 121–2).

The progressive adjustments taking place on the north side of Fleet Street were as nothing compared to the generalised reconstruction taking place to the south alongside the Inns of Court at the Temple. Between 1860 and 1914 the Corporation of London and the Metropolitan Board of Works, succeeded by the London County Council, moved through the area to powerful effect. The construction of the Embankment in the 1860s created a growing demand for effective access south of Fleet Street. The City gas works which had blighted a large part of the area was removed by the Corporation and this was followed by the construction of a new grid of streets which opened up north/south and east/west communication within the area. Almost at a stroke, a potentially user-friendly location for London newspapers was developed along the lines of Tudor Street, Temple Avenue and Carmelite Street. Meantime the approaches to Blackfriars Bridge were cleared and widened while on the south side of Fleet Street itself, the whole frontage between the Temple and Ludgate Circus was set back and rebuilt. Temple Bar was dismantled and removed to the country.[14]

From the later nineteenth century Fleet Street and its neighbourhood was constantly made over. Sequences of large and increasingly sophisticated structures began to be slotted into the densely packed environment. Based on American practice and owned by bizarre representatives of the super-rich, the buildings of the London newspaper press sprang up around Fleet Street in increasingly aggressive form. This process, extending into and through most of the twentieth century, has been clearly outlined by Susie Barson and Andrew Saint.[15] It was in and around these embattled structures that the newspapers, independently or in syndicates, engaged in ferocious competition in what is sometimes described as the free market. At the same time, whatever the increasing problems of Fleet Street as a crowded and landlocked site, the London newspapers remained rooted to the spot, held in place by their need for direct access to shared resources. Advertising and news agencies, telegraph offices and a consolidated publication system, dominated by W.H. Smith in the Strand, made escape almost impossible (see Wilson 1985). The new buildings created during reconstruction and road widening acted like a magnet to the representatives of the main local and regional papers. By the opening of the twentieth century the generalised force of Fleet Street as a crucial element in the construction and flow of news had become an inescapable fact of newspaper life.

It was in this maelstrom of activity that the concept of 'Fleet Street' emerged. It was almost inevitable that within the tightly focused nexus of interlocking activities, some sort of composite identity should emerge. Competition of various kinds did not interfere with this. Reporters struggling for exclusive stories none the less jostled together at the Central Criminal Court and in the lobbies of parliament or dashed around Europe using the same means of transport.[16] In Fleet Street itself layers of formal and informal contact offset the commercial barriers between titles. Unions linked printers and journalists with each other, whatever the normal tendency towards disintegration, while more polite and self-satisfied associations provided meeting points for editors and proprietors. The founding of the Press Club in 1875 by the most effective of Victorian journalists, George Sala, emphasised the local tendency to coalescence. The force of proximity in creating a sort of generalised *esprit de corps* was perhaps most fully developed in the public spaces long identified with the Fleet Street area. The mass of public houses offered an infrastructure through which a loose-knit form of community of interest could be identified and sustained. The pubs and cafes, many of them established in the eighteenth century, became the convivial location for an intricate and endless series of meetings organised around the daily schedules of newspaper production. Such meetings, often effectively lubricated by alcohol, contributed in themselves to a process, familiar two hundred years before, of news sharing and manufacture.

The apotheosis of Fleet Street was achieved by bringing together a variety of historical perceptions. It was directly related to a developing mythology of the newspaper itself, fostered within the industry and initially formulated during the drawn-out campaigns against the 'Taxes on knowledge'. The liberal argument for releasing the press from financial intervention had involved its characterisation in almost mystical terms. The newspaper came to be represented as the prime medium for the political education of the people while also appearing as the physical embodiment of the force of public opinion. Led by *The Times*, just about the only daily to be produced and published outside Fleet Street, the newspaper press was confirmed within the liberal ideology as 'the fourth estate' of the realm. This view was refined and reinforced in the first histories of the newspaper written from the mid-nineteenth century by practising or retired journalists (for example, Andrews 1859; Fox-Bourne 1887). In these accounts the profession was shown to have been engaged in a long march towards the establishment of what was consistently characterised as a 'free press'. The stark unreality of this view did not deter some of the journalist/historians of the mid-twentieth century who continued to offer an interpretation of the past which chimed with the romantic notions embodied in the concept of 'Fleet Street'.[17]

Part of this process, which has been identified in relation to other cultural and commercial organisations as the invention of tradition, involved placing a local emphasis on a relationship between journalism and 'serious' literature. This had the incidental benefit of distancing Fleet Street from the alternative conceptual location for literary struggle, Grub Street. Formal representations of the literary predecessors of the Fleet Street professionals began to appear in the public spaces of the street. Samuel Richardson, printer and respectable novelist, was unveiled at St. Bride's in 1889 (*The Times*, 28 November 1889), while Samuel Johnson, journalist and profound thinker, was reconstituted just beyond the site of Temple Bar in 1910. Other busts and plaques were to follow. The emergence of a self-conscious respectability coincided with a generalised improvement in the career prospects of journalists. Whatever the cultural side-effects of the Northcliffe regime, the introduction of an American-style organisation raised the status, as well as the standard of living, of the denizens of Fleet Street and contributed to the formulation of the concept.[18]

The idea of 'Fleet Street' was expressed in a variety of ways and the gradual emergence of separate but overlapping meanings is clearly identified in the two valuable bibliographies of the English newspaper press compiled by David Linton and Ray Boston (1987 and 1994). In the indexes to both, separate entries appear for 'Fleet Street (London thoroughfare)' and ' "Fleet Street" (as term referring to the London-based national press)'. The attempt to identify and separate the dual elements of the term inevitably becomes entangled in the imprecise usage of the works described. In his book on Fleet Street (1990), Ray Boston abandons the attempt and allows place and concept to blur within the text. Even so, the lists indicate that Fleet Street was taking on a variety of metaphorical attributes through the networks of print.

Through the output of journalists and ex-journalists it is possible to see the image of Fleet Street being overlaid by alternative forms. It becomes sequentially *The Highway of Letters* (1893), *The Street of Adventure* (1909), *The Pulse of the World* (1915) and *The Street of Ink* (1917). Reminiscences by journalists highlighted in their titles the jokey familiarity of a career constructed in and around the public spaces of the neighbourhood: *He Laughed in Fleet Street* (1937), *There's Fun in Fleet Street* (1938) or more rhetorically *Thirty Thousand and One Fleet Street Nights* (1937). Fleet Street had become a marker for a particular form of sub-literary activity with a real importance in the life of the nation. A sense of the combination of dignity and democratic striving that was projected through the writing of professional journalists is expressed in the tribute to Edgar Wallace erected in Ludgate Circus in 1934:

> He knew wealth and poverty yet had walked with kings and kept his bearing. Of his talents he gave lavishly to authorship – but to Fleet Street he gave his heart.

As the conjunction of place and process developed, 'Fleet Street' assumed the cast of a generalised institution with various benign characteristics and this representation overtook the physical reality of the traffic-clogged artery in central London. Its image, projected through the newspapers themselves, was reinforced through the durable stereotypes recycled in films, plays and novels identified under a variety of 'Fleet Street' titles. However, as Fleet Street (the place) developed a manic momentum as a production centre and as the product became increasingly market driven and populist the liberal underpinnning to 'Fleet Street' fell away. From the turn of the century the street itself was increasingly dominated by high-profile proprietors whose careers, gilded by the honours system, displayed some of the worst features of rampant capitalism. As their buildings marched across the area and their busts were attached to a variety of vacant walls, the cultural elite withdrew from their historical association with 'Fleet Street'.

This separation had a practical impact experienced within the principal bastions of the liberal elite, the library and university system. In these surroundings the concept of 'Fleet Street' developed a negative force. When in 1910 the British Museum moved its massive post-1800 collection of newspapers to the wastes of Colindale in north London, the decision represented more than a pragmatic response to lack of space. It contained in effect a judgement on the output of 'Fleet Street' as a subordinate and, in some respects, an undesirable element in the culture of print (Harris 1986: 54–9). This reaction, reflecting the downward mobility of the Fleet Street product, may also have played its part within the universities. Scholars located in the entrenched disciplines of literature and history, as well as in the subordinate but print-centred field of bibliography, consistently displayed an aloof disinterest in what was characterised as the ephemeral output of Fleet Street. No attempt was made to integrate the newspaper within the main lines of research and the development of the national newspaper industry slipped off the academic agenda. As the newspaper became, through the mechanisms of the mass market, an inescapable reality for the literate population, it was increasingly marginalised within the main structures of the elite culture.[19] It was left to journalists, mainly those liberated from the task itself, to represent some elements of the past and present of Fleet Street.

It was not until well into the second half of the twentieth century that the newspaper became a subject for some, initially isolated, research activity. Since the 1960s 'Fleet Street' has gradually been relocated on the academic map. This has partly resulted from a regrouping around alternative disciplines in which new lines of investigation are closely associated with serial print. In such areas as Cultural and Media Studies scholars have begun to apply some of the new technologies which, paradoxically, have dislocated Fleet Street itself.[20] The development of electronic access to data is part of the process by which 'Fleet Street' is being reunited to its past and as the research accumulates so it begins to impinge on those areas previously identified as newspaper-free zones.

The sudden upswing in the study of 'Fleet Street' has coincided with the final rupture of place and process. The introduction of electronic systems of information transfer finally tipped the balance in favour of relocation, as the print unions were overwhelmed by the brute force of international finance. What followed could be, and has been, described as the death of 'Fleet Street'. However, in most respects news of its death have been greatly exaggerated. In spite of the diaspora of titles and the disintegration of many of the networks which defined the working relationships of the street, the use of the term to describe the activity continues. 'Fleet Street' remains a collective expression for anyone engaged with the practice of journalism, a profession which forms part of an industry that requires and is receiving close investigation. The engagement of such centres of tertiary education as the City University (London) in developing links between the history and practice of journalism are, in the process, also deeply implicated in maintaining the survival of the idea of 'Fleet Street'.[21]

Meantime, the place itself remains in a state of intermediate suspension between the past and the future. The gothic structures of the newspaper business, many of them empty and decaying, are effective monuments to the manic self-publicists who built them. The chances of getting a drink in Fleet Street remain reasonably high, though the public spaces have taken on a melancholy air, and the prospect of being run over during a dash for the opposite pavement is still good. A few rather half-hearted bookshops are still located in the street and the legal profession has maintained its grip on the Temple Bar area. Only Reuters and the Press Association are engaged in a rearguard action, maintaining an uncertain link with the heyday of Fleet Street as a news centre. In some respects Fleet Street has reverted to what it was in the eighteenth century, an active, shabby, miscellaneous location in the centre of London, where the presence of the newspaper has passed like a shadow over the sun. Even so, the identification of place and process remains and in the unguessable future 'Fleet Street' will probably continue to carry its ghostly message as a term of art.

Notes

1   Under 'Fleet Street' Lillywhite (1963) listed forty-eight coffee houses. Some of the entries overlap as businesses change hands.

2   The original statement of ideas concerned with the construction and disintegration of a new public was formulated by Habermas (1989).

3   Samuel Johnson's recurrent interest in this form of publication began through his association with the *Gentleman's Magazine* and continued through his essay-papers, the *Rambler* and the *Idler*, as well as contributions to a variety of newspapers and periodicals.

4   Handbill, *At Mrs Salmon's Royal Wax-work in Fleet Street* . . . (n.d. [1770?]).

5   Handbill, *Just added to Rackstraw's anatomical exhibition* . . . (n.d. [1785?]).

6   This list of trades is compiled from items accessed through the *Eighteenth-Century Short-Title Catalogue*, CD-Rom. British Library.

7   For a full account of the location of members of the book trade around St. Paul's Cathedral see Blayney (1990).

8   Nicholas Bourne and Nathaniel Butter who were prime movers in the production of serial news between 1620 and 1640 ran shops in or immediately adjacent to the Royal Exchange.

9   David and Elizabeth Mallet had a long term interest in the serial publication of trials held at the Sessions House in the Old Bailey; see Harris (1982: 6–7).

10 For a discussion of the issues concerned with a polarisation within the London book trade see Harris (1989: 47–69).

11 For the introduction of gas to the area see reports in *The Times* (7 and 10 January 1815).

12 Some of the accidents were distinctly man made. See the report of racing omnibuses in *The Times* (1 February 1837).

13 The detail given in this section is drawn from reports of the arrest and prosecution of the arsonist, *The Times* (26 and 27 March 1866).

14 Temple Bar remains in a semi-ruined state in Theobalds Park in Hertfordshire. Plans to relocate it in the City seem to be dormant.

15 This excellent survey was published in association with an exhibition held at the Museum of London under the same title between February and May 1988.

16   This group activity was demonstrated in 1856 during the preliminary hearings of the case against William Palmer, the Rugely poisoner, when the journalists covering the case for the London papers dashed to and fro on the same trains.

17   This appears in an aggravated form in Herd 1952.

18   The shift towards a sense of generalised respectability can be identified in the comment made in the *Scots Observer* (12 March 1927): 'Shabbiness and flyblowness represent a Fleet Street tradition that has been broken.'

19   This is still a live issue. The question of how to locate the news serial in relation to the print culture generally takes on a special interest in relation to the projected and well funded 'History of the Book in Britain'. The long hiatus in research into the newspaper press from the seventeenth century makes it difficult for those entrenched in the established disciplines to acknowledge the crucial importance of the form of material.

20   I have in mind here the electronic means of accessing what has been a vast and unapproachable heap of material; not only machine-readable catalogues but scanners and indexing systems which will bring the newspaper, in its historical setting, much more clearly into view.

21   Some of the material included here was presented at a conference organised at the City University to consider changes in the newspaper business identified as 'Fleet Street'. The City has pioneered a range of courses at undergraduate and postgraduate level in which the history of the newspaper is an integral part.

References

Andrews, A. (1859) *The History of British Journalism* (2 vols), London: Richard Bentley.

Barson, S. and Saint, A. (1988) *A Farewell to Fleet Street*, London: Historic Buildings and Monuments Commission with Allison & Busby.

Blayney, P. (1990) *The Bookshops in Paul's Cross Churchyard*, London: Bibliographical Society, Occasional Paper 5.

Boston, R. (1990) *The Essential Fleet Street, Its History and Influence*, London: Blandford.

Fox-Bourne, H.R. (1887) *English Newspapers* (2 vols), London: Chatto & Windus.

Griffith, D. (ed.) (1992) *The Encyclopedia of the British Press*, London: Macmillan.

Habermas, J. (1989) *The Structural Transformation of the Public Sphere* (trans. Thomas Burger), Cambridge: Polity Press.

Harris, M. (1982) 'Trials and Criminal Biographies', in R. Myers and M. Harris (eds) *Sale and Distribution of Books from 1700*, Oxford: Oxford Polytechnic Press.

Harris, M. (1986) 'Collecting Newspapers: Developments at the British Museum during the Nineteenth Century', in R. Myers and M. Harris (eds) *Bibliophily*, Cambridge and Alexandria, VA: Chadwyck-Healey.

Harris, M. (1987) *London Newspapers in the Age of Walpole*, London and Toronto: Associated University Presses.

Harris, M. (1989) 'Paper Pirates: the Alternative Book Trade in Mid-18th Century London', in R. Myers and M. Harris (eds) *Fakes and Frauds: Varieties of Deception in Print & Manuscript*, Winchester and Detroit: St. Paul's Bibliographies/Omnigraphics.

Herd, H. (1952) *The March of Journalism: the Story of the British Press from 1622 to the Present Day*, London: Allen & Unwin.

Lewis, C. (1986) 'The Press Breaks Free', *Illustrated London News*, November.

Lillywhite, B. (1963) *London Coffee Houses*, London: Allen & Unwin.

Linton, D. (ed.) (1994) *Twentieth-Century Newspaper Press in Britain: an Annotated Bibliography*, London and New York: Macmillan.

Linton, D. and Boston, R. (eds) (1987) *The Newspaper Press in Britain: an Annotated Bibliography*, London and New York: Mansell.

Powell, K. (1987) 'Farewell to Fleet Street', *Daily Telegraph*, 7 August.

Rook, J. (1989) 'Farewell to Fleet Street', (souvenir front page) *Daily Express*, 17 November.

Smith, A. (1980) *Goodbye Gutenberg: the Newspaper Revolution of the 1980s*, New York: Oxford University Press.

Ward, N. (1924) *The London Spy* (ed. Ralph Straus), London: Casanova Society.

Wilson, C. (1985) *First with the News: The History of W.H. Smith, 1792–1972*, London: Jonathan Cape.

Chapter 26

Stuart Allan

NEWS AND THE PUBLIC SPHERE
Towards a history of objectivity and impartiality

The function of news is to signalize an event, the function of truth is to bring to light the hidden facts, to set them into relation with each other, and make a picture of reality on which men [*sic*] can act.

(Walter Lippmann, US journalist, 1922)

If once you let broadcasting into politics, you will never be able to keep politics out of broadcasting.

(Postmaster General, UK, November 1926)

The issue of whether or not journalists are capable of providing an 'objective' or 'impartial' account of the social world has long preoccupied many researchers interested in the operation of the news media in modern societies. The diverse voices participating in this debate have advanced their arguments from a variety of different epistemological positions, often seeking as they do to move beyond a consideration of the practical logistics of the reporting process in order to interrogate the ontological precepts informing journalistic configurations of what constitutes 'reality' in the first place. It is not my intention in this chapter to engage with this debate with an eye to rehearsing the main points of contention, nor to propose an alternative basis for a future elaboration of its trajectory. Rather, I will attempt to cast certain key aspects of this discussion in historical terms so as to offer a series of preliminary insights into how the codified rules of news factuality have changed since the seventeenth century. In so doing, it is my aim to contribute to the exploration of the implications that this might have for our current understanding of the democratic potential of a public sphere rapidly undergoing a process of re-definition by the news media of today.

This chapter will assume the following form. First, we will seek to elucidate the notion of the 'public sphere' as it has been developed in the historical writings of Jürgen Habermas. His account of the decisive rôle that the newspaper press played in helping to establish a discursive space for critical deliberations over public issues has proven to be highly influential within media and cultural studies, and in my view it has much to offer enquiries into the problematic at hand. Given that Habermas's account is largely an illustrative one, I shall endeavour to supplement it with additional sources, as well as with points of criticism, where appropriate.[1] In the second section, our attention will turn to the United States to examine the historical factors which gave rise to the practice of 'objective' newspaper reporting as a means to further new definitions of the public interest based on the democratisation of the public sphere. Beginning with the arrival of the 'penny dailies' during the 1830s, this assessment will proceed to consider the introduction of the electric telegraph in the 1840s (and with it the Associated Press wire service in 1848), the emergence of professionalism amongst journalists in the 1890s, and the explicit endorsement of the discursive norms and values of objectivity by journalists in the 1920s. The third section extends this discussion by investigating how these types of issues were dealt with in the early days of British broadcasting. The contested dynamics of 'impartiality' will be discerned in relation to both the British Broadcasting Corporation (BBC) and the Independent Television News (ITN) networks, paying particular attention to its invocation as a means to offset official fears about the dangers that broadcasting might pose *vis-à-vis* the articulation of popular opinion across the public sphere. Finally, the chapter will conclude with an evaluative appraisal of the continuing significance of the notions of 'objectivity' and 'impartiality' for journalism today.

The public sphere

'The usage of the words "public" and "public sphere" betrays a multiplicity of concurrent meanings.' So begins Jürgen Habermas's (1989) path-breaking study, *The Structural Transformation of the Public Sphere* (only recently translated from the 1962 publication, *Strukturwandel der Öffentlichkeit*). In the course of this enquiry into the establishment of the 'bourgeois public sphere' in the early modern period of European history, Habermas proceeds to outline the basis for a radical reconsideration of the factors informing the emergence of 'public opinion' as a social phenomenon.[2] Briefly, it is his contention that the initial appearance of a popular notion of 'public opinion' took place in Britain during the late-seventeenth century. The middle of that century had witnessed the partial displacement of terms such as 'world' or 'mankind' in popular discourse by talk of a 'public', followed by the arrival of the word 'publicity' which had been borrowed from the French *publicité* shortly thereafter

(Habermas 1989: 26). The features of this emerging lexicon were being swiftly re-drawn as the 'world of letters', that is, the literary field with its capacity for 'rational–critical debate' amongst private individuals, was being transformed in relation to the imperatives of the privatised domain of a market economy, on the one hand, and the directives of state-governed institutions, on the other.

More specifically, the usage of 'public opinion', a phrase to be differentiated at the time from 'general opinion', was contingent upon a new conception of a sphere of social life where citizens met to articulate criticisms of established authority. In Habermas's words:

> With the rise of a sphere of the social, over whose regulation public opinion battled with public power, the theme of the modern (in contrast to the ancient) public sphere shifted from the properly political tasks of a citizenry acting in common (i.e., administration of law as regards internal affairs and military survival as regards external affairs) to the more properly civic tasks of a society engaged in critical public debate (i.e., the protection of a commercial economy). The political task of the bourgeois public sphere was the regulation of civil society.
>
> (Habermas 1989: 52)

By the turn of the eighteenth century, then, a distinctive constellation of forces had arisen in Britain which led, in turn, to the advent of a public sphere of reasoned discourses circulating in the political realm independently of both the Crown and Parliament. The fledgling circumstances of this development, according to Habermas, may be linked to three key events which occurred between 1694 and 1695: the founding of the Bank of England by a group of London merchants, the inauguration of the first cabinet government, and, most importantly for our purposes here, the elimination of the institution of censorship 'which made the influx of rational–critical arguments into the press possible and allowed the latter to evolve into an instrument with whose aid political decisions could be brought before the new forum of the public' (Habermas 1989: 58).

Accordingly, in tracing the evolution of the conditions which would come to underpin the appearance of these 'unique liberties' enjoyed by the British press, Habermas focuses on the emergence of a new stage of capitalist development in the seventeenth century. Specifically, he contends that the enlarged spatialisation of early capitalist commercial relations necessitated the distribution of news in a far more public form than that which had been provided by the 'news letters' printed in political journals (this otherwise private correspondence offered current news about 'Imperial Diets, wars, harvests, taxes, transports of precious metals, and, of course, reports on foreign trade') since mid-century (Habermas 1989: 20). These journals, which were increasingly being established as commodities in their own right for the 'educated classes' (who also found news in broadsheets, learned periodicals, pamphlets, and so

forth), were also frequently used as devices in the service of public administration.[3] The steadily growing intertwinement of the interests of state
officials with those of the 'capitalists' (the merchants, bankers, entrepreneurs,
and manufacturers) was leading, in turn, to a shared recognition that social
stability could be enhanced through an appropriately informed citizenry. A
burgeoning traffic in printed materials, Habermas argues, thus developed
alongside that of other goods such that, by the end of the century, there was
a regular supply of news that was accessible to the general public.[4]

If the 'decisive mark' of this new domain of the public sphere was the
published word, as Habermas suggests, this is not to deny that at the outset
of the eighteenth century there remained in place a range of institutional
impediments to the realisation of 'press freedom'. This was despite an
improvement in the degree of press autonomy being permitted, following
the abolition in 1695 of the forms of censorship previously authorised by the
Licensing Act of 1662 (despite the pressures brought to bear on Parliament
to renew the Act by the monarchy). The law of personal libel, for example,
was a severe constraint on the reporting process, not least because of its
arbitrary re-definition in prosecutions for seditious libel.[5] Similarly, the
dictates of Crown and Parliament, often enforced on grounds of breach of
privilege, ensured that further legal restrictions could be imposed on a case
by case basis. The year 1712 saw the enactment of what were called 'the
taxes on knowledge', the most important being the stamp tax, which were
implemented not only to bolster revenues for the Crown but also to control
the right of publication. These measures had the desired effect of forcing the
more marginal – and often the more radical in political terms – titles out
of business (the stamp duty would be substantively reduced in the 1830s,
but would not be eliminated until 1855; here the selective use of subsidies
by the state was a further means to counter the radical press).

Nevertheless, over the course of the first half of the eighteenth century,
an extensive array of critical, if almost exclusively bourgeois, voices were
heard in the news journals. These voices were willing and able to take issue
with the Crown's conduct and Parliament's legislative performance. Habermas
argues that these commercially based journals were constitutive of a growing
'public spirit', one which was beginning to replace what had been until then
a 'party spirit'. If this challenging, often enraged temperament found its
expression in publications such as John Tutchin's *Observator* (1702), Daniel
Defoe's *The Review* (1704), and Jonathan Swift's *Examiner* (1710), for Habermas
(1989: 60) it is Nicholas Amhurst's *Craftsman* (1726), together with Edward
Cave's *Gentleman's Magazine* (1731), which signalled that 'the press was for
the first time established as a genuinely critical organ of a public engaged in
critical political debate: as the fourth estate'. Indeed, with the decline of the
clubs and the coffee houses, the latter being a principal forum for the circulation of news (their golden age being between 1680 and 1730),[6] the public was
now largely being 'held together' through an independent, market-based
newspaper press subject to 'professional criticism' (1989: 51).[7]

Similarly, Habermas singles out for attention the anonymously written letters attributed to 'Junius', published in the *Public Advertiser* from 21 November 1768 through to 12 May 1772, because in his view they should rightly be called 'pioneers of the modern press'. In these letters, he maintains, 'the King, the ministers, top military men, and jurists were publicly accused of political machinations, and secret connections of political significance were thereby uncovered in a manner that ever since has been exemplary of a critical press' (Habermas 1989: 61). This enhanced climate of criticism, being derivative of a wide range of different confrontations between an emboldened press and both the monarchy and government, was profoundly recasting the norms of the public sphere. Private citizens, encouraged to redefine themselves as part of a larger public force, became intent on regulating the conduct of state officials, as well as on contributing to the shaping of the direction of policy initiatives.

This transformation was made particularly visible with regard to what became a public controversy over the right to report on Parliamentary proceedings. The politicians, in seeking to preserve their general privilege of secrecy (the publication of the 'votes' had been authorised in 1681), would successfully resist efforts to formally overthrow the injunction against reporting until 1803.[8] In that year the Speaker made available a place in the gallery for journalists, but it would not be until after a new House of Parliament had been built after the fire of 1834 that stands would be erected for journalists. 'For a long time the target of critical comment by public opinion,' Habermas comments, Parliament was now being remade 'into the very organ of this opinion'. By fostering a critical engagement with the issues of the day, then, the press helped to underwrite a consensual (albeit informal) process of surveillance whereby the activities of the government could be made more responsive to the dictates of public opinion (Habermas 1989: 62).

From Habermas's vantage point, popular participation in the public sphere as a neutral space situated between the state and the market relations of the official economy was reaching its highest point at the dawn of the nineteenth century. As the arena where citizens could congregate in order to deliberate over public affairs amongst themselves, the public sphere constituted a discursive site embedded in a particular politics of representation. This site encompassed the conditions required for the formation of diverse opinions first to circulate and then, where necessary, to challenge through mediation the rationality of institutional decision making processes (the 'general interest' serving as the criterion by which this rationality was to be judged). In principle, access to the public sphere was open to each and every private individual willing to assent to the legitimacy of the 'rule of the best argument'. Journalism, as a result, was charged with the crucial rôle of ensuring that these individuals were able to draw upon a diverse spectrum of information sources to sustain their views, a responsibility which placed it at the centre of public life.

The maintenance of this critically reasoning public was therefore dependent upon a news media capable of lending expression to a richly pluralistic range of often sharply conflicting opinions.[9] This expression of views of a critical intent *vis-à-vis* established authority relations was similarly contingent, in principle, upon discursive relations free of any form of coercion associated with power and privilege. Not surprisingly, Habermas concedes that these conditions were not entirely fulfilled: formal rights should not be confused with actual, lived experiences of inequality. Even at the zenith of its inclusionary politic, participation was restricted to relative élites, namely the propertied and educated (and thus primarily white male) members of society.[10] Nevertheless, he argues, 'the liberal model sufficiently approximated reality so that the interest of the bourgeois class could be identified with the general interest . . . the public sphere as the organisational principle of the bourgeois constitutional state had credibility.' It is thus the public sphere, to the extent that it facilitates the formation of public opinion, which makes democratic control over governing relations possible.

In attempting to extend Habermas's conceptual approach to an investigation into news objectivity, then, what is evidently a rather blurred analytical distinction between the public sphere as a historical entity and as a normative ideal will require further clarification. Over the years, a number of commentators have been actively intervening in what is now an ongoing debate over how best to develop the more compelling insights generated by Habermas's study (see Calhoun 1995; Curran 1991, 1996; Dahlgren 1991, 1995; Fraser 1992; Garnham 1992; Meehan 1995; Thompson 1995; Verstraeten 1996). Five of the most pertinent lines of criticism for our purposes here may be briefly highlighted as follows.

First, the broad sweep of Habermas's mode of argument has been called into question. Some critics have insisted that his portrayal of the British press is idealistic, and that it lacks the degree of historical specificity we might ordinarily expect of such accounts. As we have seen, the scope of this enquiry encompasses a temporal period from the early 1600s through to the mid-1800s and, moreover, is spatially diffused across a range of different national contexts. Many of these commentators have proceeded to identify constitutive factors which have been glossed over, if not ignored altogether, in Habermas's treatment (hence my use of additional historical sources here). Still, should we place an emphasis on the public sphere as a normative ideal, then we might agree with Curran's (1996: 82) contention that it offers 'a powerful and arresting vision of the role of the media in a democratic society, and in this sense its historical status is irrelevant'.

A second line of criticism concerns the precise extent to which the public sphere, even in its classical (early nineteenth century) phase, was an autonomous arena for critical interactions over public affairs. Habermas does not appear to grant sufficient regard to the contested nature of this discursive space, that is, how the terrain of 'public opinion' is continually being crisscrossed with countervailing processes of transformation and incorporation.

His emphasis on how the 'neutrality' of this discursive space underpins the formation of popular consensus, defined in opposition to the interests of political and economic élites, obscures the extent to which these same élites are seeking, in turn, to extend their hegemony further by controlling access to the public sphere. That said, however, Habermas does provide a perceptive exposition of several productive mechanisms shaping this affirmation of the populace as a public, even if the attention given to communicative challenges to this consensus is inadequate. His account of the media's rôle in these conflicts is, at best, rather sketchy, but this approach does have the virtue, as Garnham (1992: 361) points out, of recognising that 'the institutions and processes of public communication are themselves a central and integral part of the political structure and process'. More to the point, in his view Habermas's approach centres 'the problem raised by all forms of mediated communication, namely, how are the material resources necessary for that communication made available, and to whom?'

To address a third and directly related limitation of Habermas's model, we need to step back to reconsider the presupposition that the public sphere is most advantageously theorised as a singular, totalised construction. That is to say, once attention turns to the possibility that there are in operation at any given moment a multiplicity of different, even competing public spheres, a series of tensions underlying Habermas's preferred (perhaps overly optimistic) formulations come to the fore. Specifically, if the limits of the public sphere are further qualified, a rich plurality of alternative discursive forums may then be identified, such as those represented by social movements, trade unions, and single-issue campaigns. By introducing this question for historical evaluation, we would be better placed to identify the means by which the socially situated logics of these alternative forums reaffirm, as well as contradict, one another over time. It is this dynamic process of mediation which, in my opinion, needs to be further accentuated in relation to the criteria by which definitions of 'the public' are being hierarchically projected by the news media, amongst other institutions.

A fourth area of concern is the distinction Habermas draws between the public and the 'private' spheres: specifically, the danger that such a dichotomy risks reifying these spheres as separate, as opposed to mutually determining, entities. Feminist researchers, in particular, have examined a number of the ways in which this separation can naturalise the displacement of a range of gender, sexual and ethnic inequalities as being exclusively matters of 'personal', 'familial' or 'domestic' concern. Consequently, as Fraser (1992: 137) argues, 'a tenable conception of the public sphere must countenance not the exclusion, but the inclusion, of interests and issues that bourgeois, masculinist ideology labels "private" and treats as inadmissible.' In a recent essay, Habermas (1992: 427–8) has acknowledged the value of this line of critique, observing that 'the growing feminist literature has sensitised our awareness to the patriarchal character of the public sphere itself [because] the exclusion of women had structuring significance.'

Finally, the fifth line of criticism directly centres the problem of news objectivity by seeking to render problematic the reliance of Habermas's model of the public sphere on a conception of normatively grounded communication. To contend that discourses of public opinion have the capacity to forge a rational–critical consensus is to assume, at the same time, that discourses circulate outside of cultural rules or conventions, that reality can be equated with objective facts. This when precisely what counts as 'rational' or 'reasoned', or even 'critical' for that matter, is always a question of definitional power: whose discourse, we need to ask, is so defined and why? Once we recognise the extent to which Habermas's model prefigures an idealised approach to discursive interaction, we may then be better able to appreciate how it needs to be recast in order to better inform our mode of enquiry. In normative terms, as Golding and Murdock (1996: 18) suggest, this 'general ideal of a communications system as a public cultural space that is open, diverse, and accessible' provides a 'basic yardstick' against which we may, in turn, measure 'the performance of existing systems and formulate alternatives'.

It is with an awareness of the heuristic value of Habermas's elucidation of the idea of a public sphere, as well as its associated difficulties, that we now turn to investigate the ascension of a US daily press committed to advancing 'the public interest' by reporting the reality of the social world in an 'objective' manner.

Factors leading to the rise of objectivity in US newspapers

Objectivity, according to a liberal mythology of the newspaper press, is a mode of interpreting evidence to meet the obligations of 'the people', that is, the needs of an informed citizenry alert to the necessity of keeping up with public affairs. In light of our discussion of Habermas's writings, it is apparent that the journalist's relationship to 'the market-place of ideas' is actively mediated through a complex array of institutional dynamics which are constantly changing over time. The question of what counts as 'rational' public dialogue at different historical conjunctures will be contingent, in part, upon the news media's dispersal of various contending definitions of the common good. News is a form of social knowledge, the evolving limits of which are shaped by normative assumptions about what the citizenry is likely to consider to be 'popular opinion', that is, the populace's image of itself as a public. Once it is recognised that news accounts are organised in accordance with certain rules or conventions which reaffirm a preferred projection of the public sphere, we may then begin to explore the conditions which have led to the authorisation of that projection in the name of 'objectivity'.

In shifting our focus from Habermas's consideration of the newspaper press in early nineteenth century Britain to that of the same period in the United States, it quickly becomes evident that the issue of objectivity possessed a much higher degree of public salience in the latter country.[11]

Most historical accounts of the rise of objectivity point to the emergence of the 'penny press' in the 1830s as the most significantly formative development in its initial phase. Briefly, it was during this decade that the dominance of the established newspaper presses, particularly the partisan titles with their highly politcised news and editorial content, came directly under threat by a press much more closely aligned with commercial imperatives. The *New York Sun*, which appeared on 3 September 1833, is generally regarded as the first of the penny papers, and it was almost immediately followed by the *Evening Transcript* and the *New York Herald* (and later by the *New York Tribune* in 1841, and the *New York Times* in 1851). From the city of New York, the penny press quickly spread to the other urban centres, beginning with Boston, Philadelphia and Baltimore. By the end of the Jacksonian era, the penny press would succeed in displacing the commercial or mercantile press, as well as the explicitly sectarian press, from the positions of prominence which they had previously enjoyed.[12]

The contours of the public sphere were being redrawn by this new type of newspaper which sought to claim for itself the status of being the people's voice in a society undergoing democratisation. Due its reliance on market-based income, namely sales and advertisements increasingly directed at consumer items, the penny press provided its customers with a much less expensive product (about five cents cheaper on average; payment was made to 'newsboys', not via annual subscription).[13] As a result, these newspapers offered a different type of access to the public sphere, since they were able to declare a greater degree of political independence from government and party. Indeed, not only did some of these newspapers define themselves as 'neutral in politics', many tended to be indifferent to elite political events. According to Schudson (1978: 21), a lead in the 9 December 1833 edition of the *New York Sun* about a 'short item of congressional news' was typical: 'The proceedings of Congress thus far, would not interest our readers.' This when the first issue of the same newspaper had proclaimed that its aim was 'to lay before the public, at a price within the means of everyone, all the news of the day.'[14]

For most of the penny newspapers, then, reporting 'the news of the day' entailed a commitment to a new, distinctive range of news values. In particular, the local 'human interest story' was to be prized above all others because it best represented the conditions of contemporary life as they touched the experiences of 'the masses'. These newspapers thus tended to restrict their coverage of party politics or issues of trade and commerce to matters of popular interest, electing instead to fill their pages primarily with news about the police, the courts, small businesses, religious institutions, and 'high society'. News from the streets and private households, especially suicides, fires and burglaries, had mass-appeal (in this way the line between 'public' and 'private' life was effectively blurred; Schiller 1981, Schudson 1978; Smith 1979). As James Gordon Bennett, founder of the *New York Herald*, declared in the 11 May 1835 edition of that penny newspaper: 'We shall give a correct picture of the world – in Wall Street – in the Exchange – in the Police Office – in the Opera – in short, wherever human nature or real life best displays its freaks and vagaries' (cited in Roshco 1975: 32). Thus in presenting to their readers a 'gastronomy of the eye' largely made up of 'the odd, the exotic and the trivial', to use Carey's (1986: 163) terms, these newspapers were expeditiously redefining what could and should qualify as news for 'ordinary people' in the context of their daily lives.

This radical re-mapping of the public sphere fundamentally transformed not only popular conceptions of what should constitute a news event, but also how that news should be communicated. In seeking to satisfy the needs of a general readership far more encompassing in class terms than that of their more established rivals, the penny newspapers utilised a language of reporting which emphasised the significance of everyday life in a 'realistic' manner. The *New York Herald*, for example, had been launched in 1835 with a pledge 'to record facts, on every public and proper subject, stripped of verbiage and coloring' (cited in Shi 1995: 95). Despite the ongoing criticisms of 'sensationalism' being levelled at the penny press by the six-penny newspapers (especially with regard to crime and scandal, the coverage of which was deemed to be 'morally dubious'), there was a conviction amongst the editors and journalists of the new titles that there was a growing 'public demand for facts'.[15] This perception that the appeal of 'facts' was intensifying for their readers encouraged them to strive harder to present the information on their pages in the most literal way possible. The penny press thus began to reflect a marked preference for factual news coverage (at its most literal this would simply consist of verbatim transcripts of official statements) over ('subjective') editorial explanation. Ironically, then, as an élite press previously preoccupied with partisan interests gave way to a popular one which sought to prioritise a public interest, the goals of explanation and critique were increasingly being played down in favour of a panorama of facts ostensibly devoid of evaluative comment.

The introduction of the electric telegraph in the 1840s has similarly been cited by press historians as a crucial contributory factor linked to the emergence of news objectivity as a professional ideal based on the presentation of facts. In 1844, an experimental telegraphic line between Washington and Baltimore was used to transmit the first 'wire' story, which was then published in the *Baltimore Patriot*. Four years later, six New York newspapers organised themselves into a monopolistic co-operative to launch the Associated Press (AP), a wire service devoted to providing equal access for its members to news from one another and, more importantly, from sources in distant sites (the Mexican War and later the American Civil War being prime examples). News reports, which had previously travelled by horse and boat (carrier pigeons were used only infrequently), took on an enhanced degree of timeliness which had significant implications for the re-definition of a public sphere. This point was underscored by Bennett of the *New York Herald* when he commented on the significance of the telegraph for the political public sphere:

This means of communication will have a prodigious, cohesive, and conservative influence on the republic. No better bond of union for a great confederacy of states could have been devised . . . The whole nation is impressed with the same idea at the same moment. One feeling and one impulse are thus created and maintained from the centre of the land to its uttermost extremities.[16]

Debates regarding the strictures of non-partisan, factual reporting took on a new resonance as AP began to train its own journalists to adopt different norms of reporting. This included the 'inverted pyramid' structure of news accounts, as unreliable telegraph lines made it necessary to compress the most significant facts into the summary 'lead' paragraph. Moreover, because newspapers of very different political orientations were subscribing to its service, the 'impartiality' of AP's 'real time' news accounts became a further selling feature. 'Opinions' were left for the client newspaper to assert as was appropriate for their 'political stripe'. In the words of the head of the AP Washington bureau, an individual who had worked for the service since its inception:

My business is to communicate facts; my instructions do not allow me to make any comment upon the facts which I communicate. My dispatches are sent to papers of all manner of politics, and the editors say they are able to make their own comments upon the facts which are sent them. I therefore confine myself to what I consider legitimate news. I do not act as a politician belonging to any school, but try to be truthful and impartial. My dispatches are merely dry matters of fact and detail. Some special correspondents may write to suit the temper of their organs. Although I try to write without regard to men or politics, I do not always escape censure.[17]

These emergent conventions of wire service reporting, apparent as they were not only in a 'dry' language of facts but also in the routinisation of news-work practices, were clearly helping to secure the codification of objectivity as a normative standard.

If it is difficult to determine precisely when 'objective' journalism was formally recognised as a professional ideal, there seems little doubt that it was the penny press in the 1830s which firmly established the institution of paid reporters (it would still take several more decades for salaried positions to become the norm, and unionisation did not begin until the 1890s). By mid-century, various social clubs and press societies were being created as informal, shared spaces for journalists to meet to discuss their concerns about what was rapidly becoming a 'profession'. These spaces were formally inaugurated after the Civil War with the opening of the New York Press Club in 1873. It was in this period, just as the newspaper was being redefined as a big business requiring financial investment on a large scale, that journalists were formally claiming for themselves a professional status deserving of public esteem. As Schudson (1978: 69) points out, this status was contingent upon the public's recognising certain differences between the so-called 'old-time reporter' and the 'new reporter':

> The 'old reporter', according to the standard mythology, was a hack who wrote for his [*sic*] paycheck and no more. He was uneducated and proud of his ignorance; he was regularly drunk and proud of his alcoholism. Journalism, to him, was just a job. The 'new reporter' was younger, more naïve, more energetic and ambitious, college-educated, and usually sober. He was passionately attached to his job.

Concomitant with this shift from reporting as a provisional occupation like any other to a 'respectable, professional career' was a growing perception amongst journalists themselves that they were assuming, at the same time, a responsibility to contribute to the general welfare of an increasingly democratic society (see also Hardt and Brennen 1995).

By the 1890s, these and related developments were being linked to the emergence of newspaper titles determined to adopt a progressive crusading rôle on behalf of the public interest. Specifically, Schudson (1978: 89) contends that the 1890s saw the emergence of two distinctive models of journalism. The first one revolved around the ideal of the 'story', with an emphasis being placed on maintaining a strong advocacy stance with regard to the public's right to know the truth (titles included Joseph Pulitzer's *New York World* and William Randolph Hearst's *New York Journal*, both exemplars of 'yellow journalism'; see also Stephens 1988; Willis 1991). The second model was based on the ideal of 'information' with an emphasis on factuality (many of which were old penny press titles, including the *New York Times*). Both of these respective models prefigured a different commercial logic of commodity production, one which was tied to the socio-economic position of a given title's 'targeted' reader. The audience for the 'story-telling' ideal was predominantly working class, whilst much of the middle class had by that time come to favour the detached 'neutrality' of the 'information' ideal (this distinction was exploited, in turn, by advertisers who welcomed the attendant standardisation of formats). The profit motive in conjunction with market forces, championed by some as the best guarantor of press freedom, were thus simultaneously engendering the decline of an advocacy or human interest journalism committed to encouraging active participation in public life.

Leading the way in 'information' journalism was the *New York Times*, a daily generally held by 'opinion leaders' to be the embodiment of reasoned, factual news coverage. Illustrative of this endorsement of 'straight' reporting is a statement made by the publisher Adolph Ochs, who purchased the title in August 1896. In the course of outlining the newspaper policies for his recent acquisition, Ochs declared:

It will be my earnest aim that *The New York Times* give the news, all the news, in concise and attractive form, in language that is parliamentary in good society, and give it as early, if not earlier, than it can be learned through any other reliable medium; to give the news impartially, without fear or favor, regardless of any party, sect or interest involved; to make the columns of *The New York Times* a forum for the consideration of all questions of public importance, and to that end to invite intelligent discussion from all shades of opinion.[18]

This quotation neatly pinpoints a convergence of the discourses of information journalism with those of professional responsibility *vis-à-vis* the public sphere, in general, and the interests of its affluent readers, in particular. With its new motto of 'All the news that's fit to Print', the *New York Times* sought to claim for itself the status of an open forum for debating public affairs.[19] This when the boundaries of its definition of 'serving the public' were recurrently projected in a way which reaffirmed existing relations of power and privilege, namely those of wealthy white males, as being consistent with American democracy.

In the years immediately following the close of the 'Great War' in Europe, the conditions were in place for the emergence of explicit appeals to 'objectivity' amongst journalists and their critics. Popular disillusionment not only with state propaganda campaigns, but also with the recent advent of press agents and 'publicity experts', had helped to create a general wariness of 'official' channels of information. For journalists, if facts could not be trusted in and by themselves as being neutral properties of the social world awaiting discovery, professionally validated rules and procedures would be required to discern how that social world was being represented from an interested or 'biased' viewpoint. In other words, objectivity demanded of journalists that they distinguish facts from values if their respective newspaper were to be recognised as a free arbiter of truth.[20] In April 1923, the American Society of Newspaper Editors announced their 'canons' of journalism, the fifth one of which reads, in its entirety, as follows:

Impartiality – Sound practice makes clear distinction between news reports and expressions of opinion. News reports should be free from opinion or bias of any kind.

1. This rule does not apply to so-called special articles unmistakably devoted to advocacy or characterised by a signature authorizing the writer's own conclusions and interpretations.[21]

Whilst the word 'objectivity' did not appear in these canons, it was becoming synonymous with this notion of 'sound practice' and was increasingly being adhered to as a guiding principle of newswork.

Over the course of the 1920s, this appeal to objective, non-'biased' reporting was gradually institutionalised throughout the growing professional culture of journalists in a variety of different ways. For example, amongst other factors, more reporters began to specialise in relation to distinct news topics (labour, science, agriculture, and so forth) using 'impersonal', fact-centred techniques of observation; there was further refinement in news interview conventions, leading to more aggressive questions being asked of public figures (the interview itself being a relatively recent invention); more prominence was given to the by-lined news account; greater emphasis was placed on new genres of 'investigative' and 'interpretive' reporting, the latter being displaced from 'hard news' into political columns; there was a more pronounced reliance on quotation marks for source attribution; and, finally, improvements in the degree of autonomy from the day to day control of both proprietors and editors were being secured by journalists. If declarations of objectivity had begun in earnest during the 1850s, it was this decade which saw a 'public service ideal', namely 'the people's right to know', enshrined as a professional ethic. This new scepticism toward the ideal of absolute truth underscored the apparent necessity of designing rules to process facts so as to minimise, if not eliminate altogether, the influence of values. In other words, the changing conventions of objectivity did not directly call into question the possibility of reasoned, rational popular debate so effectively highlighted in Habermas's account; rather, they ostensibly offered new 'scientific methods' (Lippmann 1922) for its realisation in the spirit of the public's right of access to facts.

Impartiality in the early days of British broadcasting

For broadcast journalists, the concept of 'impartiality' tends to be used in place of that of 'objectivity', although the two are virtually synonymous with respect to their application *vis-à-vis* the changing circumstances of news production.[22] The thorny question of whether or not radio or televisual news can be impartial, and if so how this impartiality is to be achieved in practical terms, has been the subject of considerable dispute in Britain from the earliest days of broadcasting. It is my aim in this section to provide an overview of a range of significant factors informing the professional invocation of impartiality in broadcast news discourse. Accordingly, our attention first turns to the emergence of impartiality as a guiding journalistic principle for BBC wireless news bulletins in the 1920s and 1930s. This investigation is then followed by a consideration of how discourses of impartiality shaped the development of televisual newscasts after the Second World War. Here it is the encodification of impartiality as a requirement enforced by Parliament, informally in the case of the BBC Charter and formally with respect to the 1954 Television Act and the creation of ITN, which is of particular interest in light of our earlier discussion of the public sphere.

When the British Broadcasting Company began its General News bulletins from London on 23 December 1922, it did not have in its employ a single journalist engaged in reporting the day's news. The cries of alarm expressed by newspaper proprietors about unfair competition from the wireless had been taken so seriously that a prescriptive injunction was inserted in the Company's licence. Specifically, BBC news reports were to be strictly limited to summaries prepared by a consortium of news agencies (Reuters, the Press Association, Exchange Telegraph and Central News), and then only broadcast after seven o'clock in the evening, so as to minimise any potential harm to the sales figures of the daily press. Improvements in this situation were only gradually achieved, even though John Reith, the Managing Director General of the BBC (he would later be the first Director General of the Corporation from 1927 to 1938), consistently petitioned the Postmaster General to reduce the restrictions on news coverage. In 1924, for example, he wrote a letter requesting 'permission to handle controversial subjects, providing we can guarantee absolute impartiality in the act' (cited in Scannell and Cardiff 1991: 27). His request was flatly denied; 'controversial' matters would continue to be prohibited for fear of their potentially dangerous influence on public opinion.

About two years later, during the General Strike of May 1926, the BBC was provided with a remarkable opportunity to proclaim its independence while, at the same time, demonstrating its willingness to obey government instructions behind the scenes. The strike having temporarily closed almost all of the newspapers, the public turned to the wireless for reports on the crisis; the BBC responded with up to five bulletins a day, most of which included at least some material it had gathered itself. At stake was the BBC's political loyalty, an issue which was framed in terms of its capacity to uphold the tenets of 'responsible' (that is, non-controversial) reporting in the name of 'impartiality'. As Reith wrote in a memorandum to Stanley Baldwin, the Prime Minister, the BBC could be trusted to endorse the Government's position against that of the trade-union movement.[23] In his words: 'Assuming the BBC is for the people and that the Government is for the people, it follows that the BBC must be for the Government in this crisis too' (cited in Burns 1977: 16–17). Government ministers were thus given direct access to BBC microphones in order to advance their definitions of the crisis, whilst voices from the opposition parties and the trade unions were virtually silenced. This 'baptism of fire' for the BBC, as it was later characterised by some newspaper commentators, underlined how the direct line of control held by the state over the Company under the legal authority of the Wireless Broadcasting Licence was being translated into self-censorship. At the same time, however, the strike proved that a national audience could be created for broadcasting. In the words of Hilda Matheson, the first head of the Talks Department, writing in 1926: 'The public and wireless listeners are now nearly synonymous terms' (cited in Curran and Seaton 1991: 141).

In the years immediately following the General Strike, Reith sought to enhance even further public trust in the BBC's 'authentic impartial news'. He recognised that a greater degree of independence would have to be established for the Company from direct government surveillance, even if the use of such pressure was the exception rather than the rule. His efforts were largely in vain, although he did achieve some success in advancing a re-visioning of the BBC, in institutional terms, as a national service in the public interest which was deserving of a more prominent reportorial rôle. By January 1927, when the BBC had achieved Corporation status by Royal Charter, an earlier time-slot of 6.30 p.m. had been secured for the news bulletins, together with further concessions regarding the use of live 'eye-witness accounts' (especially with respect to sporting contests and public events, such as the Coronation of 1937). Still forced under its licence conditions to avoid any type of programming which could be regarded as controversial, which was also taken to apply to the proceedings of Parliament, the Corporation nevertheless began to grant itself more latitude in the imposition of self-censorship despite the Postmaster General's veto power. The government's confidence in the BBC's willingness to be respectful of the limits of its 'independence' was slowly being reinforced, and the ban on controversial broadcasts was lifted in 1928 (if only experimentally at first). There was also at this time a growing sense that the mutual interests of the Post Office, the newspaper proprietors and the press agencies were inhibiting the introduction of the more interesting and informative news formats being offered by broadcasting systems in other countries. By way of an example, the BBC's extremely narrow definition of what were appropriate 'news values' meant that on Good Friday 1930 its news editors declared that in their view 'there was no news of the normal type or standard for broad-casting, and as a result no news bulletin was given.'[24] Whilst this 'no news' news bulletin cannot be regarded as typical, it does provide a telling illustration of the relative rigidity of the topical parameters within which the Corporation was attempting to operate in order to placate its administrators.

By the end of 1934, changes were underway to turn BBC News into an independent Department, a move designed, in part, to encourage further public confidence in its Corporate ethic of neutrality. The separation of News from the Talks Department was linked, in part, to charges of 'bias' being made against the latter department. If newspaper commentators framed the new division as the BBC's 'Answer to Tory Suspicions of Radicalism', within the Corporation 'it was seen as a result of a sustained campaign by the right-wing press against alleged BBC "redness"' (Scannell and Cardiff 1991: 118). Also underway at this time was a gradual shift to embrace more accessible, if not popularised, norms of reporting, particularly with respect to questions of style, tone and format. In 1936, the journalist Richard Dimbleby, who would later be recognised as perhaps the most influential radio reporter ever to work for the BBC, proposed a radical re-definition of what should constitute radio news:

> It is my impression, and I find it shared by many others, that it would
> be possible to enliven the News to some extent without spoiling the
> authoritative tone for which it is famed. As a journalist, I think I know

something of the demand which the public makes for a 'News angle', and how it can be provided. I suggest that a member or members of your staff – they could be called 'BBC reporters or BBC correspondents' – should be held in readiness, just as are the evening paper men [*sic*], to cover unexpected News for that day. In the event of a big fire, strike, civil commotion, railway accidents, pit accidents, or any other major catastrophes in which the public, I fear, is deeply interested, a reporter could be sent from Broadcasting House to cover the event for the bulletin.[25]

This configuration of a public audience for the bulletins which is demanding a 'news angle', and one which is 'deeply interested' in catastrophes (perhaps regrettably so in Dimbleby's eyes), cut against the grain of previous conceptions of the BBC's audience, in general, and the type of newscast with which it should be presented, in particular. The Corporation's self-declared responsibilities *vis-à-vis* the listening public were posited within the dictates of government influence, notwithstanding its occasional assertion to the contrary. For this and related reasons, it would be years before Dimbleby's vision was realised. In the meantime, the news bulletin's authoritative claim to impartiality relied almost exclusively on material acquired via the news agencies, even in those instances where the newer forms of technology made 'on the spot' reports possible. Deviations from this general pattern would occur only rarely until the outbreak of war, clearly the most important of which was the live broadcast (on both radio and television) of Prime Minister Neville Chamberlain's return to London from his meeting with Adolph Hitler in Munich. Still, when Britain declared war against Germany in September 1939, the BBC possessed only a tiny staff of reporters, of whom one was Dimbleby, to call into action.

Although Britain's first experimental televisual programme had been transmitted from Broadcasting House on 22 August 1932, and news had made its appearance on 21 March 1938 (a recording of radio news presented without pictures), newscasts would not be a daily feature on television until 1954. The Television Service had returned on 7 June 1946, having been closed down during the war years, in part because of fears that enemy bombers would home in on the transmitters. The radio news division prepared a nightly summary of the news to be read on television by an unseen announcer, while a clock-face appeared as the visual component. Newsreels were now manufactured in-house, due to the refusal of the cinema newsreel companies to supply them, and outside broadcasts were also regularly featured.[26] The Corporation, always fearful of the charge that its views were being broadcast in its newscasts, took elaborate care to ensure that it observed a commitment to impartiality as a professional and public duty. Given its responsibilities as a trustee in the national interest, the Corporation could not be seen to be expressing a partisan position, especially in matters of public policy. Indeed, anxieties expressed by members of the main political parties that the BBC could ultimately appropriate for itself the status of a forum for national debate to match that of Parliament led, in turn, to the implementation of the 'fourteen-day rule' beginning on 10 February, 1944 (it would stay in place until 1957). By agreeing (at first informally) not to extend its coverage to issues relevant to either the House of Commons or the House of Lords for fourteen days before they were to be debated, the BBC succumbed to pressures which severely compromised its editorial independence. No such restrictions were requested *vis-à-vis* the newspaper press, nor would their imposition have been likely to have proven to be successful.

By the early 1950s, with Britain engaged in the war in Korea (filmed coverage of which sparked public interest in the televisual reports), the arrival of competition from the commercial sector in the form of the Independent Television (ITV) network was imminent. BBC officials scrambled to get a daily newscast on the air prior to the launch of the new, commercial rival. Two weeks before the Television Act received the Royal assent, the first edition of the BBC's *News and Newsreel* was broadcast on 5 July 1954. Whilst the 7.30 p.m. programme had been heralded as 'a service of the greatest significance in the progress of television in the UK', Margaret Lane, a critic in the Corporation's own journal, the *Listener*, was not convinced:

> I suppose the keenest disappointment of the week has been the news service, to which most of us had looked forward, and for which nobody I encountered had a good word. The most it can do in its present stage is to improve our geography, since it does at least offer, in magic lantern style a series of little maps, a pointer and a voice . . . The more I see of television news in fact the more I like my newspaper.[27]

The ten minutes of news was read by an off-screen voice in an 'impersonal, sober and quiet manner', the identity of the newsreader being kept secret to preserve the institutional authority of the BBC, to the accompaniment of still pictures (as the title suggests, the news was then followed by a newsreel). Only in the final days leading up to the launch of its 'American-style' rival on the new commercial network did this practice change, and then only partially. In the first week of September 1955, the BBC introduced the faces of its newsreaders to the camera, but not their names. The danger of 'personalising' the news as the voice of an individual, as opposed to that of the Corporation, was considered to be serious enough to warrant the preservation of anonymity. This strategy, which had its origins in radio, arguably communicated an enhanced sense of detached impartiality for the newscast, and would last for another eighteen months.

The Television Act of 1954, introduced by Winston Churchill's Conservative Party government after two and a half years of often acrimonious debate, had set up the Independent Television Authority which, in turn, established Independent Television News (ITN) as a specialist subsidiary company in February 1955.[28] Contained in Clause 3 of the Act were the following instructions:

3(I) It shall be the duty of the Authority to satisfy themselves that, so far as possible, the programmes broadcast by the Authority comply with the following requirements, that is to say:

(a) that nothing is included in the programmes which offends against good taste or decency or is likely to encourage or incite to crime or to lead to disorder or to be offensive to public feeling or which contains any offensive representation of or reference to a living person;

(b) that the programmes maintain a proper balance in their subject-matter and a high general standard of quality;

(c) that any news given in the programmes (in whatever form) is presented with due accuracy and impartiality . . .

(f) that due impartiality is preserved on the part of the persons providing the programmes as respects matters of political or industrial controversy or relating to current public policy; and

(g) subject as hereinafter provided in this subsection, that no matter designed to serve the interests of any political party is included in the programmes.[29]

The imposition of these prohibitions on to the independent programme companies, especially with respect to the formal obligation to observe 'due accuracy and impartiality', was broadly consistent with the general editorial policy of the BBC. Still, an important difference with respect to how impartiality was to be achieved had been signalled, if not clearly spelt out. Where the BBC generally sought to reaffirm its impartiality over a period of time, ITN would have to demonstrate a 'proper balance' of views within each individual programme.

At 10 p.m. on 22 September 1955, ITN made its debut on the ITV network. The 'newscaster' for that evening, as they were to be called, was Christopher Chataway, a former Olympic runner who had been working as a transport officer for a brewery. The other 'personalities' hired by the network included the first female newscaster on British television, Barbara Mandell, who presented the midday bulletin, and Robin Day, then an unknown barrister with little journalistic experience. For Geoffrey Cox, who had been appointed editor just months after the launch, 'the power of personality' in presenting the news was a crucial dimension of the effort to attract public attention away from the BBC and on to ITN as a distinctive news source.[30] In contrast with the BBC's anonymous newsreaders, ITN's newscasters were given the freedom to re-write the news in accordance with their own stylistic preferences as journalists, even to the extent of ending the newscast with a 'lighter' item to raise a smile for the viewer. Cox was well aware, though, that the advantages to be gained by having newscasters who were 'men and women of strong personality' (who also tended to be 'people of strong opinions') had to be qualified in relation to the dictates of the Television Act concerning 'due accuracy and impartiality'. Given that ITN was a subsidiary company of the four principal networking companies, lines of administrative authority were much more diffuse than was the case in the BBC or, for that matter, in the newspaper press. Still, pressure from the networking companies to increase the entertainment value of the newscasts was considerable.

Consequently, Cox (1995: 75) saw in the Act's requirements the means to negotiate an even greater degree of day-to-day autonomy from institutional constraints:

> Impartiality, if it was interpreted actively, and not passively, could be a means both of protecting our independence and of strengthening our power to gather and interpret news, to arrive at the truth. It was a safeguard against pressures not only from the Government or other people of power, but also against the views and whims of the programme companies who owned us . . . These few words [Clause 3] could free a television news editor from the proprietorial pressures which were then widespread in Fleet Street – much wider than is the case today. They could give him [sic] the freedom to create something new in popular journalism.

Robin Day, who through ITN would become one of Britain's most well-known journalists, has credited Cox's editorial standards at the time for securing 'vigorous, thrusting news coverage, responsibly and impartially presented in popular style'. The question of how best to ensure that the newscast conveyed a commitment to impartiality for its audience was a serious challenge, as Day has since recalled:

> In the early formative days, he [Cox] had to inculcate a belief in impartiality into the mixed group who came together in 1955 to form the first television journalists of ITN. There was a small core of newsmen, mostly ex-BBC, headed by Arthur Clifford, the brilliant News Editor, who were trained in the discipline of impartiality. Others had no such background. There were cameramen and film editors from the cinema newsreels, where coverage had often been blatantly propagandist. There were journalists from Fleet Street, where proprietors expected their views to shape the contents as well as the policies of their newspapers. There were writers who believed that news should be seasoned by opinion.
>
> (Day 1995: viii)

In Day's view, Cox possessed a 'profound belief' in the principles of 'truth and fairness', qualities which meant that under his editorship 'ITN succeeded in combining the challenge and sparkle of Fleet Street with the accuracy and impartiality required by the Television Act' (Day 1995: ix). If this assertion is a somewhat boastful one, it nevertheless reaffirms how, from a journalistic point of view, the tenets of impartiality tend to be rendered as being consistent with professionalism.

This 'discipline of impartiality', with its appeal to the separation of news and opinion, also had implications for ITN's configuration of 'the public' for its newscasts. In its first year, ITN dramatically redefined the extent to which so-called 'ordinary' people could be presented in a televisual news account. Street-corner interviews, or 'vox pops' as they were often called by the newscasters, began to appear on a regular basis. Moreover, at a time when 'class barriers were more marked', Cox recalls that ITN sought to portray the news in 'human terms' through reports which:

> brought onto the screen people whose day to day lives had not often in the past been thought worth reflecting on the air. It gave a new meaning to the journalistic concept of the human interest story. In Fleet Street the term meant stories which were interesting because they were of the unusual, the abnormal, the exceptional. But here the cameras were making fascinating viewing out of ordinary everyday life, bestriding the gap between the classes – and making compulsive television out of it. Whether the story was hard news or not did not seem to matter. It was life, conveyed by the camera with honesty and without condescension, adding interest and humanity to the bulletins in a way unique to this new journalistic medium.
>
> (Cox 1995: 57)

Cox maintains that his sense of ITN's audience at the time was that it was 'largely working class', yet this assumption could not be allowed to 'bias' the network's news agenda. ITN's preferred definitions of 'news values', if not quite as restrictive as those of the BBC, still ensured that a potential news source's 'credibility' or 'authoritativeness' would be hierarchically determined in relation to class (as well as with regard to gender and race). The news agenda was similarly shaped by a principle of impartiality which dictated that analysis and interpretation were to be scrupulously avoided in both the spoken news and film report segments of the newscast. However, expressions of opinion could be included in the newscast through studio interviews. These 'live' segments facilitated a stronger sense of immediacy, since spontaneous or 'off the cuff' remarks added a degree of excitement that might have otherwise been denied in the name of editorial fairness or balance. Perhaps more to the point, though, they were also more 'cost-efficient' than film reports.

By 1956, the BBC had elected to follow ITN's lead. In seeking to refashion its televisual newscasts to meet the new 'personalised' standards of presentation that audiences were coming to expect, the Corporation not only began to identify its newsreaders by name but also emulated ITN in allowing them to use teleprompters in order to overcome their reliance on written scripts.[31] Further technological improvements, most notably in the quality of film processing, similarly improved the visual representation of authenticity. That said, however, the question of whether or not to use dubbed or even artificial sound to accompany otherwise silent film reports posed a particularly difficult problem for journalists anxious to avoid potential criticisms about their claim to impartiality. Much debate also ensued over what circumstances justified imitating ITN's more informal style of presentation, particularly with regard to the use of colloquial language, to enhance the newscast's popular appeal (previously BBC news writers had been told to adopt a mode of address appropriate for readers of the 'quality' press). ITN had also shown how the new 16mm film camera technology could be exploited to advantage 'in the field' for more visually compelling images, as well as how a more aggressive approach to pursuing 'scoops' (exclusives) and 'beats' (first disclosures) could attract a greater interest in news amongst viewers.[32] The same year also saw the range of newsworthy topics for both the BBC and ITN substantively extended with the suspension of the so-called 'fourteen-day rule' (it would be formally withdrawn by Prime Minister Harold Macmillan in July 1957). In the absence of this form of government control, both the BBC and ITN networks were able to redefine what could count as legitimate political coverage. It was at this point, then, that they were at last effectively positioned within the public sphere to realise their current status, arguably that of alternative forums of debate to Parliament.

It was in July of that year, however, that the stakes for a professional approach to the problem of impartiality assumed fresh significance in the eyes of many televisual journalists, as well as their critics. Egyptian President Gamal Abdel Nasser's decision that month to nationalise the Anglo-French Suez Canal Company sparked an ill-fated concerted attack, first by Israeli troops in the Sinai desert on 29 October, and continuing two days later in the form of British and French aerial bombardments of Egyptian airfields (to be followed by paratroops on 5 November). In Britain, Conservative Prime Minister Anthony Eden was of the view that opposition party criticisms of his government's military action (war would not be formally declared) should not be broadcast, but did not formally protest when the BBC granted, against his wishes, a 'right of reply' to Labour Leader Hugh Gaitskell. As the 'Suez crisis' worsened, however, the pressures brought to bear by the government on the BBC grew in intensity. Expressing fears that the Corporation was giving 'comfort to the enemy by reporting domestic divisions', Eden reportedly considered taking drastic action to curtail its independence. While some have since spoken of a 'threatened take-over' of the Corporation through a 'revival of wartime measures', others, such as F.R. MacKenzie, have suggested:

> There was real and severe pressure put on the BBC . . . This took several forms: attempts to impose pro-government speakers and curtail critics of the Suez policy; rows over the Opposition's right to reply to Ministerial broadcasts; the planting of Foreign Office liaison officers at Bush House; threats of financial cuts in the Overseas Services; and Parliamentary measures designed to clip the BBC's wings.
>
> (MacKenzie, cited in Schlesinger 1987: 36)

Despite these tensions, the BBC withstood demands that it 'rally to the nation', electing instead to prioritise its long-term reputation for being 'fair and impartial in handling matters of controversy' over the immediate political interests of the Eden cabinet (itself divided over the conflict; see also Goldie 1977). In sharp contrast with its rôle during the General Strike of 1926, therefore, the BBC maintained its apparent autonomy, although charges of 'bias' were levelled at its newscasts from all sides (evidence, for some, of their impartiality). Following its formal examination of these charges, however, the Corporation's Board of Governors concluded that 'a successful and creditable result had been generally achieved' in the news coverage, 'and that this result fulfilled the BBC's obligation for impartiality, objectivity and for telling the truth' (cited in Briggs 1979b: 216–17).[33]

Telling the truth

By the early 1960s, public opinion surveys were routinely indicating that television was beginning to displace both radio and the newspaper as the principal source of news for audiences in Britain and the United States. Today, some critics are asserting that the capacity of televisual news and current affairs programming to shape 'the public agenda' signifies that this medium is providing a positive, even democratising, function with regard to public enlightenment. This line of argument is anticipated and challenged by Habermas in *The Structural Transformation of the Public Sphere*. In the concluding sections of this study, he contends that the electronic media have become systematically implicated in the rapid state of decline of the public sphere over the course of this century. Specifically, Habermas writes:

> The communicative network of a public made up of rationally debating private citizens has collapsed; the public opinion once emergent from it has partly decomposed into the informal opinions of private citizens without a public and partly become concentrated into formal opinions of publicistically effective institutions. Caught in the vortex of *publicity that is staged for show or manipulation* the public of nonorganised private people is laid claim to not by public communication but by the communication of publicly manifested opinions.
>
> (Habermas 1989: 247–8)

His description of the conditions by which the public sphere has all but disappeared places an important emphasis on how the commercialisation of mass communication networks has virtually displaced 'rational–critical debate' into the realm of cultural consumption. This 'refeudalisation of the public sphere', as he typifies it, has not only transformed the active citizen into an indifferent consumer but also ensured that she or he is all but excluded from participation in public debates and decision-making processes in any meaningful sense.

Habermas's account is deeply pessimistic about the possibility of ever reversing the current rôle that the mass media play in controlling (in broad alignment with corporate and state interests) the public articulation of different opinions. The growing concentration and conglomeration of ownership in the media sectors of most industrialised societies, increasingly justified by state officials and corporate spokespeople in the name of 'global competitiveness', continues to re-politicise the public sphere in ways which are detrimental to public surveillance and accountability. While today we may point to the new opportunities for access to public communication which are provided by an array of emergent institutions and technologies (ranging from community access television to the Internet), it is evident that the social divisions between those with 'information capital' and those without it are widening. Moreover, precisely what counts as 'rational debate' in the age of 'public opinion management' is a matter of continuous dispute between unequal discourses of citizenship, only some of which are having their definitions of reality re-inflected as appropriate, credible or authoritative by the media (see Golding and Murdock 1996; Hallin 1996; Mosco 1996; O'Malley 1994; Thompson 1995; van Zoonen 1996).

It is here, then, that proclamations of news 'objectivity' and 'impartiality' assume particular significance. As I have attempted to demonstrate above, both concepts are historically specific in their configuration, that is, their meanings have taken on different associations in relation to the distinctive situations of their use. It follows that each concept, as the product of a convergence of contending forces (especially institutional and technological ones), will continue to evolve as the constellation of these forces changes across the public sphere (see also Allan 1995). Accordingly, we cannot expect either concept always to inform the professional ideals of journalistic practice, since there is no essential reason why this must be the case. The end of 'objectivity' and 'impartiality' as the guiding principles of an ethic of public service may soon be in sight; indeed, from the vantage point of 'reality TV' and 'infotainment' programming, it would appear that the 'tabloidization' of journalism continues apace. Meanwhile, as Habermas (1992: 437) writes, the mass media are developing the public sphere 'into an arena infiltrated by power in which, by means of topic selection and topical contributions, a battle is fought out not only over influence but over the control of communication flows that affect behaviour while their strategic intentions are kept hidden as much as possible'. In my view, it is time to engage with these 'strategic intentions' precisely as they attempt to define the contours of 'public opinion' within the limits of objective, impartial journalism. Allow me to close, then, by calling for a radical reconsideration of what constitutes 'professional' news reporting today and, even more importantly, how it will need to change in relation to the contradictory dynamics of citizenship across the public sphere tomorrow.

Notes

1   Habermas's account of British press history has been criticised by some
     commentators for relying upon a traditional Whig interpretation; for
     others, it is to be defined as an unduly romantic, even celebratory treat-
     ment (although its discussion of the eventual decline of the public sphere
     is generally considered to be overly pessimistic). Moreover, as Curran
     (1991: 53) writes: 'It hovers uncertainly between a normative account
     (what it ought to have been like) and a descriptive account (what it was
     actually like). Thus, his portrayal of the early press is presented in norma-
     tive terms; his critique of the modern media in descriptive terms; and, to
     confuse things further, this critique contains references back to an ideali-
     sation of the early press as something approximating to descriptive reality.'

2   Habermas (1992: 3) observes that the category 'public' (like 'publicity')
     is of Greek origin and has been 'transmitted to us bearing a Roman stamp.
     In the fully developed Greek city-state the sphere of the *polis*, which was
     common (*koine*) to the free citizens, was strictly separated from the sphere
     of the *oikos*; in the sphere of the *oikos*, each individual is in his own rela-
     tion (*idia*). The public life, *bios politikos*, went on in the market place
     (*agora*), but of course this did not mean that it occurred necessarily only
     in this specific locale. The public sphere was constituted in discussion
     (*lexis*), which could also assume the forms of consultation and of sitting in
     the court of law, as well as in common action (*praxis*), be it the waging
     of war or competition in athletic games.' For further discussions regarding
     the nature of the political order of the time, especially its dependency on
     what Habermas characterises as a 'patrimonial slave economy', see
     Habermas 1992, 1996; see also Calhoun 1995; Fleming 1995.

3   The extremely small size of these 'educated classes' in relation to the rest
     of the population is remarked upon by Habermas (1989: 37–8), who
     writes: 'The proportion of illiterates, at least in Great Britain, even
     exceeded that of the preceding Elizabethan epoch. Even by the start of the
     eighteenth century, more than half of the population lived on the margins
     of subsistence. The masses were not only largely illiterate but also so
     pauperised that they could not even pay for literature. They did not have
     at their disposal the buying power needed for even the most modest partic-
     ipation in the market of cultural goods.' Interesting points of comparison
     are made with Germany and France regarding the general rights of citi-
     zenship.

4   It was about this time, according to Herd (1952: 37), that competition
     between titles 'stimulated the use of what may be described as a contem-
     porary equivalent of the stop-press device in the insertion of late news,
     first written in the margins and subsequently printed on separate sheets,
     and known as Postscripts.' As he adds, however, these newspapers 'were
     still in the rough pioneer stage – inadequate, poorly written and lacking
     any professional standards'. See also O'Malley's (1986: 25) examination
     of the *London Gazette*, a state-controlled publication of this period, which
     in his view 'helped to bolster the Stuart regime by sanctioning it with

religious orthodoxy and by directing "public opinion" along the lines which government policy took at any one time'.

5   'Such actions', Harris (1978: 96) writes, 'could be expensive and difficult to follow up [for the state], and they invariably boosted the sale of the papers under attack. On the other hand, the occasional mass-arrests and the harassment of leading opposition papers had a serious impact on their organisation even when, as with most bookseller-owned papers, the personnel were indemnified against the costs of prosecution.' The Law of Libel would eventually be replaced in 1792 by Fox's Libel Act which, as Asquith (1978: 111–12) observes, 'made the public, instead of the judges, the arbiters of what could be lawfully published; the jury could give a general verdict on the question of law, as to whether the publication was libellous, instead of just a special verdict on the question of fact. A further important change was made by the Libel Act of the ex-journalist Lord Campbell in 1843 which provided that the defendant could plead, as an adequate defence, the truth of the matter provided it were in the public interest.'

6   The importance of the coffee houses for the emergence of 'public opinion' in Britain has been the subject of much scholarly attention. Habermas observes that the coffee houses were often castigated as seedbeds of political unrest, an assertion underlined in this government proclamation: 'Men have assumed to themselves a liberty, not only in coffee houses, but in other places and meetings, both public and private, to censure and defame the proceedings of the State, by speaking evil of things they understand not, and endeavouring to create and nourish an universal jealousie and dissatisfaction in the minds of all His Majesties good subjects' (cited in Habermas 1989: 59). According to Stephens (1988: 41), Britain's first coffee house opened in Oxford in about 1650, while Smith (1979: 45) suggests that the first one in London was founded in 1657. From the outset, these houses were notorious for unruly political disputes, and women were not permitted inside (a sharp point of contrast with the salons of France).

7   Smith (1979: 56–7) maintains that by the middle of that century, 'London had five daily papers, six thrice-weeklies, five weeklies and, on a far less official level, several cut-price thrice-weeklies, with a total circulation between them of 100,000 copies (up to one million readers) a week. The average weekly wage, at ten shillings, was higher in London than in the provinces, and brought the purchase of an occasional newspaper well within the reach of all but the poorest workers.'

8   If not in law, the parliamentary privilege had been rendered obsolete in practice some years earlier. Here Habermas (1989: 61–2) recounts as one example of how this problem could be overcome the story of William 'Memory' Woodfall, a man who 'was able to make the *Morning Chronicle* into the leading London daily paper because he could reproduce verbatim sixteen columns of parliamentary speeches without taking notes in the gallery of the House of Commons, which was prohibited'. Herd (1952: 73), in contrast, places the maximum number of columns at seven, but

in any case the effect on efforts to suppress accounts of the proceedings was significant.

9   The initial start-up costs of a newspaper press were relatively modest, and many could return a profit without relying on advertising. To take one example, the *Northern Star*, a leading radical newspaper with a national circulation, was launched with less than £1,000 of capital in 1837: 'A throwback to the "battle of the great unstamped" . . . it inveighed against the "reduction in stamps" for having "made the rich man's paper cheaper, and the poor man's paper dearer" ' (Koss 1984: 60). Curran and Seaton (1991: 19) point out that the radical newspapers, by the 1830s, were 'increasingly oriented towards a working class audience, and became more uncompromising in their attacks on capitalism. They were not forced to temper their radicalism or seek a more affluent readership by the need to attract more advertising. Instead they were free to respond to the radicalisation of the working-class movement because they relied on their readers rather than advertisers for their economic viability.'

10   Far from ignoring the effectivity of class, for example, Habermas (1989: 87) maintains that: 'Class interest was the basis of public opinion. During that phase, however, it must also have been objectively congruent with the general interest, at least to the extent that this opinion could be considered the public one, emerging from the critical debate of the public, and consequently, rational. It would have turned into coercion at that time if the public had been forced to close itself off as the ruling class, if it had been forced to abandon the principle of publicity. Critical debate would have become dogma, the rational insight of an opinion that was no longer public would have become an authoritarian command.' In a later essay (see Habermas 1992), he acknowledges that the issue of gender did not receive adequate consideration in this account; see also Fraser 1992; Meehan 1995.

11   This is arguably still the case today, for reasons which should become clearer below. The principal sources for this section's treatment are: Carey 1986; Hardt and Brennen 1995; Lippmann 1922; Roshco 1975; Salcetti 1995; Schiller 1981; Schudson 1978, 1995; Smith 1979; Stephens 1988; Willis 1991. For accounts of related developments in the British newspaper industry, including the emergence of the 'pauper press', see Boyce *et al.* 1978; Curran and Seaton 1991; Koss 1984; Lee 1976; O'Malley *et al.* 1997; and Weiner 1996. For a comparison with the French press, see Chalaby 1996.

12   The party press would virtually disappear by 1875, whilst the commercial press still exists today in titles such as the *Wall Street Journal* and the *Journal of Commerce*. Regarding the technological aspects of this 'commercial revolution', the invention of the steam press in the 1830s, followed by the introduction of the Hoe rotary press in 1846, enabled the mass production of newspapers on a scale never seen before. Whilst perhaps too much has been made about these technological changes by some writers who see in them a determining influence, they nevertheless significantly altered the dynamics of commodification for better (newspapers could be sold more cheaply) and for worse (the start-up costs for establishing a title quickly

became prohibitive). By the middle of the nineteenth century, as Shi (1995: 95) suggests, the US was 'awash in newsprint'; in his words: 'In 1840 there were 138 daily newspapers in the country; thirty years later there were 574; by the turn of the century the total was 2,600. Overall circulation during the same period increased from less than two million to over 24 million.' By the end of that century, the techniques of printing had been completely revolutionised; as Innis (1986: 161) writes: 'The cylinder press, the stereotype, the web press, and the linotype brought increases from 2,400 copies of 12 pages each per hour to 48,000 copies of 8 pages per hour in 1887, and to 96,000 copies of 8 pages per hour in 1893.'

13 Of the various sales strategies designed to construct a new public, none was more important than the street-distribution system; see Bekken's (1995) study of 'newsboys' in this period. At the same time, circulation further afield was enhanced through rapid improvements in transportation networks, especially canals and railroads.

14 This quotation, which goes on to highlight the advantages of this medium for advertising, is cited by Schudson (1978: 21) who, in turn, maintains that in the 1830s the penny newspapers 'began to reflect, not the affairs of an elite in a small trading society, but the activities of an increasingly varied, urban, and middle-class society of trade, transportation, and manufacturing' (1978: 22–3). This assertion is challenged by Schiller (1981), since in his view Schudson's characterisation of the new public needs to be reconsidered in a way which is more sensitive to relations of economic power. Consequently, he argues that the penny press worked to integrate working class readers (especially the artisans and mechanics) into its sphere of influence, thereby facilitating the ideological reproduction of this new phase of capitalist development.

15 Shi (1995) offers a fascinating account of the ascension of 'realism' in US culture from the mid-1800s to post-World War I, particularly with respect to science, architecture, literature and the fine arts.

16 Cited in Stephens (1988: 227). In contrast, according to Salcetti (1995: 50), the first news story 'sent by telephone' appeared in the Boston Globe on 13 February 1877.

17 Cited in Roshco (1975: 31). Moreover, as Carey (1986: 164) writes: 'The wire services demanded language stripped of the local, the regional and colloquial. They demanded something closer to a "scientific" language, one of strict denotation where the connotative features of the utterance were under control, one of fact. . . . The telegraph, therefore, led to the disappearance of forms of speech and styles of journalism and storytelling – the tall story, the hoax, much humour, irony and satire – that depended on a more traditional use of language.' Here it is also important to recall that each word of a news account had to be justified in terms of cost, a constraint which similarly conditioned the norms of reporting. In 1894, according to Stephens (1988: 258), a correspondent for The Times of London was informed that 'telegrams are for facts; appreciation and political comment can come by post'. For a historical examination of AP's main British rival, the Reuters news agency which was established in 1858, see Read 1992.

18   This quotation from Ochs is cited in Schudson (1978: 110–11). In the 1996 US election, Republican Party challenger Bob Dole had this to say about the news values of the *New York Times vis-à-vis* the public sphere: 'Don't let the media steal the election . . . the country belongs to the people, not the *New York Times*' (cited in the *Independent*, 28 October 1996: 10). The daily had formally endorsed President Bill Clinton the day before.

19   According to Willis (1991: 56), this new motto replaced an earlier slogan: 'It Does Not Soil the Breakfast Cloth'.

20   Interestingly, Lee (1976: 231) claims that this notion of objectivity also encountered criticism from abroad: 'The French condemned a worsening quality of journalism, which put facts before ideas, and attributed it to "americanisation".' To clarify the precepts informing this belief in the virtues of objectivity, Schudson (1978: 4–5) characterises it as follows: 'Facts, in this view, are assertions about the world open to independent validation. They stand beyond the distorting influences of any individual's personal preferences. Values, in this view, are an individual's conscious or unconscious preferences for what the world should be; they are seen as ultimately subjective and so without legitimate claim on other people. The belief in objectivity is a faith in "facts", a distrust of "values", and a commitment to their segregation.' In somewhat stronger language, Joseph Pulitzer declared: 'In America, we want facts. Who cares about the philosophical speculations of our correspondents?' (cited in Chalaby, 1996: 311).

21   Cited in Roshco (1975: 46). Similarly, the American Newspaper Guild's code of ethics, presented in 1935 to the US Senate Committee on Education and Labor, declared: '(1) That the newspaperman's first duty is to give the public accurate and unbiased news reports' (cited in Schiller 1981: 195).

22   This section's discussion of 'impartiality' in the early days of radio and televisual news in Britain primarily draws on the following sources: Briggs (1961, 1965, 1979a, 1979b, 1995); Burns (1977); Cox (1995); Davies (1994); Davis (1976); Goldie (1977); Paulu (1961); Pegg (1983); Scannell and Cardiff (1991); Schlesinger (1987); Sendall (1982); Smith (1973). For insights into related developments for US newscasts, see Bliss (1991); Stephens (1988); Winston (1993).

23   Lord Gainford, the BBC's Chairperson, set out the Corporation's position in a memorandum: 'As the government are sure that they are right both on the facts of the dispute and on the constitutional issues, any steps which we may take to communicate the truth dispassionately should be to the advantage of the government' (cited in Schlesinger 1987: 17). Overall, as Davies (1994: 37–8) writes: 'The aim was to provide the unvarnished truth, and during the strike the broadcasts were almost certainly a moderating influence. The organised working class, however, assumed that the Company was ranged against them and the TUC [Trades Union Congress] advised its members not to listen to the bulletins. Whatever the news given – and there is no surviving record of it – it can be assumed that it offered no portrait of the impressive unity of the workers nor any insight into the basic issues which had caused the conflict; indeed, such matters

would have been wholly outside the experience of almost all the Company's more senior employees.' Many listeners who were disgruntled with the 'one-sided' radio coverage, as Pegg (1983: 180) notes, took to using the term BFC (British Falsehood Corporation) to express their indignation.

24 Cited in Scannell and Cardiff (1991: 118) who observe, in turn, that the announcer simply declared that 'there is no news tonight'. They provide a sense of the reaction of the newspaper press by quoting the *Sunday Chronicle*: 'The BBC could have announced the death of Lady Glanely, the fire at Lord Haddo's mansion, the mountaineering accident to Professor Julian Huxley and the motor collision involving Lady Diana Cooper, among other items.' For Scannell and Cardiff (1991: 118), this example 'perfectly encapsulated the gulf between the BBC's ideas about news values at that time and those of the popular press.'

25 Dimbleby cited in Scannell and Cardiff (1991: 122), where he makes the further observation: 'I really believe that News could be presented in a gripping manner, and, at the same time, remain authentic . . . The principle of enlivening news by the infusion of the human element is being followed in other spheres . . . In this, as you may have seen, the method followed is not only that of showing the news, but telling why, and how, it happened. That is what I suggest the BBC could do with great success.' Interestingly, 1936 would also see the BBC undertake its first rudimentary forms of audience research.

26 Lord Simon of Wythenshawe, Chair of the BBC Board of Governors from 1947 to 1952, highlighted the advantages of radio over televisual newsreels, especially with regard to immediacy, when he wrote: 'A great majority of [news] items are of such a nature that they cannot, either now or ever, be shown visually; of those that could be shown on television the majority occur overseas, often in distant countries, and it will be a long time before television films can be flown from all over the world to London on the day on which they happen. Television newsreels will, of course, continue to develop and be of the greatest interest and attraction, but there is surely not the least possibility that they will ever replace the news on sound' (Wythenshawe, cited in Davis 1976: 12).

27 Lane cited in Cox (1995: 38). Shortly thereafter, Gerald Barry would comment in his television column in the *Observer* newspaper: 'The sad fact has to be recorded that news on television does not exist. What has been introduced nightly into the TV programmes is a perfunctory little bulletin of news flashes composed of an announcer's voice, a caption and an indifferent still photograph. This may conceivably pass as news, but it does not begin to be television' (Barry, cited in Davis 1976: 13). By June 1955, the title *News and Newsreel* had been dropped in favour of *Television News Bulletin*.

28 Lord Reith, speaking in the House of Lords during a major debate on commercial television on 22 May 1952, did not mince words when challenging the Conservative Government's proposal: 'What grounds are there for jeopardising this heritage and tradition? Not a single one is even suggested in the White Paper. Why sell it down the river? . . . A principle absolutely fundamental and cherished is scheduled to be scuttled. . . . The

Government are here on record to scuttle — a betrayal and a surrender; that is what is so shocking and serious; so unnecessary and wrong.' (Hansard, House of Lords, 22 May 1952, col. 1297; reprinted as Reith 1974).

29   Regarding paragraph (g) of this subsection, the Act declares that nothing shall prevent: '(i) the inclusion in the programmes of the whole (but not some only) of a series of the British Broadcasting Corporation's party political broadcasts; (ii) the inclusion in the programmes of properly balanced discussions or debates where the persons taking part express opinions and put forward arguments of a political character.'

30   The appointment of Cox followed the resignation of Aidan Crawley (ITN's founding editor) in January 1956, primarily over financial disputes with the networking companies. Crawley's departure was due, in his words, to the 'conviction that a board composed of representatives of contractors who differ so widely in their outlook towards television is incapable of maintaining a consistent policy towards the news' (cited in Paulu 1961: 92). Press reports of the time, according to Paulu (1961), also contended that Crawley and his deputy editor, Richard Goold-Adams, wanted an emphasis on serious news, while some of the representatives from the networking companies wanted priority given to entertainment and feature items. It is also interesting to note that Cox came from a newspaper tradition, namely the London *News Chronicle*, which presumably gave him a different approach to televisual news values than his counterparts at the BBC for whom radio news was the norm.

31   The policy of anonymous newsreading would continue for BBC radio until 1963 (Schlesinger 1987: 37).

32   A 1957 BBC Audience Research Report found that the '7.15 p.m. to 7.30 p.m. news bulletin on television had rather more than 4$^{1}/_{4}$ million viewers, while the 9.00 p.m. Home Service news, once the peak point of the listening day, had less than half that number of listeners' (Briggs 1995: 72). Comparisons between BBC and ITN newscasts were also being made. 'Surveys show', writes Paulu (1961: 93), 'that even while preferring to watch ITN, the public ascribes more prestige to BBC news, largely because of the BBC's past performance, especially during World War II, and that it tends to increase its BBC viewing during periods of international crisis. But opinion leaders — or, to use the British expression, Top People — are more apt to watch BBC news, as they are in fact to view the BBC at all times.'

33   Grace Wyndham Goldie (1977: 186), at the time a producer in the BBC's Television Talks Department, would later recall: 'Suez is, therefore, a salutary warning of the lengths to which a political party may go, when in power, to prevent the broadcasting of any opinions but its own. It also reveals the importance of maintaining procedures, agreed in advance by broadcasters and the Opposition as well as by Government, to which the broadcasting organisations can refer when refusing to submit to government pressures exerted at moments of tension when emotions are running high' (see also Briggs 1995).

Bibliography

Allan, S. (1995) 'News, Truth and Postmodernity: Unravelling the Will to Facticity', in B. Adam and S. Allan (eds) *Theorizing Culture: An Interdisciplinary Critique After Postmodernism*, London: UCL Press; New York: NYU Press, 129–44.

Asquith, I. (1978) 'The Structure, Ownership and Control of the Press, 1780–1855', in G. Boyce, J. Curran and P. Wingate (eds) *Newspaper History: From the 17th Century to the Present Day*, London: Constable, 98–129.

Bekken, J. (1995) 'Newsboys: The Exploitation of "Little Merchants" by the Newspaper Industry', in H. Hardt and B. Brennen (eds) *Newsworkers: Toward a History of the Rank and File*, Minneapolis: University of Minnesota Press, 190–226.

Bliss, E., jun. (1991) *Now the News*, New York: Columbia University Press.

Boyce, G., Curran, J. and Wingate, P. (eds) (1978) *Newspaper History: From the 17th Century to the Present Day*, London: Constable.

Briggs, A. (1961) *The History of Broadcasting in the United Kingdom, 1: The Birth of Broadcasting*, London: Oxford University Press.

Briggs, A. (1965) *The History of Broadcasting in the United Kingdom, 2: The Golden Age of Wireless*, London: Oxford University Press.

Briggs, A. (1979a) *The History of Broadcasting in the United Kingdom, 4: The Sound and Vision*, London: Oxford University Press.

Briggs, A. (1979b) *Governing the BBC*, London: BBC.

Briggs, A. (1995) *The History of Broadcasting in the United Kingdom, 5: Competition*, Oxford: Oxford University Press.

Burns, T. (1977) *The BBC: Public Institution and Private World*, London: Macmillan.

Calhoun, C. (1995) *Critical Social Theory*, Oxford: Blackwell.

Carey, J.W. (1986) 'The Dark Continent of American Journalism', in R.K. Manoff and M. Schudson (eds) *Reading the News*, New York: Pantheon, 146–96.

Chalaby, J.K. (1996) 'Journalism as an Anglo-American Invention,' *European Journal of Communication* 11(3): 303–26.

Cox, G. (1995) *Pioneering Television News*, London: John Libbey.

Curran, J. (1991) 'Rethinking the Media as a Public Sphere', in P. Dahlgren and C. Sparks (eds) *Communication and Citizenship*, London: Routledge, 27–57.

Curran, J. (1996) 'Mass Media and Democracy Revisited', in J. Curran and M. Gurevitch (eds) (1996) *Mass Media and Society* (2nd edn), London: Edward Arnold, 81–119.

Curran, J. and Seaton, J. (1991) *Power Without Responsibility: The Press and Broadcasting in Britain* (3rd edn), London: Routledge.

Dahlgren, P. (1991) 'Introduction', in P. Dahlgren and C. Sparks (eds) *Communication and Citizenship*, London: Routledge, 1–26.

Dahlgren, P. (1995) *Television and the Public Sphere*, London: Sage.

Davies, J. (1994) *Broadcasting and the BBC in Wales*, Cardiff: University of Wales Press.

Davis, A. (1976) *Television: Here is the News*, London: Severn.

Day, R. (1995) 'Foreword', in G. Cox, *Pioneering Television News*, London: John Libbey, vii–x.

Fleming, M. (1995) 'Women and the "Public Use of Reason"', in J. Meehan (ed.) *Feminists Read Habermas,* New York: Routledge, 117–38.

Fraser, N. (1992) 'Rethinking the Public Sphere: A Contribution to the Critique of Actually Existing Democracy', in C. Calhoun (ed.) *Habermas and the Public Sphere*, Cambridge, MA: MIT Press, 109–42.

Garnham, N. (1992) 'The Media and the Public Sphere', in C. Calhoun (ed.), *Habermas and the Public Sphere*, Cambridge, Mass: MIT Press, 359–76.

Goldie, G.W. (1977) *Facing the Nation: Television and Politics, 1936–1976*, London: Bodley Head.

Golding, P. and Murdock, G. (1996) 'Culture, Communications, and Political Economy', in J. Curran and M. Gurevitch (eds) (1996) *Mass Media and Society* (2nd edn), London: Edward Arnold, 11–30.

Habermas, J. (1989) *The Structural Transformation of the Public Sphere* (trans. Thomas Burger) Cambridge: Polity Press.

Habermas, J. (1992) 'Further Reflections on the Public Sphere', in C. Calhoun (ed.) *Habermas and the Public Sphere*, Cambridge, MA: MIT Press, 421–61.

Habermas, J. (1996) 'An Interview with Jürgen Habermas', Mikael Carleheden and René Gabriëls, *Theory, Culture and Society* 13(3): 1–17.

Hallin, D. (1996) 'Commercialism and Professionalism in the American News Media', in J. Curran and M. Gurevitch (eds) (1996) *Mass Media and Society* (2nd edn), London: Edward Arnold, 243–62.

Hardt, H. and Brennen, B. (eds) (1995) *Newsworkers: Toward a History of the Rank and File*, Minneapolis: University of Minnesota Press.

Harris, M. (1978) 'The Structure, Ownership and Control of the Press, 1620–1780', in G. Boyce, J. Curran and P. Wingate (eds) *Newspaper History: From the 17th Century to the Present Day*, London: Constable, 82–97.

Herd, H. (1952) *The March of Journalism*, London: George Allen & Unwin.

Innis, H.A. (1986) *Empire and Communications*, Victoria: Press Porcépic.

Koss, S. (1984) *The Rise and Fall of the Political Press in Britain*, London: Fontana.

Lee, A.J. (1976) *The Origins of the Popular Press in England, 1855–1914*, London: Croom Helm.

Lippmann, W. (1922) *Public Opinion*, New York: Free Press.

Meehan, J. (ed.) (1995) *Feminists Read Habermas*, New York: Routledge.

Mosco, V. (1996) *The Political Economy of Communication*, London: Sage.

O'Malley, T. (1986) 'Religion and the Newspaper Press, 1660–1685: A Study of the *London Gazette*', in M. Harris and A. Lee (eds) *The Press in English Society from the Seventeenth to Nineteenth Centuries*, London: Associated University Presses, 25–46.

O'Malley, T. (1994) *Closedown? The BBC and Government Broadcasting Policy, 1972–92*, London: Pluto.

O'Malley, T., Allan, S. and Thompson, A. (1997) 'Tokens of Antiquity: The Press and the Shaping of National Identity in Wales, 1870–1900', *Studies in Newspaper and Periodical History 1995 Annual*, Westport, CT: Greenwood, 127–52.

Paulu, B. (1961) *British Broadcasting in Transition*, London: Macmillan.

Pegg, M. (1983) *Broadcasting and Society, 1918–1939*, London: Croom Helm.

Read, D. (1992) *The Power of News: The History of Reuters*, Oxford: Oxford University Press.

Reith, J. (1974) 'Speech in the Debate on Commercial Television', in A. Smith (ed.) *British Broadcasting*, Newton Abbot: David & Charles, 103.

Roshco, B. (1975) *Newsmaking*, Chicago, IL: University of Chicago Press.

Salcetti, M. (1995) 'The Emergence of the Reporter: Mechanization and the Devaluation of Editorial Workers', in H. Hardt and B. Brennen (eds) *Newsworkers: Toward a History of the Rank and File*, Minneapolis: University of Minnesota Press, 48–75.

Scannell, P. and Cardiff, D. (1991) *A Social History of British Broadcasting, 1: 1922–1939*, Oxford: Blackwell.

Schiller, D. (1981) *Objectivity and the News*, Philadelphia, PA: University of Philadelphia Press.

Schlesinger, P. (1987) *Putting 'Reality' Together: BBC News*, London: Methuen.

Schudson, M. (1978) *Discovering the News*, New York: Basic Books.

Schudson, M. (1995) *The Power of News*, Cambridge, MA: Harvard University Press.

Sendall, B. (1982) *Independent Television in Britain, Vol. 1*, London: Macmillan.

Shi, D.E. (1995) *Facing Facts: Realism in American Thought and Culture, 1850–1920*, New York: Oxford University Press.

Smith, A. (1973) *The Shadow in the Cave*, London: George Allen & Unwin.

Smith, A. (1979) *The Newspaper: An International History*, London: Thames & Hudson.

Stephens, M. (1988) *A History of News: From the Drum to the Satellite*, New York: Viking.

Thompson, J. (1995) *Media and Modernity*, Cambridge: Polity Press.

Verstraeten, H. (1996) 'The Media and the Transformation of the Public Sphere', *European Journal of Communication* 11(3): 347–70.

Weiner, J.H. (1996) 'The Americanisation of the British Press, 1830–1914', *Studies in Newspaper and Periodical History, 1994 Volume 1*: 61–74.

Willis, J. (1991) *The Shadow World: Life Between the News Media and Reality*, New York: Praeger.

Winston, B. (1993) 'The CBS Evening News, 7 April 1949: Creating an Ineffable Television Form', in J. Eldridge (ed.) *Getting the Message*, London: Routledge, 181–209.

van Zoonen, L. (1996) 'Feminist Perspectives on the Media', in J. Curran and M. Gurevitch (eds) *Mass Media and Society* (2nd edn), London: Edward Arnold, 31–52.

Chapter 27

Michael Bromley

THE END OF JOURNALISM?

Changes in workplace practices in the press and broadcasting in the 1990s

Introduction

AS AN OCCUPATION, JOURNALISM has always been difficult to cate-gorise.[1] While, stricly speaking, neither a profession nor a craft, it has displayed many of the characteristics of both. Organisationally, it could be classified as either routine white-collar work or a largely autonomous creative process (Goffee and Scase 1995: 72–3, 137–57). During the period of the greatest expansion of the media (since *c.*1880) journalists might have been expected to have been in the forefront of the competition among the emerging 'professional class' for income, power and status (Perkin 1990: 1–29). Yet as early as 1907 journalism divided formally into those who sought profes-sional status through the Institute of Journalists (IoJ) and those who felt the need to collectivise as 'wage earners' in the National Union of Journalists (NUJ), reflecting a polarisation among journalists themselves which has led to the discounting of the possibility of a more unified 'middle way' (Bundock 1957). In the workplace, polarisation, although evident in the late nineteenth century, has increased in the 1990s (Tunstall 1996). It can be suggested that such division has disabled journalists as competitiors in 'professional society'. On the other hand, some see it as giving journalism an edge as a 'flexible' occupation.[2] Many journalists share this view, but others have associated 'flexibility' with broader damaging assaults on the function of journalism (Hallin 1996).

Function and status are clearly interdependent: at a time when the func-tion of British journalism was widely called into question, the public status of journalists was particularly low – below that of politicians – and still fell markedly, while journalists themselves had low opinions of their own ethical standards (Worcester 1994; Delano and Henningham 1996: 18–19). Among journalists there are fears that the delicate balance between the self-interest of capitalist media owners and the 'public interest' motives of journalism has been upset (Dahlgren 1992: 1–23). Although most discussed in the USA, developments such as 'total newspapering' and 'market-led journalism' are evident in the UK (*UK Press Gazette*[3] 16 October 1995). Some journalists have come to believe that the news is being stolen from them (Rosenblum 1993).

Such debates have become entangled with the processes of technological development, a tendency exacerbated by the high-profile changes which occurred in the national newspaper sector after 1986, and those which were provoked by the 1990 Broadcasting Act (Bromley 1995b; Tunstall 1993). Responses to one such development in the 1990s – the facilitation of 'multi-skilling' through the extended use of desk-top computing and communication systems – have followed this pattern.

Multi-skilling has been presented as a facet of the brave new world of late twentieth century journalism (Hammond 1995). Yet in some ways there is nothing new about it: for example, a version of multi-skilling was introduced more or less with press photography itself when at its inception the *Morning Leader* equipped its reporters with cameras (Griffiths 1992: 422). Many journalists consider the bringing together of the disparate skills of journalism and other related techniques as no more than a by-product of the introduction of 'computerised technology' which leaves unaffected 'the basic skills and standards' of journalism (Harris and Spark 1993: 220–21). On the other hand, multi-skilling represents a number of significant departures from the practices of journalism established over a century or more: as many journalists observe, news rooms have changed almost beyond recognition (Hayward 1995). Some generally welcome the changes for having reasserted what they believe is the 'natural' workplace primacy of journalists over media technicians (Wilson 1995). Others confess to having 'a Luddite streak', and feel that the uses to which journalists are asked to put 'new technology' still need to be justified in practice (MacGregor 1995: 90–3). The question posed here is whether these changes, and specifically the introduction of multi-skilling, presage a reformation of the journalist as a professional or a craft worker – or the disintegration of journalism as a specific occupation.

Journalism: craft or profession?

In the extensive and expanding body of literature addressing journalism which has been produced over the past forty years journalists appear only rarely as workers (Hardt and Brennen 1995: vii-xiii). It is not just academics who have opted largely to overlook journalists as 'operatives within a system' (Morrison and Tumber 1988: x). Journalists themselves have tended to emphasise (and often exaggerate) their closeness to and familiarity with power, celebrity and the exotic, and to gloss over the day-to-day (relative) powerlessness of employment in the news room. The subtitle of the second volume of one former national newspaper editor's autobiography, 'From Fleet Street to Show Biz', echoes journalism's real or imagined associations with glamour (Jameson: 1990). Perhaps more unwittingly it also reveals the underside of journalism, and its resemblance to work in the entertainment industry where small élites prosper at the expense of large numbers of anonymous, underemployed jobbing hacks (Tunstall 1983: 188–92; Tunstall 1996: 172ff). Like the Hollywood prototype, journalism's 'star system' is dependent on its own continual reproduction – the apparently endless capacity to discover anew 'star material'.

Since at least the 1880s, the upper echelons of journalism have been drawn from the same more or less closed source (Gross 1991: 146). For example, even during the 1930s, in what has been called 'the heyday of the *popular* press', editorial control of the left-of-centre *News Chronicle* was for the most part in the hands of men with public school and Oxford backgrounds (Cox 1996: 17–21; emphasis added). The disparities between this élite and the majority of journalists undertaking 'responsible white-collar work' (Tunstall 1983: 191) grew after 1945, influenced by the expansion of radio and television journalism. The BBC's first journalists were preponderantly the products of preparatory, public and finishing schools, Oxbridge, and 'useful' family and social connections. The preferences of the independent television (ITV) companies after 1955 were not noticeably different (Miall 1994). Journalists from less exalted backgrounds who reached the top, such as Derek Jameson and William Haley, who left school at 15 to work as a telegraphist at the *Times*, which he later edited after a period as editor-in-chief at the BBC, remained exceptional (Jameson 1990: 13–14; Miall 1994: 82).

This did not always seem to sit well with perceptions of the function of journalism or with its 'human interest' appeal. From the 1960s in particular, apologists began to claim that journalism was in fact 'classless' (Jameson 1990: 16; Randall 1988: 16). In an issue of *Twentieth Century* devoted to 'Class in Britain' James Drawbell, who had edited the *Sunday Chronicle* for more than twenty years, wrote:

> in this jungle, always struggling for survival, the make-up of a newspaper team is, in the social and educational sense, completely 'classless' . . . A newspaper has to draw its staff from every level of society if it is to be truly representative . . . I have had on my staff at the same time three ex-editors of *Isis*. Their Oxford experience was useful . . . but . . . they were indistinguishable from, and certainly not more valuable than, the other members of the paper (several of whom had left school at fifteen) . . .
>
> With this classless structure within a newspaper office, requiring ability – from whatever its background – to lead and direct it, it is not

surprising that the subject of 'class' has little immediate meaning and tends to be rejected from the minds of men clamorously engaged in turning out a newspaper for the masses.

(Drawbell 1965: no page)

Yet even Drawbell did not attempt to deny the deep social stratification of British society which he acknowledged actually shaped the newspaper business itself. A study for the third Royal Commission on the Press identified as a 'problem' the mass of 'lowly paid, lowly educated' journalists attracted to the increasing 'radicalism' of the NUJ (Tunstall 1977: 340). The idea of 'professionalism' was central to the issue. The majority view of the Commission (1977: para. 18.1) was that journalism, while not strictly speaking a profession, had become more 'professional'. The Commission had a limited view of a 'professional', however, as 'a man or woman of integrity, judgement and a sense of vocation' (1977: para. 18.3).

Similar concerns had been raised before the war by the organisation Political and Economic Planning (PEP 1938: 36–8), which called for the 'disturbing tendency to divide editorial staffs into two groups' to be 'ironed out'. When the first Royal Commission on the Press (1949: para. 633) reported – two years after the Hutchins Commission in the USA developed the 'social responsibility theory' of the self-regulation and independent monitoring of the press – it proposed a British monitoring body (later the Press Council) which was supposed to incorporate the self-regulation of journalists. In practice, this was abandoned and the Press Council narrowed its remit to that of a complaints body only (Tunstall 1983: 268). This added to the pressures, resulting from the increased commercialism of the press and the emergence of a public service broadcasting approach at the BBC, which militated against journalism developing as a self-regulating profession. While journalists had many of the appearances of being professionals, including a measure of respectability, middle-class status and individualism, in reality they were employees whose interests were subordinate to those of the organisation which hired them (Elliott 1978). Nevertheless, in the 1970s further 'limited professionalisation', exploiting the journalist's relative autonomy in the workplace, seemed likely.

A key element in this process was the extent to which journalism was moving, like teaching, towards being a graduate occupation. Implicit in this was the idea that graduates made better professionals (Tunstall 1977: 334–5). This presumed that the characteristics associated with professionalisation – the possession of skills not available to the population at large; specific behaviour associated with the group; the social cohesion of the group; and relative status (Splichal and Sparks 1994: 36) – would derive principally, if not exclusively, from their status as *graduates* rather than as journalists. This naturally placed a premium on education and training. The first Royal Commission (1949: para. 623) had bemoaned the ramshackle nature of journalism; before it sat there was no formalised training system for journalists. The National

Association of Journalists (NAJ) had drawn up proposals for a scheme in 1887–8, but it was not until 1919 that the Association's successor, the IoJ, persuaded London University to establish a two-year diploma course (Hunter 1996; Stephenson and Mory 1990: 192). Both the form and fortunes of the Diploma for Journalism reflected the ambivalent position of journalists.

The NAJ represented the first attempt to professionalise journalism, and in 1889 the IoJ had received a royal charter (Elliott 1978: 175). Even so, the university authorities clearly felt that the 'technical elements' of journalism were too lacking in academic rigour to be included in even a sub-degree course which mainly recruited students who had failed to matriculate and therefore did not qualify to enter the university as undergraduates. Practical journalism did not appear as a subject in the syllabus until 1937. By then, the course had gained a reputation in the working world of journalism for being 'too theoretical', and was never highly regarded. Despite attempts to rectify the situation, led by Northcliffe's former news editor Tom Clarke, the course was closed in 1939 (Hunter 1996). This did not signal the end of aspirations to professionalise journalism through the medium of education, however. PEP (1938: 36) urged the introduction of 'refresher courses, analogous to the staff colleges in the defence services, where higher personnel can be given advanced instruction'.

A competing view of journalism as a craft was promoted chiefly by the NUJ, which, unlike the IoJ, excluded press proprietors from membership (Lee 1978: 127). Even so, the union was not able to enforce a fully formalised apprenticeship scheme, and by the late 1940s some of the initiative on journalism training had passed to employers. Probably the most highly developed of such schemes was the Kemsley Editorial Plan started in 1947, and it is clear that it represented an attempt to wrest not only the training but also the related recruitment of journalists out of the union sphere. To do so, Lord Kemsley himself tried to stress the connection between systematic training and professionalism: Lionel Berry, the deputy chairman of Kemsley Newspapers, asserted that journalism was 'beyond question a professional occupation' (*Kemsley Manual* 1952: v-vii, 387–8). The union's position was ambiguous. It was by far the bigger of the two journalists' organisations, chiefly because it drew its members from among the majority of lower-paid non-metropolitan journalists for whom the idea of 'professionalism' had little concrete meaning. Yet it found it difficult to abandon the notion that journalists were 'above all else . . . a body of *professional* men and women' (Elliott 1978: 176; emphasis added). Uncertainty about the status of journalism manifested itself in the IoJ, too: in the late 1920s it organised a series of lectures on 'the technique of modern journalism' delivered by what it called 'masters of the *craft*' (IoJ 1932; emphasis added).

A systematic national training scheme for journalists, with a fixed curriculum and examinations, which was overseen jointly by employers and unions but which retained the primacy of the workplace as the locus for learning, emerged in the 1950s (NCTJ 1975: 7–10). Although restricted at the outset to the training of journalists in the newspaper sector, in 1964 the by then National Council for the Training of Journalists (NCTJ) expanded its activities to include the periodicals industry (NCTJ 1975: 44; Stephenson and Mory 1990: 196). The ambition to establish a more or less universal approach, under which all journalists supposedly underwent formal initial training on local and provincial newspapers before being able to move into national journalism or to broadcasting, can be seen from the apparatus it generated. In 1963 the NCTJ produced what was claimed to be the first 'comprehensive picture of the scope and techniques of British journalism' (Dodge and Viner 1963: 9); in 1966, a manual for newspaper reporting (Harris and Spark); and from 1972 a five-volume series on editing and design (Evans 1972, 1978). The third Royal Commission (1977: para. 18.10) felt that media managements and the NUJ were at last making common cause over the training of journalists; although it was one which fell short of either confirming craft status or instituting a full-blown professionalism.

Workplace practices

This approach enouraged the development of journalism which conflated craft work and professional practice. It foregrounded skills – for example, the use of shorthand – the routinisation of newsroom work, and the division of labour while simultaneously proposing a curriculum for journalism which sustained individualism and incorporated social differentiation – for instance, between editors, 'star' correspondents and columnists, and ordinary reporters and sub-editors (Elliott 1978). In this schema journalism was primarily concerned with words, not pictures (photo-journalism has always had a precarious existence in British journalism), and with writing as a practice which was distinct from editing: press journalism had a higher value than broadcast journalism.

Press photography developed from the 1890s as a specialism both within and apart from journalism. Most of the early press camera operators were studio portrait photographers who took news pictures as a sideline. This, and the reliance on support technicians, such as dark room staff, gave rise to the distinctiveness of press photography from established journalism (Smith 1948: 14–15). The first comprehensive agreement in 1918 between the NUJ and the Newspaper Proprietors' Association, representing the London daily press, excluded photographers, who were recognised only in the following year. Photographers working for the photographic agencies, the first of which had been established in 1903, were covered by an agreement reached in 1920. A separate photographers' branch of the union was formed in 1925 (Bundock 1957: 56ff). While such arrangements covered the majority of press photographers who were based in London, those in the provinces were not recognised 'as journalists for the purposes of wages and conditions' until 1934. The NUJ president at the time that the London agreements had been reached believed that photographers were overlooked chiefly because 'they were a comparatively new importation into journalism'. Photographers were particularly poorly paid (Mansfield 1943: 293, 511–12).

'Photo-reportage' and the picture essay, in which photography and lay-out dominated the text, which was often reduced to short captions, and which flourished in magazines such as *Picture Post* in the 1930s and 1940s, held out the promise of enhancing the status of the press photographer (Davenport 1991: 96–101; Kee 1989: no page). It proved to be only a brief interlude: in the long run, the photographer's work had to pass through the hands of the (journalist) editors who selected the pictures to be used and determined the lay-out (Williams 1991: 121–41). Once the picture had been taken, the press photographer tended to lose control over it (Evans 1978: no page). Photographers were viewed as adjuncts of journalism (Keeble 1994: 67, 288). As journalism training became systemised, there were still disagreements over whether press photographers were 'artists' in their own right (Cheadle 1952: 79), or simply specialised journalists (Harrison 1963: 186). The NCTJ training scheme institutionalised differences between 'journalism' and press photography. The requirements for entry into training were not the same for photographers – there was less emphasis on educational achievement – and the syllabus was significantly different (NCTJ 1989: 7). Press photographers commonly became known as 'monkeys' (Grose 1989: 63).

Press photographers were quintessentially news gatherers. Yet from the 1930s – possibly before – journalism began to be dominated by news processors. Two of the best known journalists of the twentieth century, Harry Guy Batholomew (who was said to be 'semi-literate') and Hannen Swaffer, both processed the work of photographers in the art department of the *Daily Mirror* in the 1930s. At about the same time, Arthur Christiansen, who professed a passionate interest in typography but confessed to being only an 'indifferent' reporter, was taking over the *Daily Express* which he edited for twenty-four years. Increasingly, the route to editorial advancement lay through processing other journalists' work rather than producing good writing or reporting oneself (Engel 1996: 132–5, 151–8). This separation was built into the editorial structure of the *Daily Telegraph*, where, until the 1980s, the editor was in charge of only the more literary output (leading articles, letters, book reviews, etc.) and the managing editor controlled 13 out of 16 editorial pages – the work of about 80% of the paper's journalists – with a concentration on the production process. Overall, the evidence suggests that, up to 1990, Fleet Street editorships were held chiefly by those with either wholly, or largely, news processing backgrounds (Tunstall 1996: 95–115).

While such evidence for local and provincial newspapers is less forthcoming, it is clear that many of the conglomerates which came to dominate the non-national press, such as Thomson Regional Newspapers (TRN), Westminster Press (WP), and United Provincial Newspapers (UPN), invested heavily in news processing, particularly in pre-production areas such as design, from the 1960s.[4] A survey by WP in 1993 found that two-thirds of the aggregate journalistic effort on its titles was spent on processing (*UKPG*, 14 March 1994). At about the same time, TRN was informing its journalists that the news chain was peopled by news editors, chief sub-editors, page planners, sub-editors and outputters at the expense of writers and reporters (TRN 1990).

The different technical regimes which applied in broadcasting, if anything, exacerbated the differences between both journalists and technicians, and news gatherers and news processors. Radio reporters operated in the field with sound recordists, tape was edited by dedicated technicians, and studio broadcasting was run from separate control rooms (Chantler and Harris 1992: 55–65; Schlesinger 1987: 58–9). A similar situation prevailed in television, except that both gathering and processing involved more technicians and non-journalists. Camera-operators and lighting technicians, as well as sound recordists, were needed for reporting (Boyd 1990: 275–86, 310–13). Broadcasts were controlled by studio directors. At least in theory, there existed 'a rigid distinction between technique and content' in broadcast news. The division between news gathering and news processing was perhaps even clearer (Schlesinger 1987: 58–9, 157–9). More effort was devoted to news processing in television than in radio. In the mid-1970s Schlesinger (1987: 58–9, 76–8) found that out of the 36 journalists in the BBC Radio news room, just over half (19) were reporters or special correspondents: in television, out of a news room staff of 60, only 40% (24) were primarily news gatherers.

Journalism was slow to develop in the BBC, because of the insistence of the national newspaper proprietors that the new radio service carried only headline bulletins culled from the news agencies. Although the BBC greatly expanded, and enhanced its reputation, as a news provider during World War Two, the press still set the news agenda after 1945 (Crisell 1995: 19–23; Seymour-Ure 1991: 129). Following the introduction of ITV in 1955, there was a significant increase in output of television news (Tunstall 1996: 218). Into the 1990s, television also increasingly became the first, and a more reliable, source of news for the majority of the population (Worcester 1991: 47–8). Nevertheless, television news continued to use the 'serious' press as its model (Sparks 1991: 70; Schlesinger 1987: 33). This arose in part, no doubt, because of (but it also surely reflected) the tendency of both the BBC and ITV to recruit their journalists almost exclusively from the press. This began in the 1930s. The first proper radio journalist, Richard Dimbleby, the controller of news during the Second World War, Patrick Ryan, and the head of news when a separate television news service was inaugurated in 1955, Tahu Hole, all had newspaper backgrounds (Miall 1994: 54, 123–4; Schlesinger 1987: 21, 31, 37). The practice continued at least into the 1980s with a series of newspaper journalists – William Hardcastle, Ian Trethowan, Michael Buerk and James Naughtie, to name a few – becoming senior and influential figures in broadcast news.

The NCTJ (1975: 9), in pursuing its 'one model' ideal, consciously insti-tutionalised existing practices, which placed a high value on newspaper journalism and on 'serious' rather than 'popular' journalism. This meant that young journalists ought to ground their practice in the 'serious' business of covering the traditional, formal sources of news, such as the courts, local authorities, and so on. This came as near to 'professionalism' as possible, while retaining the emphasis on craft-type skills, such as shorthand writing. The increasing incursion of more technical processes (from photography, through typography, to television production) into journalism resulted only in their incomplete incorporation. This influenced the separation of news gathering from the various forms of news processing. Journalists may have been unsure about whether they were professionals or craft workers, but, it seems, they definitely did not see themselves as technicians.

The break-up of the consensus

The 'one journalism' model came under severe strain within fifteen years of its inception. The pressures arose from four closely inter-connected factors – internal diversification within journalism; changes in the profile of jour-nalists; developments in education; and government training policy – which contributed towards and underscored changing attitudes in the media. As a result, by the early 1990s the consensus over journalism training had virtu-ally collapsed, and the debate over the nature of the professionalism of journalism was re-opened.

The idea that journalism was a single occupation practised across different media, and that there was one 'learnership' (NCTJ 1975: 9) which could serve all types of journalism, was difficult to sustain. As early as the 1940s, the BBC's news division began training its own broadcast journalists (Miall 1994: 216), and its news traineeships offered a significant alternative, and specialised, entry into journalism from the mid-1960s. A separate periodical training organisation emerged in 1970 and the Joint Committee for the Training of Radio Journalists in 1981 (Stephenson and Mory 1990: 197–8). Even under the umbrella of the NCTJ scheme, the larger provincial news-paper groups, such as TRN and WP, began setting up their own corporate training centres in the late 1960s (Johnston 1996: 1). This fragmentation was almost certainly linked to the significant growth in journalism resulting from the expansion in news provision. Although the figures are not wholly reli-able, in the thirty years up to the mid-1960s the number of journalists increased at an average rate of about 300 a year (Tunstall 1983: 188). Over the next five years the number increased by an average of around 1,000 a year, and, despite a sharp downturn in recruitment from the late 1980s, over the thirty years to the mid-1990s by an average of about 500 a year (Royal Commission 1977: para. 18.4; Bromley 1995a: 1; Corbett 1996: 4). Moreover, as the NCTJ (1975: 41) readily acknowledged, its model was less appropriate, too, for the type of person entering journalism. In 1965, no more than 5 per cent of recruits into provincial newspaper journalism were university graduates: in 1981 the figure was 30 per cent, and in 1988–9 it had reached 53 per cent (Tunstall 1983: 190; NCTJ 1989: 5).

From the outset, the NCTJ approach had been at odds with the model of journalism education adopted by UNESCO and by many other countries, including the USA. This stressed education over training, and journalism as a subject within college liberal arts courses. Graduates sought work as journalists after completing their courses. This did not appeal to employers in the UK, who preferred to recruit their journalists first, and then train them (NCTJ 1975: 41). They relied on a steady supply of school-leavers with, initially, five O-levels, and later one or two A-levels, who chose journalism as an alternative to pursuing further and higher education (Guild of Editors 1995: 3). Such training prioritised the acquisition of skills in the workplace: more educational elements, usually delivered in local colleges, were considered 'supplementary' (NCTJ 1975: 9). The expansion of higher education in the mid-1960s undoubtedly forced changes. Graduate recruitment, which had been the practice at a small number of national newspapers, including *The Times*, *Financial Times* and *The Economist*, expanded, although usually within the NCTJ scheme. In 1965 it was acknowledged that initial training could be conducted outside the workplace on college-based pre-entry courses. There was also a short-lived experiment in providing continuing occupational education at Manchester University, where experienced journalists studied a range of academic subjects one day a week leading to the award of a Certificate in Higher Education (PPITB/NCTJ 1973: 53). Meanwhile, the NCTJ raised £10,000 from the newspaper industry to fund a two-year investigation into the feasibility of starting a full-time pre-entry post-graduate university course in journalism.

Although the council did not pursue the idea, the University of Wales instituted the first post-graduate course in journalism in 1970 at Cardiff (NCTJ 1975: 42; Stephenson and Mory 1990: 197). It was clear that the potential existed for conflict between the training of journalists and the higher education system, which was beginning to offer not only more traditional university places, but also more vocationally-oriented education in the polytechnics. The NCTJ was urged in 1973 to define 'the relationship journalists' training should have with the upper echelon of the technical education system' (PPITB/NCTJ 1973: 19–23).

Changes in higher education reflected government concerns over both what was to be known as 'the skills gap' and rising unemployment. From 1968 the Printing and Publishing Industry Training Board consolidated the training effort, including the NCTJ scheme, in an attempt to spread training itself more widely and more evenly across the sector by spreading the costs similarly (NCTJ 1975: 50–2). After 1979 technical skills were not given priority, and it was assumed that some technical training could be incorporated into higher education, for which State funding was being reduced

(Hutton 1995: 187–91). For example, Department for Employment and Education bursaries for post-graduate journalism students were unilaterally withdrawn in 1994.[5] The introduction of national vocational qualifications (NVQs) and the Modern Apprenticeship scheme in the 1990s suggested the revival of the alternative, workplace-based route into journalism which emphasised occupational competence at the expense of the development of broad intellectual and creative skills (Tulloch 1990: 53–4).

NVQs more closely reflected employers' interests than university courses were likely to (Splichal and Sparks 1994: 36). In the newspaper sector, the Newspaper Society, and not the NCTJ, was made the so-called lead body (Gopsill 1995: 6). NVQs further fragmented journalism training across industry sectors (Bromley 1995a: 138–9). The decline of the 'serious' press, especially as a model for journalism, it has been noted, also weakened the notion of a unitary 'core' to journalism (Sparks 1991). Journalism training was realigned to bring it closer to the various commercial objectives of media corporations (Johnston 1996: 2). TRN and WP led an exodus from the NCTJ in 1989 (Stephenson and Mory 1990: 196). By 1990 training in journalism was 'a patchwork of different types' (Tulloch 1990: 51). One far from exhaustive survey found 30 company schemes, five pre-graduate college courses, 15 undergraduate courses, 30 post-graduate courses, and 15 NVQs with more being developed (Bromley 1995a: 138–9, 144–8).

These developments did not signal a complete break with the past, however. While some newspaper training – for example, NVQs – broke with the 'one journalism' model, the magazine industry reverted and adopted the 'core' skills approach. The distinctions between 'journalists' and photographers were maintained, and despite many complaints about the shortage of school-leaver recruits, graduates still comprised 90% of the candidates selected by editors for training at the former TRN centre (which was acquired by Trinity International in 1996) (Johnston 1996: 4). The NCTJ manuals written by Evans (1972, 1978) continued to be reprinted into the late 1980s, and a new edition of the newspaper reporting manual (Harris and Spark) was published in 1993. Finally, the higher levels of journalism remained disproportionately the preserve of the public school–Oxbridge clique (Delano and Hennington 1996: 14–15).

Nevertheless, perceptions among journalists about their occupation had clearly changed: by the mid-1990s, 51 per cent – more than at any previous time – regarded journalism as a profession, with only 16 per cent seeing it as a craft. A majority believed that they were equal in status to not only 'new' professionals, such as accountants and engineers, but also some of the traditional professionals, such as solicitors (although not barristers). This no doubt reflected in large part the changes in recruitment patterns: a majority of journalists themselves came from professional or managerial backgrounds. Nearly 49 per cent had degrees, but only 40 per cent held an NCTJ qualification. Paradoxically, more than two-thirds of journalists considered that journalism could not actually be organised as a profession, however, and between 50 per cent and 60 per cent were members of the NUJ (Delano and Henningham 1996: 9–10; Corbett 1996: 4–5). Yet these statistics led Delano and Henningham (1996: 20–22) to speculate whether the 'new journalists' of the 1990s were moving inexorably towards becoming regulated professionals. The national organiser of the NUJ argued that a post-entry closed shop, such as that which the union attempted to enforce during the decades of the consensus, and which was directed at improving pay and working conditions, remained of greater practical concern to the majority of journalists (Corbett 1996: 3–4).

It is these developments and this continuing debate which provide the context for the introduction of multi-skilling in journalism from about 1990.

Multi-skilling

As a term, 'multi-skilling' is imprecise.[6] It has been used loosely to describe the dismantling of demarcations between journalists and technicians, writers and camera operators, news gatherers and news processors, and between print, radio and television journalism. It has been categorised as an outcome of the growing convergence of the media, driven by the development of 'new technology', and finding its apotheosis in the journalism behind electronic web sites where text, sound, photography, video, and design are combined to produce a multi-media, interactive product. Stephenson and Mory opined (1990: 25) that 'Technological change, and the associated changes in working practices, are . . serving to blur even those pragmatic distinctions between journalists and non-journalists.' Such multi-skilling is not wholly new, however.

As we have seen, reporters worked also as photographers, and photo-journalism developed as a specific occupational genre from the end of the nineteenth century. It even made its appearance in television, the news agency Worldwide Television News employing journalist–camera operators (*PG*, 5 July 1996). Schlesinger (1987: 157–61) noted the extent to which the boundaries between journalism and some of the technical operations in broadcasting were in practice permeable. The advent of portable tape recorders limited the call for sound recordists in radio reporting. In independent local radio (ILR) in particular from the 1970s it became more common for journalists also to edit their own tape, and for studio control rooms to be dispensed with (Chantler and Harris 1992: 55–65). Even after the creation of a separate television news service, a number of domestic and foreign specialist correspondents continued to work for both radio and TV (Schlesinger 1987: 76). Local newspapers and magazines with small editorial staffs traditionally relied on their journalists having 'a variety of skills'. In many larger newspapers, some journalists both edited and wrote 'copy', as well as laying out pages, especially in specialist departments, such as those covering sport (*UKPG*, 24 January 1994).

This situation was recognised by the NUJ which felt that voluntary multi-skilling agreements with employers merely codified existing practices. The professional/craft regime described above might be seen as prescribing the acceptable limits to multi-skilling. At the same time, technical factors also acted as inhibitors. For instance, the introduction of electronic news gathering (ENG) in television reduced the technical crew initially by only one person, and then to a single operator, but did not obviate the need for a technician (Boyd 1990: 310–13; Yorke 1990: 62). By the early 1990s, however, the versatility of journalists was being associated less with craft/professional ideals than with business objectives, such as encouraging 'flexibility' and creating 'team-based work environment[s]' (Wilby and Conroy 1994: 94; Pritchard *et al.* 1993: no page). 'Multi-skilling', one regional editor said, 'allows newspapers to get closer to their readers' (*UKPG*, 26 December 1994). Both the NUJ and the IoJ began to believe that multi-skilling equated to 'de-skilling', and was predicated on a reduction in employment, poorer working conditions, and lower standards.[7] Journalists facing the introduction of an experiment in multi-skilling at the Brighton *Evening Argus* complained that it would reduce the journalist to 'a Jack-of-all-trades rather than a master of one' (*UKPG*, 30 August 1995). The NUJ's caricature of the journalist of the near future was 'Robohack' (*Journalist*, Sept/October 1993).

Indeed, the introduction of what were probably the first formal, contemporary multi-skilled journalists by the television company Cable News Network (CNN) in America in 1980 was greeted with scepticism from established practitioners. Young recruits to CNN were trained to write scripts, produce, edit tape, operate cameras, and work in control rooms. Their official designation as 'video-journalists' (VJs) was dismissed as masking their pivotal role in permitting CNN to establish itself as a low-cost (and by implication, low-standard) alternative to the existing US TV networks (Parker 1995: 52). Some of the practice spread, however – for example, to the BBC whose Westminster-based journalists began editing tape in 1992. In 1996 CNN founded a new network, CNN Headline News, on the interchangeability of writers and editors working with digitalised equipment. At the same time, the BBC, Granada Television, HTV and Independent Television News (ITN) were developing electronic news production systems (ENPS), which promised to eradicate most technical jobs in news processing (*UKPG*, 20 November 1995; *PG*, 12 July 1996; *Broadcast*, 16 August 1996; Marks 1996).

Digital news rooms also facilitated cross-media working, as the same networked multi-media workstation was used to process visual, audio and textual material. A number of BBC World Service radio journalists were provided with video cameras in 1992, although domestic reporters refused to carry them. Yet, while largely adhering to established working practices in analogue news rooms, many home-based BBC journalists began working simultaneously for both television and radio as bi-media correspondents in 1993 (*UKPG*, 24 May 1993). An increasing number of newspaper journalists were also expected to provide material for radio and television, as a result of greater local cross-media ownership and tie-ins. The managing director of the radio subsidiary of a provincial newspaper group argued:

> I see a future where your journalist goes out carrying a tape recorder and a video camera, records an interview, writes it up for the local paper, cuts the video for a local cable station and cuts a taped interview and report for the local radio station.
>
> (*UKPG*, 1 August 1994).

The development of digital recording equipment, particularly lightweight cameras (Franklin 1996), was expected to lead to the creation of more VJs in television news gathering, doing the work of both camera operators and journalists, and sometimes editing, too (*PG*, 26 April 1996). By the mid-1990s VJs were already at work in at least four ITV companies and the cable station Channel One (*UKPG*, 23 October 1995; 8 January 1996; 27 March 1996; *PG*, 6 September 1996). Among those who saw a synergy between VJs in the field and digital news rooms was the director-general of the BBC, John Birt (*UKPG*, 24 July 1995).

The equivalent practices in print were to equip reporters with automatic cameras, and to group writers, photographers, sub-editors and designers in 'flexible' teams (sometimes called 'pods') (*UKPG*, 13 March 1995; 12 February 1996). The extent to which the roles were interchangeable was perhaps indicated by the fact that the main instigator of these experiments, WP, preferred the term 'multi-functionalism' to multi-skilling (Slattery, 1993: 15). In some instances, it seemed that press photographers and dedicated sub-editors might disappear as distinct categories of editorial workers (Pritchard *et al.* 1993: 16ff; *UKPG*, 12 February 1996). Digitalised news rooms were seen as agents for reducing the distinctions between news gatherers and news processors in print, too (*UKPG*, 23 October 1995; 29 January 1996). Media managements and unions talked almost uniformly about these developments 'expanding journalists' skills' (Austin-Clarke 1993). It proved to be a two-way street, however.

Camera operators, researchers, tape editors and secretaries underwent retraining in journalism, wrote scripts and conducted interviews (*UKPG*, 27 March 1995; 20 November 1995; 8 January 1996). One newspaper, the *Bath Chronicle*, recruited up to 600 amateur correspondents to contribute news on a regular basis. The WP group began running courses in journalism for non-journalists, and the Periodical Publishers' Association proposed a kind of proto-journalism NVQ for secretaries who re-wrote press releases. ITN's declared objective was that each person in the news operation should be able to do the jobs of all the others, and in one instance a camera operator covered a major news story single-handedly, from research to providing the voice-over on his own final edit. A senior figure in provincial journalism claimed that basic journalism did not require any specialised skills, and another that in the electronic media journalists might easily be replaced by librarians (Sands 1996; *PG*, 12 July 1996). Similarly, news processing in many local and regional newspapers had been so routinised that sub-editing departments were known as 'vegetable patches'. More semi-automation and consolidation of newspaper production into large regional centres, each serving a number of titles, threatened to demean the status of news processors even further (*UKPG*, 19 February 1996). It appeared to some that journalism might divide in two – at one level there would be 'top quality reporters engaged on complex and important news gathering', and at another a 'lower tier of editorial assistance [*sic*]' handling routine work (Guild of Editors 1995: 8). Journalists as a whole might be 'an endangered species' (Pavlik 1996: 214–16).

Conclusion

Debate over the state of journalism in the late twentieth century and its likely future in the early part of the twenty-first century involves four inter-related areas – technological change; new business structures; the functions of news; and the coherence of journalism as an occupation (Charon 1996: 142ff). These issues are of central concern to the media organisations, such as the BBC, the provincial press groups, cable television companies, and so on, which have implemented, or plan to implement, multi-skilling. This is often couched (sometimes only accidentally) in terms of the media entering a post-Fordist phase. Many of the characteristics of post-Fordism can be traced in the development of multi-skilling (Goffee and Scase 1995: 83; Webster 1995: 145–53). First, the disempowering of trade unions has made it difficult for the NUJ in particular to influence changes in work practices (Bourne 1993). Second, multi-skilling has been closely associated with the 'downsizing' of editorial departments (Pritchard *et al.* 1993: 24). Third, multi-skilling and the extensive use of part-time, fixed contracts for journalists have clearly coincided (*UKPG*, 16 August 1996). Fourth, the use of technology has been inextricably bound up with multi-skilling. Fifth, factors such as flexibility in employment, more broadly-defined job roles, flatter hierarchies, and an emphasis on transferable skills are inherent in multi-skilling. Finally, much of the drive behind the multi-skilling initiatives can be seen as an attempt by media organisations to become more responsive to consumer demands (Hall 1996). This offers the potential for the enskilling of journalists (Scarborough and Corbett 1992: 103–9), and Austin-Clarke (1993) has argued that journalists are given 'more power and responsibility . . enhancing their job prospects'.

Yet it is also apparent that many of the factors described here existed *before* the significant introduction of multi-skilling in the British media in the early 1990s; the most obvious examples being the changes in employment patterns associated with the introduction of 'new technology' in the newspaper sector, and with the development of ILR, both of which date from the later 1970s. Other structural changes in the media industries, such as the steep decline in provincial evening newspaper sales over twenty-five years, have acted as motors for change in workplace practices (Guild of Editors 1996: 2). As the NUJ has suggested, this may indicate that multi-skilling is in fact a continuation of the process of de-skilling which can be traced back at least to the industrial organisation of the press in the late nineteenth century (Braverman 1974).

This may have been reflected in the policies of the Thatcher governments of 1979–90 of moving the training of journalists far more than it had done previously into higher education (Phillips and Gaber 1996). Many employers simply withdrew from training completely, and the overall investment of the media industries in training declined. In the mid-1990s, employers attempted to recapture the initiative on training. They began publicly attacking the education of journalists provided by colleges and universities, and putting their support behind the workplace-based alternative of NVQs and Modern Apprenticeships (*UKPG*, 13 March 1995; *PG*, 14 June 1996). The connection with work practices seems clear. The major complaint put forward by employers was that there was no guarantee that university courses concentrated on 'the basics' of shorthand, use of English, law, local government, court reporting, interviewing, and so on (Cole 1996: 46–7). Secondly, it was argued that journalism recruitment patterns had been unfavourably altered: the products of university education were ' too white, too middle-class, too rich and too south-east' (Bromley 1995a: 21).

This amounted to an attempt to turn back the clock and selectively reassert the consensus which had existed under the NCTJ from 1952 until the 1970s: significantly, the attacks were led by provincial newspaper employers, who had initially dominated the NCTJ (*UKPG*, 13 March 1995). It also reflected the intensified, and complex, bifurcation of journalism (Tunstall 1996: 136). Differentials, in areas such as pay, conditions and expectations, were widening. Many journalists on local and provincial newspapers worked in factory-like conditions (Pritchard *et al.* 1993: 21). At the start of their careers their salaries were likely to be only a half of what a comparable journalist on a local radio station was paid, and a third of what a contemporary earned in the national media (Cole 1996: 45; Bromley 1995a: 168). In such cases, multi-skilling required only reactive skills (Scarborough and Corbett 1992: 103–9; Phillips and Gaber, 1996: 65). Moreover, 'vegetable patch' journalists were likely to have a low subjective assessment of their own skills.

On the other hand, the evidence which emerged from the interviews conducted for this chapter suggested that other media organisations, especially in broadcasting, expected developments such as multi-skilling to call for a proactive response from journalists, and that broadcasters had a high subjective assessment of their skills. In the tapeless, multi-skilled television news rooms of the early twenty-first century, 'journalists will rule', one interviewee argued, and were already taking over many of the functions of technicians.

345

Multi-skilling can be expected to deskill some journalists, but it will also upskill others. In such circumstances the preservation of a unified occupation of journalism may depend on the extent to which journalists share an autonomous occupational ideology (Scarborough and Corbett 1992: 103–9). During the period of consensus, the NUJ represented up to 90 per cent of journalists (Tunstall 1996: 139–45), more or less successfully bringing together news gatherers and news processors, writers and photographers. Nevertheless, the prevailing core ideology of the NUJ (and journalism in general) remained that of 'press freedom', which was indistinguishable from that of media owners (Elliott, 1978: 189–91). It was also inconsistent with the union's own code of professional practice which permitted sanctions to be imposed on defaulting journalists. When the ideals of 'freedom of expression' came into direct conflict with professional discipline in the 1980s, it was the latter which gave way (Corbett, 1996: 3–4). Tracing a parallel 'era of professionalisation' in US journalism, Daniel Hallin (1996: 244–5) suggested that the apparent triumph of an autonomous journalistic ethic was temporary, illusory and anomalous.

In the absence of such an ethic, multi-skilling contains the potential for the final fragmentation of journalism, enskilling some as 'entrepreneurial editors' (Tunstall, 1996: 116), but deskilling others to the status of machine hands and extensions of the computer. In between, there may develop several levels of employment as media technicians-with-words (and pictures) (Tunstall 1996: 136). None, however, will be journalists as such.

Notes

1   A version of this chapter was presented in the form of a report, 'Multi-skilling in journalism', to the European Journalism Training Association – British and Irish Section in February 1995. I am grateful to various individual members of EJTA–BIS for their comments, and in particular to Hugh Stephenson.

2   A common theme among interviewees consulted for this study (see notes 4 and 6 below).

3   Hereafter, *UKPG*. The *UK Press Gazette* changed title to *Press Gazette* (*PG* here) in March 1996.

4   Author's own experiences as a regional newspaper journalist, 1965–9 and 1972–87; and interviews conducted between 5 and 13 January 1995 with Colin Bourne (NUJ), Keith Elliott (PMA Training), Rodney Bennett-England (IoJ/NCTJ); Don Mildenhall (Guild of Editors/NCTJ), Bob Norris (NUJ) and Peter Sands (WP).

5   Personal experience of the author. Funding aid for about 13 students on City University's post-graduate diploma course in Newspaper Journalism was withdrawn.

6   This section is based, unless otherwise indicated, on interviews conducted on 12 and 16 January and on 17 April 1995 and in May 1996 with Martin

Hurd (ITN), Ivor Yorke and Neil Everton (both formerly BBC); on interviews conducted between March and August 1996 with a number of journalists with experience of working at CNN and Channel 1, but who wished to remain anonymous; and on the interviews listed in note 4.

7   These fears were expressed in a resolution adopted by the annual delegate meeting of the NUJ in April 1993, which commits the union to supporting members who are resisting attempts to introduce multi-skilling in the workplace.

References

Austin-Clarke, P. (1993) 'Reshaping the *T&A*: a radical revolution', *Newspaper Focus* (December): 12–13.

Bourne, C. (1993) 'Sold down the river', *Journalist* (September–October): 13.

Boyd, A. (1990) *Broadcast Journalism: Techniques of Radio and TV News* (2nd edn), Oxford: Heinemann.

Braverman, H. (1974) *Labor and Monopoly Capital,* New York: Monthly Review Press.

Bromley, M. (1995a) *Media Studies: An Introduction to Journalism*, London: Hodder & Stoughton.

Bromley, M. (1995b) 'From conciliation to confrontation: industrial relations, government and the Fourth Estate, 1896–1986', in A. O'Day (ed.) *Government and Institutions in the post-1832 United Kingdom*, Lampeter: Edwin Mellen, 357–85.

Bundock, C.J. (1957) *The National Union of Journalists: A Jubilee History, 1907–1957*, Oxford: NUJ.

Chantler, P. and Harris, S. (1992) *Local Radio Journalism*, Oxford: Focal Press.

Charon, J.M. (1996) 'Journalism mutations', in A. Agostini (ed.) *New Media, New Journalism*, Maastricht: European Journalism Training Association, 160–71.

Cheadle, E.W. (1952) 'Picture editing', *Kemsley Manual of Journalism* (2nd edn), London: Cassell, 79–96.

Cole, P. (1996) 'Are journalists born – or trained?', *British Journalism Review* 7(2): 42–8.

Corbett, B. (1996) 'Could the shop be closed again?', paper delivered to conference *Turning 21: Journalists for the New Century*, London Institute (April).

Cox, G. (1996) 'The editor who made love – and great news', *British Journalism Review* 7(3): 16–24.

Crisell, A. (1995) *Understanding Radio* (2nd edn), London: Routledge.

Dahlgren, P. (1992) 'Introduction', in P. Dahlgren and C. Sparks (eds) *Journalism and Popular Culture*, London: Sage.

Davenport, A. (1991) *The History of Photography: An Overview*, Oxford: Focal Press.

Delano, A. and Henningham, J. (1996) *The News Breed: British Journalists in the 1990s*, London: London Institute.

Dodge, J. and Viner, G. (eds) (1963) *The Practice of Journalism* London: Heinemann.

Drawbell, J. (1965) 'The press and class', *Twentieth Century* (Spring).

Elliott, P. (1978) 'Professional ideology and organisational change: the journalist since 1800', in G. Boyce, J. Curran and P. Wingate (eds) *Newspaper History: From the 17th Century to the Present Day*, London: Constable, 172–91.

Engel, M. (1996) *Tickle the Public: One Hundred Years of the Popular Press*, London: Gollancz.

Evans, H. (1972) *Newsman's English*, London: Heinemann.

Evans, H. (1978) *Pictures on a Page: Photo-journalism, Graphics and Picture Editing*, London: Heinemann.

Franklin, C. (1996) 'The news gatherers' technology war', *Combroad* 110 (March): 11.

Goffee, R. and Scase, R. (1995) *Corporate Realities: The Dynamics of Large and Small Organisations*, London: Routledge.

Gopsill, T. (1995) 'What about the workers?', paper delivered to the NUJ conference *Media v. the People*, London (March 18).

Griffiths, D. (ed.) (1992) *The Encyclopedia of the British Press, 1492–1992*, Basingstoke: Macmillan.

Grose, R. (1989) *The 'Sun'-sation: Behind the Scenes of Britain's Best-selling Newspaper*, London: Angus & Robertson.

Gross, J. (1991) *The Rise and Fall of the Man of Letters: English Literary Life since 1800*, Harmondsworth: Penguin.

Guild of Editors (1995) *Survey of Editorial Training Needs*, London: Guild of Editors.

Guild of Editors (1996) *Tomorrow's Journalist: A 'Green Paper' on Training*, London: Guild of Editors.

Hall, T. (1996) 'BBC News – glimpsing the future' (BBC News and Current Affairs Publicity), London: BBC.

Hallin, D.C. (1996) 'Commercialism and professionalism in the American news media', in J. Curran and M. Gurevitch (eds) *Mass Media and Society*, London: Edward Arnold, 243–62.

Hammond, R. (1995) 'You ain't seen nothin' yet', *UK Press Gazette* 30 Years Anniversary supplement (27 November): 37.

Hardt, H. and Brennan, B. (eds) (1995) *Newsworkers: Toward a History of the Rank and File*, Minneapolis: University of Minnesota Press.

Harris, G. and Spark, D. (1993) *Practical Newspaper Reporting* (2nd edn), Oxford: Focal Press.

Harrison, N.K. (1963) 'Press photography', in J. Dodge and G. Viner (eds) *The Practice of Journalism*, London: Heinemann, 183–93.

Hayward, D. (1995) 'Quiet revolution', *UK Press Gazette* 30 Years Anniversary supplement (27 November) 22.

Hunter, F. (1996) 'Teenage girls as journalism students at London University, 1919–39', paper delivered to the Institute of Contemporary British History conference *A Century of the Popular Press*, University of London (9–10 September).

Hutton, W. (1995) *The State We're In*, London: Jonathan Cape.

Institute of Journalists (1932) *Journalism – by Some Masters of the Craft: A Series of Lectures on the Technique of Modern Journalism Delivered under the Auspices of the Institute of Journalists*, London: Pitman.

Jameson, D. (1990) *Last of the Hot Metal Men: From Fleet Street to Show Biz*, London: Ebury Press.

Johnston, T. (1996) 'Trinity editorial training', paper delivered to conference *Turning 21: Journalists for the New Century*, London Institute (April).

Kee, R. (1989) *The Picture Post Album*, London: Barrie & Jenkins.

Keeble, R. (1994) *The Newspapers Handbook*, London: Routledge.

Keene, M. (1993) *Practical Photo-journalism: A Professional Guide*, Oxford: Focal Press.

Kemsley Manual of Journalism (1952 edn) London: Cassell.

Lee, A. (1978) 'The structure, ownership and control of the press, 1855–1914', in G. Boyce, J. Curran and P. Wingate (eds) *Newspaper History: From the 17th Century to the Present Day*, London: Constable, 117–29.

MacGregor, B. (1995) 'Our wanton use of the technology: television news gathering in the age of the satellite', *Convergence* 1(1): 80–93.

Mansfield, F.J. (1943) *Gentlemen, the Press! Chronicles of a Crusade*, London: W.H. Allen.

Marks, N. (1996) 'How BBC's digital news will change journalism', *UK Press Gazette* (26 February): 17.

Miall, L. (1994) *Inside the BBC: British Broadcasting Characters*, London: Weidenfeld & Nicolson.

Morrison, D.E. and Tumber, H. (1988) *Journalists at War: The Dynamics of News Reporting during the Falklands Conflict*, London: Sage.

National Council for the Training of Journalists (1975) *Training in Journalism*, Epping: NCTJ.

National Council for the Training of Journalists (1989) *How Journalists are Trained*, Epping: NCTJ..

Parker, R. (1995) *Mixed Signals: The Prospects for Global Television News*, New York: Twentieth Century Fund Press.

Pavlik, J.V. (1996) *New Media Technology: Cultural and Commercial Perspectives*, Needham Heights, MA: Allyn & Bacon.

Perkin, H. (1990) *The Rise of Professional Society: England since 1890* (pbk edn), London: Routledge.

Phillips, A. and Gaber, I. (1996) 'The case for media degrees', *British Journalism Review* 7(3): 62–5.

Political and Economic Planning (1938) *The British Press*, London, PEP.

Printing and Publishing Industry Training Board and National Council for the Training of Journalists (1973) *The Training of Regional Newspaper Journalists*.

Pritchard, C., Kelly, G. and Ward, M. (1993) *The Changing Vision*, Preston: Lancashire Business School.

Randall, M. (1988) *The Funny Side of the Street*, London: Bloomsbury.

Rosenblum, M. (1993) *Who Stole the News?* New York: John Wiley.

Royal Commission on the Press (1949) *Report*, Cmnd 7700, London: HMSO.

Royal Commission on the Press (1977) *Report*, Cmnd 6810, London: HMSO.

Sands, P. (1996) 'A training task facing editors', *UK Press Gazette* (8 January): 16.

Scarbrough, H. and Corbett, J.M. (1992) *Technology and Organization: Power, Meaning, Design*, London: Routledge.

Schlesinger, P. (1987) *Putting 'Reality' Together: BBC News* (pbk edn), London: Methuen.

Seymour-Ure, C. (1991) *The British Press and Broadcasting Since 1945*, Oxford: Blackwell.

Slattery, J. (1993) 'Mission: imperative', *UK Press Gazette* (18 October): 15, 17.

Smith, W.H. (1948) 'The growth of pictures in the press', *The Press, 1898–1948*, London: Newspaper World, 114–15.

Sparks, C. (1991) 'Goodbye, Hildy Johnson: the vanishing "serious press"', in P. Dahlgren and C. Sparks (eds) *Communication and Citizenship*, London: Routledge: 58–74.

Splichal, S. and Sparks, C. (1994) *Journalists for the 21st Century*, Norwood, NJ: Ablex.

Stephenson, H. and Mory, P. (1990) *Journalism Training in Europe*, Brussels: European Commission.

Thomson Regional Newspapers (1990) *The Key*.

Tulloch, J. (1990) 'The United Kingdom', in K. Nordenstreng (ed.) *Reports on Journalism Education in Europe*, Tampere: University of Tampere, 47–54.

Tunstall, J. (1977) '"Editorial sovereignty" in the British press', *Studies on the Press*, London: HMSO, 249–341.

Tunstall, J. (1983) *The Media in Britain*, London: Constable.

Tunstall, J. (1993) *Television Producers*, London: Routledge.

Tunstall, J. (1996) *Newspaper Power: The New National Press in Britain*, Oxford: Clarendon Press.

Webster, F. (1995) *Theories of the Information Society*, London: Routledge.

Wilby, P. and Conroy, A. (1994) *The Radio Handbook*, London: Routledge.

Williams, V. (1991) *The Other Observers: Women Photographers in Britain, 1900 to the Present* (2nd edn), London: Virago.

Wilson, J. (1995) 'Survival!', *UK Press Gazette* 30 Years Anniversay supplement: (27 November) 20.

Worcester, R.M. (1991) 'Who buys what – for why?', *British Journalism Review* 2(4): 46–52.

Worcester, R.M. (1994) 'Demographies and values: what the British public read and what they think about their newspapers', paper delivered to the first Conference on the Press, City University, London (5 February).

Yorke, I. (1990) *Basic TV Reporting*, Oxford: Focal Press.

Chapter 28

Sally Bailey and Granville Williams

MEMOIRS ARE MADE OF THIS
Journalists' memoirs in the United Kingdom, 1945–95

ROBERT EDWARDS ENDS HIS MEMOIR, *Goodbye Fleet Street*, in the pivotal year 1985. Effectively, in January 1986, with the move to Wapping of the News International titles – *The Sun*, *News of the World*, *The Times* and *The Sunday Times* – the foundations of Fleet Street were knocked away in a process which continued through to 1988 with the exodus of the Associated Newspapers group (Lord Rothermere's *Daily Mail*, *Mail on Sunday* and *Evening Standard*) from the Carmelite Street area. The last, large scale manufacturing industry left in inner London was decanted to various sites in Battersea, Kensington and the Docklands.

Fleet Street disappeared, destroyed by a combination of soaring site values (a consequence of the so-called Big Bang in the City of London), the application of new technology in newspaper design and production, and the use by newspaper groups of anti-trade union legislation, introduced by the Conservative government, to emasculate trade union rights and recognition amongst print workers and journalists on national newspapers.

Robert Edwards provides one insight and perspective into Fleet Street, and the power and privileges generated by an enormously profitable industry in the period before the great change. He edited *Tribune* from 1951 to 1954 and, in a move which paralleled one earlier by the Labour politician Michael Foot, he went to work for Beaverbrook on the *Evening Standard*. He became editor of the *Daily Express* (twice), edited the *People* from 1966 to 1972 and edited the *Sunday Mirror* for thirteen years. He was there, too, for the take-over of the Mirror group by Robert Maxwell, and the proprietor's grandiose personal projection in his papers' columns. *Goodbye Fleet Street* is one of a number of memoirs forming part of an extensive collection of material written by reporters and editors about their early lives, their entry into journalism, often on local and regional newspapers, and the transition to work in Fleet Street (Edwards 1988).[1]

Many of these memoirs are amusing and informative about all sorts of Fleet Street personalities, proprietors and practices. Keith Waterhouse in *Streets Ahead* lovingly describes Fleet Street in the early 1950s, when he was taken on by the Features Editor of the *Daily Mirror*. In a lyrical passage, introduced by an obligatory reference to Sir Philip Gibbs' novel *The Street of Adventure*, which seemed to inspire a generation of young readers to work in newspapers, he describes the titles, terrain and structures which sustained the vibrant and expanding national newspaper and publishing industry based in and around Fleet Street. Later he gives an enthusiastic account of the Fleet Street drinking establishments, the pubs used by journalists from different papers, and the nuances of pub etiquette. All of this meticulously recalled detail conveys a vivid sense of the social life and day-to-day activities of journalists working in Fleet Street, and also helps us to place the author's career in the social and cultural changes which he lived through and wrote about to such effect (Waterhouse 1995: 32–34, 38–40).

Obviously many of the memoirs are uneven in quality, not only in terms of content and style, but also because of the motive behind their creation. In *The Universal Journalist* David Randall dismisses in particular 'editors' memoirs [which] seem often to be written to settle old scores, drop names or justify expenses' (Randall 1996: 198). Other memoirs explore the more seedy aspects of tabloid journalism, with the authors going into great detail about how they got a scoop or exposed crime and corruption.

This chapter analyses some of the distinctive features of these memoirs and their value for students of journalism, and suggests some of the limits which they have as a source of evidence, insight and information on the development and transformation of the newspaper industry since 1945. In particular, it argues that on some of the crucial issues of proprietorial intervention, and the pressures on journalists to work within the parameters set by the newspaper owners and editors, with rare exceptions most of these memoirs contain very little analysis or information, being mainly descriptive, opinionative or anecdotal. Even these are not without value, however, and, in much the same way as films such as *Ace in the Hole* with Kirk Douglas as the ruthless reporter can give us powerful images, information and insights into the workings of journalism, journalists' memoirs have been an underused source in helping us to understand some of the dilemmas, pressures and practices facing journalists in their work (French and Rossell 1991).[2]

To place the memoirs in some kind of perspective in terms of the changes in Fleet Street, including the varying fortunes of different titles and the issues influencing the industry, we start with a short summary of the key factors impinging on the working lives of journalists. Jeremy Tunstall has a useful sub-division of the fifty-odd years under review from the end of the Second World War in his *Newspaper Power* where he identifies different phases, beginning with the period 1945–55, which was relatively quiet for two reasons (Tunstall 1996: 31–5).

Newsprint rationing was eased slightly in 1949 but was not ended completely until 1956. It distorted changes in the popularity of newspapers in the immediate post-war years because paper-rationing was based on pre-war circulation figures. Rationing also meant that editions of newspapers were limited in terms of the number of pages they could print, and consequently the amount of advertising they could carry. Newsprint prices also rose remorselessly: in 1945 it was costing £25 a tonne, ten years later the price had more than doubled to £58. By 1977 it was costing £250 a tonne, £450 in 1995 and £520 a tonne in 1996. Also, seen from the perspective of the increasingly cluttered multi-channelled media world of the late 1990s, it was a period of relative stability with broadcasting consisting of the two BBC radio channels, the Home and Light programmes, a fledgling BBC television, and, for those who could twiddle with the radio tuning dial, Radio Luxembourg.

Newspapers were widely read, and people often purchased more than one title. Circulation, compared with figures for 1996, shows dramatic differences. At the end of 1949 the *News of the World* sold seven million copies, the *Sunday Pictorial* five million; in 1950 the *Daily Express* had the largest daily readership (4.2 million) but by June 1954 the *Daily Mirror* had passed the five million mark and could boast that it was the newspaper with the biggest daily sale in the world.

In the years 1955–60 there was frantic competition between press and television as ITV was launched in 1955 (indeed, in the lobby against commercial television, newspaper owners were heavily involved because of the perceived threat to advertising revenue). Newspapers which were struggling in the circulation wars of the 1930s now found the same problems re-emerging. Papers with high circulations but without reasonably affluent readers were squeezed as commercial television became an alternative outlet to catch the same people. Also, as papers started getting bigger, the habit of buying more than one paper began to weaken. This was also the period which saw the demise of the liberal *News Chronicle* (circulation 1.2 million a day) and its sister London evening paper, the *Star*, which were sold to the second Viscount Rothermere, who then killed them off to reduce competition for his own *Daily Mail* and *Evening News*. Sunday papers also closed – the *Sunday Chronicle* (1955), the *Sunday Graphic* (1960), and the *Sunday Dispatch* (1961).

The 1960s are identified by Tunstall as the 'golden years' when the Press Council had the support of two leading newspaper employers, Cecil King and Lord Thomson. Cecil King, chairman of Mirror Group Newspapers since 1951, played a key role in building the sales and power of the Group. In December 1958 the Mirror Group acquired Amalgamated Press, 'the largest periodical and specialist publishing house in the world, consisting of 42 weeklies, 27 monthlies and 20 annuals', as *Time and Tide* described it. In March

1961 they also took over Odhams, whose titles included the *Sunday People* and the *Daily Herald*. This powerful new grouping was renamed the International Publishing Corporation (IPC) in 1963. The other key change in newspaper ownership was the purchase of the Kemsley newspapers by the Canadian Roy (later Lord) Thomson, which created an industrial group spanning a stake in Scottish commercial television, the *Scotsman*, travel interests, as well as *The Sunday Times*, *Empire News*, *Sunday Graphic* and a string of provincial local and regional newspapers. He also added *The Times* to his newspaper titles in 1966.

The support of these two figures gave the Press Council credibility in a period when papers avoided sensationalist excesses, in stark contrast with later years. The Press Council, established in July 1953 at the instigation of the 1947–49 Royal Commission on the Press, was criticised by the second Royal Commission on the Press, chaired from 1961 to 1962 by Lord Shawcross, for failing to engage in the wide range of activities envisaged by the previous Royal Commission, including monitoring issues of ownership, monopoly and journalist training. From 1964 to 1969 the Press Council, chaired by Lord Devlin, had widespread support and made a number of 'Declarations of Principle' including one in 1965 on chequebook journalism. It was also a time when ITV, in the wake of the Pilkington Report, eschewed its more populist programming and moved towards the establishment of the BBC/ITV duopoly.

This relatively tranquil period for the UK press came to an end with the acquisition by Rupert Murdoch in 1969 of the *News of the World* and *The Sun*, which ushered in a new competitive era, with the brash tabloid *Sun* under Larry Lamb's editorship challenging the *Daily Mirror*, and the *Daily Mail* absorbing the *Daily Sketch* and being launched under its new editor David English in direct, and successful, competition with the middle-market *Daily Express*. These changes occurred in 1969–71, and were followed by three other dramatic phases of intense competition, beginning with the period 1979–81 when the *Daily Star*, which introduced bingo, was launched to compete with the *Sun* and *Mirror*. Also, Rupert Murdoch acquired *The Times* and *Sunday Times* from Lord Thomson, and quickly set out to expand the already profitable *Sunday Times*, taking readers from the struggling *Observer*.

The third competitive phase, 1986–88, was the move to Wapping and the end of the national newspaper industry in Fleet Street. This move, which included the introduction of new printing technology, and journalists working to computer screens in brightly lit, open-plan environments in stark contrast from those in Fleet Street, also meant the end of the complex of pubs, clubs, restaurants and other networks which sustained the romantic aura of Fleet Street which Philip Gibbs and many other journalists evoked in memoirs and novels over the decades. Newspaper groups cut costs and boosted profits, and increased the size of the papers substantially, with specialist sections on finance, lifestyle, culture, and much more. There were brave predictions that the post-Wapping world of national newspapers would see a wide range of new titles flourish, but amongst the welter of new launches only *The Independent* and *Independent on Sunday* survived as part of Mirror Group Newspapers, with *Today*, which was launched in March 1986 by Eddie Shah and closed by Rupert Murdoch's News International in November 1995 as newsprint costs rose dramatically.

Another phase of intense competition centred on the use of savage price cutting to weaken and drive out rival titles. *The Sun* cut its price from 25 to 20 pence, to eat into the circulation of the *Mirror* and *Star*. In 1993 *The Times* reduced its price from 45 to 30 pence − its targets were the *Daily Telegraph* and *The Independent* − and in 1996 it cut the price of its Monday edition to 10 pence.

Amidst all of these changes, the status, confidence and working lives of journalists were inevitably drastically affected. If nothing else, the migration of journalists to News International's fortress at Wapping, with its razor wire, security passes and CCTV, symbolised a sense of the beleaguered position in which many journalists felt that they were placed. Although January 1996 was the tenth anniversary of Wapping, we will have to wait for the book-length memoirs that cover this period in any detail, but the pre-Wapping period provides us with a rich resource from which to gain insights into the working lives of journalists and the pressures of the Fleet Street newspaper world.

Fleet Street remembered: 1945–85

Point of Departure by James Cameron provides a useful introduction to the early post-war journalistic world. Cameron started his journalistic career in Manchester in the late 1920s on a Thomson publication, *Weekly News*. He moved to Dundee and Glasgow, started work for the *Scottish Daily Express* and then moved to London to work on the *Daily Express*, becoming an international reporter covering events such as the 1946 US Bikini A Bomb tests. Incidentally, the *Daily Express* at this time was selling more than 4.5 million copies a day − in Cameron's words, 'the highest circulation newspaper on the face of the earth, God help us' − and had a network of eighteen foreign correspondents, the envy of Fleet Street. In 1996 the *Express* had just two staff reporters in New York, plus ten super-stringers who provided a daily page of world news which mainly consists of gossipy and insubstantial reports of murder, royal visits and off-beat stories (Cameron 1967; Leapman 1996).

There is a section in *Point of Departure* where Cameron reflected on his journalistic work at this time. He realised that in reporting on the various events, 'my relationship with the newspaper could be likened only to that of a very remote and insignificant curate to the Holy See; I accepted their authority, and paid no attention at all to their doctrine . . . I wrote copiously and enthusiastically on all the themes that my employers held in scant regard.' He wrote with clear sympathy, for example, about the lengthy process leading to India's independence, and reflected in his writing his friendship and affection for Jawaharal Nehru, whereas the *Express* proprietor, Lord Beaverbrook, was opposed to Indian independence, had a strong dislike for Nehru, and used his papers to advance his old protectionist and imperialist policies.

Cameron commented, 'I cannot remember how often I have been challenged, and especially in America, for disregarding the fundamental tenet of honest journalism, which is objectivity.' He considered the notion of 'objectivity' meaningless and impossible in certain circumstances, and in a key passage argues:

> I still do not see how a reporter attempting to define a situation involving some sort of ethical conflict can do it with sufficient demonstrable neutrality to fulfil some arbitrary concept of 'objectivity'. It never occurred to me, in such a situation, to be other than subjective, and as obviously as I could manage to be. I may not always have been satisfactorily balanced; I always tended to argue that objectivity was of less importance than the truth, and that the reporter whose technique was informed by no opinion lacked a very serious dimension. It can easily be misrepresented. Yet as I see it – and it seems to me the simplest of disciplines – the journalist is obliged to present his attitude as vigorously and persuasively as he can, insisting that it *is* his attitude, to be examined and criticized in the light of every contrary argument, which he need not accept, but must reveal.
>
> (Cameron 1967: 71–72)

But in 1950 Cameron moved back to London, and to what he described as 'the rough-and-tumble of the English post-war newspaper scene' where he was soon embroiled in two dramatic issues which challenged his notion of journalistic independence. Lord Beaverbrook's press empire – the *Daily Express*, *Sunday Express* and *Evening Standard* – was at the height of its power, and his opposition to the Labour government was clearly stamped on the political stance of his papers. In the spring of 1950 the Labour government appointed John Strachey the Secretary of State for War, but this coincided with the conviction of Klaus Fuchs, the German-born Communist atomic physicist who was sentenced as a Soviet spy. The *Evening Standard* linked the stories and carried the headline on 2 March 1950, 'FUCHS AND STRACHEY: A GREAT NEW CRISIS. War Minister Has Never Disowned Communism.'

The association of these two events shocked Cameron because the 'evidence' in the item was two quotations from Strachey's books which he had written fifteen years before, expressing a sympathy for Soviet communism, and which he had long since repudiated. It forced Cameron to consider his position, and when the *Express* also appeared with editorial support and endorsement for the *Standard*'s attitude, he wrote to the *Express* editor, Arthur

Christiansen, asking to be released at once from his position as chief foreign correspondent. A subsequent letter to *The Times* on 11 March 1950, in which he explained his resignation, generated a burst of publicity and public meetings.

Cameron describes his action as part of the 'minutiae of Fleet Street history' but it does serve as a useful benchmark from which to measure and judge future blatant political distortions by newspapers, and the response by journalists to them. In his letter to *The Times* Cameron argued that the particular incident was of less importance than the longer term implications of the technique used against Strachey: 'we have now set the precedent for the purge-by-Press, which could end at last only in a race of people talking behind their hands, knowing that the words that they said yesterday, in a very different world mood, are the words they may swing for tomorrow.' He also wondered 'whether the best judge of political reliability is an industry whose own caprices of principle and accommodations of policy have seldom been marked over the years by a rigid ethical consistency'. These are remarkably prescient comments, when we consider the techniques used increasingly since 1979 by partisan newspapers seeking to discredit political opponents by trawling through their utterances of years before.[3]

In his memoirs, with the elapse of sixteen years 'which have seen so much worse, so much more awful and meaningful', Cameron thought his action pretentious; that it was a professional objection, and that if the *Daily Herald* had used the same tactics on Eden or Churchill he would have objected just as strongly and on the same grounds. Also, he thought it hardly reasonable to 'put the exclusive responsibility on the management, since however rotten their policy it could not be expressed in print without the active co-operation of journalists, and while they were prepared to co-operate in this way, reserving their protests to mutual commiseration later in the bar, then quite clearly this dismal state of affairs could go on forever.'

If this incident focused strongly on the issue of journalistic ethics, Cameron was soon embroiled in another which sharply raised the issues of proprietorial power and censorship. Shortly after he left the *Express* he was offered a job as staff writer on *Picture Post* by the editor Tom Hopkinson and was off to Korea to report the war with photographer Bert Hardy.

Cameron's reports for the magazine – particularly the record of General MacArthur's landing at Inchon published in *Picture Post*, 7 October 1950 – were strong pieces and Hardy's photos gave added impact. Still following his belief in the journalist's role as the exposer of the unpalatable and unjust, Cameron filed a report on the brutal treatment meted out to North Korean prisoners of war and the excesses of the Synghman Rhee regime in South Korea. *Picture Post* editor, Tom Hopkinson, has an account of this incident in his own memoirs, *Of This Our Time: A Journalist's Story, 1905–1950*. The proprietor of Hulton Press, Edward Hulton, had during the war years, and until eighteen months or so into the post-1945 Labour government, supported the general direction that the magazine took, with its emphasis on reform and broad support for Labour. It was also successful; sales in December 1943 were 950,000 and increased to over 1,422,000 in September 1949. But by 1950, whilst *Picture Post* remained neutral in the February general election, Edward Hulton wrote in his own personal column the reasons why he would vote Conservative. Tom Hopkinson found a gap opening up between his and the proprietor's views, and he was bombarded with complaints from Hulton and the top management about the magazine being 'too left-wing'. He was advised to study the popular weeklies, *Weekend* and *Reveille*, and to make the magazine more 'bright' and entertaining (Hopkinson 1982: 282–9).[4]

The crunch came for Hopkinson over Cameron's article and the accompanying Bert Hardy photographs. Cameron described how it 'had been written with the best restraint and care of which I was capable; I had done my best to drain it of emotion, and it was documented in detail. Since even the most arid words can be pejorative in such situations, I had made sure that they were substantiated by a considerable file of photographs.' But it was too much for the proprietor, who prevented publication of the feature, and sacked Hopkinson. The Communist Party paper, the *Daily Worker,* got hold of the story and printed it and another major furore engulfed Cameron in debates about proprietorial censorship.

Cameron's report, and the subsequent controversy it generated, also raised issues which remain relevant today about how journalists should report issues which involve criticism of 'our side' in military conflicts. During both the Falklands and the Gulf wars there were tensions between the journalists who were happy to accept restrictions on reporting in order to get access to the war arena and those, such as Robert Fisk of the *Independent*, covering the Gulf War, who would not accept military restrictions when filing reports.

Cameron's account of the 'sad scuttling of a decent newspaper', the *News Chronicle*, a paper for which he worked as an international correspondent until shortly before its demise, raised again an issue which was to come to the fore more and more in the ruthlessly combative world of newspaper competition and proprietorial power. The paper's unbroken line of descent, over nearly 115 years from its original title as the *Daily News*, came to an end in October 1960. Cameron described the paper as 'at least the most worthy amongst the papers of the day, standing out in a fairly shoddy company' and the way in which it closed symbolized for him 'the melancholy condition of the British press, in which a simple and secret financial deal between two proprietors, Lawrence Cadbury and Lord Rothermere, could bring about literally overnight the elimination of something on which a million and a quarter people had come to rely.' He was withering in his comments on Cadbury's statement to the effect that in his view the *News Chronicle* and the *Daily Mail* 'had so much in common in the integrity of their reporting and honesty of outlook'. Cameron wrote, 'Thus was blessed the absorption of a liberal and radical paper which had taken issue against Franco and Hitler and Suez by a paper which had reconciled the Nazis and sustained every cause the old guard of the *News Chronicle* had opposed.' In an obituary piece, written pointedly for the *West London Press* because Cameron 'was damned if I was going to be paid by its rich competitors to write a wreath for its funeral', he raised the key issues about diversity and pluralism in the press which have become so pressing in the late twentieth century.

> Not only has a key vehicle of public opinion been removed, and a quality of views that may not find any other means of expression, but by its removal the things for which it tried to stand are undermined. Here is the most insoluble problem of what we rather fulsomely call the 'Free Press':
>
> How is it possible to equate the commercial success that is indispensable to a liberated newspaper with the business interests which will always encroach upon that liberty?

And on the issue of choice he asked where the million-odd readers would go now:

> The creeping block-ownership of the industry still leaves them some choice – but not much, and not for long.
>
> (Cameron 1967: 275–83)[5]

There is much more in *Point of Departure* which is of value to students of journalism – including Cameron's involvement in the early years of CND, and marvellous accounts of his various international forays. Most importantly, it is a book which helps us to gain a sense of perspective, and comparison, on debates about the roles and responsibilities of journalists, and the various pressures they face, which were to emerge more strongly later in the century, and how they responded to them. One reason for the value of the book's insights into early post-war journalism is Cameron's own rugged independence as a witness (*Witness* was the title of his 1966 book on Vietnam). He wasn't wedded to carving out some great career as a newspaper editor, and he remained remarkably determined, after the 'cheapjack death' of the *News Chronicle,* not to attach himself to any other newspapers, a decision which resulted in his living for many years in 'an endemic condition of cashlessness'.

The fact that Cameron's main work was as an international reporter obviously gives his memoirs a different emphasis to that of someone involved in the hurly-burly world of political reporting within Britain, but being away from the country regularly can give a sense of scale and comparison with which to judge the national press and politics. It certainly did in his case.

In contrast with the thoughtful and measured tone of Cameron's memoirs, those of Hugh Cudlipp have a different, more combative and confident quality. His first work, *Publish And Be Damned* (1953) was a lively history of the *Daily Mirror*. It contains some interesting material both on the fraught relationship between the paper and the wartime Prime Minister, Winston

Churchill, and on the famous cartoon by Philip Zec of a merchant seaman clinging to a raft, with the caption 'The price of petrol has been increased by one penny – official'. This cartoon, one of a series on black market activities and their impact on the war effort, came at a particularly sensitive time in the Second World War as U-boats were taking a heavy toll of merchant shipping in the North Atlantic. The Home Secretary, Herbert Morrison, sought to suppress the paper for its 'reckless indifference to the national interest and to the prejudicial effect on the war effort' (Cudlipp 1953: 175–98).[6]

His second book on the British press, *At Your Peril* (1962), takes a wider view of the state of the press and some of the controversies. The memorable *Observer* photograph by John Hedgecoe of all the Mirror–Fleetway–Odhams publications on one news-stand accompanies Cudlipp's account of the take-overs. Both of these books contain a great deal of information on the personalities and the journalistic approaches which shaped the creation of the *Daily Mirror* in the war and post-war years, but the final volume, *Walking On The Water* (1976), which is more specifically his own autobiography and was written two years after he stepped down as chairman of International Publishing Corporation, presents his views on a number of journalistic issues.

As a young reporter on the *Manchester Evening Chronicle*, a Conservative paper owned by Lord Kemsley and other members of his family, Cudlipp wrote a sympathetic story about a bitter dispute in the Lancashire cotton industry after making a lightning tour of the mill towns – Oldham, Rochdale and Bury. His story, which he dictated by telephone, was a page-one lead in the first edition but it was missing from the final edition. When he returned to the office he was asked to call in and see the Managing Editor, Nathaniel Booth. Cudlipp observed that in moments of crisis Booth sank his hands deep into the seat of his pants and scratched his backside, and he was doing exactly that when Cudlipp entered the room: 'Sorry, Cudlipp, I want you to know that I agree it was a great story, but I had to take it out of the final. The proprietors have interests in the cotton industry. And . . . well . . .' The final edition would be dispatched to London and it was considered circumspect to erase the story. Cudlipp says that this was the only occasion, in nearly fifty years of newspaper work, that a story was ever suppressed, but it does raise the wider question about whether journalists learn the professional codes for survival and write accordingly for particular papers, editors or proprietors (Cudlipp 1976: 43).

One of the interesting features of the memoirs of senior newspaper figures is the way in which they blithely accept the contradictions between their own political views and those of their proprietors.

> Battling over the politics of their newspapers is by no means a common interest among all Editors. Most of them are content to obey His Master's Voice and express their own views with a cross on a secret

ballot paper . . . Percy Cudlipp, as Editor of Beaverbrook's *Evening Standard*, did not personally endorse many of the paper's policies: 'That is not the point,' he said to me. 'I am an advocate, like a lawyer in court, rewarded for my skill in putting my client's case.' It was not an attitude I could assume with the same bland professional aplomb. I was always in the propaganda business myself so far as a newspaper's opinions were concerned.

(Cudlipp 1976: 401)

It was perhaps fortunate that for the bulk of his journalistic life Cudlipp could work at a senior level on papers which were shaped by his own pro-Labour views. Other editors sought to address this apparent tension between their political views, and those of their proprietors, but not always with great conviction.

Robert Edwards details the ways in which Lord Beaverbrook guided the *Express* on policy issues through critical memos and ideas for leaders which were dictated and passed on to a corps of leader-writers to be worked on, and comments that 'he always maintained the fiction that the editor is in command'. A number of journalists with left-leaning views worked for Beaverbrook, including Ian Aitken, Michael Foot and Tom Driberg; indeed the notorious 'SOCIALIST GESTAPO' headline in the 1945 election was written by a socialist, Brian Chapman. Robert Edwards, himself 'a known socialist', seemed to have no difficulty in reconciling his political views with editing the *Daily Express* under Beaverbrook. He points out that the paper then was not a 'conventional Tory paper' — over 40 per cent of its readers expressed an allegiance to Labour — and on a range of issues, such as opposition to the Common Market, and a commitment to full employment and decent wages, it often had a populist stance.

However when Lord Beaverbrook's son, Max Aitken, a more conventional Tory than his father, took over the reins after his father's death in June 1964 there was hostility towards Edwards, as the former editor of *Tribune*, and Edwards in turn thought that Aitken lacked business and editorial flair. At the start of the election campaign in October 1964 the paper pronounced that its first duty was to 'give each of the parties in the contest a fair show in the news'. However the paper's political correspondent, Ian Aitken, 'rather than face what he thought might be the horrors of working for the *Express* during the election in that role', resigned and went to work for the *Guardian*. Edwards thought that it was the warm relationship with Beaverbrook which had kept Ian Aitken at the *Express* — 'he had none of the flak inflicted on editors'. The paper came out half-heartedly for the Conservatives on polling day, too late according to Edwards to have any influence on the result, and the following year Max Aitken fired him as editor (Edwards 1988: 152–3).

In a review of the relationships between editors and proprietors from the perspective of the mid-1970s, Cudlipp could describe varying approaches ranging from Roy Thomson, who 'rigorously edits the balance sheet of the *Sunday Times* and *The Times* and publicly acknowledges that he leaves the journalism to the journalists', to Lord Hartwell, who held the posts of Chairman and Editor-in Chief of both the *Daily* and *Sunday Telegraph*. He concluded:

> It is nonsense to expect any proprietor to say to his Editor, 'Here it is. I will take all the financial risks in this precarious industry, but you can say what the hell you want to say in my newspaper any time you like.' It is manifestly greater nonsense to accept the current notions of the militants who advocate that the editorial staff, and maybe the compositors and doormen, should decide the policy of the newspaper and hire and fire (but not pay) the Editor.
>
> (Cudlipp 1976: 408)

Cudlipp was referring to the growing demand by journalists and print workers in the 1970s for some involvement in and control of the products which they helped to produce. In the period of heightened industrial militancy under Edward Heath's Conservative government from 1970 to 1974 a series of disputes and strikes led to action against particular cartoons or reports. One dramatic protest by print workers at the *Evening Standard* was over an offensive cartoon by Jak of a power worker during the power workers' dispute, and the editor, Charles Wintour, conceded that a letter by the Federated House Chapel should be printed to express their view (Wintour 1972: 77–90).[7]

Harold Evans' memoir, *Good Times, Bad Times*, has some extremely valuable insights into *The Times* and *Sunday Times* under Murdoch, compared with the benign regime under which Lord Thomson allowed the *Sunday Times* to develop when Evans edited it from 1967 to 1981. It is an extremely informative book, packed with detail on journalists and on key events in which the paper played a role. Evans quotes the Thomson creed: 'I do not believe that a newspaper can be run properly unless its editorial columns are run freely and independently by a highly skilled and dedicated professional journalist.' Whilst Thomson was concerned about balance sheets, budgets and circulation figures, Evans asserts, 'There was no pressure to seek circulation by any means. He disapproved of sex and violence in newspapers' (Evans 1994: 4–5).

Evans felt that 'the quality press practised invertebrate journalism. It recycled speeches and statements, and delivered stylish opinions on routine public affairs. It mistook solemnity for seriousness, and by seriousness I mean a serious scrutiny of institutions and activities which affect the lives, safety and happiness of millions of people.' It was this emphasis on investigative journalism, notably through the Insight team, linked to a powerful sense of a paper's social and political responsibility on issues such as the plight of the Thalidomide victims, which fuelled the growth in circulation and respect for the *Sunday Times* under Evans (Evans 1994: 366–7).

When Murdoch took over *The Times* and *Sunday Times* in 1981 Evans was appointed editor of *The Times* until his dramatic resignation a year later. The remorseless pressure that Murdoch deployed to reshape the papers is vividly described in such incidents as that arising from the publication of an important two-page report from Poland by Roger Boyes after the military crackdown on Solidarity in December 1981. A day or two after it was published Murdoch went over to the reading rack in his room and flicked open a copy of the *Sun*, pointing at a few paragraphs in the paper: 'There,' he said, '*that*'s all you need on Poland.'

When Murdoch took over the papers, guarantees of editorial independence were sought and agreed, but they were swiftly broken as Murdoch subordinated editorial independence to his other commercial interests. In a damning judgement, Evans described the difference between the Thomson and Murdoch eras:

> in *The Sunday Times* years all our energies were directed outwards, and at *The Times* they were turned fatally inwards. It was the external restraints of the law and executive secrecy that tried to constrain the editorial freedom and excellence of *The Sunday Times*. But at *The Times* the pressures came from within: from a proprietor in breach of his guarantees to Parliament and from a debilitating introspection about the role and identity of the paper.
>
> (Evans 1994: 460)

Good Times, Bad Times is an important, indeed essential, source not only for anyone who wants to understand the strength and confidence of the journalistic culture associated with the *Sunday Times* when it was at the peak of its power under Evans, but also for the detail on the techniques that Murdoch used to take over the Thomson titles, and the consequences of this for the journalists, for editorial independence and for the political stance which the papers took.

If Evans gives us an insight into the titles on which he worked which were termed the 'qualities', the final book that we consider in this section, John Pilger's *Heroes*, deals with his experiences while working for over a decade on a popular, campaigning tabloid, the *Daily Mirror*, until it came under competition from the *Sun* and declined dramatically under Robert Maxwell. The book has many of the qualities associated with James Cameron's *Point of Departure*, with Pilger interspersing reports based on his international assignments and comments on changes in the press and society in Britain, with reflections on the pressures that journalists face from proprietors and other sources. Pilger worked as a cadet journalist on the Sydney *Daily Telegraph*, a paper owned by Sir Frank Packer who was a strong supporter of Robert Menzies, Australia's conservative prime minister for much of the 1950s and 1960s. As Pilger comments,

> The *Telegraph* was extremely right-wing. However, many of its jour-
> nalists were vociferous supporters and members of the Labour Party;
> it seemed that writing one thing and believing another was the way the
> system worked, and to do otherwise was to risk not working at all.
> This apparent contradiction, which I soon discovered was universal, left
> an impression on me. For one thing, it helped to explain why so many
> young journalists assumed a fake cynicism towards their craft, their
> readers and themselves.
>
> (Pilger 1986: 41)

Pilger arrived in England and was soon working for the *Daily Mirror* when
it was at the height of its circulation and influence under editorial director,
Hugh Cudlipp. Pilger pays tribute to his personality and flair, including the
invention of the 'shock issue' where the paper devoted most of its space to
an urgent social or political theme. He cites one such issue, preceding the
October 1964 general election, where beneath a banner headline 'IS THIS
THE PROMISED LAND?' there was a picture of a woman hanging out her
washing in a squalid back yard (Pilger 1986: 51).

Later on in *Heroes* there is a key chapter, 'You write. We publish',
written just after Murdoch's move to Wapping, in which Pilger sees the
decline of the *Mirror* as crucial to the erosion of press freedom and other
freedoms. The paper he worked for in the 1960s – 'once the greatest-selling
paper in the Western world and the only mass-circulation newspaper to offer
consistent political dissent in Britain' – encouraged journalists to try new
approaches, covered world events and had popular appeal. But when Cudlipp,
as chairman of IPC, sold the title of the old, ailing *Sun* to Murdoch in 1969
the paper's dominance was gradually challenged. The wrong response, Pilger
thought, was for the *Mirror* to follow the *Sun* on to its own low ground:

> Somebody in charge had to decide whether the *Daily Mirror* was to be
> a popular newspaper or a popular comic, to retain its humanity or be
> a copy of the *Sun* . . . But nobody made the decision and the *Mirror*
> deteriorated.
>
> (Pilger 1986: 511–13).

When in 1983 Reed International, who had taken over IPC in 1970,
decided to sell Mirror Group Newspapers it pledged not to put the company
under the control of one individual or corporation, but this was abandoned
when Maxwell took over in June 1984. The result was disastrous, with over
half a million readers lost in eighteen months, and constant interference in
the work of the editor and journalists. Pilger, his ideas and stories no longer
accepted, left the paper at the end of 1985.

Pilger's proposals to remedy the excessive power of the press proprietors might seem positively utopian ten years after they were written. He
urged the rewriting of the monopoly laws, 'so that ownership of more than

one daily and Sunday newspaper is illegal, and to legislate the right of employees to share ownership of their newspapers and the right of editorial freedom'. The 1996 Broadcasting Act, which jettisoned ownership restrictions between press and broadcasting, was designed to encourage the growth of media groups on a scale which it would have been difficult to predict in the mid-1980s. But Pilger was also concerned about how individual journalists defended freedom of expression. He quotes Henry Fairlie: 'Men such as Murdoch can operate only if they can find pliant men to assist them.' Pilger goes on to list a number of journalists 'who reject the notion of themselves as functionaries and sycophants, of barkers in one man's circus' and who left the *Sunday Times* after Murdoch took over, and another group who refused to go to Wapping. Pilger, a courageous and independent-minded journalist, is clear that the onus to develop a more responsible press lies with journalists themselves; otherwise they will pursue a debased craft (Pilger 1986: 533–4).

Wapping and after: 1986–96

Harold Evans, in the preface to the third edition of *Good Times, Bad Times*, hopes that *The Times* editor Peter Stothard and the (former) *Sunday Times* editor Andrew Neil will one day share with readers their experiences of 'how they work out their responsibilities with Rupert Murdoch hovering over them on the satellite'. Ten years after Wapping there was a spate of accounts from different sides of the barricades but they were sharply focused on the specifics of the action rather than concerned with broader analysis and description. Andrew Neil no longer works for Murdoch, and his memoir, *Full Disclosure* (1996), is surprisingly critical of the policies Murdoch pursued.

Also, of course, we should not focus only on News International; post-Wapping action by most national newspapers resulted in the derecognition of the National Union of Journalists, increasing work-loads, and heightened job insecurity. These experiences are not to be found in book-length memoirs, but are gleaned from surveys, short articles, the trade press, and material in books such as Tunstall's *Newspaper Power*. Geoffrey Goodman, for many years a distinguished industrial correspondent on the *Daily Mirror*, drew up a kind of balance sheet in *British Journalism Review*

> Some new jobs have been created for journalists though nearly all of them lack any form of security. Everywhere the drive is on to reduce costs (which usually means cutting jobs) and the degree of vulnerability for most people in the media today is greater than it has ever been. To be sure this factor is paralleled in many other industries, where the robot has taken over from human hands. But it is no special pleading that we emphasise the crucial nature of individual creative work in our own trade . . . The danger now is of a combination of ever-more

powerful tycoonery armed with new technology driving out, or
certainly limiting, that creative, independent, non-conforming quality.
(Goodman 1996: 4–5)

It will be interesting to see if, in the shiny, strip-lit offices scattered
around London, journalists are writing and recording their experiences in
the same way as the generations before them did. One thing is certain –
they won't be doing it in the firm's time on their computer screens which
they log on to.

The Street of Shame: how they 'made their excuses and left'

Much of the current debate on ethical issues in journalism centres around
the practices of the tabloid press – the 'public interest versus privacy' question; the 'doorstepping' of public figures, especially politicians and members
of the Royal Family; and whether the motive for publication of many of the
sensational revelations of the tabloid press can be defended as being true
investigative journalism that is 'in the public interest' or whether it is solely
a question of market forces and commercial interests. These are among the
issues that will concern students of journalism. The tabloid press is possibly
the most subject to commercial pressures. Commercial success is dependent
on the scoop, the exclusive, the necessity of reading it first in a particular
paper. Consequently the practices that tabloid journalists employ in order to
secure these exclusives, and the content of the resulting articles, provide
much of the fodder for debate on the profession's integrity.

While the memoirs of tabloid journalists provide some insight into the
commercial pressures under which they worked, and their working practices, they fail, on the whole, to address the moral and ethical questions that
will interest students of journalism. Working pressures are their theme –
beating the rival paper to be first on the scene or hiding the vital witness
are their prime concern. The bottom line, the editorial pressure under which
the tabloid journalist works, is to get the story before someone else does
and to ensure that it is sufficiently factually accurate and water-tight to avoid
a libel suit.

Most of the tabloid memoirs tend to be factual, anecdotal accounts of
how the writer exposed a particular scandal or obtained a scoop, with only
scant mention of, or debate about, the ethical issues. They do, however,
provide detailed revelations of their working practices written, for the most
part, in true 'confession' style, and some entertaining images of the arche-
typal cynical tabloid 'hack', who it seems is not entirely a figment of literary
imagination but the product of plenty of real-life role-models. Although there
are few published accounts by tabloid journalists, it is interesting to compare
an early work, *The Street of Disillusion: Confessions of a Journalist* written by
Harry Procter in 1958, with two recent memoirs – *Dog Eat Dog: Confessions*

of a Tabloid Journalist (1990) by Wensley Clarkson, and *Exposed!* (1995) by Gerry Brown, a former *News of the World* reporter and freelance.

The most notable difference in what are, in style and content, very similar books is the fact that, where Clarkson and Brown make little contribution to any of the ethical debates surrounding tabloid journalism, Procter ventures on to a much higher moral ground. According to the book's sleeve notes, Procter wrote the book 'in a state of spiritual disgust' as a man 'whose high hopes foundered in disillusion'.

Working in Fleet Street in the immediate post-war period on the *Sunday Pictorial*, he was billed as 'Harry Procter, Special Investigator', the newspaper's exposure expert. In all three accounts the image of the tabloid journalist is strongly aligned to that of the private detective. Procter's editor, Colin Valdar, instructed him that, 'exposures sell the *Pic*. We must be first with every important exposure – but they must be genuine.' Procter expresses his doubts about the justification for some of the stories which he was required to cover:

> The power of exposure on a big Sunday newspaper is a weapon to be used, I think, with every care. I have not turned squeamish in middle age. News is news, and I believe that real news should be pursued ruthlessly, accurately, speedily and completely.
>
> But to be exposed in bold headlines is a terrible thing for a victim – far worse than a heavy prison sentence. By it, lives are completely ruined – not only the life of the subject of the exposure – but of his wife, his children, his parents, his friends.
>
> Exposure of poverty, injustice, crime, is a good thing: but if this weapon is used carelessly and ordinary innocent people become its victims, then this is a terrible thing indeed. To focus the spotlight of publicity on the shadows of misery, despair and injustice is a noble task for a newspaper to perform – Charles Dickens was the first exposist in Fleet Street.
>
> But when the headlines hit the innocent, a great crime is committed.
>
> (Procter 1958: 140–1)

Procter's perception of the role of the tabloid journalist and his paper as philanthropic crusaders may appear naive and ingenuous in contrast to comparable accounts published in the 1990s. Brown's contribution in *Exposed!* to the ethical debate ranges from, 'Yeah, I know a lot of people say I ruined Frank Bough's private life. But I didn't. Honestly, it was like that when I got there,' to his concluding comment, 'Don't complain to me about invasion of privacy. If it's in the public interest, I prefer to call it the invasion of secrecy. Listen, pal, I don't tell you how to do your job.'

In *Dog Eat Dog,* Clarkson admits that, after the death of a tabloid 'victim', 'even hard-bitten hacks have a heart, and sometimes even a conscience. Inevitably things happen to you occasionally that really make you think twice about ignoring people's feelings – events that ruin other people's lives and leave you with a sick feeling in the stomach' but that is the nearest we get to profound debate on the issue of privacy versus the public interest (Clarkson 1990: 156).

In *Exposed!* Gerry Brown explains the methodology behind successful tabloid journalism thus:

> You ditch the press release you've been offered on the warm, loveable leading character of a top soap opera and you root around in the dirt and reveal that he or she left his or her old mum to live in poverty in a run-down block of council flats. While the pop reporter for a rival tabloid is on tour with the latest chart-topping group of wholesome teen heroes, you expose the fact that the lead singer has done time in a young offenders' institution for de-railing commuter trains and mugging pensioners.
>
> If the interview with the Hollywood star is too boring and he's going on about doing his own macho stunts in his movies and his ambitions to be a serious director, you check out the rumours that he is a serial wife-beater who's waiting for the results of his latest AIDS test. And if you think there's a fair chance you won't get sued, you publish the rumours anyway . . .
>
> There might be helpless, homeless teenagers squatting in the stairwell, heroin dealers on the balconies and a mad axeman living across the landing, but the average British family tucked up in their flat in a tower block will be too busy worrying about whether Deidre and Ken on *Coronation Street* will get back together to pay any attention.
>
> (Brown 1995: 146)

One of the most noticeable differences between tabloid journalism of the 1950s and that of the present day which is apparent from these memoirs is the present day predilection for stories that cover 'personalities' rather than incidents and facts. Procter and his newspaper were concerned with exposing vice, crime, scandal and sin; the tabloids of the 1990s are more intent on exposing personalities. The three accounts give us the opportunity to compare and contrast the difference in the nature of the coverage of one tabloid perennial, the prostitution exposure, and how, variously, the writers 'made their excuses and left'. Procter describes his exposure of the 'London Call-Girl Syndicate' as a 'great service to the community'. He writes:

> We hated mixing with the brazen, shameless hussies; we sickened at having to enter scented boudoirs, confirm our suspicions, then beat hasty, embarrassing retreats. It was hard work and it was rotten work. But it was a job worth doing, and we did it.

In addition to providing this 'service to the community', Procter adds,

> Of course we sold papers by this startling exposure which ran for several weeks and was billed throughout Britain. And why not? Selling newspapers to the public is, in the phrase of that famous television team, 'the end product' of the Mirror Group; the final act which makes their millions.
>
> (Procter 1958: 205)

However, it was the exposure of the prostitutes that made the story, even though Procter obtained, in the course of his investigations, a list of their illustrious clients which included politicians and sporting and media personalities. If we compare the accounts in Brown's *Exposed!* of Jeffrey Archer's denial of his liaison with Monica Coghlan, and the exposure of Pamella Bordes, or Clarkson's chapter in *Dog Eat Dog* entitled 'Make your excuses and leave', the difference in emphasis becomes apparent – it is the high profile of the clients rather than any flouting of morality that is the focal point of the story.

None of these accounts addresses in any depth the external pressures under which the journalists worked. *Dog Eat Dog* is concerned primarily with the rivalry among journalists to secure the vital scoop, the underlying assumption being that commercial pressure was the prime motive behind the entire exercise of obtaining the exclusive. *Exposed!* deserves consideration as an informative 'working guide' to some aspects of investigative journalism. Brown, as well as writing for the *News of the World*, worked for the BBC and *World in Action*. Perhaps the value of Brown's and Clarkson's accounts is in the glimpse that they provide of the reality of the world of tabloid journalism; they are, as all good tabloid stories purport to be, frank, revealing and sensational while lacking any in-depth analysis of the situation. While Procter in *The Street of Disillusion* portrays himself as the people's champion exposing evil and corruption for the common good, Clarkson has no illusions about the image of the tabloid 'hack':

> I'll never forget Bob Edwards' great brainchild – the *Sunday Mirror* glow-worm campaign. This highly unlikely piece of journalism involved giving away little badges that glowed in the dark during the winter months. It was without doubt an admirable attempt to reduce the number of tragic accidents involving schoolkids on the streets of Britain, but it so nearly sparked off a number of near arrests when well-meaning teams of *Sunday Mirror* reporters were assigned the arduous task of hanging around school gates to hand out these badges to young children.
>
> Not surprisingly, the sight of tatty raincoated hacks loitering outside schools at the end of class created some potentially ugly incidents between concerned parents and 'those dirty old men trying to lure our

children with the offer of a free badge'. The campaign went on literally for years and covering it became the most dreaded task of every
reporter on the paper.

(Clarkson 1990: 23)

Stafford Somerfield's *Banner Headlines* (1979), an account of his years as
editor of the *News of the World*, explores the wider picture of tabloid journalism. Somerfield spent twenty-five years at the *News of the World* and edited
the paper from 1960 to 1970 when he was fired by Rupert Murdoch. His
memoirs relate the history of the *News of the World* from 1891 and cover, in
the post-war period, Somerfield's disagreements with the Press Council over
the reporting of the Christine Keeler affair. The Press Council criticised the
paper for exploiting Christine Keeler by printing her story for which she was
paid £21,000. In this section of the book Somerfield addresses the issues of
both 'cheque-book' journalism and exposure that is in the public interest.
He wrote,

> My sin, I was told, was to sell the story for commercial ends. But what
> is wrong with good, honest commercial ends? That is what the news-
> paper business is all about. My job of telling the truth was just as
> honourable as that of others who complained.
>
> (Somerfield 1979: 141)[8]

In his reply to the Press Council's statement that 'by this exploiting vice
and sex for commercial reward the *News of the World* has done a disservice
both to the public welfare and to the Press', Somerfield maintained that

> The only difference between the *News of the World* and other newspa-
> pers is that we were the first to publish material with an authentic
> basis. In order to provide those facts we had to pay. The complaints
> you mention appear to be mainly directed to the profits which accrue
> to unworthy persons who capitalise on their notoriety. Such a criticism
> may in particular cases be true, but when directed at this newspaper
> in this instance it is clearly misconceived . . . A healthy society must
> surely demand exposure, however sordid, in the context of recent
> events. Nothing published in the *News of the World* by way of comment
> has sought to disguise as virtue that which is vicious, but in the belief
> that the public is entitled to know what is going on, and to know
> authentically, we have discharged our prime duty of giving the news.
>
> (Somerfield 1979: 143)

Somerfield's book also covers the commercial aspect of newspaper
production, the question of balance and political independence, and,
inevitably in the chapters that deal with Rupert Murdoch's take-over of the
paper, the issue of editorial independence and proprietorial intervention.

There was, between Somerfield and Murdoch, a clash of both temperaments and principles. Somerfield said, quite simply, 'He did not understand that, in this country, the Editor is wholly responsible' and within a few months of Murdoch's take-over of the paper he departed. In what may be seen as the forerunner of Harold Evans' account of Murdoch's take-over of *The Times*, there seems to have been no attempt by either man to reach a compromise:

> Murdoch was used to telling editors what to do, and I was used to having my own way. That, in a nutshell, was the difficulty. To the Royal Commission on the Press, Carr [the former proprietor] had said: 'I cannot remember issuing a directive to the Editor. The policy of this paper is laid down by the board and the Editor interprets it.' I was resolved to change the situation, for I believed it to be right, no matter who was chief shareholder and Chairman.

> Murdoch's way was different. 'I did not come all this way not to interfere,' he said. He might have talked about co-operation or working together, but not 'interfering'.

> (Somerfield 1979: 187)

Overview

Journalists present a peculiarly split image. On the one hand their activity is perceived as seedy and unethical, a callous and cynical group chasing stories of gruesome murders or sensational scandals, with all the associated activities of cheque-book journalism and body-snatching; side by side with this are the awards for journalists courageously reporting conflicts, or working tirelessly on investigations to uncover miscarriages of justice or corruption. There is ample evidence in the memoirs we have surveyed to support both views of journalists but what else can we extract from them which is valuable to students of journalism?

Memoirs offer an indicator of changes in the way in which journalists work, the economic and ethical factors influencing what they write, and how they obtain material. Take, for example, the description by Robert Edwards of the range of stories covered by *The People* which he edited from 1966 to 1972. They included reports on the new suburban practice of wife-swapping, 'which we ran and ran to prove to the staff that the new editor knew which side his paper's bread was buttered'. But beside this kind of familiar Sunday scandal story, the paper had a skilled investigative team under Laurie Manifold who first exposed the corruption at the top of Scotland Yard involving the head of the flying squad, Commander Frank Drury, and the pornographer James Humphreys. It also campaigned on issues which cut across readers' views when Enoch Powell made his 'rivers of blood' speech in 1968. The paper carried a picture of fifty people of forty-seven nationalities at a hospital in Essex under the headline: 'DEAR ENOCH

POWELL, IF YOU EVER HAVE TO GO INTO HOSPITAL, YOU'LL BE *GLAD* OF PEOPLE LIKE THESE'. Of course we shouldn't inflate these examples, or romanticise popular newspapers in the pre-Murdoch era, but there is evidence that both editors and journalists were aware of the importance and impact of the power of the press when it was directed at people, or used to campaign on particular issues. There was also a sense of what was unacceptable, and boundaries which should not be crossed, which was due partly to the Press Council but also to an acceptance by editors and journalists of the need for honesty and ethical standards (Edwards 1988: 167).[9]

But time and again memoirs also provide the focus for the crucial break in Fleet Street which came with the take-over by Rupert Murdoch of the *News of the World* and *The Sun,* and saw the plummet downmarket which other titles were eager to emulate. The crucial entry of Rupert Murdoch into national newspapers in England, and the subsequent powerful impact that he had, is something that memoirs such as Cudlipp's *Walking On The Water*, written in 1976, could only partially assess. Whilst the Murdoch *Sun* rapidly won readers after its first new tabloid edition came out on Monday 17 November 1969, it is only from the perspective of the later 1990s that we can see how crucial the acquisition of newspaper titles was in the subsequent creation by Rupert Murdoch of a global media empire, with dominance in the United Kingdom in newspapers, satellite television and book publishing. It is interesting therefore to look back at the chapter, 'The Sun That Didn't Rise', where Cudlipp, after devoting several chapters to an up-beat description of the great days of the *Daily Mirror*, deals with the sequence of events leading to the sale of the *Sun* to Rupert Murdoch.

When Cecil King took over Odhams Press in 1961 and the *Daily Herald* came into the Mirror Group, Cudlipp commented, 'Nobody sane in publishing would have paid a penny to acquire the *Herald*: it was part of the package', which included a seven-year guarantee to sustain the paper's existence. Three years later, and after failed attempts to inject new life into the paper, the statistics showed that it had the highest proportion of men amongst its readers of any national newspaper (59%); only 33% of its readers were housewives; and it had the highest C2 and DE readership. But the biggest problem was the absence of a new, younger generation amongst its readership. And so the idea of re-launching the old *Herald* as the new *Sun* was born. But the problem was that the terms of the guarantee meant that nobody could be fired, and therefore only a few new journalists could be taken on to give the paper a new direction; also, the paper had to continue to be printed in the same physical shape and surface size because of the mechanical inflexibility of the Odhams rotary presses (Cudlipp 1976: 246–53).

Nonetheless the project to launch *The Sun* sent nervous tremors through the rest of Fleet Street; Cudlipp was closely associated with the project and other papers took pre-emptive measures to prevent circulation losses. Robert Edwards mentions that the *Daily Express*, at Max Aitken's prompting, turned several of the pages of the Saturday edition into a magazine called

'Leisurescope'. Edwards thought the title hideous but it was designed 'to compete with similar pages everyone in Fleet Street knew were to appear in Cudlipp's *Sun*. The *Daily Mail* did the same, so great were the fears about the new publication and the man behind it' (Edwards 1988: 150–1).

The new *Sun*, launched in 1964 with the slogan 'born of the age we live in', started with the *Herald*'s circulation of 1.5 million but by the spring of 1969 sales had slumped to 850,000 and the combined losses of the *Herald* and *Sun* over a period of eight years had reached £12.7 million. The IPC board, with Hugh Cudlipp as chairman (after the dramatic departure of Cecil King following the penning of a front page article in the *Mirror* urging that the Labour Prime Minister, Harold Wilson, should go), resolved that it was unable to continue publication of the *Sun* after the guarantees expired in January 1970. Robert Maxwell offered to take over the paper from Cudlipp for nothing, but said that there would have to be redundancies, especially among the printers. It was this fact which swung the printers to support Murdoch's bid, who promised fewer redundancies, and so he got the paper for the bargain price of £800,000, payable in instalments, and within one hundred days of the launch of the new *Sun* he had boosted the readership to 1.5 million, compared with the figure of 650,000 for the last editions of the old *Sun*. In *Walking On The Water* Cudlipp analysed all of the options that he had had in 1969 regarding the decision to sell to Murdoch, and concluded:

> I would come to the same conclusions if confronted today by the same problem, and so I believe would my colleagues . . . Murdoch's *Sun* rose and shone. He inherited no labour problems by buying it. He was conditioned by no pledges from the past. His machines could produce a tabloid-size newspaper, and to produce a paper to compete with the *Mirror* was precisely what he planned to do. Nobody could say he has not been successful.
>
> (Cudlipp 1976: 252; Edwards 1988: 209)

Hugh Cudlipp, writing in 1990, surveyed a scene where

> The four or five most popular of the nationals circle monotonously in the same orbit, chasing their tails like hounds with rabies in a breathless Royal gossip hunt. As an encore they savage any randy pop star, wayward football manager, erring priest or two-timing MP they happen to spy in the hedgerows during the chase and proclaim the sleazy end-product as yet another front page 'world exclusive'.
>
> (Cudlipp 1990: 4)

But many media commentators would attribute the responsibility for this state of affairs to Rupert Murdoch. Ian Aitken, reviewing a biography of Rupert Murdoch by William Shawcross, pointed to the vulgarity, cruelty and unapologetic dishonesty of the two tabloid comics, *The Sun* and the *News of the World*, and asserted, 'It is beyond dispute that the Dirty Digger has dragged the rest of the UK's popular press into the gutter along with his nasty sheets. He now looks like doing the same to television on a worldwide scale' (Aitken 1993).

The result, according to MORI opinion polls in the 1990s, is that the public rank journalists lower than politicians, and popular newspapers are not to be trusted for the accuracy of their contents. More importantly, journalists themselves and their own sense of the value of their work is demeaned:

> We have reached the stage where journalists refer to each other in print as hacks and deride rival newspapers as rags. Investigative journalism is degraded to the level of spying . . . The excesses of the down-market tabloids have desecrated the press as a whole.
>
> (Cudlipp 1990: 9)

Whilst this is one reason for the changed perception of journalists and their work, there are two other factors which again have emerged since the 1970s, and which have increased in intensity post-Wapping: proprietorial and editorial pressures on journalists, combined with a deterioration in working conditions and loss of trade union organisation on most of the national newspapers. Again we need to keep a sense of perspective. Proprietors pre-Wapping had varying attitudes towards their involvement in the day-to-day running of their newspapers. Lord Beaverbrook, for example, inspired great affection, and fear, amongst his journalists and editors but he controlled, and often dictated, what his newspapers published almost to his last breath. Indeed, an obituary for George Malcolm Thomas, chief leader writer of the *Daily Express* under three editors, Arthur Christiansen, Edward Pickering and Robert Edwards, is scathing about his subservience: he was 'his master's pen, the obedient leader-writer who did the bidding of Lord Beaverbrook, press baron and politician manqué'. Sometimes he would go riding with Beaverbrook, struggling to stay in the saddle as he noted down the press lord's thoughts: 'It made him feel, he said, like Marshall Ney to Beaverbrook's Napoleon. "You mean Marshall Yea," snorted another journalist when he heard about this conceit' (*Economist* 1996).

But as the press has become more and more dominated by proprietors with explicit interventionist styles, and editors eager to do their bidding, we have had some startlingly frank pieces by journalists on the problems that this creates. Antony Bevins, who has worked for the *Sunday Express*, *The Sun*, the *Daily Mail*, *The Times*, *The Independent* and *The Observer*, has written a key piece on the pressures on journalists. He argues that reporters who deliver what is demanded of them are exceedingly well rewarded, but

> dissident reporters who do not deliver the goods suffer professional death. They are ridden by newsdesks and backbench executives, they have their stories spiked on a systematic basis, they face the worst form

of newspaper punishment – by-line deprivation. Such a fate is not always a reflection of professional ability. Over the last 20 years, I have known fine journalists broken on that wheel; they lose faith in themselves, and are tempted to give up the unequal struggle.

(Bevins 1990: 15)

He also has some damning comments about the professional practices of news reporters, including the herd instinct

the front line reporter's cultivated craving for safety in numbers. If all reporters and newspapers carry the same inaccuracy, there is much less chance of the dreaded midnight call from newsdesks, or a comeback from editors' ritual inquests the next morning.

(Bevins 1990: 15)

Memoirs have their value and limitations; examples of the kind of reflectivity which Cameron and Pilger demonstrate when they consider issues such as objectivity, journalistic ethics or the impact of proprietorial power are the exception rather than the rule. In part this is due to the nature of journalistic work which involves immediacy, deadlines, established routines to obtain and record stories, and also increasingly a desperate sense to be ahead of the competition. For most journalists wider professional or ethical concerns are unlikely to impinge on their work, especially when, according to Jeremy Tunstall, 'between the 1960s and the 1990s the amount of words written and space filled by each national newspaper journalist certainly doubled and perhaps trebled'. The number of national newspaper journalists remained about the same in London, but, with the closure of the Manchester offices in the 1980s, the journalists had to handle more editions of fatter newspapers as well as do work formerly controlled by compositors such as proofing, integrating advertising and editorial space and finalising pages (Tunstall 1996: 136).

The changes in the national press post-Wapping have seen a major shift of power away from journalists and compositors to owners, managers and editors, and the breaking of the complex patterns of work and social life that were associated with Fleet Street. Journalists' memoirs, for all their omissions, self-justifications and fallibilities, allow us to gain insights into and re-create aspects of a vanished world.

Notes

1   This chapter is a preliminary review of some of the memoirs published since 1945, and we plan to produce a more comprehensive account.

2   French and Rossell (1991) is a very useful dossier, including essays which cover over sixty films dealing with print journalism which were shown at the National Film Theatre, London, to commemorate the first edition of

The Observer, which has been in continuous weekly production since 1791.

3   Peter Hitchens writes for the *Daily Express*, specialising in reports on Labour leaders and Labour Party 'slur' stories. In a move designed to discredit Labour leader Tony Blair's wife, Hitchens advertised in the *Thanet Times* in March 1996 requesting 'mementoes of Cherie Booth's parliamentary campaign in early 1983. We would like to see leaflets and election addresses, and would also like to hear about speeches she made in Margate and Ramsgate.' Cherie Booth stood unsuccessfully for the Labour party in 1983, but the *Express* was seeking to portray her as an unreconstructed left-winger. According to a *Guardian* report, 8 March 1996, by Patrick Wintour and Andrew Culf, 'In the past year Mrs Blair, a barrister, has been targeted by the *Daily Mail* and the *Daily Express* with reporters trailing her on obscure court cases.' The intention of the stories was to portray her as the power behind Tony Blair, and to diminish electoral support in much the same way as attacks on the US President's wife, Hillary Clinton, damaged Bill Clinton's popularity.

4   See also Hopkinson (1984), edited and with a new Foreword by Tom Hopkinson, which has an evocative selection of the features by Kenneth Allsop, James Cameron and Robert Kee, amongst others, and photographs by Bert Hardy and Bill Brandt.

5   An account of the demise of the *News Chronicle* is in Glenton and Pattinson (1963).

6   For another interesting perspective on the government's reaction to the Zec cartoon see Challinor (1995: 70–71).

7   Wintour (1972) summarises an editor's view of the Jak cartoon and the broader movement for workers' control. This period, and particularly the work of the Free Communications Group, which Wintour briefly mentions, deserves more research.

8   Murdoch insisted that Somerfeld pay £21,000 for a rehashed version of the Christine Keeler memoirs of the Profumo affair (Chippindale and Horrie 1990: 6).

9   See also Press Council (1966: 4–7), where the Press Council unequivocally condemned as 'immoral the practice of financially rewarding criminals for disclosure of their nefarious practices by way of public entertainment'.

Bibliography

Aitken, I. (1993) 'Prince of Darkness', *London Review of Books*, 28 January

Bevins, A. (1990) 'The Crippling of the Scribes', *British Journalism Review* 1(2).

Brown, G. (1995) *Exposed!*, London: Virgin Books.

Cameron, J. (1967) *Point of Departure: Experiment in Bibliography*, London: Arthur Barker.

Challinor, R. (1995) *The Struggle For Hearts and Minds: Essays on the Second World War*, Newcastle: Bewick Press.

Chippindale, P. and Horrie, C. (1990) *Stick It Up Your Punter!*, London: Heinemann.

Clarkson, W. (1990) *Dog Eat Dog: Confessions of a Tabloid Journalist*, London: Fourth Estate.

Cudlipp, H. (1953) *Publish And Be Damned*, London: Andrew Dakers.

Cudlipp, H. (1962) *At Your Peril*, London: Weidenfeld & Nicolson.

Cudlipp, H. (1976) *Walking On The Water*, London: Chatto & Windus.

Cudlipp, H. (1990) 'The Deathbed Repentance', *British Journalism Review* 1(2).

Economist (1996) 'Obituary: George Malcolm Thomson', 1 June.

Edwards, R. (1988) *Goodbye Fleet Street*, London: Jonathan Cape.

Evans, H. (1994) *Good Times, Bad Times* (3rd edn), London: Orion Books.

French, P. and Rossell, D. (1991) *The Press Observed and Projected*, London: British Film Institute.

Glenton, G. and Pattinson, W. (1963) *The Last Chronicle of Bouverie Street*, London: George Allen & Unwin.

Goodman, G. (1996) 'Please Pass The Typewriter', *British Journalism Review* 7(1).

Hopkinson, T. (1982) *Of This Our Time: A Journalist's Story, 1905–1950*, London: Hutchinson.

Hopkinson, T. (ed.) (1984) *Picture Post 1938–1950*, London: Chatto & Windus.

Leapman, M. (1996) 'Foreign Bureaux Resist Economic Pressure', *IPI Report*, February/March, London: International Press Institute.

Neil, A. (1996) *Full Disclosure*, London: Macmillan.

Pilger, J. (1986) *Heroes*, London: Jonathan Cape.

Press Council (1966) *The Press and the People*, London: Press Council.

Procter, H. (1958) *The Street of Disillusion: Confessions of a Journalist*, London: Allan Wingate.

Randall, D. (1996) *The Universal Journalist*, London: Pluto Press.

Somerfield, S. (1979) *Banner Headlines*, London: Scan.

Tunstall, J. (1996) *Newspaper Power: The New National Press in Britain*, Oxford: Clarendon Press.

Waterhouse, K. (1995) *Streets Ahead*, London: Hodder & Stoughton.

Wintour, C. (1972) *Pressures On The Press*, London: Andre Deutsch.

Wintour, P. and Culf, A. (1996) 'Express puts Cherie Blair in the Dock', *Guardian*, 8 March.

Chronology

THIS LIST OF SELECTED DATES is intended to provide information for readers unfamiliar with the major phases of press, broadcasting and political history.

1819	'Gag Acts' against the radical press
1821	*Manchester Guardian* founded
1837–1901	Queen Victoria
1840s	Development of electric telegraph for transmission of news
1842	*Lloyd's Weekly Newspaper* founded
1843	*News of the World* founded
1848	Rotary action press first used
1850	*Reynold's Newspaper* founded
1851	Reuters news agency opened
1853	Advertisement Duty abolished
1855	Stamp Duty abolished
	Daily Telegraph founded
1861	Paper Duties repealed
1880	*Tit Bits* founded
1888	*Answers* founded
1889	First Official Secrets Act
1896	*Daily Mail* founded

1880–1914 Age of Empire: UK, Germany, France, USA, Italy, Netherlands, Belgium and Japan establish colonies

1895–1902 Conservative Government – Prime Minister Lord Salisbury

1900 *Daily Express* founded
Labour Representation Committee formed – becomes Labour Party in 1906
1901–10 Edward VII [Edwardian period]
1903 *Daily Mirror* founded as a women's paper
1904 *Daily Mirror* changed to a general illustrated paper
1907 National Union of Journalists founded
1902–05 Conservative Government – Prime Minister, A.J. Balfour
1905–08 Liberal Government – Prime Minister H.H. Asquith
1908–10 Liberal Government – Prime Minister H.H. Asquith

1910–15 Liberal Government – Prime Minister H.H. Asquith
1910–36 George V
1912 *Daily Herald* founded (as *Herald*)
1913 Lord Beaverbrook acquires control of the *Daily Express*
1914–18 First World War
1915–16 Wartime Coalition Government – Prime Minister H.H. Asquith
1916–18 Wartime Coalition Government – Prime Minister David Lloyd George
1916 Easter Rising in Dublin – Irish Nationalists rebel against British rule
1917 Russian Revolution
1918–22 Coalition – Prime Minister David Lloyd George

1922–23 Conservative Government – Prime Minister A. Bonar Law
1922 Harmsworth Newspaper Group founded
British Broadcasting Company set up
TUC and Labour Party take over *Daily Herald*
1923 Harmsworth buys the Hulton chain
1923–24 Conservative Government – Prime Minister Stanley Baldwin
1924 January–November: first Labour Government – Prime Minister J.R. McDonald
1924–29 Conservative Government – Prime Minister Stanley Baldwin
1926 General Strike in Britain
British Broadcasting Company is granted a Royal Charter and becomes British Broadcasting Corporation
Berry Brothers buy Lord Rothermere's Amalgamated Press Ltd
1927 Kemsley Newspapers founded
Westminster Press founded

	British Broadcasting Company becomes British Broadcasting Corporation
1928	Lord Rothermere forms Northcliffe Newspapers Ltd
1929–31	Labour Government – Prime Minster J.R. McDonald
1929	Stock Exchange crashes in USA
1929–35	World economic depression
1930s	Circulation war between popular dailies
	Daily Chronicle amalgamates with *Daily News* to form *News Chronicle*
	Provincial Newspapers founded
1931–35	National Government – Prime Minister J.R. McDonald
1936	Edward VII – abdicated to marry Mrs Simpson
	First experimental BBC TV services transmitted
1936–52	George VI
1937–39	Conservative Government – Prime Minister Neville Chamberlain
1939–40	National Government – Prime Minister Neville Chamberlain
1939–45	Second World War
1939	BBC TV closes down for the duration of the war
1940–45	Coalition Government – Prime Minister Winston Churchill
1940	Statutory newsprint rationing introduced
1945	Germany surrenders – war in Europe ends
	Labour withdraws from Coalition
	Allies drop two atom bombs on Japan – war with Japan ends; Berlin partitioned between USA/UK/France on one side and USSR on other; onset of Cold War
1945–50	Labour Government – Prime Minister Clement Attlee; introduction of sweeping reforms in health, education, welfare and key industries
1945–73	World economy enters phase of sustained economic growth based on dominance of USA – known as 'Long Boom' or 'Age of Affluence'
1946	BBC TV resumes after the war
1947	India gains independence from Britain; this signals a slow 30–40 year period of British formal withdrawal from most of her colonies
1947–49	First Royal Commission on the Press
1949–51	Beveridge Committee on the BBC
1950	First television coverage of a general election
1950–51	Labour Government – Prime Minister Clement Attlee
1951–55	Conservative Government – Prime Minister Winston Churchill
1952–	Elizabeth II
1953	Press Council established
1954	Television Act establishes Independent Television in the UK

1955–57	Conservative Government – Prime Minister Anthony Eden
1955	First commercial television stations on air
1956	Statutory newsprint rationing ended
1957–59	Conservative Government – Prime Minister Harold Macmillan
1957	USSR launches first satellite
1959	Lord Thomson buys Kemsley Newspapers
1959–63	Conservative Government – Prime Minister Harold Macmillan
1960s	Decade in which Japan and West Germany emerge as main global economic rivals to USA; decade of escalating US involvement in Vietnam
1960	*News Chronicle* closes
1961	Mirror Group buys Odhams
	Lord Thomson buys Illustrated Newspapers chain; *Sunday Dispatch* closes and *Sunday Telegraph* launched
1961–62	Second Royal Commission on the Press
1962	Pilkington Commission reports on broadcasting
1963	International Publishing Corporation (IPC) founded
1963–64	Conservative Government – Prime Minister Sir Alec Douglas Home
1964	First 'pirate' radio station, Caroline, on air
1964–66	Labour Government – Prime Minister Harold Wilson
1964	*The Sun* launched by IPC, replacing *Daily Herald*
	BBC2 on air
1966–70	Labour Government – Prime Minster Harold Wilson
1966	Lord Thomson buys *The Times*
1967	BBC Radios 1, 2, 3 and 4 launched
	First regular colour television transmission
1969	Rupert Murdoch buys *News of the World* and *The Sun*
1970	Reed International Paper acquires IPC
1970s	*Sun* catches up with *Daily Mirror*
1970–74	Conservative Government – Prime Minister Edward Heath; takes UK into the EEC and engages in major confrontations with trade unions
1971	*Daily Sketch* closes
1972	Sound Broadcasting Act establishes legal commercial radio in the UK
1973	Middle East military crisis and oil price rises signal onset of sustained economic problems for world economy
	First commercial radio stations go on air
1974–76	Labour Government – Prime Minister Harold Wilson, until his resignation in 1976
1974–77	Third Royal Commission on the Press
	Annan Commission on Broadcasting

1975	Margaret Thatcher is elected as Leader of the Conservative Party
1976–79	Labour Government – Prime Minister James Callaghan
1978	First regular sound broadcasting of parliament
1979–83	Conservative Government – Prime Minister Margaret Thatcher
1980	Broadcasting Act establishes Channel 4 and S4C
1981	Murdoch buys *Sunday Times* and *Times*
	First subscription cable TV authorised
1982	Falklands War
	Channel 4 and S4C on air
1983–87	Conservative Government – Prime Minister Margaret Thatcher
1983	First breakfast time television
1984	First satellite television, Sky, on air
	Legislation for cable TV
1984–85	Coal dispute; Government defeats NUM
1985	Robert Maxwell acquires *Daily Mirror*
	Televised proceedings of the House of Lords
	Gorbachev becomes leader of USSR; dawn of *glasnost* and *perestroika*
1986	*The Independent* founded
	Murdoch moves his newspaper business to Wapping
	BBC starts daytime television
1986–87	Murdoch confronts and defeats trade unions over new technology in Wapping dispute
1987	Murdoch acquires *Today*
1987–90	Conservative Government – Prime Minister Margaret Thatcher, until ousted in Tory Party coup in November 1990
1989	Collapse of Soviet Bloc
	First televising of proceedings of the House of Commons
	Murdoch launches full direct satellite broadcasting by Sky
	First 'incremental' commercial radio stations on air
1990	Broadcasting Act increases commercial competition in UK broadcasting
	Sky TV takes over British Satellite Broadcasting to form BSkyB
	BBC Radio 5 launched
1990–92	Conservative Government – Prime Minister John Major
1991	*Radio Times* and *TV Times* lose monopolies on publishing television programme schedules
1992–97	Conservative Government – Prime Minister John Major
1992	First national commercial radio stations on air
1994	Mirror group acquires major share in *The Independent*
1995	Murdoch closes *Today*
1996	Broadcasting Act relaxes rules governing cross-media ownership
	MAI media group merges with Express newspapers
1997	Labour government – Prime Minister Tony Blair
	Channel 5 television on air

Contributors

Stuart Allan is Senior Lecturer in Media and Cultural Studies at the University of Glamorgan.

Sally Bailey is a graduate in Public Relations of Leeds Metropolitan University.

J.O. Baylen is Regents' Professor of History, Emeritus, at Georgia State University.

Michael Bromley is Lecturer in Journalism and Deputy Director of the Communications Policy and Journalism Research Unit at City University, London.

Cynthia Carter lectures in Mass Communication Studies, School of English, Communication and Philosophy, University of Wales, Cardiff.

Alan Doig is Professor of Public Services Management, Liverpool Business School, Liverpool John Moores University where he runs the Unit for the Study of White Collar Crime. He is author of the only book on corruption in British politics and co-editor with Professor Fred Ridley of a book on sleaze in British politics.

Matthew Doull is President of Hollinger Digital, the new media arm of one of the world's leading newspaper groups. He was previously Associate Publisher of *Wired* magazine.

Bob Franklin is a Reader in the Department of Sociological Studies, the University of Sheffield.

Gregor Gall is Lecturer in Industrial Relations at the University of Stirling. He has published widely in the field of industrial relations, in the printed media and on trade unionism in general.

Michael Harris is Senior Lecturer in History, Centre For Extra-Mural Studies, Birkbeck College, University of London.

Chandrika Kaul graduated in history from Balliol College, Oxford, and has been a doctoral student at Nuffield College, Oxford. Her research interests include the British press and politics, imperialism and nationalism in South Asia, and she has published widely in these areas.

Julian Petley is an 'ologist' at Brunel University, and a member of the editorial board of the *British Journalism Review*.

Tom O'Malley is Senior Lecturer in Media Studies at the University of Glamorgan.

David Murphy lectures in the School of Management, University of Manchester Institute of Science and Technology

Andrew Thompson lectures in Sociology at the University of Glamorgan.

Granville Williams edits *Free Press*, the journal of the Campaign For Press and Broadcasting Freedom, and teaches Journalism and Media Policy at the University of Huddersfield.

Index